Harvard-Yenching Institute Studies, II

AN ANNOTATED BIBLIOGRAPHY OF SELECTED CHINESE REFERENCE WORKS

Third Edition

Compiled by Ssu-yü Teng, Indiana University
and Knight Biggerstaff, Cornell University

Harvard University Press, Cambridge, Massachusetts, 1971

© Copyright, 1950, 1971 by the Harvard-Yenching Institute
Distributed in Great Britain by Oxford University Press, London
Library of Congress Catalog Card Number 77-150012
SBN 674-03851-7

Foreword

The original *Annotated Bibliography of Selected Chinese Reference Works* was published in China as Monograph No. 12 of the *Yenching Journal of Chinese Studies*, 1936, subsidized by the Harvard-Yenching Institute. The second edition, somewhat revised, appeared in 1950 as Volume II of these Harvard-Yenching Institute Studies, with the prior consent of Yenching University. This third edition, bearing the same number, is so extensively revised that it may be considered practically a new work by the same compilers. Like the second, this edition is financed from the residue of funds provided by the Rockefeller Foundation during World War II for the printing of Chinese and Japanese dictionaries.

Glen W. Baxter
Associate Director
Harvard-Yenching Institute

Preface to the Third Edition

This is the second time *An Annotated Bibliography of Selected Chinese Reference Works* has been revised, the first revision having been published in Cambridge by the Harvard University Press in 1950. The original edition was published in 1936 by the Peiping Office of the Harvard-Yenching Institute.

Approximately a hundred titles that appeared in the second edition have been dropped because they have been superseded or for some other reason are no longer considered useful. Nearly two hundred new titles have been added, including some twenty-five written in Japanese, mostly indexes, which can be used by persons who, though knowing little or no Japanese, can read Chinese. We have included very few works that are devoted entirely to developments since 1949 because of the availability of *Contemporary China: A Research Guide*, by Peter Berton and Eugene Wu (Stanford: The Hoover Institution on War, Revolution and Peace, 1967), which is concerned almost entirely with the 1950's and 1960's.

A large proportion of the older books described in our second edition have been reprinted in Taiwan, in mainland China, or in Hong Kong, and we supply data on as many of the best of these new editions as we can, though we doubtless have missed some because of the large number of publishers involved in this business. Where several editions of a work are listed, we sometimes mark the best one with a cross (+); and a few titles generally recognized as of outstanding importance are marked with a star (*).

The organization of the second edition has been retained with only minor modification to meet changing emphases in book publishing. The Chinese characters for the titles of *ts'ung-shu* and for the names of book publishers that appear more than twice in the text are to be found in the Index and Glossary, which also defines a few terms. The Wade-Giles system of romanizing Chinese characters is used throughout except where we have followed the romanization used by a particular author or publisher.

We wish to express our gratitude to the librarians and Chinese libraries in the United States, Japan, Taiwan, and Hong Kong without whose assistance and facilities a revision of this kind would not be possible. We are especially grateful to those who opened their libraries for us on weekends and at other times when they are normally closed. We thank the members of the staffs of the Far Eastern Library of the University of Chicago, especially T. H. Tsien; of the Harvard-Yenching Library, especially Eugene Wu, Zunvair Yue and Liu Kai-hsien; of the Hoover Institution Library at Stanford, especially John Ma; of the University of California at Berkeley, especially Charles E. Hamilton, and Ch'en Chih-p'ing of the Center for Chinese Studies; of the Library of Congress, especially Edwin G. Beal and K. T. Wu; of the Chinese and Japanese Library of Columbia University, especially Tong Te-kong; of the Indiana University Library, especially Mrs. Liu Wu-chi and Hsü Chia-pi; of the Wason Collection on China and the Chinese at Cornell University, especially William C. Hu and Richard C. Howard; of the University of Hawaii Library; of the University of Hong Kong Library; of the United College and New Asia Libraries of the Chinese University of Hong Kong; of the Research Institute of Humanistic Sciences Library of Kyoto University; of the Library of the Institute of Modern History, Academia Sinica, at Nankang in Taiwan; of the National Central Library in Taipei; of the Gest Oriental Library of Princeton University, especially Tung Shih-kang; and of the National Taiwan University Library. We are grateful to Robert L. Irick and staff members of the Chinese Materials and Research Aids Service Center in Taipei, who made their extensive files available to us and were helpful in other ways. It should be pointed out that all Taiwan publications mentioned in this bibliography may be purchased through that Center (P.O. Box 22048, Taipei, Taiwan). We appreciate the suggestions and assistance received from Derk Bodde, K'ai-ming Ch'iu, Chow Tse-tsung, John K. Fairbank, A.F.P. Hulsewé, D. R. Jonker, Liu Shih-chi, Nathan Sivin, Etsuko Terasaki and many others.

We are grateful to Arthur F. Wright, chairman, and the other members of the Committee on Studies of Chinese Civilization of the American Council of Learned Societies for the grant that has helped meet a number of the expenses connected with this revision. We also thank the Center for East Asian Studies (China Program) of Cornell University, which sent Mr. Biggerstaff to Taipei to work on this project. Finally we express our gratitude to Margaret S. Teng and Camilla M. Biggerstaff for their assistance with copying, indexing and proofreading, and for their constant encouragement.

Ssu-yü Teng
Knight Biggerstaff

September 15, 1970

Preface to the Original Edition

The present bibliography was compiled with the intention of providing Western students in the field of Sinology with an elementary guide to the most important Chinese reference works. A few of the best editions available are listed under each title, followed by a note briefly describing the contents of the work or giving directions regarding its use. Criticisms are frequently added, but only for the purpose of helping the student to determine whether the work is likely to meet his needs. It has not been our intention to make the list of works exhaustive, but rather to include only the most important ones, always keeping in mind the needs of the student seeking general information rather than those of the specialist.

We have perhaps tended to overemphasize certain fields in spite of our attempt to represent all fairly, and probably many scholars will disagree with our choice of works and also with our classification. The works marked with an asterisk are generally recognized as being indispensable to all Sinologues, and at the same time they are the ones which should be consulted first by beginners. The notes are without exception based upon a personal examination of the works themselves, although we sometimes quote the opinion of the compilers of the *Ssu-k'u ch'üan-shu tsung-mu.* Occasionally we have listed editions which we have not seen ourselves, but only when the data we give concerning them appear in two or more library catalogues. In order to keep this bibliography up to date, we recommend that the *Quarterly Bulletin of Chinese Bibliography,* which is edited and published by the National Library of Peiping for the Chinese National Committee on Intellectual Understanding, be consulted.

The Wade system of romanization, as modified by Giles, is used throughout this bibliography except for place-names which are better known by the Post Office romanization. Chinese words which appear in the text without the characters may be found, with their characters, in the combined glossary and index at the back, along with definitions of certain terms which recur throughout the text, full citations of *ts'ung-shu,* dates of dynasties and reign periods, and book titles and compilers' names.

We are very happy to express our appreciation to the following persons, who have made suggestions and corrections, and helped us in many other ways: Professor L. C. Porter 博晨光, Professor William Hung 洪業, Mr. Derk Bodde 卜德, Mr. Nieh Ch'ung-ch'i 聶崇岐, Mr. Ku T'ing-lung 顧廷龍, Mr. T'an Ch'i-hsiang 譚其驤, Mr. Chu Shih-chia 朱士嘉, Dr. A. K. Ch'iu 裘開明, Dr. Cyrus H. Peake 畢格, Dr. L. C. Goodrich 富路特, Mr. Yoh Liang-mu 岳良木, Mr. Chang Erh-t'ien 張爾田, Professor Teng Chih-ch'eng 鄧之誠, Dr. A. W. Hummel 韓慕義, Dr. Charles S. Gardner, Professor Wang Li 王力, Mr. Chou I-liang 周一良, Mrs. Biggerstaff, Miss Hilda Hague 海松芬, Miss Yü

Shih-yü 于式玉, and Mr. T'ien Hung-tu 田洪都 and the staff of the Yenching University Library. We are also indebted to the Harvard-Yenching Institute and to the Social Science Research Council respectively, whose fellowships we have held during the time this bibliography was being compiled.

We realize that we have probably made numerous errors in judgment, and we shall be very grateful for criticisms and suggestions.

Ssu-yü Teng
Knight Biggerstaff

Peiping
June 6, 1936

Contents

I BIBLIOGRAPHIES

Although bibliographies were compiled in China as early as the first century B.C. little use has been made of them until modern times except by those, such as custodians of imperial collections, compilers of encyclopedias, recollectors of lost works, and private book collectors, who, because of the nature of their work, found it necessary to devote special attention to them. During the past half century, however, as a consequence of the development of a more scientific approach to scholarship in China, a greater general interest has been shown in bibliography, and it is now generally recognized that the first step a serious student must take in beginning research in any branch of Chinese studies is to acquaint himself with the most important bibliographies related to his subject.

In selecting the works to be included in this section, only the more important bibliographies were admitted, no attempt being made to make the list exhaustive. Only a fraction of the available bibliographies and library catalogues are here described, so that scholars who wish to find further works along any particular line are advised to consult the bibliographies of bibliographies listed in the subsection devoted to such works. All bibliographies included in other works, bibliographies relating to specific localities, general university library catalogues, and catalogues in which specimen pages of rare editions are reproduced, have been omitted.

It should be pointed out that many Chinese bibliographies do not give definite data on such things as the time of writing and publication, and that the number of *ts'e* given for the same edition of a work, if given at all, is frequently different in different catalogues. Furthermore, the author's name and even the dynasty during which a work was written are often not known, so that when the compilers of the present work say in their description of a bibliography that the name and dynasty of the authors of the works listed in it are given, certain exceptions to that general statement must be expected since in many cases such information is not available. Exact figures given for the number of titles listed in the different bibliographies are, unless attributed to other sources, based upon the count of the compilers of the present bibliography. As in other parts of this work, the system of classification followed has been determined by a desire to make the material as accessible to Western students as possible.

A. BIBLIOGRAPHIES USEFUL FOR GENERAL REFERENCE

For general research, the first two titles listed below are useful guides. For establishing a new sinological library, the *Shu-mu ta-wen pu-cheng*, compiled by two outstanding Ch'ing scholars and revised in the 1930 s, is a very important bibliography of selected works. The two most useful checklists are the *Naikaku bunko kanseki bunrui mokuroku* and the *Kyōto daigaku, Jimbun kagaku kenkyūjo: Kanseki bunrui mokuroku*.

Chung-wen ts'an-k'ao-shu chih-nan 中文參考書指南. Compiled by Ho To-yüan 何多源, and first published in 1936. (1) Revised edition published in 1938 by the Commercial Press as one of the series entitled *Ling-nan ta-hsüeh t'u-shu-kuan ts'ung-shu* 嶺南大學圖書館叢書. [26] 961 pp. (2) Taipei: Ku-t'ing shu-wu, 1970 (photocopy).

This is a reference guide to 2350 works. It is divided into two parts. The first part, after a discussion of reference works in general, takes up dictionaries, encyclopedias, general catalogues or bibliographies, *ts'ung-shu*, periodicals and newspapers, publications by academic institutions, and government publications. The second part deals with reference works on libraries, journalism, the classics, philosophy and religion, social sciences, philology, natural sciences, applied sciences, arts, literature, history and geography, and with maps, atlases, and travelers' guides. In appendixes at the end are a list of a hundred selected reference works, a very brief list of Chinese reference works in English, a guide to publishers throughout the country—now of course obsolete—and a combined index of authors and titles arranged by number of strokes. Under each category there is a brief introduction; under each work there is a short descriptive note usually followed by a brief criticism. One of the special features of this reference guide is a list of dictionaries in Manchu, Mongolian, Tibetan, Arabic, Latin, and a number of other foreign languages. Another good feature is that the scope is broader than that of the *Annotated Bibliography of Selected Chinese Reference Works*. However, many of the annotations seem to be roughly done; information on editions is very limited; furthermore, the definition of a reference work and the system of classification leave room for discussion.

Chung-kuo li-shih yen-chiu kung-chü-shu hsü-lu (kao-pen) 中國歷史研究工具書叙錄(稿本). Compiled by Tseng Ying-ching 曾影靖. Hong Kong: Lung-men shu-tien 龍門書店, 1968. 8, 325 pp.

"Research Tools for Chinese History: An Annotated Bibliography" was originally a B.A. thesis of the University of Hong Kong. It includes a total of 719 entries: 268 bibliographies, 125 indexes, 59 works on chronology, 81 geographic aids, 93 biographical works, 32 dictionaries, and 61 yearbooks. English and Japanese reference works are included as well as Chinese. This compilation contains much useful information even though it lacks author and title indexes.

Shu-mu ta-wen pu-cheng 書目答問補正, 5 *chüan*. Compiled by Chang
    Chih-tung 張之洞, with the assistance of Miao Ch'üan-sun 繆荃孫, Chang's
    preface dated 1875. Revised and enlarged by Fan Hsi-tseng 范希曾. (1)
    Nanking: Kuo-hsüeh t'u-shu-kuan 南京國學圖書館, 1931. 2 *ts'e*. (2) Peking:
    Chung-hua shu-chü, 1963. 7, 233 pp. (3) Taipei: Hsin-hsing shu-chü, 1956.
    238 pp. (4) **Shu-mu ta-wen pu-cheng so-yin** 索引. Hong Kong: Ch'ung-
    chi 崇基 shu-tien, 1969, with an index compiled by Wang Mien 王緜. 1, 2,
    309, 233 pp.

This carefully selected bibliography of 2266 important Chinese works still
extant at the end of the Ch'ing dynasty was originally compiled by a great
scholar during the 1870's to serve as a handbook for elementary students. It
was originally called the *Shu-mu ta-wen* 書目答問, and was published in numerous editions. The original compilation was revised and enlarged during
the 1920's by a contemporary bibliographer whose additions appear in the
present edition under the character *pu* 補. Works are arranged in the first four
chüan according to the traditional four-branch classification, and under each
title there are given the number of *chüan*, the author's name and dynasty,
together with a minimum of information concerning all of the different editions known to the compiler and reviser. There are also frequent brief notes
concerning the contents and value of the works listed. The fifth *chüan* lists a
number of *ts'ung-shu*, making this the first important Chinese bibliography to
classify *ts'ung-shu* separately. And in the fifth *chüan* there is also a list of what
the compiler considered to be the most important works in various fields.
Finally, there is a list of the names of the most important writers of the Ch'ing
dynasty, arranged chronologically under fourteen different classifications, the
hao and ancestral home of each man being given the first time his name appears. Although there are occasional mis-classifications such as the *Hsüan-ho
i-shih* 宣和遺事, which should be classified under fiction instead of history,
this is the most important and the most widely used bibliography compiled
since the *Ssu-k'u ch'üan-shu tsung-mu*, and while it is not sufficiently exhaustive
for scholars who are working intensively in special fields, it is indispensable
for anyone desiring a general selected list of Chinese works. Wang Mien
corrects a number of mistakes in the earlier editions. In his edition the text of
the bibliography follows an index to authors and titles arranged by the number
of strokes.

Chiang-su sheng-li kuo-hsüeh t'u-shu-kuan tsung-mu 江蘇省立國學圖書
    館總目, 44 *chüan*. **Chiang-su sheng-li kuo-hsüeh t'u-shu-kuan tsung-
    mu pu-pien** 補編, 6 *chüan*. Compiled by Liu I-cheng 柳詒徵 and others.
    (1) Published in a movable-type edition by the Kiangsu Provincial Sinolo-
    gical Library 江蘇省立國學圖書館, Nanking 1933–1935, 24 *ts'e*, and the *Pu-
    pien*, 1937. 3 *ts'e*. (2) Taipei: Kuang-wen shu-chü, 1970. 15 vols. (photocopy).

This is the general catalogue of the Kiangsu Provincial Sinological Library in Nanking, as it existed prior to the Japanese occupation. It is arranged according to the traditional four-branch system with the addition of three separate divisions, and modern publications are classified with older editions rather than separately, as is the case with most modern catalogues. According to the figure given at the end of the catalogue, 37,002 works in 198,922 *ts'e* are listed, although the sum of the figures given at the end of the seven divisions differs somewhat. The work is divided as follows:

Classics:	10 sections	94 subsections	4,295 titles
Histories:	18	92	8,007
Philosophers:	28	197	12,068
Belles-lettres:	4	73	9,907
Gazetteers:	3	27	1,681
Maps and Atlases:	9		414
Ts'ung-shu:	5	23	1,006

On the whole the arrangement combines the best points of the old system with convenient innovations developed to meet modern conditions. Particular attention has been paid to distinguishing between different fields of knowledge in the choice of section and subsection headings. Under each of the classics, for instance, separate subsections list the following types of works: the bare text, commentaries, glossaries, related works on divination, histories of the classic itself, the evolution of different schools, bibliography, etc. A separate section lists collections of the classics. Among other typical innovations are the following: under history, there is a section devoted to historical tables; there is a *nien-p'u* 年譜 subsection in the biography section; there are subsections on Buddhist and Taoist temples, ancestral temples, gardens, and old-style provincial colleges, in the geographical section; modern governmental publications are placed at the end of the section on institutions 政書; and there is a special section for histories of foreign countries, although many works are listed under it which do not properly fall within the field of history. Under philosophers there are separate subsections for different branches of the Sung School in the section on the Confucian School. Under belles-lettres works are arranged by dynasties, and those written during recent dynasties are further classified geographically; there is a special subsection listing poems written by women. Individual works published in *ts'ung-shu* are listed separately under their proper classification. Each title is followed by the number of *chüan* and *ts'e*, the name and dynasty of the author, and essential information concerning different editions.

Because modern works are classified in this catalogue according to the old Chinese system, it is sometimes difficult for those not acquainted with that system to find the titles they are looking for. Magazines, modern medical works, and works on education and languages, for instance, are all listed under the third or philosophers branch, the first in the miscellaneous section 雜家, the second in the *fang-ch'i* 方技 section, and the last two in the section on social sciences 社會科學. Several of the subsection headings are misleading, and works are frequently incorrectly classified, as for instance, yearbooks, which are listed in the section on historical tables. There are also numerous typographical errors. On the whole, however, this is a carefully compiled, useful catalogue, and it no doubt marks a not inconsiderable advance in the science of Chinese bibliography.

The *Pu-pien* follows the same system of classification as the catalogue itself. It contains about 10,000 entries, most of which are titles of works included in *ts'ung-shu*.

According to Liu I-cheng, 6803 *ts'e* of block-printed *ts'ung-shu* and gazetteers belonging to the library were burned during the Japanese occupation and thousands of cases of other books were removed. However, three-fourths of the library's holdings ultimately were recovered, including all Sung editions, ninety-two percent of Yüan and ninety-three percent of Ming editions.[1] Although this catalogue is no longer a reliable guide to present holdings, it remains a useful checklist.

Naikaku bunko kanseki bunrui mokuroku or **Nei-ko wen-k'u Han-chi fen-lei mu-lu** 內閣文庫漢籍分類目錄. Tokyo: Naikaku bunko, 1956. 5, 7, 598, 3, 9, 125 pp.

This is a catalogue of the Chinese books in the Cabinet Library, Tokyo, which inherited a few old collections handed down from the Tokugawa period. The Library is especially well known for its collection of the early printings of popular Chinese literature and for its numerous early Japanese reprints of Chinese works. The *ts'ung-shu* are all analyzed and the entries are indexed. This catalogue has proven to be particularly useful to cataloguers of Chinese libraries faced with the task of identifying book titles.

Kyōto daigaku, Jimbun kagaku kenkyūjo: Kanseki bunrui mokuroku or **Ching-tu ta-hsüeh, Jen-wen k'o-hsüeh yen-chiu-so: Han-chi fen-lei mu-lu; fu, Shu-ming, jen-ming t'ung-chien** 京都大學, 人文科學 研究所: 漢籍分類目錄; 坿, 書名, 人名通檢. Compiled by Kurata Junnosuke 倉田淳之助. Kyoto: Jimbun kagaku kenkyūjo, 1963. 2 vols. 12, 343, 427; 15, 1126 pp.

This catalogue of more than 60,000 Chinese works in the library of the Research Institute of Humanistic Sciences of Kyoto University is classified according to the *Ssu-k'u* system for old books and according to the Japanese

---

1. For the holdings of the Kiangsu Provincial Sinological Library in 1947 see **Chiang-su sheng-li kuo-hsüeh t'u-shu-kuan hsien-ts'un shu-mu**. (1) Nanking, 1947, 2 vols. (2) Taipei: Kuang-wen shu-chü, 1970 (photocopy).

decimal system for modern publications, the last section of the catalogue, the *Hsin-hsüeh pu*, 新學部, listing works published since 1911. *Ts'ung-shu* are listed separately under the heading *Ts'ung-shu pu*. The second volume has author and title indexes arranged by number of strokes. This catalog is an unusually useful reference tool for research scholars and the cataloguers of Chinese libraries.

Ssu-k'u ch'üan-shu hsüeh-tien 四庫全書學典. Compiled by Yang Chia-lo 楊家駱. Shanghai: Shih-chieh shu-chü, 1946. [1077] pp.

This "bibliographical encyclopaedia" is divided into 9 chapters. The second chapter explains the classification system of the *Ssu-k'u ch'üan-shu* and is followed by a chart showing the history of the Chinese classification system. The third discusses the organization, the research on, and the editorial board of the *Ssu-k'u ch'üan-shu*, the buildings in which the seven copies of that collection were preserved, and finally the problem of printing the huge collection. The fourth chapter tells how many works were copied into each section and how many were merely listed by title. The fifth lists a hundred works which are either special studies of the *Ssu-k'u* or reference works on the use of the *Ssu-k'u ch'üan-shu*. This is a particularly informative section. The sixth chapter discusses the history of the Chinese intellectual world before the compilation of the *Ssu-k'u ch'üan-shu* and the new tendencies in intellectual circles after its compilation. This chapter also contains a history of *ts'ung-shu*. The main part of this big volume is based on and is largely the same as Yang Chia-lo's **Ssu-k'u ta-tz'u-tien**.[2] While the latter work is arranged by the four-corner system, this one is arranged by the K'ang-hsi system. Any item in the *Ssu-k'u* can be found in this work. Beginning with the Chinese character *wu* 伍 (Part V, p. 179), there is an annotated list of works which the compiler believes might be included in an enlarged compilation of the *Ssu-k'u ch'üan-shu*. Not only are Chinese books listed there, but also such Western works as *The Outline of History* by H. G. Wells, and the *Encyclopaedia Britannica*. On the whole, while this work furnishes some useful information, it is poorly arranged and presented.

B. BIBLIOGRAPHIES RELATED TO HISTORICAL PERIODS

The special importance of the bibliographies and catalogues included in this subsection lies in their relationship to specific historical periods. A scholar who

---

2. First published in 1935. (Taipei: Chung-kuo tz'u-tien-kuan fu-kuan ch'ou-pei-ch'u, 1967). 1690, 1, 411 pp.

knows the name of a writer and who wishes to determine the titles of books written by him or the period in which he lived, or who knows the title of a book and wishes to find out the name of the author or the period during which it was written, or who is trying to determine whether or not a work was extant at a certain time or whether it varied in title, number of *chüan*, etc., at different times, should first consult the *I-wen-chih erh-shih-chung tsung-ho yin-te*. If the information sought cannot be found in the bibliographical sections of dynastic histories or in the bibliographical supplements to dynastic histories which are indexed in that work, resort should then be made to catalogues of public collections, as the *Ch'ung-wen tsung-mu*, and to catalogues of private collections, as the *Chün-chai tu-shu-chih* and the *T'ien-i-ko shu-mu*. The works included in this subsection also give an indication of Chinese cultural development through different periods by giving some idea of the number and variety of books extant at different times. The bibliographical section of the *Wen-hsien t'ung-k'ao*, which is the most nearly complete pre-Yüan bibliography available, is not described in this subsection because it is not an independent work.

Han-shu i-wen-chih 漢書藝文志, 1 *chüan*. Compiled by Pan Ku 班固 (A.D. 32–92). (1) *Ch'ien-Han-shu* 前漢書, *chüan* 30. (2) *Pa-shih ching-chi-chih, ts'e* 1. (3) Hong Kong: T'ai-p'ing shu-chü, 1963. 1, 100 pp., with a four-corner author and title index. (4) *Mu-lu-hsüeh ming-chu*, series 3, *ts'e* 1. + (5) Shanghai: Commercial Press, 1955. 1, 100, 15 pp., with a four-corner index.

The bibliographical section of the *Ch'ien-Han-shu*, called the *Han-shu i-wen-chih*, is the earliest Chinese bibliography extant. The earliest known Chinese bibliography was the *Pieh-lu* 別錄, compiled between B.C. 26 and B.C. 6 by Liu Hsiang 劉向. It was an annotated catalogue of the works which were gathered during the early Han period in the course of an imperial campaign to bring together surviving copies of the books which had been ordered destroyed by Ch'in Shih Huang-ti 秦始皇帝. Liu Hsiang's son, Liu Hsin 劉歆, compiled the *Ch'i-lüeh* 七略, basing it upon his father's catalogue; he arranged the titles under seven divisions, including, however, no descriptive notes. When Pan Ku compiled the *Han-shu i-wen-chih*, he based it upon the *Ch'i-lüeh*, but instead of making a separate division of the introductions to sections as Liu Hsin had done, he scattered them among the other six categories. He also added a few titles and probably changed the classification of some of the works.

Altogether 677 works are listed in Pan Ku's catalogue, beginning with the very earliest books written in China and including works written in the first century A.D. The titles are classified as follows:

Liu-i lüeh   六藝略,   9 sections (classics, including histories under the
                          Ch'un-ch'iu 春秋 section)   103

Chu-tzu lüeh	諸子略,	10 sections (philosophical works)	189
Shih-fu lüeh	詩賦略,	5 sections (poetry)	106
Ping-shu lüeh	兵書略,	4 sections (military tactics)	53
Shu-shu lüeh	術數略,	6 sections (astronomy, genealogy, divination, and other pseudo-sciences having to do with numbers)	190
Fang-ch'i lüeh	方技略,	4 sections (medicine, popular religions, etc.)	36

It is estimated that of the 677 works listed, 47 have been preserved almost in their entirety until the present time, 41 have been preserved in incomplete form, 65 have been re-collected from other sources, and the others have been entirely lost. Under each title are to be found the number of *chüan*, the author's name and period, and sometimes very brief notes concerning the contents of the book or indicating a relationship between the author and other authors. The notes were written by Pan Ku except in cases where the names of other commentaries are given. At the end of each section the total number of titles and *chüan* listed in it are given, after which there is an introduction giving a brief history and discussion of the type of writing included in that section. These introductions are extremely important, serving as reliable sources for the early history of Chinese culture, and stressing in particular the development of different schools of thought.

The principal strong points in the *Han-shu i-wen-chih*, besides the special attention paid to different schools of thought, are the excellence of the classification of works under the different sections, based strictly upon content, and the distinctive and appropriate headings chosen for the different sections. Among its defects are its failure to list certain earlier works, and an occasional carelessness in the order of the works listed within a section. This bibliography has been a model with some modifications for all later ones, and so important has it been considered by later scholars that many special studies have been made of it.[3]

Sui-shu ching-chi-chih 隋書經籍志, 4 *chüan*. Compiled under Imperial auspices by Chang-sun Wu-chi 長孫無忌 and others, and presented to the emperor in A.D. 656. (1) *Sui-shu* 隋書, *chüan* 32–35. (2) *Pa-shih ching-chi-chih, ts'e* 2–3. (3) Shanghai: Commercial Press, 1957. 2, 155, 58 pp., with

3. Three of the best of these are: Yao Chen-tsung's 姚振宗 *Han-shu i-wen-chih t'iao-li* 漢書藝文志條理, 8 *chüan*, preface dated 1892, and *Han-shu i-wen-chih shih-pu* 漢書藝文志拾補, 6 *chüan*, probably of about the same time, both published in the *K'uai-ko shih-shih shan-fang ts'ung-shu*, and in the *Erh-shih wu-shih pu-pien* and Ku Shih's 顧實 *Han-shu i-wen-chih chiang-su* 漢書藝文志講疏, preface dated 1922, published by the Commercial Press in 1925. [12] 262 pp. The second of these also appears in the 1955 Commercial Press edition of the *Han-shu i-wen-chih*. pp. 73–100.

a four-corner index. (4) *Mu-lu-hsüeh ming-chu*, series 3, *ts'e* 1. 2, 155, 58 pp., with a four-corner index.

After the compilation of the *Han-shu i-wen-chih*, the number of books dealing with certain subjects increased so rapidly that a revision of the system of classification was necessary. Historical works became so numerous that they were removed from the *Ch'un-ch'iu* 春秋 section under classics and made into a separate division. Increasing numbers of mystical writings led to the removal of that type of work from the philosophers division, to be combined with works on Buddhism in an appendix. And the belles-lettres category came into use for the first time. In the middle of the third century A.D., the first four-branch classification appeared in Cheng Mo's 鄭默 *Chung-ching* 中經, to be repeated in 264 by Hsün Hsü 荀勖 in his *Hsin-pu* 新簿. In these works the divisions were classics, philosophers, histories, and belles-lettres, in the order given. Between 317 and 322, Li Ch'ung 李充 compiled a catalogue, the *Chin Yüan-ti shu-mu* 晉元帝書目, in which he used the same four divisions but reversed the positions of the second and third. Between that time and the beginning of the T'ang dynasty, thirteen other catalogues were compiled which followed the four-branch system in the order found in Li Ch'ung's catalogue, and in general it is the system which has been followed ever since. The *Ch'i-lüeh* 七略 classification was not entirely forgotten, however, for several pre-T'ang catalogues used it with certain modifications. Among these was Juan Hsiao-hsü's 阮孝緒 *Ch'i-lu* 七錄, which was compiled between 520 and 526.

The compilers of the *Sui-shu ching-chi-chih*, which is the bibliographical section of the *Sui-shu* 隋書, took over the four-branch classification and certain other things from Li Ch'ung's catalogue, but at the same time they incorporated certain features from the *Ch'i-lüeh*. There are ten sections under classics listing 627 works, thirteen under histories with 817 works, fourteen under philosophers with 853 works, and three under belles-lettres with 554 works. In addition, 1064 titles of works from the *Ch'i-lu* which were no longer extant in the Sui period were included, that many works having been lost since the *Ch'i-lu* was completed. Under each title the number of *chüan* and the name and period of the author are given. Finally, a supplement lists collections containing 377 Taoist and 1950 Buddhist works. There is a general historical introduction of considerable value at the beginning of the *Sui-shu ching-chi-chih*, and there are also useful remarks at the end of each section. This bibliography is a very important one, since it is the only one compiled between the Han and T'ang dynasties which is still preserved in its entirety. There are two good special studies.[4]

4. Yao Chen-tsung's 姚振宗 *Sui-shu ching-chi-chih k'ao-cheng* 隋書經籍志考證, 52 *chüan*, preface dated 1897, published both in the *K'uai-ko shih-shih shan-fang ts'ung-shu*, and in the *Erh-shih-wu-shih pu-pien*. (2) Chang Tsung-yüan's 章宗源 work of the same title, 13 *chüan*, Hu-pei ts'ung-wen shu-chü 湖北崇文書局 block-print edition of 1877. Chang, who died in 1800, devoted his entire life to study the history division of the *Sui-shu ching-chi-chih*.

Pa-shih ching-chi-chih 八史經籍志. (1) Japanese block-print edition of 1825. 16 *ts'e*. (2) Chang Shou-jung 張壽榮 re-cut block-print edition of 1883. 16 *ts'e*.

This is a collection of the bibliographical sections of the six dynastic histories having such sections, and of four supplementary bibliographies compiled during the Ch'ing period. The following works are included: *Han-shu i-wen-chih, Sui-shu ching-chi-chih, Chiu T'ang-shu ching-chi-chih* 舊唐書經籍志, *T'ang-shu i-wen-chih* 唐書藝文志, *Sung-shih i-wen-chih* 宋史藝文志,[5] *Sung-shih i-wen-chih pu* 宋史藝文志補, *Pu Liao-Chin-Yüan i-wen-chih* 補遼金元藝文志, *Pu san-shih i-wen-chih* 補三史藝文志, *Pu Yüan-shih i-wen-chih* 補元史藝文志, and *Ming-shih i-wen-chih* 明史藝文志.[5] The bibliographies in the dynastic histories provide valuable material on the works extant in their respective periods, not only presenting a fairly reliable list of the books written within each particular dynasty but also making it possible, to a considerable extent, to find out when earlier books were lost. Unfortunately very few of the dynastic histories have bibliographical sections, and even these sections are by no means exhaustive.

To meet the need for additional bibliographical material of this variety, Ch'ing scholars compiled a number of bibliographical works called "supplements 補," which are based upon material in the biographical sections of dynastic histories, upon other catalogues published either during the particular dynasty being dealt with or later, and upon actual works extant at the time of compilation. Four of the bibliographies included in the *Pa-shih ching-chi-chih* are of this "supplementary" type. With the exception of the *Han-shu i-wen-chih*, in which the works are divided into six classes, all of the bibliographies included in the *Pa-shih ching-chi-chih* follow the traditional four-branch classification. Titles are arranged in the *Han-shu i-wen-chih* in such a way as to show the development of different schools of thought, but in the other nine bibliographies the titles are as a rule merely arranged chronologically under from forty to fifty classified section headings. In all ten bibliographies, besides the title of each work listed, the author's name and dynasty and the number of *chüan* are given. Possibly the most important feature about these bibliographies is the long introduction at the beginning of each which gives a comprehensive survey of the chief bibliographical facts and developments of that dynasty.

Chung-kuo li-tai i-wen-chih 中國歷代藝文志. Shanghai: Ta-kuang shu-chü 大光書局, 1936. [7] 623 pp. Photo-reprint entitled **Chung-kuo li-tai t'u-shu ta-tz'u-tien** 中國歷代圖書大辭典. Taipei: Yüan-tung t'u-shu kung-ssu 遠東圖書公司, 1956. 6, 623 pp.

---

5. Useful reprints: *Sung-shih i-wen-chih*, Shanghai: Commercial Press, 1957. 10, 560 pp. *Ming-shih i-wen-chih*, Peking: Commercial Press, 1959. 2 vols.

This is a reproduction of ten historical bibliographies: namely, the *Han-shu i-wen-chih* (q.v.); Wang Ying-lin, *Han-shu i-wen-chih k'ao-cheng* 考證; *Sui-shu ching-chi-chih* (q.v.); Chang Tsung-yüan, *Sui-shu ching-chi-chih k'ao-cheng;* the bibliographies of the two T'ang histories; the bibliography of the Sung history; and a comparative list of the books in the bibliography in the Sung history together with those of the *Sung-shih hsin-pien* 宋史新編; the *Yüan-shih hsin-pien i-wen-chih* 元史新編藝文志; and the *Ming-shih i-wen-chih* 明史藝文志. It is handy for librarians to have these materials in one volume, and the text is punctuated throughout. But, having been reproduced by the modern movable type process, it is not without typographical errors.

*I-wen-chih erh-shih-chung tsung-ho yin-te 藝文志二十種綜合引得. Compiled by William Hung 洪業, Nieh Ch'ung-ch'i 聶崇岐 and others. (1) Peiping: Harvard-Yenching Institute, 1933. (Index No. 10) 4 vols. [iv] 92; 143, 133; 300, 42; 395 pp. (2) Taipei: Ch'eng Wen Publishing Co., 1966 (photocopy).

This is a combined *kuei-hsieh* index to twenty dynastic bibliographies. Besides the ten either taken directly from dynastic histories or compiled as supplements to dynastic histories which were published together in the *Pa-shih ching-chi-chih*, four more of the latter type are here indexed: *Hou-Han-shu i-wen-chih* 後漢書藝文志, *San-kuo i-wen-chih* 三國藝文志, *Pu Chin-shu i-wen-chih* 補晉書藝文志, and *Pu Wu-tai-shih i-wen-chih* 補五代史藝文志. Of the remaining six, the *Cheng-fang Ming-chi i-shu-mu* 徵訪明季遺書目 is a bibliography of books written toward the end of the Ming dynasty and at the beginning of the Ch'ing and the *Ch'ing-shih-kao i-wen-chih* 清史稿藝文志, *Chin-shu tsung-mu* 禁書總目, *Ch'üan-hui shu-mu* 全燬書目, *Ch'ou-hui shu-mu* 抽燬書目, and *Wei-ai shu-mu* 違碍書目 are Ch'ing bibliographies. Books are indexed both by title and by author's name, the index being especially useful for locating the titles of books by the names of authors and vice versa, and for tracing the existence of particular works down through various dynasties. In a preface (1, pp. 1–39), Mr. Nieh briefly characterizes each of the twenty works indexed, after which he discusses the history of Chinese bibliography in some detail. No information is given about any individual work in the index itself beyond the title, author's name, and its location in one or more of the twenty bibliographies. However, at the back of the first volume (pp. 87–89) there is a table by which one may calculate under which section heading the work is classified in any of the fourteen bibliographies and supplementary bibliographies to dynastic histories or in the *Ch'ing-shih-kao i-wen-chih*.

T'ang-shu ching-chi, i-wen ho-chih 唐書經籍, 藝文合志. (1) Shanghai: Commercial Press, 1956. 4, 472, 69 pp. (2) *Mu-lu-hsüeh ming-chu*, series 3, ts'e 2. 4, 472, 34, 2, 18 pp.

This is a combination of the bibliographical sections of the old T'ang and new T'ang dynastic histories with supplements (pp. 385–472) by Lo Shih-lin 羅士琳 and others. There is a four-corner author and title index.

Sung-shih i-wen-chih 宋史藝文志, by T'o-t'o 脫脫 of the Yüan dynasty; **Sung-shih i-wen-chih pu** 補 (Additions), by Lu Wen-ch'ao 盧文弨 (1717–1796); and **Sung-shih i-wen-chih fu-pien** 附編 (Supplements), by Hsü Sung 徐松 (1781–1848) and four others. Shanghai: Commercial Press, 1957. 9, 560, 159, 2 pp.

This may be the best available source of bibliographical information on the Sung dynasty, for it brings together the bibliographical sections of the dynastic history, Lu Wen-ch'ao's very important supplement, and five additional supplements. Particularly useful is the combined four-corner index to book titles and authors' names.

Sung-shih yen-chiu lun-wen yü shu-chi mu-lu 宋史研究論文與書籍目錄. Compiled by Sung Hsi 宋晞. Taipei: Chung-kuo wen-hua hsüeh-yüan 中國文化學院, 1966. 111, 82 pp.

A classified catalogue of articles and books in Chinese relating to the history of the Sung dynasty published between 1905 and 1965, with an index.

Liao, Chin, Yüan i-wen-chih 遼金元藝文志. Compiled by Huang Yü-chi 黃虞稷 (1629–1691), Ni Ts'an 倪燦 (1764–1841), Ch'ien Ta-hsin 錢大昕 (1728–1804) and others. (1) Peking: Commercial Press, 1958. 3, 1, 4, 76, 248, 320, 111 pp. (2) *Mu-lu-hsüeh ming-chu*, series 3, *ts'e* 5–6 (photocopy).

This is a comprehensive bibliographical guide to these three dynasties, none of the three dynastic histories having an *i-wen-chih* or bibliographical section. The Commercial Press compilers have brought together a total of 23 bibliographies of the Liao, Chin, Yüan periods. While they are reproduced separately, there is one author and one title index to all of them.

Ming-shih i-wen-chih, pu-pien, fu-pien 明史藝文志, 補編, 附編. (1) Shanghai: Commercial Press, 1959. 2 vols. 7, 1288, 385 pp. (2) *Mu-lu-hsüeh ming-chu*, series 3, *ts'e* 7–10 (photocopy).

This work brings together six book catalogues of more than 29,000 titles relating to the Ming period: the *i-wen-chih* section of the Ming dynastic history; the *Ming-shu, ching-chi-chih* 明書, 經籍志, by Fu Wei-lin 傅維鱗, in *Ming-shu, chüan* 75–76, based on a modified version of the *Wen-yüan-ko shu-mu*

文淵閣書目; the *Hsü wen-hsien t'ung-k'ao, ching-chi-k'ao* 經籍考 (q.v.); Chiao Hung 焦竑, *Kuo-shih ching-chi-chih* 國史經籍志; and a supplement to Chiao's compilation. There is a combined author and title index by the four-corner system.

Mindaishi kenkyū bunken mokuroku or **Ming-tai shih yen-chiu wen-hsien mu-lu** 明代史研究文獻目錄. Compiled by Yamane Yukio 山根幸夫. Tokyo: Tōyō bunko, Mindaishi kenkyūshitsu 東洋文庫明代史研究室, 1960. 7, 258 pp.

This mimeographed catalogue lists 2373 articles and 128 books in Chinese and Japanese dealing with the Ming period. The pages of the magazine articles are not indicated. The titles are arranged under the following headings: general history, Japanese-Ming relations, biographies and *nien-p'u*, historical geography, social history, economic history, political and religious history, relations with the West, intellectual conditions, science, literature, fine arts, archaeology, folklore, philology and bibliography. There are six indexes including Japanese author index, Chinese author index, eminent Chinese of the Ming period, eminent non-Chinese, and eminent Europeans. The catalogue was prepared under the auspices of the Project Committee for the Ming Biographical Dictionary and is designed for the use of sinologists who do not read Japanese.

Wan-Ming shih-chi k'ao 晚明史籍考, 20 *chüan*. Compiled by Hsieh Kuo-chen 謝國楨. (1) Peiping: National Library of Peiping, 1932. 10 *ts'e*. (2) Taipei: I-wen yin-shu kuan, 1968. 3 vols. 1198 pp. (photocopy).

This annotated bibliography of some 1400 titles from late Ming (1621–1662) is indispensable to research scholars on this period because of the many works that were destroyed by the Manchu conquerors. Hsieh Kuo-chen devoted several years to searching for such rare materials in many parts of China and Japan. Following the style of Chu I-tsun's *Ching-i-k'ao* (q.v.), he brought together prefaces, comments, and pertinent information about each book written during this period and indicated its whereabout in libraries or *ts'ung-shu* and what parts if not the whole work have survived. There are author and title indexes.

Ch'ing-shih i-wen-chih, ch'ung-hsiu, 清史藝文志, 重修. Compiled by P'eng Kuo-tung 彭國棟. Taipei: Commercial Press, 1968. 3, 4, 338 pp.

The compiler claims that his 18,059 book titles almost double the number listed in the bibliographical section of the *Ch'ing-shih*. The sources for the additional works are private and public book catalogues. The classification is traditional, but the arrangement of titles makes this catalogue inconvenient to use.

Ch'ung-wen tsung-mu 崇文總目, 5 *chüan*. Compiled under Imperial auspices by Wang Yao-ch'en 王堯臣 (1001–1056) and others between 1034 and 1038; re-collected and re-edited by Ch'ien T'ung 錢侗 and others in 1799. +(1) *Yüeh-ya-t'ang ts'ung-shu, ts'e* 172–176. (2) *Kuo-hsüeh chi-pen ts'ung-shu*. [13] 407 pp. (3) *Ts'ung-shu chi-ch'eng*. (4) *Shu-mu hsü-pien,* 2 vols. 299 pp.

This is a catalogue of 3445 works with a total of 30,669 *chüan*, which constituted the imperial collection of the Sung dynasty in the middle of the eleventh century. The titles are arranged in the customary chronological order under each of the forty-five section headings, all of the sections being grouped according to the traditional four-branch system. Two of the sections, which list Taoist and Buddhist works, are rather unusual for the Sung period. The *Ch'ung-wen tsung-mu* was originally an annotated catalogue of 66 *chüan*,[6] but according to Ch'ien T'ung's preface, an edition from which the descriptive notes had been excluded was published in 1142 under the same title and issued to local officials throughout the empire with the hope of thus re-collecting those works listed in the unabridged edition which had been wholly or partially lost in the meantime. Ultimately the original annotated catalogue was lost, but a manuscript of the abridged edition was preserved in the T'ien-i-ko 天一閣 library. At the time of the compilation of the *Ssu-k'u ch'üan-shu*, this manuscript was sent to the capital and copied into that great collection of Chinese literature.

In 1799, Ch'ien T'ung and others re-collected 980 of the original descriptive notes and thirty of the original section introductions from various Sung works, most of them from the collected writings of Ou-yang Hsiu 歐陽修. In the modern editions listed above, the original descriptive notes are always preceded by the characters *yüan-shih* 原釋, and followed by the names of the sources from which they were re-collected. The insertion of the character *ch'üeh* 闕 indicates that the work was missing or incomplete in 1142, and the character *an* 案 precedes comments added by Ch'ien T'ung and his four collaborators. At the end of the work a brief supplement lists the names of nineteen works which were not listed in the T'ien-i-ko abridged edition but which, according to other sources, were included in the original annotated catalogue. There is also a short appendix containing notes on the history of the work. The *Ch'ung-wen tsung-mu* is a famous catalogue and it is an extremely useful checklist of the works extant in the middle of the eleventh, as well as in the

---

6. Different Sung works variously say that this work originally consisted of 60, 64, 66, or 67 *chüan*. The number given here, however, seems to be the most reliable.

middle of the twelfth century. The descriptive notes reassembled in the modern editions are clear and comprehensive, and it is a great pity that nearly eighty per cent of those in the original work have been lost. There is a table of sections at the beginning.

*Chün-chai tu-shu-chih 郡齋讀書志 (also entitled **Chao-te hsien-sheng chün-chai tu-shu-chih** 昭德先生郡齋讀書志). Compiled by Ch'ao Kung-wu 晁公武, compiler's preface dated 1151. +(1) Wang Hsien-ch'ien 王先謙 block-print edition published in Changsha in 1884. 10 *ts'e*. (2) The *ch'ü* 衢 edition, 20 *chüan*, arranged by Yao Ying-chi 姚應績, a pupil of Ch'ao Kung-wu, Wu-men Wang-shih i-yün ching-she 吳門汪氏藝芸精舍 re-cut block-print edition of 1819. 8 *ts'e*. (3) *Kuo-hsüeh chi-pen ts'ung-shu*. 4 vols. (4) *Shu-mu hsü-pien*. 4 vols. 1617 pp.

This is a famous annotated catalogue of two private Sung collections, those of Ch'ao Kung-wu and of Ching Meng-hsien 井孟憲. Ch'ao scrutinized all of the books very carefully, and for each work he wrote a note giving information concerning the author, the number of *chüan*, the general contents, the value, and occasionally some discussion of the authenticity. These notes are of unequal length, occasionally being very long and sometimes very brief. The bibliographical section of the *Wen-hsien t'ung-k'ao* (q.v.) is based mainly upon this work and the *Chih-chai shu-lu chieh-t'i* (q.v.), and all three are considered by Chinese scholars to be very important bibliographies.

The problem of unraveling the history of the different editions of the *Chün-chai tu-shu-chih* is a complicated one. After Ch'ao Kung-wu had finished writing his descriptive notes, two editions were published in Szechwan, one in four *chüan* and the other in twenty *chüan*, the latter arranged by Ch'ao's pupil, Yao Ying-chi, who added a number of works. In 1249 the twenty-*chüan* edition, which has since been known as the *ch'ü-pen* 衢本, was republished by Yu Chün 游鈞. The next year Li An-ch'ao 黎安朝 republished the original four-*chüan* edition, together with a one-*chüan* supplement 附志 by Chao Hsi-pien in which he catalogued his own library, and still another two-*chüan* supplement 後志 also compiled by Chao and made up of the works which had been added to the twenty-*chüan* edition by Yao Ying-chi. This edition has since been known as the *yüan-pen* 袁本. The first edition indicated above, published by Wang Hsien-ch'ien, is based upon the *ch'ü-pen*, although Wang compared it with a Ch'ing edition of the *yüan-pen* and with certain other earlier editions and added Chao Hsi-pien's one-*chüan* supplement as well as notes in smaller-sized characters in which he pointed out the differences between all of them.

The books listed in the *ch'ü-pen* are arranged under thirty-seven section headings, and those in the *yüan-pen* under thirty-nine. The classification of the individual works differs somewhat in the two editions, but the descriptive notes are the same, with only an occasional slight difference in the wording. There are 1461 titles listed in the twenty-*chüan ch'ü-pen*, compared with 1033 in the principal four-*chüan* and 435 in the two-*chüan* supplement 後志, of the *yüan-pen*. The Chao Hsi-pien one-*chüan* supplement 附志 lists 471 more. Wang Hsien-ch'ien's edition, which is the easiest of the first two to use, is preceded by a table of sections and a list of the works included.[7]

*Chih-chai shu-lu chieh-t'i 直齋書錄解題, 22 *chüan*. Compiled by Ch'en Chen-sun 陳振孫, who is known to have been an official in Chekiang between 1234 and 1236. Published in one separate edition, that of the Kiangsu shu-chü 江蘇書局, in 1883, in 6 *ts'e*, and in two different editions of the *Wu-ying-tien chü-chen-pan ts'ung-shu:* (1) Fukien re-cut block-print edition of 1868, *ts'e* 564–575; +(2) Fukien enlarged block-print edition of 1895, *ts'e* 397–408. Also, (3) *Kuo-hsüeh chi-pen ts'ung-shu.* 2 vols. 617 pp.; (4) *Shu-mu hsü-pien.* 3 vols. 332 pp.

This is an annotated catalogue of the works preserved by the compiler, who is said to have copied books from the private libraries of such famous scholars as Cheng Ch'iao 鄭樵, and to have had the largest private collection of books in existence in the middle of the thirteenth century. The titles are classified under fifty-three section headings, arranged in the order of the traditional four-branch system: 370 titles under classics, 838 under histories, 830 under philosophers, and 1032 under belles-lettres, a total of 3070. The descriptive notes, like those in the *Chün-chai tu-shu-chih,* are simple, clear, and to the point. The original edition was lost, the present edition having been re-collected from the *Yung-lo ta-tien* 永樂大典, and edited to a certain extent by the compilers of the *Ssu-k'u ch'üan-shu,* who added occasional notes in smaller-sized characters. There is a table of contents at the beginning. The *Chih-chai shu-lu chieh-t'i* and the *Chün-chai tu-shu-chih* are the most famous and probably the most important of the Sung bibliographies. The bibliographical section of the *Wen-hsien t'ung-k'ao* is based to a large extent upon them and they are extremely useful both because they present information concerning works now lost, and because they provide a basis for judging the authenticity of old works still in existence.

Nei-ko ts'ang-shu mu-lu 內閣藏書目錄, 8 *chüan*. Compiled in 1605 by Sun Neng-ch'uan 孫能傳, Chang Hsüan 張萱 and others. (1) *Shih-yüan ts'ung-shu, ts'e* 9–12. (2) *Shu-mu hsü-pien.* 2 vols. 565 pp.

This catalogue of the Ming Imperial Library lists 2552 titles. A brief descrip-

7. For a special study see *Ch'ao Kung-wu chi ch'i chün-chai tu-shu-chih* 晁公武及其郡齋讀書志 by Liu Chao-yu 劉兆祐. Taipei: National Taiwan Teachers' College, Chinese Research Institute Series (國立臺灣師範大學國文研究所集刊), 13 (1969), 463–574.

tive note was written for each work, giving the name and official title of the author, a statement concerning the contents, and necessary information regarding editions and missing parts. The books are classified as follows: first *chüan*, the writings of various emperors, works compiled under imperial auspices, and books on institutes and laws; second *chüan*, classics, histories and philosophers; third *chüan*, writings of individuals in the general category of belles-lettres; fourth *chüan*, anthologies of essays and poems, encyclopedias, works on archaeology, and charts and maps; fifth *chüan*, works on music and calligraphy, works on the Sung school of philosophy, and memorials to the throne; sixth *chüan*, biographies, natural science, and fine arts; seventh *chüan*, gazetteers; eighth *chüan*, miscellaneous works not fitting easily into other categories. This catalogue is particularly useful to those interested in Ming writings or in gazetteers.

Ch'ien-ch'ing-t'ang shu-mu 千頃堂書目, 32 *chüan*. Compiled by Huang Yü-chi 黃虞稷 (1629–1691). (1) *Shih-yüan ts'ung-shu, ts'e* 13–24. (2) Shanghai Chung-kuo shu-tien 中國書店 photolithographic edition of the above, [1935]. 16 *ts'e*. (3) *Shu-mu ts'ung-pien*. 6 vols. 2266 pp.

This is a bibliography of Ming works, at the end of each section of which there is a supplement listing Sung, Liao, Chin, and Yüan works. None of the Sung works listed appear in the bibliographical section of the *Sung-shih* 宋史, and at the time of compilation the bibliographical supplements to the other three dynastic histories had not yet appeared. The *Ch'ien-ch'ing-t'ang shu-mu* follows the traditional four-branch system, the titles being classified under fifty-two section headings. 14,907 Ming works are listed and 2907 from the earlier dynasties, making a total of 17,814. Besides the title, the author's name and the number of *chüan* are always given, and occasionally a few words which give some idea of the contents of the book. A very brief biographical note is included the first time an author's name appears. This is probably the most reliable bibliography which has been compiled for the Ming period, the bibliographical section of the *Ming-shih* 明史 being largely based upon it. The belles-lettres division is the largest, works being arranged in it according to the period of the Ming dynasty in which the writer took his literary degree. The sections listing gazetteers and civil service examination papers are also very large.

T'ien-i-ko shu-mu 天一閣書目, 4 *chüan*. Compiled by Juan Yüan 阮元, during the years 1803–1804. **Pei-mu** 碑目, 1 *chüan*, compiled by Fan Mou-min 范懋敏, and edited by Ch'ien Ta-hsin 錢大昕 (1728–1804). Yang-chou Juan Yüan wen-hsüan-lou 揚州阮元文選樓 block-print edition of 1808. 10 *ts'e*.

This catalogue lists the contents of the T'ien-i-ko 天一閣, a famous private library located at Ningpo in Chekiang, and also includes brief descriptive notes on all of the books in that library at the beginning of the nineteenth century. The library, which was founded toward the end of the Ming Chia-ching period by Fan Ch'in 范欽 (*chin-shih*, 1532), was collected from three sources. (1) Many works were bought from the Wan-chüan-lou 萬卷樓, a library belonging to one Feng Fang 豐坊, which was claimed to date from the Sung dynasty. (2) Works were bought or copied by Fan Ch'in in the course of his travels. (3) The libraries of Fan Ju-tzu 范汝梓 and Fan Ta-ch'e 范大徹, both of Ningpo, were consolidated with the books collected by Fan Ch'in. Very strict rules were enforced forbidding fires of any kind in the buildings and holding all of Fan Ch'in's descendants jointly responsible for the loss of books, with the result that the library ranked, during most of the Ch'ing period, as one of the four largest private collections in China.

This catalogue, which was the fourth to be published in the course of the library's history, is classified according to the system of the *Ssu-k'u ch'üan-shu*, and lists 4094 titles, with a total of 53,799 *chüan*. The number of historical works is extraordinarily large, being larger than that of the works in any of the other three general divisions. Under each title there is a short descriptive note giving information such as the name of the author, whether the work is printed or in manuscript form , and the names of the writers and the dates of prefaces and postfaces. Informative paragraphs are frequently quoted directly from prefaces.

The T'ien-i-ko collection was particularly strong in five respects: rare works, manuscripts including many Chinese civil service examination papers, different editions, gazetteers, and rubbings from stone inscriptions, and although most of the works were lost in the course of the T'aip'ing Rebellion and the Revolution of 1911, the catalogue is still useful.

C.   MODERN CRITICAL ANNOTATED BIBLIOGRAPHIES

The bibliographies included in this subsection are largely made up of critical notes which describe the contents of the works included in them. In general, material is presented concerning the contents, the author, the authenticity, and the value of each work, with the critical opinion of the compiler expressed in each case. The four works published together in the *Ku-shu pien-wei ssu-chung* differ somewhat from the others in that they are primarily devoted to the question of authenticity.

*Ssu-k'u ch'üan-shu tsung-mu, Ch'in-ting 四庫全書總目, 欽定, 200 *chüan*. Compiled under Imperial auspices by Chi Yün 紀昀 and others, and completed in 1782. (1) Wu-ying-tien 武英殿 block movable-type edition, published during the Ch'ien-lung period. 100 *ts'e*. (2) Kuang-tung shu-chü 廣東書局 re-cut block-print edition of 1868. 112 *ts'e*. (3) Shanghai Tien-shih-chai 點石齋 lithographic edition of 1894. 40 *ts'e.* +(4) Shanghai: Ta-tung shu-chü lithographic edition of 1930. 10 volumes or 44 *ts'e.*[8] (5) Commerical Press movable-type edition of 1934. 4 vols. [73] 4490 [133] pp. (6) Taipei: I-wen yin-shu-kuan, 1957. 16 vols. 62, 4820 pp. (photocopy of the Ta-tung edition).

This, the most important and the most useful of all Chinese annotated bibliographies, catalogues not only the 3461 works included in the *Ssu-k'u ch'üan-shu* 四庫全書 collection, but also 6793 other works which were extant at the time of the compilation of the *Ssu-k'u* but which were not considered important enough by the editors to be copied into it. The *Ssu-k'u ch'üan-shu*, which was compiled between 1773 and 1782 under the patronage of Emperor Ch'ien-lung, represents an attempt to bring together all the works known at the time which the compilers considered worthy of preservation. The editorial board consisted of 361 scholars, with Chi Yün 紀昀 and Lu Hsi-hsiung 陸錫熊 as chief editors, and Tai Chen 戴震, Shao Chin-han 邵晋涵, Chou Yung-nien 周永年, and Chi Yün, each in charge of one of the four branches into which the collection was divided. The works incorporated into the *Ssu-k'u* were copied from: the *Yung-lo ta-tien* 永樂大典, imperial publications and books in other imperial collections, books presented by provincial authorities and private collectors, and books gathered from various sources by the editors in the course of the compilation. The first copy was completed in 1782 and deposited in the Wen-yüan-ko 文淵閣, which had been built in the Peking Palace especially to house it, and during the years immediately following six other manuscript copies were made and deposited in other parts of the empire.[9]

Every work copied into the *Ssu-k'u ch'üan-shu* was preceded by a long descriptive note which was written under the direction of the editor of the particular section in which the work was classified. Later, by order of the emperor, these descriptive notes were gathered together and re-edited by Chi Yün, and

8. This edition, which is a reissue, with the addition of two new appendixes, of a first edition published in 1926, is definitely the best now available. It includes, besides the original bibliography; (1) the **Ssu-k'u wei-shou shu-mu t'i-yao** 四庫未收書目提要, in 5 *chüan*, compiled by Juan Yüan 阮元 in the Chia-ch'ing period, which lists 173 works not included in the original bibliography, with descriptive notes for each; (2) the **Ssu-k'u so-yin** 四庫索引, an author index in 4 *chüan*, compiled by Ch'en Nai-ch'ien 陳乃乾 and arranged according to the number of strokes; (3) the **Ch'ing-tai chin-hui shu-mu ssu-chung** 清代禁燬書目四種, a list of all the works said to have been partially or wholly proscribed by Ch'ien-lung. The best bibliography of the banned books is the **Ch'ing-tai chin-shu chih-chien-lu** 清代禁書知見錄 compiled by Sun Tien-ch'i 孫殿起 (Shanghai: Commercial Press, 1957). 341, 252, 75, 66, 7 pp. It has number-of-strokes and four-corner indexes. See also **Ch'ing-tai chin-hui shu-mu yen-chiu** 清代禁燬書目研究 by Wu Che-fu 吳哲夫. Taipei: Chia-hsin shui-ni kung-ssu 嘉新水泥公司, 1969. [6], 512 pp.

9. For more information, see *Ssu-k'u ch'üan-shu tsuan-hsiu-k'ao* 四庫全書纂修考, a study of the compilation of the *Ssu-k'u ch'üan-shu* by Kuo Pai-kung 郭伯恭, published by the Commercial Press, 1937. [6], 295 pp.

published, together with similar notices concerning the works listed but not copied into the collection, in the *Ssu-k'u ch'üan-shu tsung-mu*. In this annotated bibliography, as in the *Ssu-k'u* itself, the classics branch is divided into ten sections, the history branch into fifteen, the philosophers branch into fourteen, and the belles-lettres branch into five. At the beginning of each section of the bibliography there is a brief introduction, after which the works are listed chronologically, the titles of the works actually copied into the *Ssu-k'u* preceding those merely listed, each title followed by a descriptive note.

The notes give information concerning the number of *chüan*, the source of the copy made use of by the *Ssu-k'u* editors, and the nature and style of the work; the whole of, or a summary of the table of contents is included, examples of the work's strong and weak points are given, and finally there is a critical evaluation. A brief biographical sketch of the author is included the first time a work written by him appears in the catalogue. These descriptive notes, although containing some mistakes and occasionally showing prejudice, particularly against Ming writings, are very well written and, on the whole, show excellent judgment. Each was written by a specialist in the field in which it is classified, and all were finally edited and their style made uniform by one of the greatest scholars of the Ch'ien-lung period. Even though the *Ssu-k'u ch'üan-shu tsung-mu* has one serious defect in that it gives no information on different editions, no other annotated bibliography can be compared with it either in the number of works included or in the clarity and thoroughness of its descriptive notes. 10,254 works, with a total of 171,796 *chüan* (414 works not divided into *chüan*), are included in the catalogue, divided as follows.[10]

		Copied				Listed	
Classics	695	works	10,360	*chüan*	1,081	works	10,169	*chüan*
Histories	564	"	21,960	"	1,572	"	16,342	"
Philosophers	925	"	17,832	"	2,016	"	41,449	"
Belles-lettres	1,277	"	29,026	"	2,124	"	25,658	"
Total	3,461	"	78,178	"	6,793	"	93,618	"

Because of the unwieldiness and rather complicated arrangement of the *Ssu-k'u ch'üan-shu tsung-mu*, it is advisable to consult one of the indexes that have been compiled to make the bibliography easier to use.[11]

10. These figures are based upon a count made of the titles included in the Ta-tung shu-chü edition.

11. **Ssu-k'u ch'üan-shu tsung-mu chi wei-shou shu-mu yin-te** 四庫全書總目及未收書目引得. Compiled by James R. Ware and revised by Weng Tu-chien 翁獨健. (1) Peiping: Harvard-Yenching Institute, 1932. (Index No. 7) 2 vols. [xxii], 195; 210 pp. (2) Taipei: Ch'eng Wen Publishing Co., 1966 (photocopy). This is a *kuei-hsieh* index to both titles and authors' names, based on the Ta-tung shu-chü edition, with a table making it possible to apply the index to other editions.

Ssu-k'u ts'ai-chin shu-mu 四庫採進書目 (Original name: **Ko-sheng chin-ch'eng shu-mu**. 各省進呈書目). Compiled by Wu Wei-tsu 吳慰祖. Peking: Commercial Press, 1960. 2, 2, 460 pp.

This general list claims to include the titles of more than 20,000 books presented by provincial and metropolitan officials to the *Ssu-k'u* editors. They were not all examined by the editors; therefore this catalogue includes many titles which are not to be found in the *Ssu-k'u ch'üan-shu tsung-mu*. Such works are indicated in the author-title index by "*wei-shou* 未收." Also included are many proscribed books that managed to survive, adding bibliographical information to that available in the *Ch'ing-tai chin-hui shu-mu ssu-chung* (q.v.). Banned books are indicated in the index by "*chin-shu* 禁書." Finally, many good editions are presented in this catalogue which were unnoticed by the *Ssu-k'u* editors. Since there were numerous duplications and copying errors in the booklists submitted by various provinces and government offices, Wu Wei-tsu compared them with other *Ssu-k'u* lists, corrected errors, and prepared a combined author-title index which is arranged by the number of strokes.

Fan-shu ou-chi 販書偶記, 20 *chüan*. Compiled by Sun Tien-ch'i 孫殿起. Peking: Chung-hua shu-chü, 1959. 3, 4, 797 pp. **Ssu-k'u ch'üan-shu hsü-pien** 四庫全書續編, 20 *chüan*. Compiled by Sun Yao-ch'ing 孫耀卿. Taipei: Shih-chieh shu-chü, 1961. 3, 4, 563 pp.

This is a kind of supplement to the *Ssu-k'u ch'üan-shu tsung-mu* (q.v.). Sun Tien-ch'i (T. Yao-ch'ing, 1894–1958), who was a book dealer for many years, took careful notes on books written since the beginning of the Ch'ing dynasty that were not described by the *Ssu-k'u* editors and put together in this work titles, authors' names, place and time of publication, number of *chüan*, and other pertinent information. The catalogue includes not only pre-*Ssu-k'u* works but others published down to the 1930's. There is a combined four-corner index to titles and authors' names. The Taipei edition has a different title, but it is exactly the same as the Peking edition except for the changing of a few words in the publisher's explanation and omission of the index.

Ssu-k'u t'i-yao pien-cheng 四庫提要辨證. Written and published by Yü Chia-hsi 余嘉錫, 1937. 6 *ts'e.* +(1) Peking: K'o-hsüeh ch'u-pan-she, 1958. 55, 1605 pp. (2) Taipei: I-wen yin-shu-kuan, 1957. 2 vols. 441 pp.

This is a critical study of the annotations in the *Ssu-k'u ch'üan-shu tsung-mu*. The author, who spent many years making this study, was particularly interested in historical and philosophical works. He re-examined 55 of the former and 171 of the latter. In each case the author read the original annotation so carefully that he was able to point out each mistake and to document it. He also supplied new information about the author, editions, and other things. The 1958 edition adds notes on 264 works, mostly in classics and belles-lettres, making a total of 490, arranged in 24 *chüan*. All should be read together with material on the same works supplied by editors of the *Ssu-k'u ch'üan-shu*.

Ssu-k'u ch'üan-shu tsung-mu t'i-yao pu-cheng 四庫全書總目提要補正. Compiled by Hu Yü-chin 胡玉縉 (1858–1940) and Wang Hsin-fu 王欣夫. Shanghai: Chung-hua shu-chü, 1964. 2 vols. 3, 104, 1764 pp.

These corrections of and addenda to the book reviews in the *Ssu-k'u ch'üan-shu tsung-mu* (q.v.) were written by Hu Yü-chin, a famous scholar of Wu-hsien, Kiangsu, who spent a lifetime carefully reading many books and correcting many errors of the *Ssu-k'u* editors. This book resembles Yü Chia-hsi's *Ssu-k'u t'i-yao pien-cheng* (q.v.), except that Yü reexamined only 226 titles, while Hu scrutinized more than 2300. Some of Hu's notes are very long, others are of uneven length and quality. His manuscript appears to have been unfinished and unchecked when he died at the age of 82. Wang Hsin-fu devoted much time to editing Hu's notes and to arranging them according to the *Ssu-k'u* classification and order. The text is punctuated and the titles of books are indexed by the four-corner system.

Ssu-k'u ch'üan-shu chien-ming mu-lu, Ch'in-ting 四庫全書簡明目錄; 欽定, 20 *chüan*. Compiled under Imperial auspices by Chi Yün 紀昀 and others, and completed in 1782. (1) Kuang-tung shu-chü 廣東書局, 1868. 12 *ts'e*. (2) Kuang-chou ching-yün-lou 廣州經韻樓 block-print edition of the T'ung-chih period. 8 *ts'e*. (3) *Mu-lu-hsüeh ming-chu*, series 1, *ts'e* 1–2. 6, 964 pp. (4) Shanghai: Chung-hua shu-chü, 1964. 2 vols. 964, 69 pp.

Because of the bulkiness of the *Ssu-k'u ch'üan-shu tsung-mu*, the Emperor Ch'ien-lung ordered the compilation of this shorter bibliography, which lists only the works actually copied into the *Ssu-k'u* collection, and provides only a minimum of bibliographical material. For each work listed there is a note indicating the number of *chüan* and the author's name and dynasty, and giving a very brief criticism which is usually a summary of the original descriptive note but occasionally differs somewhat from it. The classification and arrangement of this catalogue are on the whole the same as those of the larger *Ssu-k'u* bibliography, and while the notes are very brief, they are sufficiently full to give the person consulting them an accurate idea of the nature and value of the work described. The Chung-hua shu-chü edition has a combined author-title index arranged according to the four-corner system.

Cheng-t'ang tu-shu-chi 鄭堂讀書記, 71 *chüan*. Compiled by Chou Chung-fu 周中孚(1768–1831). +(1) Wu-hsing Liu-shih chia-yeh-t'ang 吳興劉氏嘉業堂 block-print edition of 1921. 24 *ts'e*. (2) *Wan-yu wen-k'u ti-erh-chi*. (3) *Kuo-hsüeh chi-pen ts'ung-shu*. (4) Shanghai: Commercial Press, 1959, with a supplement **Pu-i**. 3 vols. (5) *Mu-lu-hsüeh ming-chu*, series 1, *ts'e* 3–4. 694 [47] pp.

This annotated bibliography is similar to the *Ssu-k'u ch'üan-shu tsung-mu* both in classification and in the style of its descriptive notes. There is a total of 2609 works listed and annotated, 1802 of which are also included in the *Ssu-k'u ch'üan-shu tsung-mu*. The remainder, amounting to 807, are of two kinds: those which were for some reason omitted from the *Ssu-k'u*, and those which were written too late to be included in it. Each descriptive note indicates the number of *chüan*, the particular edition, and whether or not the work was included in the *Ssu-k'u*. In addition, it gives a brief summary of the contents, some information concerning the style and arrangement, a few lines of criticism, and occasionally a comparison of different editions. The names of the writers of prefaces and their dates are given and also a brief biographical sketch of the author the first time a work written by him appears. The notes are a little shorter than those in the *Ssu-k'u*, the material, particularly that of a critical nature, being less detailed. Not infrequently the figures given in the bibliography are incorrect. The work as it is now known is almost unquestionably incomplete, for the original manuscript is known to have consisted of one hundred *ts'e;* furthermore, the belles-lettres division is very short, listing only 132 titles. However, the descriptive notes which have survived are very helpful, particularly those for works not included in the *Ssu-k'u*.

Ku-shu pien-wei ssu-chung 古書辨偽四種. (1) Shanghai: Commercial Press, 1935. 2, 169 pp. (2) *Kuo-hsüeh chi-pen ts'ung-shu*.

This is a collection of four critical studies of early books. The authors of all four were great scholars, and between them they established a new critical approach to China's ancient writings which ultimately flowered in the modern critical movement. (1) The **Chu-tzu-pien** 諸子辨,[12] written by Sung Lien 宋濂 in 1458, was intended primarily to present othodox interpretations concerning some forty philosophic works examined, and the writer's investigation of their authenticity was merely incidental. (2) The **Ssu-pu cheng-e** 四部正譌,[13] written by Hu Ying-lin 胡應麟 in 1586, is devoted to an examination of more than one hundred works primarily with a view to determining their authenti-

---

12. Published separately. Hong Kong: T'ai-p'ing shu-chü, 1962. 4, 7, 48 pp.
13. Published separately. Peiping: Ching-shan shu-she 景山書社, 1929, with a preface by Ku Chieh-kang 顧頡剛.

city. A special technique was worked out by Hu, and more or less scientific principles of critical analysis are outlined in this work. (3) Eighty-nine works are examined by Yao Chi-heng 姚際恒 (1647–1715?) in the **Ku-chin wei-shu-k'ao** 古今偽書考.[14] Yao further developed Hu's methods and dared to attack traditional ideas at a time when heterodoxy was extremely unpopular. (4) The **K'ao-hsin-lu t'i-yao** 考信錄提要 of Ts'ui Shu 崔述 (1740–1816) severely attacks the authenticity of a number of works and also discusses methods for judging forged works among classics, classical commentaries, histories, and philosophic works. A fifth work of the same general type, K'ang Yu-wei's 康有爲 **Hsin-hsüeh wei-ching-k'ao** 新學偽經考,[15] might well have been included in this collection. For a list of a number of the critical writings of modern scholars, the **Ku-shih-pien** 古史辨 should be consulted.[16]

Wei-shu t'ung-k'ao 偽書通考. Compiled by Chang Hsin-ch'eng 張心澂. (1) Shanghai: Commercial Press, 1939. 2 vols. [11] 1142 pp. (2) Revised edition, Shanghai: Commercial Press, 1959. 2 vols. 1318 pp., with a four-corner index.

This is a general review of forged books. It sums up the total achievements of Chinese textual criticism in determining the authenticity of many books. After briefly discussing motives for forgery and methods of detecting forged books, the compiler proceeds to discredit 1059 works as forgeries, semi-forgeries, and suspected forgeries. These are classified as follows: classics, 73; history, 93; philosophy, 317; belles-lettres, 129; Taoist canons, 31; Buddhist literature, 416. Under each title, material from ancient and modern critical bibliographies is quoted with clear indication of sources. Although the compiler presents his own position regarding the authenticity of certain books, the novice may at other times be perplexed by the many varying opinions submitted without indication of any definite conclusion. The 1959 edition clears some of the works previously thought to have been forgeries.

T'ung-shu i-ming t'ung-chien 同書異名通檢. Compiled by Tu Hsin-fu 杜信孚. Hong Kong: T'ai-p'ing shu-chü, 1963. 4, 8, 228 pp.

This is a catalogue of books dating from ancient times to 1949 that have been published under more than one title, in many cases in order to mislead

14. Published separately. Hong Kong: T'ai-p'ing shu-chü, 1962. 10, 19, 71, 10, 18 pp.
15. (1) K'ang-shih wan-mu-ts'ao-t'ang 康氏萬木草堂 block-print edition of 1891. 6 *ts'e*. (2) *Wan-yu wen-k'u ti-erh-chi*. 3 *ts'e*. (3) Taipei: Shih-chieh shu-chü, 1962. 4, 426 pp.
16. Published in 1935 by the Peiping Ching-shan shu-she. [44] pp. This is a reprint of the tables of contents of the first five volumes of the *Ku-shih-pien* 古史辨, which is a symposium of critical essays written by contemporary scholars, and of the *Pien-wei ts'ung-k'an ti-i-chi* 辨偽叢刊第一集, which is a collection of ten critical studies published by the Ching-shan shu-she.

the buying public. Librarian Tu Hsin-fu has collected more than 4,000 titles, indicating under each the number of *chüan*, the author's name, time and place, different editions, and the different names under which the work has been issued. The titles are arranged according to the number of strokes. At the beginning there is an index of first characters, making it easy to locate any title. This is a very useful compilation especially for librarians. It is hoped that a supplement will be prepared covering post-1949 publications, among which there are many pirated editions of which the title or the author's name has been changed.

D.   BIBLIOGRAPHIES OF EDITIONS

Most Chinese bibliographies list only a limited number of editions, making it necessary for scholars and librarians who wish to know how many editions of a work there are—particularly rare editions—to consult the special bibliographies described in this subsection. Although the information given about each edition is very limited, it is sufficient to identify the edition and to make consultation of the catalogues listed in the two following subsections more intelligible.

Ssu-k'u chien-ming mu-lu piao-chu 四庫簡明目錄標注, 20 *chüan*; supplement, 1 *chüan*. Compiled by Shao I-ch'en 邵懿辰 (1810–1860). (1) Jen-ho Shao-shih pan-yen-lu 仁和邵氏半巖廬 block-print edition of 1911. 6 *ts'e*. (2) Peking: Chung-hua shu-chü, 1959, with supplements.[17] 2, 11, 1185 pp. (3) *Mu-lu-hsüeh ming-chu*, series 2, *ts'e* 5–6. 3, 1038 pp.

Neither the *Ssu-k'u ch'üan-shu tsung-mu* nor the *Ssu-k'u ch'üan-shu chien-ming mu-lu* contains material on editions, but Shao I-ch'en wrote on the margin of his copy of the latter work notes concerning all of the different editions that he was able to examine. He made the acquaintance of many famous book-collectors and secured permission to look through their libraries for editions which he had not previously seen. After his death his notes passed through the hands of various scholars, among them Miao Ch'üan-sun 繆荃孫 and Tung K'ang 董康, and were finally published by one of Shao's descendants. The classification and order of titles follow exactly those of the *Ssu-k'u ch'üan-shu chien-ming mu-lu*, and under each title all editions are listed which were known to the compiler or to those scholars who later had access to his manuscript. Unfortunately the number of *ts'e* is only occasionally given, and there are few exact dates.

17. *Shan-pen shu-pa chi ch'i-t'a* 善本書跋及其他; *Ssu-k'u wei-ch'uan-pen shu-mu* 四庫未傳本書目; *Tung-kuo shu-mu* 東國書目 (Chinese books in Korea and Japan). This edition has a four-corner index to titles and authors' names.

Lü-t'ing chih-chien ch'uan-pen shu-mu 邵亭知見傳本書目, 16 *chüan*. Compiled by Mo Yu-chih 莫友芝 (1811–1871). (1) Movable-type edition published in Peking by Tanaka Keitaro 田中慶太郎 in 1909. 16 *ts'e.* (2) Shan-yin Wu-shih hsi-ling yin-she 山陰吳氏西泠印社 movable-type edition of about the same time. 6 *ts'e.* +(3) Chiang-an Fu Tseng-hsiang 江安傅增湘 movable-type edition published after 1911. 8 *ts'e.* (4) Shanghai Sao-yeh shan-fang 上海掃葉山房 lithographic edition of 1923. 8 *ts'e.*

This bibliography, based on the titles listed in the *Ssu-k'u ch'üan-shu chien-ming mu-lu*, presents data on all of the editions seen or heard of by the compiler. Particularly good editions are indicated by the character *chia* 佳, and poor editions by the character *lieh* 劣. Editions which are not so designated may either be undistinguished or may not have been seen by the compiler. This bibliography and the *Ssu-k'u chien-ming mu-lu piao-chu* are the two best sources for material on different editions. While the latter gives more detailed information and is more reliable because the compiler himself examined every edition included, the former includes very many more editions, and it is easier to use.

Shui-ching-chu teng pa-chung ku-chi yin-yung shu-mu hui-pien 水經注等八種古籍引用書目彙編. Compiled by Ma Nien-tsu 馬念祖. Shanghai: Chung-hua shu-chü, 1960. 4, 133 pp.

This is a catalogue of ancient books quoted in the commentaries of four works: *Shui-ching* by Li Tao-yüan 酈道元; *San-kuo chih* 三國志 by P'ei Sung-chih 裴松之; *Shih-shuo hsin-yü* 世說新語 by Liu Hsiao-piao 劉孝標; *Wen-hsüan* 文選 by Li Shan 李善; and in the texts of four encyclopedias: *I-wen lei-chü* (q.v.), *I-ch'ieh ching yin-i* 一切經音義, *T'ai-p'ing yü-lan* (q.v.), and *T'ai-p'ing kuang-chi* (q.v.). More than 6,000 books are quoted in these eight works, a majority of them no longer extant. This is a useful handbook for students of bibliography and of ancient and medieval Chinese culture.

E.   REFERENCE CATALOGUES OF RARE EDITIONS

Although there are thousands of rare editions scattered through numerous Chinese and foreign libraries, probably the largest collections are those in the Peking Library and in the National Central Library in Taipei. The catalogues of those collections are included in this subsection because they provide convenient and useful checklists.

Pei-ching t'u-shu-kuan shan-pen shu-mu 北京圖書館善本書目. Compiled in the rare book section of the Peking Library. Peking: Chung-hua shu-chü, 1959. 8 vols.

This collection of more than 11,000 rare books is said to be the best of its kind in China. The Peking Library inherited a good portion of the rare works that had belonged to the Ch'ing government and also secured the Tunhuang manuscripts that remain in China. In 1949 the People's Liberation Army turned over more than 4,000 *chüan* of Chao Ch'eng-chin's 趙城金 famous library that had been taken away by Japanese soldiers a few years earlier. At the same time many private bibliographers such as Chou Shu-tao 周叔弢 and Fu Chung-mo 傅忠謨 offered their valuable collections to the Library for permanent custody, and the Soviet Union and other friendly nations returned many volumes of the *Yung-lo ta-tien* that had been bought or seized earlier by foreigners. From these various sources and through purchase, a magnificent collection of rare books has been built up. The catalogue is classified according to the *Ssu-k'u* system and bibliographical data are carefully indicated. There is neither an author nor a title index.

Kuo-li chung-yang t'u-shu-kuan shan-pen shu-mu, tseng-ting pen

國立中央圖書館善本書目，增訂本. Taipei: National Central Library, 1967. 4 vols. 2, 2, 3, 14, 1872 pp.

This enlarged and revised catalogue of 143,000 *ts'e* of rare books in the National Central Library is classified according to the *Ssu-k'u* system. In addition to the rare works it had collected in Nanking, the National Central Library has custody over the rare book collection of the Northeastern University Library and over those sent from the National Library of Peiping to the American Library of Congress for safe keeping at the time of the Japanese invasion and ultimately shipped to Taiwan. A good number of unusual works have also been purchased during the last decade.

T'ai-wan kung-ts'ang Sung Yüan pen lien-ho shu-mu 臺灣公藏宋元本

聯合書目. Compiled by Ch'ang Pi-te 昌彼得. Taipei: The National Central Library, 1955. 70 pp.

This is a union list of over 1,000 Sung, Chin, and Yüan editions that were shipped to Taiwan from continental China during the late 1940's and are now in various public libraries there. A very terse description of each work is given and its present location.

Kuo-hui t'u-shu-kuan ts'ang, Chung-kuo shan-pen shu-lu 國會圖書館藏,

中國善本書錄 (*A Descriptive Catalog of Rare Chinese Books in the Library of Congress*). Compiled by Wang Chung-min 王重民, edited by T. L. Yuan. Washington: Library of Congress, 1957. 2 vols. 2, 2, 1305 pp.

This descriptive catalogue of 1,777 rare works accumulated by the Library of Congress during the last generation or more was compiled by library experts and has author and title indexes arranged by the number of strokes. Although not available on interlibrary loan, the books in this collection may be consulted in the library, and microfilms or photostats of all or parts of them may be secured through the Library's photoduplication service.

Kuo-li Pei-p'ing t'u-shu-kuan shan-pen shu-mu i-pien 國立北平圖書館善本書目乙編, 4 *chüan*. **Hsü-mu** 續目, 4 *chüan*. Compiled by Chao Lu-cho 趙錄綽. National Library of Peiping 國立北平圖書館, 1935–1937. 2 *ts'e*.

This is a catalogue of the old National Library collection of valuable Ch'ing dynasty works, including rare editions, drafts, and manuscripts, works annotated by famous scholars, and certain especially well printed or otherwise valuable editions. It follows the traditional four-branch arrangement, listing, according to the calculation of the compiler, a total of 2779 titles, divided as follows: classics 212, histories 1864, philosophers 182, belles-lettres 408, and 113 less important works listed in supplements to the various subsections into which the catalogue is divided. Under each title the number of *chüan*, the name and dynasty of the author, the time of publication, writing (if a draft), or copying, and the names of writers of postfaces are given. If an edition is incomplete, the number of *chüan* remaining is indicated, and the titles of works included in *ts'ung-shu* are listed under each *ts'ung-shu* title. This collection is important for its more than a thousand rare gazetteers, its almost complete set of provincial taxation records for the Shun-chih and K'ang-hsi periods, its approximately five hundred dramas performed in the Palace since the Ch'ien-lung period, and its rare editions and not-yet-published drafts. The supplement lists 1350 titles of rare Ch'ing editions and manuscripts. There are some entries written in Manchu.

Tun-huang i-shu tsung-mu so-yin 敦煌遺書總目索引. (1) Peking: Commercial Press, 1962. 2, 552 pp. (2) Tokyo: Kyokutō shoten 極東書店, 1963 (facsimile reproduction).

This is a union catalogue of some 22,500 scattered Tunhuang manuscripts: (1) more than 8000 in the Peking Library; (2) 6780 selected and brought from Tunhuang by Sir Aurel Stein, now in the British Museum[18] (there are microfilm copies of these in the Peking Library); (3) 3378, mostly in the Chinese language, in the Bibliothèque Nationale in Paris, where they were deposited

---

18. The British Museum collection of Tunhuang manuscripts is the best because Sir Aurel Stein had first access to the cave where they were found and took the neatest and best manuscripts to England. For an expert, careful description, see Lionel Giles, *Descriptive Catalogue of the Chinese Manuscripts from Tunhuang in the British Museum* (London: Trustees of the British Museum, 1957). xxv, 334 pp.

by Paul Pelliot; and (4) scattered manuscripts in Japan and in fourteen other collections in China, the information on these last being based on library and collection catalogues. The entries are arranged by the number of strokes.

F. ANNOTATED CATALOGUES OF RARE EDITIONS

Most of the works included in this subsection are annotated catalogues of collections of rare editions which have been scattered or destroyed, the permanent value of the catalogues being due to their descriptive notes. While most of the catalogues contain a certain amount of material descriptive of the works themselves, the primary interest of the compilers was in editions. Form and make-up are described, significant prefaces and postfaces are reproduced, and information is given concerning publication, copying, and the history of ownership. Such problems as dating, the determination of the publisher or copyist, and the transcription of seals, require experience and technical knowledge far beyond those of the ordinary scholar, so for reliable information on such matters it is necessary to turn to catalogues such as these, which were compiled by experts.

Tu-shu min-ch'iu-chi chiao-cheng 讀書敏求記校證, 4 *chüan*, with supplements. Compiled by Ch'ien Tseng 錢曾 (H. Tsun-wang 遵王, 1630—after 1699). Collated by Kuan T'ing-fen 管庭芬 (b. 1797), enlarged and published by Chang Yü 章鈺, block-print edition of 1926. 6 *ts'e*. (2) *Ts'ung-shu chi-ch'eng, ts'e* 49. (3) *Shu-mu ts'ung-pien*. 3 vols. 14, 1046 pp.

This is the annotated catalogue of a private library of 634 selected works, classified according to the traditional four-branch system. Ch'ien Tseng was a book collector who was particularly interested in fine editions, and in this catalogue are published the notes which he wrote describing the works in his library. In his notes, besides making brief statements concerning the content and value of the works themselves, Ch'ien discussed in some detail the characteristics of the different editions in his collection. Furthermore, if his copy of a work was an unusually rare or fine one, he traced the history of its ownership or designated the person from whose library it was copied. The *Ssu-k'u* editors criticised Ch'ien's classification of works and said of his notes that they are inconsequential, but it should be pointed out that in most of the notes in the *Ssu-k'u ch'üan-shu tsung-mu* in which editions discussed in the *Tu-shu min-ch'iu-chi chiao-cheng* are mentioned, Ch'ien's work is referred to; and most Chinese scholars who are interested in editions keep it near at hand. The notes were kept in manuscript form for a generation or more, but various incomplete printed editions appeared from time to time after 1726. This edition was re-collected by Chang Yü, a contemporary scholar, who collated various editions and published the results in 1926. The work itself takes up only one fourth of the present edition, the rest of it consisting of Chang's supplementary notes, and prefaces and postfaces reproduced from a number of earlier editions. There is a table of contents at the beginning.

T'ien-lu lin-lang shu-mu, Ch'in-ting 天祿琳琅書目, 欽定, 10 *chüan*. Compiled under Imperial auspices in 1744, and revised in 1775 by Yü Min-chung 于敏中 and others. **T'ien-lu lin-lang shu-mu hou-pien** 天祿琳琅書目後編, 20 *chüan*. Compiled under Imperial auspices by P'eng Yüan-jui 彭元瑞 and others, and completed in 1798. (1) Changsha Wang-shih 長沙王氏 block-print edition of 1884. 10 *ts'e*. (2) *Shu-mu hsü-pien*. 5 vols. 1810 pp.

These are catalogues of a collection of rare editions preserved in the Imperial Library during the Ch'ien-lung period. The *T'ien-lu lin-lang shu-mu*, which lists a total of 415 editions including duplicates, is divided into four parts: *chüan* 1–3 lists Sung editions; *chüan* 4 lists traced copies of Sung editions; *chüan* 5–6 lists Yüan editions; and *chüan* 7–10 lists Ming editions. In each of the four parts the works are arranged according to the traditional four-branch system. Under each title the following information is given: the number of *chüan*, the number of *ts'e* and *han*, a very brief biography of the author, a summary of the table of contents, the date of publication, a history of the ownership, and the state of preservation. Imperial notes, and all prefaces and postfaces are reproduced in full and also the seals of previous owners.

The supplement, which lists a total of 665 editions including duplicates, is arranged in the same way as the original catalogue: *chüan* 1–7 lists Sung editions; *chüan* 8, traced copies of Sung editions; *chüan* 9–11, Yüan editions; and *chüan* 12–20, Ming editions. There is one Chin edition listed in each catalogue and a Liao in the supplement. All are famous works and the catalogues are particularly useful for purposes of checking editions. Nearly all of the books listed in the *T'ien-lu lin-lang shu-mu* were lost when the Chao-jen-tien 昭仁殿, in which the special collection was housed, was burned in 1797, those which escaped destruction being later listed in the supplement.

Ku-kung tien-pen shu-k'u hsien-ts'un-mu 故宮殿本書庫現存目, 3 *chüan*. Compiled by T'ao Hsiang 陶湘. Peiping: The Palace Museum 北平故宮博物院, 1933. 3 *ts'e*.

This is an annotated catalogue of 1290 Ch'ing "Palace editions" and other works compiled under imperial auspices during the Ch'ing dynasty which were preserved in the Palace Museum. It is divided into twenty sections, following in general the classification of the bibliographical sections of the *Kuo-ch'ao kung-shih* 國朝宮史 and the *Kuo-ch'ao kung-shih hsü-pien* 續編. Among the types of works listed are *Shih-lu* 實錄, *Sheng-hsün* 聖訓, imperial writings

御製, *Fang-lüeh* 方略, the twenty-four dynastic histories, the thirteen classics, and the twenty-eight Buddhist canons. Under each title, in addition to giving the number of *chüan* and *ts'e*, the author's or compiler's name, and the period of publication, the history of the compilation or publication is usually traced by quoting from relevant imperial prefaces, poems, and essays. Explanatory notes are also frequently added, giving the compiler's conclusions regarding certain problems, comparing editions, and dealing with related matters, as, for example, the different editions of the *Wu-ying-tien chü-chen-pan ts'ung-shu* 武英殿聚珍版叢書. Although not very conveniently arranged, this catalogue is a useful guide to Ch'ing Palace compilations and publications. For a more conveniently arranged list of Palace publications, which, however, gives only the title, the author's name, the number of *chüan* and *ts'e*, and very brief notes on the nature and time of publication, see the **Ku-kung so-ts'ang tien-pen shu-mu** 故宮所藏殿本書目, published in one *ts'e* in 1933 by the Palace Museum.

Ai-jih ching-lu ts'ang-shu-chih 愛日精廬藏書志, 36 *chüan;* supplement, 4 *chüan*. Compiled by Chang Chin-wu 張金吾, compiler's preface dated 1826. (1) Wu-hsien Ling-fen-ko Hsü-shih 吳縣靈芬閣徐氏 block-print edition of 1887. 10 *ts'e*. (2) Chao-wen Chang-shih 昭文張氏 block-print edition of 1826. 8 *ts'e*.

This is the descriptive catalogue of a private library of 706 works, mostly Sung and Yüan editions. The classification follows the traditional four-branch system, with 136 titles listed under classics, 182 under histories, 123 under philosophers, and 265 under belles-lettres. In the supplement, 58 additional works are listed. Following the method used in the bibliographical section of the *Wen-hsien t'ung-k'ao*, all prefaces and postfaces to pre-Ming editions are quoted exactly as they appear in the original edition, unless they have already been published in the collected works of the writer or in the *Ching-i k'ao*, the *Hsiao-hsüeh k'ao*, or the *Ch'üan-T'ang wen* 全唐文. In addition, notes made by previous owners or by other scholars in any of the works listed are reproduced in full. The title given is always that appearing in the work itself, even when it differs from one more commonly used, and different editions of the same work are always dealt with separately. When the name or dynasty of an author has had to be ascertained through independent research on the part of the compiler, it is given in incised characters. This catalogue is useful both because of the many early prefaces reproduced in it and because some of the works listed are now very rare.

T'ieh-ch'in t'ung-chien-lou ts'ang-shu mu-lu 鐵琴銅劍樓藏書目錄, 24 *chüan*. Compiled by Ch'ü Yung 瞿鏞, who lived during the second half of the nineteenth century. (1) Ch'ang-shou Ch'ü-shih ku-li chia-shu 常熟瞿氏罟

里家塾 block-print edition of 1898. 10 *ts'e*. (2) Tung K'ang 董康 Sung-fen-shih 誦芬室 block-print edition of 1897. 10 *ts'e*. (3) *Shu-mu ts'ung-pien*. 5 vols. 16, 1510 pp.

This annotated catalogue lists the rare works preserved in one of the four great private collections of the latter part of the Ch'ing dynasty. 1228 works are included: classics 165, histories 246, philosophers 343, and belles-lettres 474. Most of the works listed are Sung and Yüan editions, the remainder being principally old manuscripts. Under each title there are given the number of *chüan*, the dynasty of publication, the name and dynasty of the author, a summary of the contents, a comparison with more modern editions, and the names of famous scholars who had examined or annotated it. The descriptions of editions are particularly detailed, it being the purpose of the compiler to demonstrate the superiority of Sung and Yüan editions.

Pi-sung-lou ts'ang-shu-chih 皕宋樓藏書志, 120 *chüan*; supplement, 4 *chüan*. Compiled by Lu Hsin-yüan 陸心源 (1834–1894). (1) Shih-wan-chüan-lou 十萬卷樓 block-print edition of 1882. 32 *ts'e*. (2) *Shu-mu hsü-pien*. 12 vols. 5578 pp.

This is a descriptive catalogue of the collection of rare editions preserved in another of the four great private libraries of the latter half of the Ch'ing period, and it includes many works which do not appear in the *Ssu-k'u ch'üan-shu tsung-mu*. 1913 titles are listed, classified according to the four-branch system as follows: classics 226, histories 316, philosophers 530, and belles-lettres 841. According to a preface there were more than 200 Sung editions and more than 400 Yüan editions in the collection, but in the catalogue there are 251 Sung editions, 166 Yüan editions, and 210 traced or re-cut copies of Sung and Yüan editions listed. Where works have already been described in the *Ssu-k'u ch'üan-shu tsung-mu* or in the *Ssu-k'u wei-shou shu-mu t'i-yao*, only brief summaries of the notes in those bibliographies are given in this one, but for those works not included in the two earlier bibliographies, the brief notes here included are modeled after those in the *Chün-chai tu-shu-chih* and the *Chih-chai shu-lu chieh-t'i*. The prefaces and postfaces of all pre-Ming editions, unless they have previously appeared in the collected writings of the authors or in the *T'ung-chih-t'ang ching-chieh* 通志堂經解, the *Ch'üan-T'ang-wen* 全唐文, or the *Shih-wan-chüan-lou ts'ung-shu* 十萬卷樓叢書, are exactly reproduced, and the editions themselves are minutely described. Reading notes of early and contemporary scholars, and notes and seals of previous owners are also included; and the taboo characters substituted for in each work are indicated. Twelve years after the death of Lu Hsin-yüan the works still left in the collection were sold to the Seikado Library 靜嘉堂文庫, near Tokyo, Japan. Already, however, many of the early editions had disappeared, for according to the catalogue of the Seikado Library, it secured only 121 Sung and 109 Yüan editions by the transaction.

I-ku-t'ang t'i-pa 儀顧堂題跋, 16 *chüan*; supplement 16 *chüan*. Compiled and published between 1890 and 1892 by Lu Hsin-yüan 陸心源. 14 *ts'e*. (2) *Shu-mu hsü-pien*. 4 vols. 1490 pp.

This annotated catalogue was compiled by Lu Hsin-yüan, who was a famous book collector and bibliographer of the last part of the Ch'ing dynasty. The last three *chüan* in the main work and the last two in the supplement are made up of postfaces written by Lu for the examples of calligraphy, the rubbings of stone inscriptions, and the pictures in his private collection, and the remainder consists of notes written by him describing his rare books. The classification is according to the four-branch system, with 266 titles listed in the main work and 270 in the supplement, most of them Sung and Yüan editions. Under each title there are given the number of *chüan*, a description of the edition and a comparison with other editions, and material concerning the author. This last type of material is the most important in the bibliography, particularly that relating to writers not dealt with at all or not adequately in the *Ssu-k'u ch'üan-shu tsung-mu*. Lu was a specialist in Sung history, so Sung writers are particularly well handled; however, all of his biographical sketches are important, as the data were drawn from a wide variety of sources. Several weaknesses are apparent in this catalogue, among them being occasional unsound or contradictory conclusions, a lack of uniformity in style, and a failure to indicate sources in sufficient detail. On the whole, however, the *I-ku-t'ang t'i-pa* is a very useful work, there being much valuable material in the notes. At the beginning of both the main work and the supplement there is a table of titles indicating the approximate location of each.

Shan-pen shu-shih ts'ang-shu-chih 善本書室藏書志, 40 *chüan*; supplement, 1 *chüan*. Compiled by Ting Ping 丁丙, compiler's preface dated 1898. (1) Ch'ien-t'ang Ting-shih 錢塘丁氏 block-print edition of 1901. 16 *ts'e*. (2) *Shu-mu ts'ung-pien*. 6 vols. 2126 pp.

This is an annotated catalogue of the rare editions in the Pa-ch'ien-chüan-lou 八千卷樓 collection, most of which were later acquired by the Kiangsu Provincial Sinological Library in Nanking. There are 2668 works listed, including 283 different editions of titles counted more than once, divided as follows: classics 370, histories 462, philosophers 598, and belles-lettres 1238. The descriptive notes combine the style of the notes in the *Ssu-k'u ch'üan-shu* with that of the notes in the catalogues of most private collections, not only presenting material on the contents and value of the works themselves, but also describing the editions and reproducing a few significant sentences from prefaces, postfaces, and the notes of previous owners. This bibliography is useful not only because of the material on rare editions but also because of the simple and concise descriptions of the works themselves.

Ku-wen chiu-shu k'ao 古文舊書考, 4 *chüan*. Written by Shimada Fumi 島田翰, writer's preface dated 1903. (1) Minyusha 民友社 movable-type edition of 1905. 4 *ts'e*. (2) Peking Tsao-yü-t'ang 北京藻玉堂 movable-type edition of 1927 (also including the *Fang-yü lu* 訪餘錄). 5 *ts'e*.

The author of this work was a noted Japanese bibliographer and collator of books who had access to the Japanese Imperial Library and who took advantage of his privilege to examine the rare Chinese editions preserved there. In this work which is written in Chinese, he presents material on fifty-three rare editions, giving the history and a detailed description of each. Fifteen old Japanese manuscripts, fourteen Sung editions, twelve old Japanese printed editions, and twelve Yüan, Ming, Ch'ing, and Korean editions are discussed, the Japanese manuscripts being particularly important because they are based upon Chinese manuscripts of the T'ang dynasty or earlier. The *Ku-wen chiu-shu k'ao* is especially useful to those interested in early texts, for in it each work is minutely and competently examined and the author explains his technique and criteria in considerable detail. Of added interest are two essays, one on the history of Chinese book-binding in the first *chüan*, and one on the invention of Chinese printing in the second.

G. BIBLIOGRAPHIES FOR SPECIAL SUBJECTS

The compilation of bibliographies for special subjects is a comparatively recent development in China. Many of the bibliographies of this type published during recent decades are neither exhaustive nor wholly reliable, and they also leave much to be desired in the matter of arrangement, although recently there seems to be a tendency toward improvement.

I. MODERN CHINA

Chung-kuo chin-tai-shih ts'an-k'ao shu-mu ch'u-pien 中國近代史參考書目初編. Compiled by the Source Material Room of the Department of History, East China Teachers University 華東師範大學, 歷史系資料室. [Shanghai], 1962. 93 pp.

This catalogue of reference works on modern Chinese history from the

1840's to the 1950's is divided into four parts: general reference, gazetteers, Japanese books, and Western books. The first part (pp. 1–70) is the best, listing a large number of books, writings in *ts'ung-shu*, articles in magazines, and individual chapters in larger works. Many rare items, including manuscripts and pamphlets with ephemeral circulation, appear in these pages. The material is to be found under headings arranged by the number of strokes. Thus under *hsin-hai* 辛亥 are many accounts of the 1911 revolution. The remaining three parts are of lesser quality and usefulness. The arrangement throughout is crowded, limiting the amount of bibliographical data supplied.

Gendai Chūgoku kankei Chūgokugo bunken sōgō mokuroku or **Hsien-tai Chung-kuo kuan-hsi Chung-kuo-yü wen-hsien tsung-ho mu-lu** 現代中國關係中國語文獻總合目錄. Tokyo: Ajia keizai kenkyūjo (The Institute of Asian Economic Affairs), 1967. 8 vols.

This "Union Catalogue of Chinese Literature on Modern China" provides essential bibliographical information on 36,000 books published or republished between 1912 and 1965 that are to be found in twenty-two libraries in Japan. The subjects covered are by no means confined to the modern period. Book titles are arranged under the following headings: social sciences (vols. 1–3), natural sciences and general (vol. 4), and humanities (vols. 5–6). In each of these sections the titles are arranged alphabetically according to the Japanese *on* reading of the first character; different characters having the same sound are arranged in order of the number of strokes; and the same order is used for second and subsequent characters when the first and later characters are the same. The contents of *ts'ung-shu* are given; and the Japanese libraries in which the books may be found are indicated. In volume 7 are indexes to the names of individual and of corporate authors and compilers, arranged alphabetically following the same system as the earlier volumes. Volume 8 has indexes to the first characters of titles and authors' names arranged by (1) the Japanese *on* reading, (2) the Chinese Phonetic Scheme (of 1958), (3) the Wade-Giles system, and (4) the number of strokes. An English explanation is provided at the beginning of each volume.

Chūgokubun shimbun zasshi sōgō mokuroku or **Chung-kuo-wen hsin-wen tsa-chih tsung-ho mu-lu** 中國文新聞雜誌總合目錄. Compiled by Ichiko Chūzō 市古宙三 *et al.* Tokyo: Kindai Chūgoku kenkyū iinkai, 1959. 16, 171 pp.

This is a union catalogue of some 3,000 Chinese-language newspapers and magazines scattered among twenty-three major research institutes and libraries in Japan.

T'ai-p'ing t'ien-kuo tzu-liao mu-lu 太平天國資料目錄. Compiled by Chang Hsiu-min 張秀民 and Wang Hui-an 王會庵, edited by Chin Yü-fu 金毓黻. Shanghai: Jen-min ch'u-pan she, 1957. 4, 2, 224 pp.

This catalogue of material on the Taiping Rebellion is divided into four parts: Taiping documents, official publications and leaders' statements; accounts of the movement by people on the Ch'ing government side; recent studies of the movement; and foreigners' accounts. Sources on the Heaven and Earth Society are appended. On the whole the bibliographical data supplied on Chinese-language sources are adequate.[19]

Chiao-an shih-liao pien-mu 教案史料編目. Compiled by Wu Sheng-te 吳 盛德 and Ch'en Tseng-hui 陳增輝. Peiping: Yenching School of Religion, Yenching University, 1941. xxviii, 227 pp.

This is a "Bibliography of Chinese Source Materials dealing with 328 Local or International Cases Involving Christian Missions," during the period from 1840–1908. The materials are arranged under the four imperial reign periods of the time covered. In the first three periods the cases are arranged chronologically; in the last they are arranged first by provinces, then in chronological order. Under each case there is a brief summary; then articles, memorials, and reports concerning the case are listed, with sources carefully indicated. The collection was compiled with care and is fairly complete.

There are two useful appendixes: a bibliography of Chinese sources on the Boxer uprising, called **"Keng-tzu ch'üan-luan shu-mu** 庚子拳亂書目" and a list of documents, regulations and articles concerning missionary work in China. There is also a supplement giving material on various missionary cases which are not included in the main text. An index to the names of persons involved in the cases, arranged according to the number of strokes, is placed at the end.

"I-ho-t'uan shu-mu chieh-t'i 義和團書目解題." Compiled by Chien Po-tsan 翦伯贊. In *I-ho-t'uan* (Shanghai: Hsin-hua 新華 shu-tien, 1957), IV, 529–621.

This is an annotated bibliography of 278 Chinese works on the Boxer uprising, followed by an annotated list of 102 Western language sources. The Chinese list is classified under sixteen headings, including imperial edicts and memorials, three kinds of official despatches, local reports, private diaries,

---

19. For other bibliographies of the Taiping Rebellion see: Kuo Ting-yee, *T'ai-p'ing t'ien-kuo shih-shih jih-chih* (q.v.), pp. 179–266; Chien Yu-wen 簡又文, "Wu-shih-nien lai T'ai-p'ing t'ien-kuo shih chih yen-chiu 五十年來太平天國史之研究," in *Symposium on Chinese Studies commemorating the Golden Jubilee of the University of Hong Kong, 1911–1961* (Hong Kong University Press, 1964), pp. 237–314; Ssu-yü Teng, *Historiography of the Taiping Rebellion* (Cambridge: East Asian Research Center, Harvard University, 1962). vii, 180 pp.

miscellaneous writings, biographical materials, poetry, fiction and drama, and others. Although not exhaustive, especially on Western sources, this is an informative study aid.

"Min-kuo shih-liao shu-mu, ch'u-pien 民國史料書目, 初編.**"** Compiled by Su Te-yung 蘇德用 in *Hsüeh-shu chi-k'an* 學術季刊. Part one, Vol. 1, No. 3 (March 1953), 210–227; Part two, Vol. 1, No. 4 (June 1953), 152–176; Part three, Vol. 2, No. 1 (September 1953), 160–181.

This is a preliminary but very useful and informative list of books on the history of the Republic of China. It is divided into many sections: general, cultural, educational, political, constitutional, diplomatic, financial, and economic history, as well as communications and transportation, overseas Chinese, military history, the Northern Expedition, the anti-Japanese war, suppression of rebellions, local history, literature, and biography. Each section is further subdivided and for each book listed the title, author, publisher and date are given. Many general reference works are included. This bibliography was preceded by a catalogue of 370 works on the history of the Kuomintang by the same compiler.[20] Although somewhat inaccessible in this form, the "Min-kuo shih-liao shu-mu" is quite useful for the study of Chinese history since 1912.

Chung-kuo hsien-tai-shih tzu-liao tiao-ch'a mu-lu 中國現代史資料調查目錄. Kuo Ting-yee 郭廷以 and Li Yü-chu 李毓澍, editors-in-chief. Taipei: Institute of Modern History, Academia Sinica 中央研究院近代史研究所, 1968–1969. Limited mimeographed edition. 11 vols.

This is a catalogue of historical source materials from the first half of the twentieth century preserved in two major collections in Taiwan, those deposited with the Historical Archives Commission of the Kuomintang (vols. 1–8), and the diplomatic archives of the Institute of Modern History (vols. 9–10). The first volume lists newspapers, magazines, and government bulletins published from 1902 to 1949. The second volume lists documents dating from 1894 to 1923 under the headings of Hsing-chung hui 興中會, T'ung-meng hui 同盟會, Kuomintang 國民黨 (1912–1913), Chung-hua ko-ming tang 中華革命黨, and Chung-kuo Kuomintang (1919–1923). The third, fourth, and fifth volumes list documents relating to the Chung-kuo Kuomintang from 1924–1936, 1937–1945 and 1946–1949. Volume 6 lists documents relating to Sun Yat-sen, and volumes 7 and 8 list documents relating to other members of the Kuomintang, arranged by the number of strokes in their names, commencing with a large section devoted to Chiang Kai-shek. There are further subdivisions under the headings mentioned. The diplomatic documents in

20. **"Chung-kuo kuo-min-tang tang-shih ts'an-k'ao shu-mu** 中國國民黨々史參考書目,**"** *Hsüeh-shu chi-k'an*, Vol. 1, No. 2 (December 1952), 205–216.

volumes 9 and 10 are arranged under forty-seven topics. The eleventh volume (附錄) contains two kinds of keys to the material in the first volume and an alphabetical index to the approximately 2400 personal names (in Wade-Giles romanization) under which the references in volumes 7 and 8 are arranged. There are tables of contents at the beginning of most volumes.

T'ai-wan wen-hsien mu-lu 臺灣文獻目錄. Compiled by Li Tao-hsien 李道顯 and Ho Chin-chu 何金鑄. Taipei: Chung-kuo wen-hua hsüeh-yüan, T'ai-wan yen-chiu so 中國文化學院, 臺灣研究所, 1965. 3, 1, 10, 264, 2 pp.

This catalogue of books about Taiwan published before 1964 is divided into history, geography, sociology, literature, etc., a total of 27 sections which are listed in a table of contents at the beginning. Although there is no index, this is a useful source of bibliographical information about Taiwan.

Chung-kuo kung-ssu ching-chi yen-chiu chi-kuan chi ch'i ch'u-pan-wu yao-lan 中國公私經濟研究機關及其出版物要覽. Compiled by the Chung-kuo kuo-min ching-chi yen-chiu-so 中國國民經濟研究所 and published in 1936. [10] 176 pp.

This is a bibliography of Chinese economic affairs, classified under such section headings as: general economics, finance, currency, industry, commerce, communications, social problems, land problems, co-operatives. In each section the title, author, price, and publisher of each book are indicated. The materials were collected from both government and private sources. This is a useful bibliography of writings on economic affairs before 1936.

Chung-kuo she-hui wen-t'i ts'an-k'ao tzu-liao so-yin 中國社會問題參考資料索引. Compiled by Yü Ch'ing-t'ang 俞慶棠. Wu-hsi 無錫: Kiangsu Provincial Educational Academy 江蘇省立教育學院, 1936. 162 pp.

This is an index to some 1600 books and articles dealing with Chinese social questions, including population, national characteristics, geography, economic conditions, social organizations, racial problems, rural labor, poverty, unemployment, family, women and children. Bibliographical data are given in full.

2.   TAOISM AND BUDDHISM

Tao-ts'ang mu-lu hsiang-chu 道藏目錄詳註, 4 *chüan*. Supplement: **Ta-Ming hsü-tao-ts'ang-ching mu-lu** 大明續道藏經目錄, 1 *chüan*. Compiled by Po Yün-chi 白雲霽, and completed, according to the *Ssu-k'u ch'üan-shu tsung-mu*, in 1626. (1) T'ui-keng-t'ang 退耕堂 lithographic edition of the Wen-chin-ko 文津閣 copy of the *Ssu-k'u ch'üan-shu*, published by Hsü Shih-ch'ang 徐世昌 sometime after 1911. 4 *ts'e*. (2) *Wan-yu wen-k'u ti-i-chi*. 2 *ts'e*. (3) *Kuo-hsüeh chi-pen ts'ung-shu*.

This is the only general annotated bibliography of Taoist writings extant. It is divided into seven sections, the first three of which are each divided into twelve subsections. Under each title there are given the name of the author, the number of *chüan* (if the work is so divided), the *hao* under which it is to be found in the Taoist canon,[21] information as to whether there are charms to be found in it, and usually a descriptive note. The descriptive notes may give the table of contents, discuss the nature of the work, and reproduce a few important lines; sometimes they give the names and describe the contents of commentaries. Many important works, particularly philosophic writings, which have no direct connection with Taoism are included both in this cata-logue and in the Taoist canon. While a few works included in the canon have been left out of the catalogue, and although the descriptive notes are inferior to those in the *Ssu-k'u ch'üan-shu tsung-mu*, it is still an important tool for those desiring either a general introduction to Taoist literature or a brief introduc-tion to individual Taoist writings.

Chung-wai Lao-tzu chu-shu mu-lu 中外老子注述目錄. Compiled by Yen Ling-feng 嚴靈峯.[22] Taipei: Chung-hua ts'ung-shu wei-yüan hui, 1957. [8] 380, 5 pp.

This is a bibliography of writings about Lao-tzu, including special studies, desultory notes, and translations by scholars in China and foreign countries from the third century B.C. to 1956. Yen Ling-feng has combed numerous bibliographies and catalogues and accumulated some 1600 books and articles about Lao-tzu, which are arranged dynasty by dynasty. Yen's important con-tribution is the indication of which book or article is "extant," "lost," "par-tially lost," "still in manuscript form," "not known in detail," or "unseen." Various editions, Tun-huang manuscripts, and apocrypha on Lao-tzu are also listed. In spite of some typographical and other errors and the incompleteness of the list of translations of Lao-tzu into Western languages, this biblio-graphy should be useful to students of the ancient philosopher.

21. The Taoist canon is divided into 512 *hao* 號, each of which is designated by a character in the *Ch'ien-tzu-wen* 千字文; those *hao* from *t'ien* 天 to *tu* 杜 make up the old canon, and the remainder the new canon compiled during the Ming dynasty. The **Tao-ts'ang tzu-mu yin-te** 道藏子目引得, which was compiled by Weng Tu-chien 翁獨健, provides *kuei-hsieh* indexes to the titles and names of the authors of the works included in the *Tao-ts'ang* 道藏, the *Tao-ts'ang chi-yao* 道藏輯要 and a similar catalogue no longer extant, and also to the names of persons mentioned in seventy-seven historical and biographical works included in the *Tao-ts'ang*. (1) Peiping: Harvard-Yenching Institute, 1935. (Index No. 25) xxxvi, 216 pp. (2) Taipei: Ch'eng Wen Publishing Co., 1966 (photocopy).

22. The same author has also compiled **Lieh-tzu Chuang-tzu chih-chien shu-mu** 列子莊子知見書目 (Hong Kong: Wu-ch'iu-pei chai 無求備齋 1961). 2, 405 pp.; and **Mo-tzu chih-chien shu-mu** 墨子知見書目 (Taipei: Hsüeh-sheng shu-chü, 1969).

Yüeh-ts'ang chih-ching 閱藏知津, 44 *chüan;* table of titles, 4 *chüan.* Compiled by the Buddhist monk Chih-hsü 智旭, compiler's preface dated 1654. (1) Re-cut block-print edition published in Peking by Chang Hsing 張珩 in 1792. 12 *ts'e.* (2) Chin-ling k'o-ching ch'u 金陵刻經處 re-cut block-print edition of 1892. 10 *ts'e.* (3) *Wan-yu wen-k'u ti-i-chi.* 6 *ts'e.* (4) *Kuo-hsüeh chi-pen ts'ung-shu.*

This is a collection of reading notes on the Chinese Buddhist canon which answers very well as an annotated bibliography of Buddhist writings and translations. There are a number of good Chinese catalogues of Buddhist works, among them the *Ch'u-san-ts'ang chi-chi* 出三藏記集 (compiled in A.D. 520), the *Ta-T'ang nei-tien-lu* 大唐內典錄 (completed in A.D. 664), and the *K'ai-yüan shih-chiao-lu* 開元釋教錄 (compiled in A.D. 730), but there are only two usable annotated bibliographies, the *Ta-ts'ang sheng-chiao fa-pao piao-mu* 大藏聖教法寶標目 and the present work. This work, which is the more useful of the two, is divided into four parts: canonical writings 經藏, disciplinarian writings 律藏, metaphysical writings 論藏, and miscellaneous writings 雜藏. Each part is divided into two sections, each of the first three into Mahāyāna 大乘 and Hinayāna 小乘 writings, and the fourth into the writings of the sages of India and the writings of the wise men of China. The sections are further broken up into subsections within which titles are arranged according to the nature of the work. Under each title the number of *chüan* and the name, dynasty, and native place of the writer or translator are given, then if there are several translations of a work the best one is indicated, the others being listed after the descriptive note. The note, which is based upon the compiler's own reading, describes the contents of the work with necessary explanations, gives a brief account of the story when there is a story, and compares different translations. These notes are inferior to those in the *Ssu-k'u ch'üan-shu tsung-mu* but somewhat better than those in the *Tao-ts'ang mu-lu hsiang-chu;* taken altogether, they provide a useful guide to Buddhist literature. The tendency to over-emphasize T'ien-t'ai 天臺 writings is probably due to the compiler's affiliation with that particular school. A comprehensive index to the names of authors and titles of works in four great collections of Buddhist writings has been published by the Harvard-Yenching Institute.[23]

---

23. **Fo-ts'ang tzu-mu yin-te** 佛藏子目引得. Compiled by Hsü Ti-shan 許地山 and others. (1) Peiping: Harvard-Yenching Institute, 1933. (Index No. 11) 3 vols. xvi, 266; 460; 412 pp. (2) Taipei: Ch'eng Wen Publishing Co., 1966 (photocopy). This is a combined *kuei-hsieh* index to the titles of works included in four collections published in Japan: (1) *Daizōkyō* 大藏經, published by Kōkyō Shoin 弘教書院, 1881–1885; (2) *Daizōkyō*, published by Zōkyō Shoin 藏經書院, 1902–1905; (3) *Zokuzōkyō* 續藏經 also published by Zōkyō Shoin, 1905–1912; and (4) *Taishō Shinshū Daizōkyō* 大正新修大藏經, published by Taishōissaikyō Kankō-kai 大正一切經刊行會, 1922–1932; also to the chapter headings in the first of these collections. There is an index to the names of the authors of works included in the four collections and cross references to variations in names and to the Chinese and Sanscrit renderings of terms.

Fo-hsüeh shu-mu 佛學書目. Published by the Fo-ching liu-t'ung-ch'u 佛經流通處. Peiping: Ta-fo-ssu 大佛寺, 1940. 2, 168 pp.

"This sales-catalogue of the Buddhist bookstore in the Ta-fo-ssu is a very useful bibliography of Buddhist publications in China. It lists over 3500 titles." —*Monumenta Serica*, 8 (1943), 351.

Chung-kuo Fo-chiao shih-chi kai-lun 中國佛教史籍概論. Compiled by Ch'en Yüan 陳垣. Peking: Chung-hua shu-chü, 1962. 3, 2, 161 pp.

This is an introduction to thirty-five famous works that deal with the history of Buddhism in China, from the *Ch'u-san-ts'ang chi-chi* 出三藏記集 (an account of the translation and production of the Tripitaka, by Seng-yu 僧佑, 445–518) to a book of the seventeenth century. Consisting of lectures by a leading historian, the discussion of each work includes the name and background of the author, its organization and importance, and relevant information as well as the correction of misjudgments of the book by the editors of the *Ssu-k'u ch'üan-shu*. Though informal in style, this book provides an interesting and useful introduction to Chinese Buddhist literature.

Hui-lin i-ch'ieh-ching yin-i yin-yung-shu so-yin 慧林一切經音義引用書索引. Compiled by the Division of Literature and History, Graduate School of the National Peking University 國立北京大學研究所文史部 and published by the Commercial Press, Changsha, 1938, as No. 6 of the *Kuo-li Pei-ching ta-hsüeh yen-chiu-so wen-shih ts'ung-k'an* 國立北京大學研究所文史叢刊. 5 ts'e. 3, 1548, 3 pp.

This is an index to the titles and chapter and section headings of and to terms used in all the works quoted in the *I-ch'ieh-ching yin-i* (100 *chüan*) by Hui-lin (737–820), a learned monk of the T'ang period, and in the supplement, *Hsü-yin-i* 續音義, by a later scholar. It was the purpose of the two authors to furnish a well documented commentary for all Buddhist sutras, indicating the T'ang or pre-T'ang pronunciation of all non-Chinese words. They quote a large number of Buddhist and non-Buddhist works on philology and etymology, many of which have since been lost. This index, which eliminates the necessity for consulting the *I-ch'ieh-ching yin-i* itself, is of great help to students of early Chinese Buddhist and secular literature. It is arranged according to the number of strokes and was compiled under the supervision of Shen Chien-shih 沈兼士, an outstanding philologist. Many errors and inconsistent indications of sources in the original work have been corrected.

3. CLASSICS AND PHILOLOGY

★Ching-i k'ao 經義考, 300 *chüan* (of which *chüan* 286, 299, and 300 exist only in bare outline). Compiled by Chu I-tsun 朱彝尊 (1629–1709). +(1) Techou Lu Chien-tseng 德州盧見曾 block-print edition of 1755. 32 *ts'e*. (2) Che-kiang shu-chü 浙江書局 block-print edition of 1897. 50 *ts'e*. (3) *Ssu-pu pei-yao*. 32 *ts'e* or 8 vols.

This is a descriptive bibliography of all of the classical commentaries and other studies of the classics written between the beginning of the Han dynasty and the end of the K'ang-hsi period. The first *chüan* deals with Ch'ing dynasty works containing imperial commentaries and works compiled under imperial auspices. *Chüan* 2–238 take up the *Thirteen Classics* one by one. After *chüan* 238, works are classified under the following headings: collections of the classics, as the *Five Classics*, the *Nine Classics*, etc.; the *Four Books;* lost classics; ancient and medieval commentaries on the classics; imitation classics and supplements to the classics; the transmission of differing interpretations by different schools; stone inscriptions of the classics; wall inscriptions of the classics; studies of the bibliographical sections in the dynastic histories and in important private bibliographies; and general discussions of the classics. Within each section titles are arranged chronologically, and each is preceded by the name and dynasty of the author. After each title the number of *chüan* is indicated, and also information is given as to whether the work is extant as a whole, incomplete, completely lost, or merely not seen by the compiler. All prefaces and postfaces in the editions upon which the bibliography is based are reproduced, bibliographical data are copied from the dynastic histories, and reading notes, discussions, and criticisms are collected from as many sources as possible. Brief biographical notes are given for each author, and finally Chu I-tsun includes some comments of his own. Altogether 8317 titles are listed, and although there are certain weaknesses, such as the failure to include any works commonly classified under the *hsiao-hsüeh* 小學 section of classics except those under the subsection on the *Erh-ya* 爾雅, the needless inclusion of many useless prefaces, and the citation of sources only by the author's name, still this is the most comprehensive bibliography of its kind. A number of the works which Chu declared lost have since been found, most of them probably having been recovered in connection with the compilation of the *Ssu-k'u ch'üan-shu*. In 1792 a twelve-*chüan* supplement was published giving more than a thousand additions and corrections, arranged in the original order.[24]

Hsiao-hsüeh k'ao 小學考, 50 *chüan*. Compiled by Hsieh Ch'i-k'un 謝啓昆, compiler's latest preface dated 1802. +(1) Shu-ching-t'ang 樹經堂 block-print edition of 1816. 16 *ts'e*. (2) Sun Chih-ch'ing 孫質卿 re-cut block-print

24. **Ching-i k'ao pu-cheng** 經義考補正, 12 *chüan*. Compiled by Weng Fang-kang 翁方綱. (1) *Su-chai ts'ung-shu, ts'e* 164–175. (2) *Yüeh-ya-t'ang ts'ung-shu, ts'e* 58–60. (3) Shanghai Po-ku-chai 上海博古齋 photolithographic edition of the *Su-chai ts'ung-shu*, 1924, *ts'e* 22–25. (4) *Shu-mu hsü-pien*.

edition of 1852. 16 *ts'e*. (3) Chekiang shu-chü 浙江書局 block-print edition
of 1888. 20 *ts'e*. (4) *Shu-mu san-pien*. 5 vols. 44, 2457 pp.

This annotated bibliography was compiled to redress the deficiencies in the
Ching-i k'ao arising out of the failure of Chu I-tsun to deal with any of the
subsections classified under the *hsiao-hsüeh* 小學 section of classics except that
on the *Erh-ya* 爾雅. The *hsiao-hsüeh* section is placed in the first, or classics,
division of Chinese bibliographies because the *Erh-ya* is recognized as one of
the *Thirteen Classics*. However, the works listed in it have little direct relation
to the other classics, being more of the nature of dictionaries. This bibliography, after giving special treatment in the first two *chüan* to eight works
compiled during the Ch'ing period under imperial auspices, is divided into
four sections. (1) *Hsün-ku* 訓詁, works such as the *Erh-ya*, in which characters
and phrases are arranged according to subject matter; since the *Ching-i k'ao*
includes such a section, this is merely a supplement, although the section is
here enlarged to include works on dialects and colloquialisms. (2) *Wen-tzu*
文字, works in which characters are arranged by their radicals, after the model
of the *Shuo-wen* 說文. (3) *Sheng-yün* 聲韻, works in which characters and
phrases are arranged according to their rhyme. (4) *Yin-i* 音義, dictionaries
which give the pronunciation and definition of characters according to their
usage in specified works. 1099 titles are listed, the arrangement and the kind
of information given about each work being similar to those of the *Ching-i
k'ao*. While the *Hsiao-hsüeh k'ao* is inferior to its model, in that it is less carefully
arranged and it also tends to ignore the researches of contemporary scholars,
it is indispensable to scholars working in the field with which it is concerned.
A supplement to the *wen-tzu* section, listing 206 studies of the *Shuo-wen chieh-
tzu* written since the *Hsiao-hsüeh k'ao* was compiled, has been published.[25]

4. ARCHAEOLOGY

Wu-shih-nien chia-ku-hsüeh lun-chu mu 五十年甲骨學論著目. Compiled
by Hu Hou-hsüan 胡厚宣. Shanghai: Chung-hua shu-chü, 1952. 273 pp.

This list of 728 periodical articles and 148 books dealing with the oracle
bones of the Shang dynasty during the fifty years from their discovery in 1899
to 1949 was prepared by an authority in this field. During that half century
about 160,000 pieces of oracle bones were unearthed and nearly 300 students
scattered all over the world were working on the new material. The 876
studies written in Chinese, Japanese, English, French, German and Russian
are divided into ten sections, and each entry is accompanied by full biblio-

---

25. **Hsü-hsüeh k'ao** 許學考, 26 *chüan*. Compiled and published by Li Ching-kao 黎經誥
in 1927. 16 *ts'e*.

graphic data. To facilitate consultation of this list, there are three indexes: author, title, and chronology. In the last, for example, the earliest study of oracle bones appears under 1903, and the four works issued in 1916 are listed under that year.

"Chia-ku-hsüeh chuan-shu t'i-yao chi lun-wen mu-lu 甲骨學專書提要及論文目錄**."** Compiled by P'eng Shu-chi 彭樹杞 and published in *Chinese Culture*, Vol. 6. No. 3 (June 1965), 97–149.

This bibliography of writings on oracle bones includes books and magazine articles written by Chinese, Japanese and Western scholars. It is divided into two parts: books, with annotations; and articles, which are not annotated but for which adequate bibliographical data are supplied. All entries are arranged by the number of strokes. There is an alphabetical index to Western authors.

Chin-shih-shu mu-lu 金石書目錄, 10 *chüan*, with two appendixes. Compiled by Jung Yüan 容媛, and edited by Jung Keng 容庚. Revised and enlarged edition published in 1936 by the Institute of Philology and History of the Academia Sinica 中央研究院歷史語言研究所. 1 *ts'e*. **Pu-pien** 補編. *K'ao-ku t'ung-hsün* 考古通訊, No. 3 (1959), 70–80.

This bibliography of the archaeological works owned by or known to the editor was first published in 1929 and enlarged and republished seven years later. There are 977 titles listed and classified under ten section and forty-seven subsection headings. The section headings are: general works, bronzes, coins, seals, stones, jade, bones, pottery, bamboo and wooden slips, and works related to particular localities. The number of *chüan* and the name and dynasty of the author are indicated under each title, and also the publisher's name with the date and place of publication whenever that information was known to the editor. Those editions which had not actually been seen by the editor are designated by a dot, and 173 of the titles are indented one space to indicate that those works are less useful than the others. The first appendix lists 190 gazetteers which have archaeological sections, and the second appendix lists the works included in twelve archaeological *ts'ung-shu*. There are two indexes, one to 545 authors' names, arranged first by dynasty and then according to the number of strokes, and the other to titles, arranged according to the number of strokes. This is a convenient catalogue, and the list of works included in it is very nearly complete.

5. PALEOGRAPHY

While the works described in this subsection are not bibliographies, they serve somewhat the same purpose, as catalogues of bone, bronze, coin and stone inscriptions. Some might, in fact, be classified as dictionaries of the characters found in such inscriptions.

Yin-hsü pu-tz'u tsung-shu 殷虛卜辭綜述. Compiled by Ch'en Meng-chia 陳夢家 (*K'ao-ku-hsüeh chuan-k'an* 考古學專刊, Series A, No. 2). (1) Peking: K'o-hsüeh ch'u-pan she, 1956. 9, 674, 10, 24 pp., with charts, maps and illustrations. (2) Tokyo: Daian Bookstore, 1964 (photocopy).

This is a comprehensive survey of most of the research that has been done on the oracle inscriptions excavated at the old Shang-Yin capital near modern Anyang. The introductory chapter traces the history of the discovery and study of the oracle bones. This is followed by a chapter on bone inscriptions, names of court diviners, and the dating of various bones. Ch'en has his own views concerning the chronology. Also discussed are ancient geography, ancestors' and posthumous titles of the Shang-Yin dynasty, religion, agriculture, society, and other aspects of the period. Although there is no index, there is a good bibliography.

Pu-tz'u t'ung-tsuan 卜辭通纂, 1 *chüan*, **K'ao-shih** 考釋, 3 *chüan*, **So-yin** 索引, 1 *chüan*. Compiled by Kuo Mo-jo 郭沫若. Tokyo: Bunkyūdō 文求堂, 1933. 4 *ts'e*.

This work contains eight hundred oracle bone inscriptions, most of them selected from Japanese collections. The classification is under eight sections: the stems and branches, numerical figures, genealogy, astronomical phenomena, agricultural matters, military expeditions, hunting, and miscellaneous. The arrangement of classes is according to a sequence of ideas, and individual inscriptions are classified by the subject to which they relate or by the frequency with which certain characters occur. The oracle bones are numbered from one to eight hundred, and are skillfully reproduced by collotype, with careful indication of sources. Kuo has noted those instances in which bones that had been broken into several pieces have been published separately by different collectors, and he has re-united the broken parts.

In the *K'ao-shih* or explanatory section, which is arranged according to the numerical order of the bones, many of the inscriptions are reproduced and enlarged to increase their legibility; there are also explanations and discussions of previous studies by other scholars. Kuo's new ideas and criticisms are summarized in his preface and postface. Though not accepted in its entirety by all experts in this field,[26] this is a good text from which beginners may learn the rudiments of the study of oracle bone inscriptions.

The book is furnished with four appendixes: (1) a photolithographic reproduction of the *Ta-kuei* (four large pieces of tortoise shell belonging to the

---

26. See the review of this book in *Yen-ching hsüeh-pao* 燕京學報 13 (June 1933), 253–256, probably by Jung Keng.

Academia Sinica); (2) twenty-two pieces of oracle bone discovered by the Academia Sinica; (3) sixteen pieces from Ho Sui's 何遂 collection of oracle bones; and (4) eighty-seven carefully selected pieces from twelve Japanese collections. All these pieces are reproduced by collotype and are very valuable materials. At the end there is a character index, arranged by number of strokes.

Yin-hsü wen-tzu lei-pien 殷虛文字類編, 14 *chüan*. **Tai-wen pien** 待問編, 13 *chüan*. Compiled by Shang Ch'eng-tso 商承祚. Block-print edition of 1926, 6 *ts'e*, including **Yin-hsü shu-ch'i k'ao-shih** 殷虛書契考釋, 1 *chüan*, by Lo Chen-yü 羅振玉.

This work is commonly used as a dictionary of oracle bones. It includes 789 characters arranged according to the *Shuo-wen* radicals. The character in seal form appears at the top of a page, followed by the oracle inscription, with detailed source references and explanations. Shang Ch'eng-tso was a pupil of Lo Chen-yü, and he has based this book almost entirely upon the researches of his teacher. At the end of the fourth *ts'e* there is an index arranged by the number-of-strokes system. The *Tai-wen pien* lists undeciphered characters for further research. The book is beautifully printed and convenient to use.

Chia-ku wen-pien 甲骨文編, 14 *chüan*. **Ho-wen** 合文, **Fu-lu** 附錄, **Chien-tzu** 檢字, and **Pei-ch'a** 備查, each 1 *chüan*. Compiled by Sun Hai-po 孫海波. (1) Peiping: Harvard-Yenching Institute, 1934. 5 *ts'e* (lithographic edition). (2) Taipei: I-wen yin-shu-kuan, 1958. 2 vols. 788 pp.

This collection of oracle bone inscriptions contains more characters than any earlier work. Altogether 1006 characters are listed in the main collection, 150 phrases in the *Ho-wen*, and 1110 uncertain characters in the *Fu-lu*. The method of compilation is patterned after that of Shang Ch'eng-tso's *Yin-hsü wen-tzu lei-pien*. The characters are arranged according to the *Shuo-wen* radicals, and sources are indicated in detail, making it easy to check the original works. The *Chia-ku wen-pien* may be considered a companion book to Jung Keng's *Chin-wen pien*. However, it is incomplete because it is based on only eight sources.

Hsü chia-ku wen-pien 續甲骨文編, 16 *chüan*; **Fu-lu** 坿錄, 2 *chüan*; **Chien-tzu** 檢字, 1 *chüan*. Compiled by Chin Hsiang-heng 金祥恒. Taipei: I-wen yin-shu-kuan, 1959. 4 *ts'e*.

This supplement to Sun Hai-po's *Chia-ku wen-pien* increases the total number of oracle bone characters in the two works to 2,630, about half of which have been deciphered. While patterned after Sun Hai-po's work some forty later sources have been used. Especially important is the inclusion of the materials excavated at Anyang before the Second Sino-Japanese War by the Academia Sinica. The arrangement is in accordance with the *Shuo-wen* radicals. There is a supplement with some three hundred undeciphered characters in the last *ts'e* and near the end there are indexes to the characters in oracle bone inscriptions that have *Shuo-wen* equivalances and to 1585 characters which were not included in the *Shuo-wen*. Chin gives precise references to the original oracle bones on which the characters are to be found.

Chin-wen pien 金文編, 14 *chüan*, appendix 1 *chüan*, index 1 *chüan*. Compiled by Jung Keng 容庚. Commercial Press, for the Academia Sinica, 1939 (first edition 1925). 5 *ts'e*. Supplement, **Chin-wen hsü-pien** 金文續編, 14 *chüan*, appendix 1 *chüan*, **Ming-wen** 銘文, 2 *chüan*, index 1 *chüan*. Compiled by Jung Keng. Commercial Press, for the Academia Sinica, 1934. 2 *ts'e*. Revised edition, Peking: K'o-hsüeh ch'u-pan-she, 1959. 34, 1034, 166 pp.

The historical value of inscriptions on bronze vessels was first recognized by scholars of the Sung dynasty. Since that time many special studies of such inscriptions have been made. Jung Keng has tried to bring the efforts of previous scholars together in one place and thus to make them all available to students of history. The *Chin-wen pien* is a collection of bronze inscriptions of the Shang (Yin) and Chou dynasties. The 1925 edition contains 1382 characters, with an appendix of 924 characters which are hard to decipher. The 1939 edition contains 1804 characters, with an appendix of 1165 characters which are difficult or illegible. The 1959 edition increases to 1894 the number of legible characters and to 1199 the number of undeciphered ones. Under each character the source is indicated, and occasionally an explanation is given.

The *Chin-wen hsü-pien* catalogues 951 characters on bronze vessels of the Ch'in and Han dynasties. The method of compilation is the same as that of the main work. Jung is a careful scholar whose particular contribution is the collecting of material from different sources. His inclination to write characters in their abbreviated form may create some difficulty for Westerners at first, but with a little practice it is easy to read his handwriting. At the end of each collection is an index to the characters, arranged by the number-of-strokes system.

Liang-Chou chin-wen-tz'u ta-hsi k'ao-shih 兩周金文辭大系考釋 (1935), 3 *ts'e*. **Liang-Chou chin-wen-tz'u ta-hsi t'u-lu** 兩周金文辭大系圖錄 (1934), 5 *ts'e*. Compiled by Kuo Mo-jo 郭沫若. Tokyo: Bunkyūdō 文求堂. Revised edition: Peking: K'o-hsüeh ch'u-pan-she, 1957. 8 vols.

This is a systematic study and explanation of bronze inscriptions. Some of the passages included are almost five hundred characters long, and are of no less value than a chapter of the *Book of History* in the verifying of historical records. The compiler has carefully examined the shape, design, personal and place names, etc., of each vessel in order to decide its date. By this method he has designated 162 vessels as of the Western Chou period, discussing them in the first part of the *K'ao-shih*. The 161 vessels treated in the second part are of the Eastern Chou period and are classified as coming from 32 states; the vessels from each state are arranged chronologically if they can be dated. The original texts, which are reproduced in the compiler's own handwriting, are legibly written and punctuated. The explanations are clear, and in some cases new ideas are introduced.

The *T'u-lu* also is divided into two parts. One, *t'u*, contains diagrams or pictures of bronze vessels; the other, *lu*, consists of photolithographic reproductions of bronze inscriptions. The *t'u* section is introduced by a well-prepared pioneer study of designs and patterns which attempts to find the characteristics of each of the four periods within which the compiler classifies the bronzes, from Yin (Shang) to the end of the Period of Warring States. Although Kuo's interpretations are not without error, his diligence and brilliance have produced two charming large-scale studies of Chinese bronzes.

Chin-shih ts'ui-pien 金石萃編, 160 *chüan*. Compiled by Wang Ch'ang 王昶. Compiler's Ching-hsün-t'ang 經訓堂 block-print edition of 1805, 64 *ts'e*. **Chin-shih hsü-pien** 金石續編, 21 *chüan*. Compiled by Lu Yao-yü 陸耀遹. (1) Pi-ling shuang-pai yen-t'ang 毗陵雙白燕堂 block-print edition of 1874. 16 *ts'e*. (2) Taipei: Kuo-feng ch'u-pan-she, 1964. 4 vols. Facsimile reproduction.

This is a collection of more than 1500 bronze and stone inscriptions from Chou down to the end of the Chin 金 dynasty. The original text of most of the inscriptions is given with many critical notes chiefly collected from other works and with sources carefully indicated. At the beginning is a detailed table of contents. This reference work[27] deals mainly with stone inscriptions. It is said that the compiler took more than fifty years to prepare it and that he intended to include all important information on the subject. However, there are many omissions and errors, part of which have been corrected in the supplement listed above which adds 450 stone inscriptions. For another supplement see the *Chin-shih-shu mu-lu, chüan* 1.

27. For those who are interested in a more complete list of stone inscriptions in various periods and areas of China, an important reference work is the **Huan-yü fang-pei lu** 寰宇訪碑錄, 12 *chüan*, compiled by Sun Hsing-yen 孫星衍 and Hsing Chu 邢澍, and published in 1802. This work lists the headings of 7849 stone inscriptions, but does not give the texts. For supplements to this work, see Jung Keng, *Chin-shih-shu mu-lu, chüan* 5, p. 1b.

Liu-i chih-i-lu mu-lu fu yin-te 六藝之一錄目錄附引得. (1) Peiping: Harvard-Yenching Institute, 1940. (Supplement No. 15) xx [482] pp. (2) Taipei: Ch'eng Wen Publishing Co., 1966 (photocopy).

The *Liu-i chih-i-lu* is a collection of bronze and stone inscriptions and models of calligraphy of various dynasties compiled by Ni T'ao 倪濤 of the early Ch'ing period. The *Ssu-k'u* editors considered it a complete collection of discussions of calligraphy since the T'ang and Sung dynasties. The only available edition is in the *Ssu-k'u ch'üan-shu chen-pen ch'u-chi* 四庫全書珍本初集. Since the work is cumbersome to use, this index was prepared to facilitate consultation. It is in two parts: first a 265-page table of contents, following the arragement of the *Liu-i chih-i-lu*, and second an index to the table of contents.

Li-tai chu-lu chi-chin mu 歷代著錄吉金目. Compiled by Fu K'ai-sen 福開森 (John C. Ferguson). Changsha: Commercial Press, 1939. [8] 208, 1365, 196 pp. (lithographic edition).

This is a catalogue of all the recorded bronzes of successive dynasties. While other catalogues have listed only bronzes which bear inscriptions and have been based upon ten to twenty-odd works, the *Li-tai chu-lu chi-chin mu* includes more than ten thousand articles, with or without inscriptions, gathered from more than eighty different sources published prior to the end of 1935. Previous catalogues do not list descriptive notes; this one does. All the bronzes included are well classified, with cross references. The classification is according to the use of the object, as: musical instrument, wine vessel, water vessel, military implement, Buddhist figure. While the catalogue is well compiled and easy to use, it is not without mistakes, omissions, and the indiscriminate inclusion of dubious objects. On the whole, however, it is an important reference work which will save students of archaeology a great deal of time.

Kuo-li Pei-p'ing t'u-shu-kuan kuan-ts'ang pei-mu: Mu-chih lei 國立北平圖書館館藏碑目: 墓誌類. Compiled by Tuan T'eng-tuan 段騰端. Shanghai: K'ai-ming shu-tien, 1941. 142, 12 pp. (Published for the National Library of Peiping)

This is a catalogue of rubbings of tomb inscriptions in the National Library of Peiping, which is said to have the largest collection of such material in existence. It lists 3407 tomb inscriptions from the Later Han to the end of the Ming dynasty, but a majority (2601) belong to the T'ang dynasty. These inscriptions furnish valuable biographical and historical information. The entries are arranged chronologically, and under each item the title, the date, and the style of inscription are given. There is a statistical chart showing the number of stones dating from the reign period of each emperor.

Shih-k'o t'i-po so-yin 石刻題跋索引. Compiled by Yang Tien-hsün 楊殿珣 under the auspices of the National Library of Peiping. Commercial Press, 1941. 14, 834, 4 pp. Enlarged edition, Shanghai: Commercial Press, 1957, with a four-corner index to the first characters of titles and authors' names. 10, 807 pp.

This is a classified index to stone inscriptions from the Chou period to the end of Yüan. As the texts of stone inscriptions are reprinted and scattered in a large number of different works, it is often difficult to locate them. In order to facilitate the study of such inscriptions, therefore, the National Library of Peiping has compiled the present index to more than forty thousand entries in 140 works. These are classified in seven categories: (1) *Mu-pei* 墓碑, tomb tablets, including tombstones, tomb pagoda inscriptions, and memorial inscriptions; (2) *Mu-chih* 墓誌, tomb records; (3) *K'o-ching* 刻經, inscribed classics; (4) *Tsao-hsiang* 造像, inscriptions on statues or pictures; (5) *T'i-ming t'i-tzu* 題名題字, inscriptions of names or other characters; (6) *Shih-tz'u* 詩詞, poems; and (7) miscellaneous inscriptions including those on bricks, tiles, and calligraphs. The items of each class are again arranged either chronologically or according to subject matter. Each entry includes indication of the author and the book and page where the item originally appeared.

Ku-ch'ien ta-tz'u-tien 古錢大辭典, 12 *ts'e*, and **Shih-i** 拾遺, 1 *ts'e*. Compiled by Ting Fu-pao 丁福保. (1) Shanghai: I-hsüeh shu-chü 醫學書局, 1938–1939. (2) Taipei: Shih-chieh shu-chü, 1962. 5 vols. 110, 2312 pp.

This dictionary of old coins, containing most of the available material, follows the plan of the *Shuo-wen chieh-tzu ku-lin* (q.v.) but omits the obviously unreliable coins. The compiler's prefaces and introductions give a general discussion of various forms of coins in successive dynasties. Pictures of coins show the original sizes, although the reproductions are not very clear. The explanatory note under each coin consists of photolithographically reproduced quotations from various works, with sources indicated in each instance. Arrangement is by the number of strokes of the first character of the inscription on each coin. At the beginning of the first *ts'e* there is a table of all the inscriptions, also arranged by number of strokes. The supplement gives additional material, arranged according to the same plan as the main work.

6. PAINTINGS, CALLIGRAPHY AND MUSIC

Shu-hua shu-lu chieh-t'i 書畫書錄解題, 12 *chüan*. Compiled by Yü Shao-sung 余紹宋. (1) Peiping: National Library of Peiping, 1932. 6 *ts'e*. (2)

Taipei: Chung-hua shu-chü, 1968. 2 vols. +(3) Hong Kong: Chung-mei t'u-shu kung-ssu 中美圖書公司, 1968. 2 vols. (photocopy). **Fu-k'an** 坿刊, 1969. 1 vol.

This is an annotated bibliography of 860 works on Chinese painting and calligraphy. It is divided into ten sections and a number of subsections; among the section headings are the following: historical biographies, technical studies of calligraphy and painting, works on criticism and appreciation, eulogistic writings on calligraphy and painting, works on calligraphy and painting in public and private collections, works on calligraphy and painting included in *ts'ung-shu*. The descriptive notes give for each title the number of *chüan*, the name, dynasty, native place and alternative names of the author, and a brief statement concerning the nature, contents, and value of the work, with particular stress on style, authenticity, critical value, and different editions, and frequently include the compiler's valuable critical evaluations. Whether the work is extant, lost, or merely not seen by the compiler is also indicated in each case. The first *chüan* is a classified list of all the titles included, giving in each case the number of *chüan*, the name and dynasty of the author, and often a brief statement of the nature of the work. The last *chüan* has a chronological table of authors, giving the titles of their works, followed by an author index which is arranged according to the number of strokes. The *Fu-k'an* contains four useful reference works: *Tsen-yang chien-ting shu hua* 怎樣鑑定書畫 by Chang Heng 張珩, 28 pp.; **Chung-kuo pan-hua yen-chiu chung-yao shu-chi** 中國版畫研究重要書籍 by Fu Hsi-hua 傅惜華, 20 pp.; **Yin-p'u chih-chien chuan-pen shu-mu** 印譜知見傳本書目, by Wang Tun-hua 王敦化, 52, 3 pp.; and *Ch'ing-tai chiang-tso tse-li hui-pien* 清代匠作則例彙編 by Wang Shih-hsiang 王世襄, 184 pp. The last is a collection of blueprints and examples of commercial art objects such as stone statues, Buddhist images, bronzes and paper gate gods.

Li-tai chu-lu hua-mu 歷代著錄畫目. Compiled by Fu K'ai-sen 福開森 (John C. Ferguson). Institute of Chinese Cultural Studies, University of Nanking 金陵大學, 中國文化研究所, 1934. 6 *ts'e*. (2) Taipei: Chung-hua shu-chü, 1968. 2 vols. 13, 1162, 34 pp.

This is a catalogue of paintings which have been mentioned or annotated in Chinese bibliographies. The names of the artists are arranged by the number-of-strokes system, and each name is followed by an indication of the time when the artist lived and a list of his paintings. About 1700 artists are listed, and 108 works on Chinese art are quoted. At the end are appendixes on (1) collaborative paintings, that is, pictures painted by more than one artist; (2) anonymous and undated pictures; (3) unidentified fancy names requiring further research; (4) *k'o-ssu* 緙絲 or brocade and embroidery. At the end of the last volume are indexes to surnames, to full names, to alternative or fancy names, and to names in the Wade-Giles romanization arranged alphabetically. Although the work is not without mistakes and typographical errors, it is convenient to use because of the indexes, and it can serve as a guide for curators and amateur connoisseurs who wish to learn whether certain famous paintings have been listed in books on Chinese art.

Li-tai Chung-kuo hua-hsüeh chu-shu mu-lu 歷代中國畫學著述目錄. Compiled by Yü Fu 虞復. Peking: Chao-hua mei-shu ch'u-pan-she, 朝花美術 出版社, 1962. 106 pp.

This bibliography of works on Chinese painting from A.D. 280 to the time of compilation is divided into three parts: (1) book titles, with the names of authors, arranged by dynasties; (2) book titles, with the names of authors and the time they lived, arranged by the number of strokes in the first character; and (3) authors' names, with their time and the titles of their books, arranged by the number of strokes. Although the catalogue is informative, the bibliographic data are incomplete.

Chung-kuo ku-tai yin-yüeh shu-mu 中國古代音樂書目. Compiled by the Chinese Music Research Institute of the Central Academy of Music 中央 音樂學院中國音樂研究所. Peking: Yin-yüeh ch'u-pan-she 音樂出版社, 1961. 131 pp.

This is a catalogue of books on Chinese music written from ancient times to 1840. It is divided into three parts: works which are now extant and have been seen by the compilers (about 1200 titles), works which may be located after further search, and works known to have been lost. The first part is divided into sections such as musical theory and history, lyric music, light opera music (with talking and singing), dramatic music, musical instruments, religious music, and encyclopedias of music. There is a list of reference works on music (pp. 101–108) and an index to titles arranged alphabetically according to the new official system of romanization.

7. MAPS, ATLASES, AND GAZETTEERS

Kuo-li Pei-p'ing t'u-shu-kuan Chung-wen yü-t'u mu-lu 國立北平圖書館 中文輿圖目錄; **Hsü-pien** 續編. Compiled by Wang Yung 王庸 and Mao Nai-wen 茅乃文. Peiping: National Library of Peiping, 1933–1937. 2 vols. 2, 174 pp.; [8] 398, 30 pp.

This is a catalogue of approximately two thousand atlases and maps that were preserved in the National Library of Peiping. It is divided into three parts: (1) world and continental maps and atlases; (2) general and provincial maps and atlases of China; and (3) special maps and atlases, as historical maps and atlases, and those related to mountains, rivers, famous places, historical sites, products, etc. Under each title the following data are given: scale, size, whether colored or not, the name of the compiler or draughtsman, the year and place of publication, the publisher's name, and the number of plates or *ts'e*. The supplement adds more than 2300 atlases and and maps purchased by the library between 1934 and 1936. There is a table of contents at the beginning of each of the two volumes.

Chung-kuo ku fang-chih k'ao 中國古方志考. Compiled by Chang Kuo-k'an 張國淦. Shanghai: Chung-hua shu-chü, 1962. 4, 782 pp.

Chang Kuo-k'an made a life-long study of early local histories or gazetteers, following the example of Chu I-tsun who compiled the *Ching-i k'ao* (q.v.). He collected the available sources concerning local history from the Chin (A.D. 265–420) to the Yüan dynasty. Many ancient and medieval geographical names and works can be identified with current names by means of this tool. At the beginning of the volume there is a list of more than 1,000 local histories arranged by province, and at the end there is a title index by the number-of-strokes system.

★Chung-kuo ti-fang-chih tsung-lu 中國地方志綜錄. Compiled by Chu Shih-chia 朱士嘉. Commercial Press, 1935. 3 *ts'e* (lithographic edition). Revised and enlarged edition, Shanghai: Commercial Press, 1958. 318, 105 pp.

This began as a union catalogue of the gazetteers preserved in fifty different collections: thirty-five public and fifteen private, of which forty-two are in China, six in Japan, and two in the United States. The gazetteer, or local history, is a record of all important facts pertaining to a limited geographical area, and of all significant activities occurring in it. Among the data to be found in most gazetteers are: a detailed history of the area—political, cultural; a discussion of the topography, including past changes in the political boundaries; a history of the changes in the local government and in local officials; population figures, studies of economic conditions, customs, education, communications, and archaeological and historical relics; biographies of famous persons native to the area; reproductions of poems and essays by local authors, and often a bibliography of well known works by local authors.

The first Chinese gazetteer was written in the third century A.D., although the earliest one listed in this catalogue dates from the Sung dynasty. Many were written during the Ming dynasty and the first half of the Ch'ing, but it was not until the great historian Chang Hsüeh-ch'eng 章學誠 (1738–1801)

pointed out their importance as historical sources and urged that more care be given to their compilation that they began to be carefully enough done to be comparable to other first class historical works. The sources upon which most gazetteers are based are: documents belonging to the local government, archaeological materials, earlier gazetteers, dynastic histories, classics, and the collected writings of individuals. Usually these sources are supplemented by the special investigations of the board entrusted with the task of making the compilation.

The gazetteers listed in this catalogue are arranged according to the political subdivisions outlined in the *Ta-Ch'ing i-t'ung-chih* 大清一統志, with some modifications to meet post-Ch'ing changes. Each page is divided into seven columns, giving the following information: (1) title, (2) number of *chüan*, (3) names of chief compilers, (4) date of compilation, (5) dates of editions, if differing from the date of compilation, (6) in which of the eighteen largest Chinese collections and five largest foreign collections there exist copies, (7) miscellaneous notes: as a brief description of the edition, changes in the name of the place since the compilation of the gazetteer, rare editions to be found in the twenty-seven collections not listed in the previous column, etc. In the middle of the third *ts'e* there are thirty-two statistical tables and charts showing the total number of gazetteers compiled in various dynasties and in different provinces, the total number in the different libraries, etc. The revised edition adds 1581 titles to the 5832 listed in the first edition, making a total of 7413 gazetteers that are available in one or more of twenty-nine libraries in mainland China. Chu has also corrected more than a thousand errors in the 1935 edition. At the end of the work there is an index to titles, arranged by the number-of-strokes system. This is easily the best catalogue of gazetteers yet compiled.

Kuo-li Pei-p'ing t'u-shu-kuan fang-chih mu-lu 國立北平圖書館方志目錄, and **Erh-pien** 二編. Compiled by T'an Ch'i-hsiang 譚其驤 and others. Peiping: National Library of Peiping, 1933–1936. 4 *ts'e*; 1 *ts'e*. (2) A poor duplicate of the original work, with an index to titles: Hong Kong: Kuo-chi t'u-shu kung-ssu 國際圖書公司, 1968. 5 *ts'e*.

This is a catalogue of the more than 5200 gazetteers accumulated by the National Library of Peiping before the War, the largest collection of its kind in the world. The collection was begun with more than a thousand works taken over from the Nei-ko ta-k'u 內閣大庫 and several hundred each from the Kuo-tzu-chien 國子監 and the Ch'ing Board of Education 清學部, and it was added to thereafter by gift and purchase. Titles are classified according to the political subdivisions of the Ch'ing period, which are in turn arranged under the thirty provinces into which China was divided in 1933. Under each title the number of *chüan* and *ts'e*, the name and dynasty of the compiler, and the date of publication are given. When a gazetteer has bibliographical or archaeological sections, the *chüan* in which they occur are indicated immediately after the title. At the end there is an index to titles, arranged according to the number of strokes. The assignment of gazetteers to their proper geographical areas, which is often an exceedingly difficult task, is particularly well done in this catalogue, as the compiler is a specialist in historical geography. A supplement, published in 1934, lists 314 additional titles, and the *Erh-pien* lists 862 local histories received by the library from 1933 to June 1936.

Kuo-hui t'u-shu-kuan ts'ang Chung-kuo fang-chih mu-lu 國會圖書館藏中國方志目錄. Compiled by Chu Shih-chia 朱士嘉. Washington: U.S. Government Printing Office, 1942. xi, 552, 19 pp.

This is a catalogue of the Chinese gazetteers in the American Library of Congress. The total number of these histories of Chinese provinces, prefectures, and districts is 2,939, making it the largest collection of its kind at the time except for that of the National Library of Peiping. Chu Shih-chia, an expert cataloguer of local histories, not only lists the title, author, and editions of each work, but also points out, for the benefit of research scholars, important articles or treatises it contains. Most of these local histories were compiled during the Ch'ing dynasty. Entries are arranged by provinces, and two indexes are included in which the titles are arranged by number of strokes and alphabetically according to the Wade-Giles romanization.

T'ai-wan kung-ts'ang fang-chih lien-ho mu-lu 臺灣公藏方志聯合目錄. Compiled by the National Central Library. Taipei: Cheng-chung shu-chü, 1960. 2, 103, 30 pp.

This is a union catalogue of the gazetteers available in eleven libraries in Taiwan, arranged by province. The total number of entries is estimated at about eighteen hundred, including a number of rare items. There is an index.

Chūgoku chihōshi sōgō mokuroku or **Chung-kuo ti-fang-chih tsung-ho mu-lu** 中國地方志總合目錄. Tokyo: Kokuritsu kokkai toshokan, sankō shoshibu 國立國會圖書館參考書誌部, 1969. v, 350 pp.

This is a union catalogue of an estimated 2900 Chinese local gazetteers in fourteen major libraries and research institutes in Japan. The titles are arranged under twenty-nine provinces and Tibet and Mongolia. Under each entry the title, compiler, date of publication, number of *chüan* and *ts'e* and the location in a library or libraries, if the work is available in more than one. There is a title index arranged by the Japanese alphabet and an index to Chinese characters by the Wade-Giles system to serve as a guide to the Japanese index.

8. LITERATURE AND DRAMA

Chung-kuo wen-hsüeh pai-k'o ch'üan-shu 中國文學百科全書. Compiled by Yang Chia-lo 楊家駱. (1) Nanking: Chung-kuo tz'u-tien kuan 中國辭典館, 1936–1937. Part I, three vols.; Part II, one vol. 44, 32, 1276; 1270; 1033; 1102 pp. (2) Taipei: Shih-chieh shu-chü, 1967. 4 vols.

This compilation of Chinese literature was planned to consist of three parts in eight volumes. It is a combined bibliography and dictionary of authors, book titles (often also chapter titles), and literary terms. The information under the various entries varies in fullness. Available editions of books are mentioned. Some articles on literary terms and names are very long, some very short. Sources are only occasionally mentioned in a vague way. The entries are arranged by the four-corner system; the last number is 3912, indicating the incompleteness of the work. There is at the beginning a list of works of literature published in the early years of the Republic (**Min-kuo i-lai so-ch'u-pan wen-hsüeh lun-chu tsung-mu** 民國以來所出版文學論著總目, 31 pages), giving titles, authors, and publishers.

The *Chung-kuo wen-hsüeh pai-k'o ch'üan-shu*, like other works of this compiler, is informative and useful. The lithographed type is beautiful and legible. Unfortunately Mr. Yang is so prolific a compiler that his books have to be used with caution. The broad scope and unsystematic presentation of material make his works difficult to classify. This one might be considered a bibliography, an encyclopedia, or a dictionary. The new edition adds a table of contents prepared by Lu Ch'ien 盧前 at the end of each volume, a great help in locating material.

Ch'u-tz'u shu-mu wu-chung 楚辭書目五種. Compiled by Chiang Liang-fu 姜亮夫. Peking: Chung-hua shu-chü, 1961. 2, 3, 525 pp.

These five bibliographies on the poetic anthology *Ch'u-tz'u* catalogue most of the editions and studies of this subject from the Han dynasty to the present time. The first is an annotated bibliography of 228 works; the second contains a descriptive list of 47 paintings, illustrations, maps, and specimens of calligraphy relating to certain parts of chapters of the *Ch'u-tz'u*; the third is a list of imitations and supplements in the *Ch'u-tz'u* style; the fourth registers 802 notes on this ancient piece of literature by famous scholars; and the last lists 447 modern articles dealing with various facets of the great work. There is a combined index to books, articles and authors' names, arranged by the four-corner system.

Ch'ü-hai tsung-mu t'i-yao 曲海總目提要, 46 *chüan*. Originally compiled under Imperial auspices by Huang Wen-yang 黃文暘 and others between

1777 and 1781. Collated by Tung K'ang 董康, collator's preface dated 1926. (1) Shanghai: Ta-tung shu-chü, 1928. 4 vols. or 16 *ts'e*. (2) Taipei: Hsin-hsing shu-chü, 1967. 3 vols. (3) Reprint of Ta-tung edition, Peking: Jen-min wen-hsüeh ch'u-pan-she, 1959. 3 vols. 45, 2173 pp. **Pu-pien** 補編. Compiled by Pei-ying 北嬰 [pseud.]. Peking: Jen-min wen-hsüeh ch'u-pan-she, 1959. 11, 5, 298 pp.

This is an annotated bibliography of the Chinese musical dramas known as *ch'ü* 曲 written between the beginning of the Yüan dynasty and the middle of the Ch'ien-lung period. Most of the plays listed are well written in a combination of the literary and colloquial styles, their authors generally being good scholars even though without great reputation as such. The present edition of the catalogue was collated from three earlier incomplete editions of the original work appearing under different names. It was originally called **Ch'ü-hai** 曲海, and when first published had 20 *chüan*. The plays are arranged chronologically, and under each title there are given the dynasty in which it was written, the author's name if known, a very brief summary, a more detailed outline of the play, a critical study of the origin and history of the story, and sometimes a glossary of difficult terms. The notes are well written and clear cut, and they are helpful both in providing background for a general study of Chinese drama and as guides to the individual plays. The present edition catalogues 685 plays, the titles of which are listed at the beginning in the order in which they appear in the bibliography. The supplement adds seventy-two new dramas and a general index to titles arranged according to the Chinese national phonetic alphabet (注音字母).

Chung-kuo hsi-ch'ü tsung-mu hui-pien 中國戲曲總目彙編. Compiled by Lo Chin-t'ang 羅錦堂. Hong Kong: Universal Book Co. 萬有圖書公司, 1966. 2, 1, 368 pp.

This is *A Comprehensive Bibliography of Chinese Drama* from the Yüan to the 1960's, publication of which was subsidized by the Harvard-Yenching Institute. Although the material is arranged chronologically and is well classified, there is neither author nor title index.

Yüan-tai tsa-chü ch'üan-mu 元代雜劇全目. Compiled by Fu Hsi-hua 傅惜華. Peking: Tso-chia ch'u-pan-she, 1957. [10] 429 pp.

The Research Institute of Chinese Drama (Chung-kuo hsi-chü yen-chiu yüan, 中國戲劇研究院) in Peking has made a great effort to accumulate materials relating to early Chinese drama, a field to which Fu Hsi-hua has long devoted himself. With government encouragement this "complete" list of *tsa-chü* (a variety of northern play of the Yüan dynasty) has been compiled, listing a total of 737 titles. Of these, some 550 were composed by Yüan playwrights, while the remaining 187 were written by anonymous authors who lived during the Yüan or early Ming dynasties.

Under each entry are given the title, edition, whether lost or still available in a named library, and a short biography of its author, if known. Appended are an annotated bibliography of works cited in this volume and author and title indexes arranged alphabetically according to the official phonetic system.

Ming-tai tsa-chü ch'üan-mu 明代雜劇全目. Compiled by Fu Hsi-hua 傅惜華. Peking: Tso-chia ch'u-pan-she, 1958. 1, 1, 328 pp.

This is a "complete" list of Ming dynasty *tsa-chü*, totaling 523, of which 349 are attributed to named authors while 174 remain anonymous. The information given under each title and the three appendixes, are similar to the *Ming-tai ch'uan-ch'i ch'üan-mu*.

Ming-tai ch'uan-ch'i ch'üan-mu 明代傳奇全目. Compiled by Fu Hsi-hua 傅惜華 . Peking, Jen-min ch'u-pan-she, 1959. 580 pp.

This is a "complete" list of "*ch'uan-ch'i* (romantic dramas)" written during the Ming dynasty. Of a total of 950 plays, 618 have known authors, while 332 remain anonymous. Under each title the editions, their availability, and a short biographical note about the author are given. The appendixes offer the reader an annotated bibliography of cited works, an index to authors and their alternate names, and another index to the titles of the plays included.

Pei-ching ch'uan-t'ung ch'ü-i tsung-lu 北京傳統曲藝總錄. Compiled by Fu Hsi-hua 傅惜華. Peking: Chung-hua shu-chü, 1961. 2, 3, 1, 3, 1008 pp.

This is a general list of all sorts of popular songs and short dramas prevalent at one time or another in the Peking area from the Yüan dynasty to the 1950's. Some of these were called "flower-drum (*hua-ku* 花鼓)," "big-drum (*ta-ku* 大鼓)" or "*lien-hua-lo* 蓮花落," the last accompanying the singing with a rattle made from bamboo slips. The purpose of this compilation is to supply a handy reference for students of folk literature. Under each of several thousand songs and dramas are given the author, if known, the edition, collector, and source. A combined index of authors and titles is arranged according to the four-corner system.

Ching-chü chü-mu ch'u-t'an 京劇劇目初探. Compiled by T'ao Chün-ch'i 陶君起. Peking: Chung-kuo hsi-chü ch'u-pan she 中國戲劇出版社, 1963. 1, 9, 23, 558 pp.

This is a descriptive catalogue of more than 1200 old dramas which had been often performed before the 1950's, mainly in Peking and Shanghai theaters. The compilation has been revised and enlarged twice before the present edition. The old dramas are discussed in Part A, new ones written between 1949 and 1962 in Part B. The information supplied on each drama is intended to contribute to an understanding of its performance. There is a title index at the end of the volume.

Wan-Ch'ing hsi-ch'ü hsiao-shuo mu 晚清戲曲小說目. Compiled by A-ying 阿英 [Ch'ien Hsing-ts'un 錢杏邨]. Shanghai: Chung-hua shu-chü, 1959. 5, 2, 10, 178 pp.

This catalogue of plays and short stories written or translated into Chinese during the late Ch'ing period was prepared by a famous collector and compiler of new Chinese literature. Under each of the 185 titles included, author, edition, time, and place of publication are given. The material is classified under stories, plays, local and modern drama (*hua-chü* 話劇) and, according to the compiler, all reflect China's socio-political conditions. Some of the dramas were very popular and widely circulated. Under each classification the entries are arranged by the number of strokes.

Chung-kuo hsien-tai hsi-chü t'u-shu mu-lu 中國現代戲劇圖書目錄. Compiled and published by the United College Library, Hong Kong, 1967. ii, 109 pp.

This catalogue of modern Chinese dramas published from 1924 to about 1966 is arranged according to the number of strokes in the titles. Under each play the number of acts, names of author and publisher, the date of publication and the number of pages are given. Chinese translations of dramas from foreign languages are listed separately, classified by nation of origin, such as Japan, India, ancient Greece, modern Europe, Great Britain, the United States, France, and Russia. Under each translated title are given the names of author and translator, the original title, the publisher's name and year of publication of the translated edition, and the number of pages and size of the book. Books and articles discussing the theory of drama and movies by Chinese and foreign authors are also included. There is an index to Chinese authors and translators arranged by the number of strokes and an alphabetical list of foreign authors and titles.

Chung-kuo t'ung-su hsiao-shuo shu-mu 中國通俗小說書目, 12 *chüan*. Compiled by Sun K'ai-ti 孫楷第. (1) Peiping: National Library of Peiping, 1933. [24] 384 [86] pp. (2) Peking: Tso-chia ch'u-pan she, 1957. [10] 323 pp.

This is a bibliography of Chinese fiction written in the colloquial style. More than 600 works are listed, dating from the beginning of the Sung dynasty down to the end of the Ch'ing, and including, besides works known to the compiler, lost works and works not seen by him. The main part of the bibliography fills the first seven *chüan* and is divided into four sections: the first, Sung and Yüan fiction; the second, Ming and Ch'ing historical fiction; and the third and fourth, Ming and Ch'ing general fiction. The fourth section is divided into four subsections, the first listing love stories, the second mythological stories, and the third and fourth heroic and satirical stories. The eighth *chüan* lists works which the compiler was unable to classify because he had not seen them, the ninth *ts'ung-shu* made up entirely of fiction, the tenth Chinese fiction translated into Japanese and annotated by Japanese, the eleventh Chinese fiction translated into Western languages, and the twelfth Chinese fiction translated into Manchu. In all sections the works are listed chronologically according to the time of writing except the historical writings which are arranged chronologically according to the time of the story. Under each title, besides giving the number of *chüan*, the editions, and the name of the writer, brief notes are added describing rare editions, pointing out that certain works having different titles are the same work, and discussing the value of the work itself. Different titles of the same work are indented one character, and when the author's name is not given or when only a pen name is given in the book, an attempt is made by the compiler to supply the real name. There are two indexes arranged according to the *kuo-yü* 國語 system, one to titles and one to authors' names.

9. AGRICULTURE AND MEDICINE

Chung-kuo nung-shu mu-lu 中國農書目錄. Compiled by Mao Yung 毛雝.
  (1) Nanking: Nanking University Library 金陵大學圖書館, 1924. 214 pp.
  (2) Taipei: Ku-t'ing shu-wu, 1970 (photocopy).

This is a bibliography of works on agriculture and allied subjects, the titles of which were collected from seventy-three catalogues. It is divided into twenty-one sections, two of which are subdivided, and the titles are arranged in each section or subsection according to the number of strokes. On each page there are five columns: (1) the title, (2) the number of *chüan* or volumes, (3) the name and dynasty of the author, (4) the original catalogue from which the title was taken, or, if included in a *ts'ung-shu*, the name of the *ts'ung-shu*, (5) miscellaneous notes, mostly cross-references. Sections in encyclopedias relating to agriculture are listed as though they were separate works. While the list is not exhaustive, it was carefully compiled and is quite useful as a guide to available material. Besides strictly agricultural topics such related subjects as famine, tea culture, silk culture, gardening and domestic economy are included. There is a table of contents at the beginning. The photocopy changes the title to **Chung-kuo nung-shu mu-lu hui-pien** 彙編 and the compiler's name to Mao Chang-sun 毛章孫.

Chung-kuo nung-hsüeh shu-lu 中國農學書錄. Compiled by Wang Yü-hu 王毓瑚. Peking: Chung-hua shu-chü, 1957. 232 pp.

This is an annotated bibliography of books dealing with Chinese agriculture, including techniques and instruments, horticulture, sericulture, livestock breeding, and fishery. At the end there are three indexes: classification, authors, and titles.

Chung-kuo i-chi k'ao 中國醫籍考. Compiled by Tamba Mototane [Taki Mototane] 丹波元胤 [多紀元胤]. Peking: Jen-min wei-sheng ch'u-pan she 人民衞生出版社, 1956. 5, 85, 1404, 97 pp.

This is an annotated bibliography of more than 3,000 books and articles dealing with Chinese medicine from ancient times to the 1840's. Sources are carefully indicated, and author and title indexes are furnished.

10. LAW

Chung-kuo li-tai fa-chia chu-shu-k'ao 中國歷代法家著述考. Compiled by Sun Tsu-chi 孫祖基 and first published in 1934. Taipei: Ku-t'ing shu-wu, 1970. 166 pp.

This is a descriptive bibliography of 574 works on Chinese law, the titles having been collected principally from the bibliographical sections of dynastic histories and from other bibliographies. The work is divided into six sections: the first, philosophy of law; the second and third, law making; the fourth, legal procedure; the fifth, coroner's inquests; and the sixth, works in which practical legal experiences are recorded. Under each title the number of *chüan* and the name and dynasty of the author are given, and notes are added for most of the works giving a certain amount of material concerning the author and the history of the compilation, and the contents and nature of the work. Scholars who are interested in Chinese legal and constitutional history will find this bibliography of considerable interest, although it must be pointed out that its general usefulness is very much lessened by the compiler's failure to indicate which of the works listed are still extant.

Chung-kuo fa-chih-shih ts'an-k'ao shu-mu chien-chieh 中國法制史參考
書目簡介. Compiled by the Fa-chih chü 法制局 of the Kuo-wu-yüan 國務院.
Peking: Fa-lü ch'u-pan she 法律出版社, 1968. [5] 228 pp.

This bibliography of 932 works (with a total of 10,607 *ts'e*) on Chinese
legal history and modern legal practice before 1949 was compiled by Li Tsu-
yin 李祖蔭 and others. Li was for many years a highly respected professor of
law at Yenching University. The work is divided into ten sections such as
writings by famous jurists, source materials on legal history, codes and institutions, precedents, regulations, by-laws, prosecution and the collection of
evidence. In each section the books are listed with terse summaries of their
contents but without comment or criticism. Although there is neither author
nor title index, this bibliography is informative and useful.

11.   OFFICIAL PUBLICATIONS

**Pei-ching t'u-shu-kuan hsien-ts'ang Chung-kuo cheng-fu ch'u-pan-
p'in mu-lu** 北京圖書館現藏中國政府出版品目錄. Peking: Metropolitan Library 北京圖書館, 1928. 80 pp. (Part I). **Kuo-li Pei-p'ing t'u-shu-kuan
hsien-ts'ang kuan-shu mu-lu** 國立北平圖書館現藏官書目錄. Peiping: National Library of Peiping, 1932. 91 pp. (Part II).

These are catalogues of Chinese official publications collected first in the
Peking Metropolitan Library, and after its amalgamation with the National
Library of Peiping, in the latter library. The first lists publications dating from
1911 to the end of March 1928, and it also includes a few related publications
dating from the last few years of the Ch'ing dynasty. There are 820 titles arranged according to the departments and bureaux of the government to which
they are related, while the publications of various local governments are listed
in a supplement. Under each title there are given the name of the author,
editor, or translator, the publishing bureau and date of publication, and the
number of volumes. The second catalogue is divided into two parts, one devoted to the publications of the National Government—both central and local
—and the other to the publications of the Kuomintang. Of the 1009 titles
listed, most are periodicals dating from the establishment of the Nationalist
Government at Canton in 1924 to the end of 1932. The same type of information is given under each title as in the first catalogue. Each catalogue is preceded by a table of the different departments and bureaux into which it is
divided. A similar catalogue, the **Kuo-li chung-yang t'u-shu-kuan ts'ang
kuan-shu mu-lu**[28] was published in Nanking in 1933 by the National Central
Library.

28. 國立中央圖書館藏官書目錄 (第一輯) Compiled and published by 國立中央圖書館籌備處
[11], 318 pp.

12. MINORITY PEOPLES

Man-wen shu-chi lien-ho mu-lu 滿文書籍聯合目錄. Compiled by Li Te-ch'i 李德啓 and edited by Yü Tao-ch'üan 于道泉. National Library of Peiping and the Library of the Palace Museum. 國立北平圖書館, 故宮博物院, 1933. 26, 126 pp.

This is a union catalogue of the Manchu books, and also of a very few Mongol and Tibetan books, preserved in the National Library of Peiping and in the Palace Museum. There are 472 works classified under ten section headings: general, philosophy, religions, natural sciences, applied sciences, social sciences, philology, literature, fine arts, and history and geography. Each section, except the first, is subdivided into a number of subsections. In so far as possible the following information is given concerning each of the works included: the Chinese title, the romanized form of the Manchu title, the number of *chüan*, *ts'e* and *han*, whether printed or in manuscript, the date of publication or copying, and whether or not there are missing parts. When a work has no Manchu title, the Chinese title is romanized, and when there is only a Manchu title, this is phonetically written in Chinese characters. In either case the characters *pu-i* 補譯 are inserted to show what has been done. When a work has no title at all one is invented for it by the compiler, in which case the character *pu* 補 is inserted. When a work is written in both Manchu and Chinese, or in Manchu, Mongol, and Chinese, the characters *man-han* 滿漢 or *man-meng-han* 滿蒙漢 are inserted. The characters *p'ing* 平 and *ku* 故 are used to distinguish between the works in the National Library and those in the Palace Museum. At the beginning of the catalogue there is a table of contents, and at the end there are the following indexes: one to the Chinese titles, by the four-corner system; one to the Chinese form of the names of Manchu writers, by the four-corner system; one to the Manchu titles, in Manchu; one to the names of Manchu authors, in Manchu, each followed by the Chinese form of the name; one to the Mongol titles, in Mongol; one to the Tibetan titles, in Tibetan; and one to the romanized form of the Manchu titles, arranged in alphabetical order.

Meng-ku ts'an-k'ao shu-mu 蒙古參考書目. Compiled by Chang Hsing-t'ang 張興唐. Taipei: Chung-hua ts'ung-shu wei-yüan hui, 1958. 8, 6, 2, 278 pp.

This reference work on Mongolia lists 1831 selected books, monographs, and articles written in Chinese, Japanese, Mongolian, and European languages except Russian, with brief compiler's remarks on the author, the contents, or the value of most of the entries. An interesting preface sums up Mongol history and relations with China over four thousand years and also discusses the evolution of Mongolian studies in China and other parts of the world. The bibliography is divided into history, geography, travel accounts, culture, linguistics, religion, institutions, sociology and economics, ethnography, and miscellaneous, with an eleventh section which lists 305 English, French, and German works on Mongolia. In the history section there are 289 works, 185 of which are in Chinese, written from the Sung to and including the Republican period, 10 in Mongolian, and 94 in Japanese. In the culture section there are 333 works, 287 in Chinese, from Yüan to the 1950's, 9 in Mongolian, and 37 in Japanese. In the miscellaneous section there are 51 works on statistics, yearbooks, biographical lists, and encyclopedias, 41 of which are in Chinese compiled from Yüan to 1953, and ten in Japanese. Since this is a selected bibliography, it can hardly be expected to meet with the approval of all readers. Nonetheless, it is a useful key to Mongol history and culture.

Chung-kuo pien-chiang t'u-chi lu 中國邊疆圖籍錄. Compiled by Teng Yen-lin, 鄧衍林. Shanghai: Commercial Press, 1958. 4, 329, 64, 37, 4 pp.

The study of Chinese minority groups and of the history and problems of China's border regions has become popular recently, but it remains hard to find material. To meet this difficulty a comprehensive catalogue of nearly 10,000 essays, articles, maps, atlases, and books has been compiled by a famous bibliographer and librarian, Teng Yen-lin. In this catalogue general works on the topography of the borderlands and on relations with Korea, Russia, Burma, and Annam are presented first. Then follow sources on the border relations between Sung China and the Tangut (*Hsi-hsia* 西夏 kingdom), Khitan, Jürched, and Mongol peoples, on Ming frontier troubles, and on *Wo-k'ou* 矮寇 or Japanese pirate attacks. Materials on these subjects found in *ts'ung-shu* and periodicals are listed in a special section. Thereafter materials dealing with the Northeast, Mongolia, the Northwest, the ancient West Region or Turkestan, Sinkiang, Tibet, and the Southwest, and with minority groups in the Southwest, Yünnan, and Kwangsi as well as in Taiwan, and with Maritime and River Defense are arranged geographically. Although the classification is somewhat confusing, the book is informative, and the author and title indexes arranged by the four-corner system are helpful. The original manuscript was completed in 1939 but, because of the war, it was not published until two decades later and then without much revision with the result that many recent studies of border problems are not listed.

13. SOUTHEAST ASIA

"Nan-yang wen-hsien hsü-lu ch'ang-pien 南洋文獻叙錄長編." Compiled by Hsü Yün-Ts'iao 許雲樵. Singapore: *Nan-yang yen-chiu* 南洋研究. Vol. 1, No. 1 (1959), 1–170.

This is an annotated bibliography of Chinese works on Southeast Asia other than dynastic histories, encyclopedias, collections of documents, and the contents of the *Hsiao-fang hu-chai yü-ti ts'ung-ch'ao*. There are 1101 titles listed in alphabetical order according to the compiler's own system of romanization, with detailed bibliographical data and succinct descriptive notes. There is an alphabetical index to authors' names at the end, again using the compiler's system of romanization.

Hua-ch'iao wen-t'i tzu-liao mu-lu so-yin ch'u-pien 華僑問題資料目錄索引初編. **Hsü-pien** 續編. Compiled by the Chung-kuo ch'iao-cheng hsüeh-hui 中國僑政學會. Taipei: Hai-wai ch'u-pan she 海外出版社, 1956, 5, 141 pp.; 1957, 19, 99 pp.

This is a catalogue of books and articles available in Taiwan that are concerned with overseas Chinese. The titles are arranged first under continents, then under countries, and finally under political subdivisions. More than half of the material deals with Southeast Asia. Adequate bibliographical information is supplied.[29]

14. TRANSLATIONS

Ming-Ch'ing-chien Yeh-su hui-shih i-chu t'i-yao 明清間耶蘇會士譯著提要. Compiled by Hsü Tsung-tse 徐宗澤. (1) Shanghai: Chung-hua shu-chü, 1949. 2, 18, 482, 8 pp. (2) Taipei: Chung-hua shu-chü, 1958. 19, 481, 8 pp.

During the seventeenth and eighteenth centuries many Jesuits and members of other Catholic orders in China wrote or translated 214 books, copies of which were still preserved in the 1940's in the mission library at Zikawei 徐家滙. These works are described by Hsü Tsung-tse, who claims to follow the style of the *Ssu-k'u ch'üan-shu tsung-mu* (q.v.).

An informative introduction includes discussion of the sciences introduced by the Jesuits near the end of the Ming, the influence of their writings on the Chinese intellectual world, their religious pamphlets, and their translating done in cooperation with Chinese converts. The book notes that make up the body of the work are arranged under the following headings: sacred books, arguments against the challenge of Taoists and other non-Christians to Christian tenets, theology and philosophy, ecclesiastical history, the calendar, science, and famous sayings. Under each title are given the author's name, the time and place of publication, and the preface or table of contents. There are author and title indexes near the end.

29. For later writings see the **Hua-ch'iao wen-t'i yu-kuan tzu-liao so-yin** 華僑問題有關資料索引. (Taipei: Ch'iao-wu wei-yüan hui 僑務委員會, 1965–1966). 2 vols. 454; 158 pp.

Appended is a union list of missionary writings in Chinese in the libraries at Zikawei, Paris, and the Vatican. *Chüan* 9 contains the authors' (or translators') Chinese names, Western names, dates of arrival in China and dates of death, as well as short biographies translated from Louis Pfister, S.J., *Notices biographiques et bibliographiques etc.*

Chin-pai-nien lai Chung-i hsi-shu mu-lu 近百年來中譯西書目錄. Compiled by the National Central Library. Taipei: Chung-hua wen-hua ch'u-pan shih-yeh wei-yüan hui, 1958. 1, 7, 328 pp.

This list of 5047 translations into Chinese, including some duplicates from different European languages, is arranged under the following headings: general, philosophy, religion, natural sciences, applied sciences, social sciences, history and geography, linguistics, and fine arts. In each section the Chinese title, translator's name, publication place (but no date) and publisher are given, followed by the original author's name and book title; no information is given regarding the original edition or publisher. There are neither author nor title indexes.

H.   CATALOGUES OF *TS'UNG-SHU*

The *ts'ung-shu* 叢書 is a collection of independent works which are published together in order that they may not be lost, or in order to give wider circulation to the writings of a particular locality, of one person, or of one family. Generally the works included in a *ts'ung-shu* are miscellaneous in nature, although occasionally *ts'ung-shu* have been published the contents of which have been limited to one subject. The name *ts'ung-shu* came from the title of a work which was not a *ts'ung-shu* but a collection of miscellaneous essays: the *Li-tse ts'ung-shu* 笠澤叢書, which was compiled by Lu Kuei-meng 陸龜蒙 during the latter half of the ninth century. The earliest *ts'ung-shu* extant is the *Ju-hsüeh ching-wu* 儒學警悟, a collection of seven works, which was published by Yü Ting-sun 俞鼎孫 in 1202. Since that time more than twenty-eight hundred *ts'ung-shu* have been published.

As the number of *ts'ung-shu* increased rapidly during the Ch'ing dynasty, catalogues were published, the earliest one being the *Hui-k'o shu-mu* 彙刻書目, compiled by Ku Hsiu 顧修 at the end of the eighteenth century. The largest thus far compiled is the *Chung-kuo ts'ung-shu tsung-lu;* it includes practically all of the *ts'ung-shu* listed in earlier catalogues and is more conveniently arranged than any of its predecessors, thus superseding almost all of them.

Ts'ung-shu tzu-mu shu-ming so-yin 叢書子目書名索引. Compiled by Shih T'ing-yung 施廷鏞. Peiping: The Library of Tsing Hua University 清華大學圖書館, 1936. 58, 1254 [204] pp.

This is an index to the titles of more than 40,000 works contained in the 1275 *ts'ung-shu* preserved in the Tsing Hua University Library. The titles are arranged according to the number of strokes, and under each there are given the name and dynasty of the author, the call number in the Tsing Hua Library, and the abbreviated title of the *ts'ung-shu* with the number of the *ts'e* in which it is to be found. At the beginning of the work there are two indexes to first characters (including the abbreviated forms of characters), one arranged according to the number of strokes and the other by radicals. At the end there are three lists: (1) A classified list of the *ts'ung-shu* indexed, giving for each title the library call number, the number of works included in it, the name and dynasty of the compiler, the year and place of publication, the number of volumes or of *han* as rearranged by the Tsing Hua Library, and the original number of *ts'e*. (2) A list of the *ts'ung-shu* in which their full titles are arranged according to the number of strokes, giving under each full title the abbreviated title used in the index, the library call number, and the location of the work by *chüan* and page in eight catalogues of *ts'ung-shu*. (3) A list of the *ts'ung-shu* arranged under the abbreviated titles used in the index, the abbreviated titles being arranged according to the number of strokes and followed by the same information as is given in the preceding list. This work does not contain an author index, nor are the works included in the Buddhist and Taoist canons indexed because of their having been indexed separately in the *Fo-ts'ang tzu-mu yin-te* and the *Tao-ts'ang tzu-mu yin-te*. Although there are occasional mistakes and omissions, this was at the time of publication the most nearly complete and the most conveniently arranged index to the contents of *ts'ung-shu* available.

*Chung-kuo ts'ung-shu tsung-lu 中國叢書綜錄. Compiled by the Shanghai Library 上海圖書館. Shanghai: Chung-hua shu-chü, 1959–62. 3 vols. 4, 1186; 3, 8, 1752; xl, 791 pp.

This is probably the most useful reference work compiled thus far by scholars in continental China; it is indispensable to every Chinese reference library. It is a comprehensive catalogue of 2797 *ts'ung-shu* or Chinese collectanea, excluding only those on Buddhism and on new studies (新學). It includes more than twice as many *ts'ung-shu* as the *Ts'ung-shu tzu-mu shu-ming so-yin* (q.v.), heretofore the largest catalogue.

The first volume lists the titles of the 2797 *ts'ung-shu* largely according to the *Ssu-k'u* classification system with analytical subheadings to facilitate quick and easy reference. Near the end of the volume (pp. 958–1133) there is a long list of the different editions of the 2797 *ts'ung-shu* which are available in the forty-one major libraries in continental China, serving as a union catalogue. At the end there is a four-corner index and a number-of-strokes index to the titles of the *ts'ung-shu*.

Volume 2 is a classified catalogue of the more than 70,000 titles of the works included in the 2797 *ts'ung-shu*, also arranged according to the *Ssu-k'u* system. Volume 3 contains indexes to these titles and to their authors, both using the four-corner system. There are also keys to first characters, arranged by the number of strokes and by the romanization used in the People's Republic of China.

I. BIBLIOGRAPHIES OF BIBLIOGRAPHIES

The compilation of bibliographies of bibliographies is a comparatively recent development in China, the earliest one (the *Shu-mu chü-yao* 書目舉要, compiled by Chou Chen-liang 周貞亮 and Li Chih-ting 李之鼎) having been published in 1920. The National Library of Peiping published a more extensive catalogue of bibliographies fourteen years later.

Kuo-li Pei-p'ing t'u-shu-kuan shu-mu: Mu-lu lei 國立北平圖書館書目: 目錄類. Compiled by Hsiao Chang 蕭璋. Peiping: National Library of Peiping, 1934. 2 *ts'e*.

This is the catalogue of the bibliographies preserved in the National Library of Peiping in 1934. It is divided into three parts. The first part, subdivided into six sections, lists works which discuss editions, authenticity, collation, and other matters having to do with the physical make up of books. The second part has nine sections of special bibliographies, such as annotated bibliographies, bibliographies of *ts'ung-shu*, and bibliographies of special fields, and three sections of catalogues of public and private collections. The third part lists works on library science, classified under seven section headings. Under each title there are given the number of *chüan* and *ts'e*, the name and dynasty of the compiler or author, and the date and place of publication. Different editions of the same work are treated separately, a special effort being made to give as definite information concerning the date and place of publication as possible. A total of 896 works are listed, the bibliographical sections of dynastic histories, gazetteers, and encyclopedias being omitted. There is a table of contents at the beginning, and at the end there are two indexes, both arranged according to the number of strokes, one to the titles of works and the other to the names of writers and compilers.

Chung-kuo li-tai shu-mu tsung-lu 中國歷代書目總錄. Compiled by Liang Tzu-han 梁子涵. Taipei: Chung-hua wen-hua ch'u-pan shih-yeh wei-yüan hui, 1953. 5, 484 pp.

This is a classified bibliography of bibliographies, divided into general, historical, subject, special, and public and private library catalogues. A large number of titles are to be found in each category, with detailed bibliographical data. Unfortunately, there is no author or title index.

Chung-kuo mu-lu-hsüeh nien-piao 中國目錄學年表. Compiled by Yao Ming-ta 姚名達 and published by the Commercial Press in 1940 in the *Kuo-hsüeh hsiao ts'ung-shu* 國學小叢書. 19, 175, 17 pp. (2) Taipei: Commercial Press, 1967. 2, 2, 17, 175, 17 pp.

This a chronological catalogue of bibliographies. It gives detailed accounts of all private and official bibliographical compilations during the period from 213 B.C. to A.D. 1936, as well as accounts of the founding and destruction of various public and private libraries. There is an index to the bibliographies included, arranged by the four-corner system.

J. BIBLIOGRAPHIES OF RECENT PUBLICATIONS

T'u-shu nien-chien 圖書年鑑. Compiled by Yang Chia-lo 楊家駱. Nanking: Chung-kuo t'u-shu ta-tz'u-tien pien-chi-kuan 中國圖書大辭典編輯館, 1933. 2 vols. 15, 503 pp.; 41, 1888 pp. Fourth printing, 1935, one vol.

This is a combined library yearbook and annotated bibliography of books published in China between 1912 and May 1933, listing, according to the introduction, a total of 8474 titles. The first volume presents material on the history, equipment, and contents of all libraries in China, reproduces all Chinese laws and governmental mandates concerning publications of all kinds, and gives a list of all publishers. The titles of books and the notes describing them are arranged in the second volume, which is divided into fourteen sections and over a thousand subsections. The fourteen section headings are: general, philosophy, languages, writings on literature, Chinese literature, translations from foreign literature, writings on the arts, education, the natural sciences, practical knowledge (including agriculture, medicine, engineering, etc.), the social sciences, economics, political science and law, and history and geography. Under each title the author's name, the publisher, the number of *ts'e* (if more than one), and the price are given. Under most titles there are notes describing the contents and value of the work, sometimes long and sometimes short, as a rule based upon prefaces or book reviews. Besides the Chinese titles of translations, the original titles and authors' names are given in the original language. The titles of works published in *ts'ung-shu* are classified and listed as though they were independent works. The list of titles is far from complete, the system of classification is not very logical, much of the material in the first volume is copied without acknowledgment from the writings of others, and the publication dates of the works listed are not given.

In spite of these serious faults, this is still the best descriptive guide to books published since the establishment of the Republic. There is a table of contents at the beginning, but there is no index to titles.

Sheng-huo ch'üan-kuo tsung shu-mu 生活全國總書目. Compiled by P'ing Hsin 平心. Shanghai: Sheng-huo shu-tien, 1935. [42] 716 [213] pp.

This volume lists books published in China between 1911 and 1935. It is divided into ten sections and a great many subsections. The ten section headings are: general, philosophy, the social sciences, religions, subjects related to both the social and natural sciences, natural sciences, literature, languages, history and geography, and practical knowledge. Under each title the name of the author, the price, and the abbreviated name of the publisher are given. If the book is a translation from a foreign language, the title and author's name are also given in their original form. A star placed before a title is meant to indicate that that work is intended for the use of specialists and advanced students, although the compiler's judgment is not always reliable. The classification of works is frequently faulty, no publication dates are given, and the list of titles is far from exhaustive. However the catalogue is quite useful to scholars and historians as a checklist of recent publications. There are indexes to titles, arranged according to the four-corner system, to countries, arranged by continents and subdivided according to subsection headings, to the names of Western authors whose works have been translated, arranged alphabetically, and to the names of Japanese writers of translated works, arranged according to the four-corner system.

Ch'üan-kuo hsin shu-mu 全國新書目. Compiled and published in Peking by the General Bureau of Publications 全國出版總署 from 1951 to 1953 and thereafter by the Acquisitions Library of the Bureau of Publications of the Ministry of Culture 文化部出版事業管理局版本圖書館. Frequency varies.

This bibliography of all books and pamphlets published in mainland China during the period covered, has sometimes appeared monthly and sometimes two or three times a month, although the first issue covered publications from October 1949 through 1950, and the next two issues were quarterlies. For a fuller description see Peter Berton and Eugene Wu, *Contemporary China: A Research Guide* (Stanford, 1967), p. 8. Microfilms of the 1959 and 1960 issues may be purchased from the Library of Congress, and issues from May 1962 through 1964 from the Hoover Institution at Stanford.

Ch'üan-kuo tsung shu-mu 全國總書目. The 1949–1954 and 1955 issues were compiled and published in Peking in 1956 and 1957 respectively by the

Hsin-hua shu-tien 新華書店. The 1956, 1957 and 1958 issues were compiled by the Acquistitions Library of the Bureau of Publications of the Ministry of Culture 文化部出版事業管理局版本圖書館 and published in Peking by the Chung-hua shu-chü in 1957, 1958 and 1959 respectively.

This is a cumulative list of publications in continental China. The latest issue to appear abroad, that for 1958, is in three volumes (45, 1688 pp.) and lists 28,090 titles, arranged under 19 section headings beginning with works on Marx and ending with works of general reference. The largest section, on technology and techniques, lists 5,564 titles, the second largest, on literature, lists 4,916, and the third, illustrated books, lists 1,304. Under each title the author's name, the publisher, the month and year of publication and the price are given. Russian works with Chinese translations are indicated bilingually. There is a title index to the 1958 issue arranged by a new system explained on pp. 1422–23, and there is a detailed classification table on pp. 7–45. Microfilms of the first four issues may be purchased from the Library of Congress and of the 1958 issue from University Microfilms, Ann Arbor, Michigan.

Chung-hua min-kuo ch'u-pan t'u-shu mu-lu hui-pien 中華民國出版圖書目錄彙編. Taipei: National Central Library, 1964. 2 vols. 4, 846 pp.

This is essentially a catalogue of books published in Taiwan from 1949 to the end of 1963, though a small number of books published in Hong Kong and Macao and some complimentary copies sent by overseas authors are also included. There are 15,000 titles classified under general, philosophy, religion, natural science, applied science, social science, history and geography, language and literature, and fine arts. The process of registration, title, author's name, date and place of publication, publisher's name, number of pages, size of the book, and finally the price, if known, are given. At the end of volume II, there is a list of English books published in Taiwan.

Chinese Bibliography 中華民國出版圖書目錄. Taipei: National Central Library. February 1970+.

This cumulative listing of new books published in Taiwan is expected to appear monthly. Each entry follows a catalogue card format giving author and title (in Wade-Giles romanization as well as in Chinese characters), date of publication, price, and classification number according to the Chinese system. Each issue is divided into two sections: general books and government publications. Maps, music and cheap novelettes are excluded. Annual author and title indexes are expected to appear in the December issue. This periodical is intended to provide complete coverage.

Ch'üan-kuo Chung-wen ch'i-k'an lien-ho mu-lu 全國中文期刊聯合目錄. Compiled by Ch'üan-kuo t'u-shu lien-ho mu-lu pien-chi tsu 全國圖書聯合目錄編輯組. Peking: The Peking Library, 1961. 36, 1252 pp.

This is a union list of 19,015 Chinese serials published between 1833 and 1949. It includes most of the "reactionary publications" considered to be of academic value for domestic use but excludes Communist party papers and documents, which were to appear in a separate compilation. These nineteen thousand periodicals are deposited in fifty participating libraries scattered throughout the country, with each library assigned a certain number. The entries are arranged by the number of strokes, and under each are given the title, frequency of publication, name of the editor, publisher, date and place of the first issue, date of suspension, and the holding libraries. Cross references and brief remarks are abundant. The compilers were aware of their handicap in not being able to examine all of the scattered publications which made it impossible to classify them according to their contents. Nevertheless, it is still the best checklist of its kind in existence.

K.   INDEXES TO PERIODICALS AND NEWSPAPERS

Three types of indexes are included in this section: general indexes to periodicals, indexes to magazine articles in special fields, and general indexes to newspapers. There are special indexes to articles relating to Sinology, literature, geography, law, medicine, agriculture, and mining.

Jen-wen yüeh-k'an 人文月刊. Compiled and published in Shanghai by the Jen-wen yüeh-k'an she 人文月刊社. Vol. 1, No. 1 (Feb. 15, 1930)—Vol. 8, No. 10 (Dec. 15, 1937); Vol. 9, No. 1 (April 1947).

More than half of the space in this magazine is devoted to indexing the articles in the current issues of some 250 Chinese periodicals (including the supplements of the *Ta-kung-pao* 大公報), the articles being carefully classified under subdivisions of the various branches of modern knowledge. For each article indexed the title, the author's or translator's name, the name of the magazine with volume, number and page, and the date of publication are given. A list of the magazines indexed, with the publisher's name, dates, and volume and numbers, precedes the index in each issue, and after the index there is a classified list of newly published books, which, besides the title and author's name, gives the name of the publisher of each book and the price.

The remainder of the magazine consists of articles which very often are annotated diaries or collected notes having historical value, and a table of important events. The latter is divided into four columns: (1) Kuomintang and National Government affairs, (2) diplomatic events specifically related to

China, (3) other events in China, and (4) events in the rest of the world. The index to periodical articles in the *Jen-wen yüeh-kan* is not as complete or as well classified as the index published in the *Ch'i-k'an so-yin*; however it was published for nearly four years before the first number of the *Ch'i-k'an so-yin* was issued, and it occasionally indexes magazines which are neglected by the latter.

Ch'i-k'an so-yin 期刊索引. Vol. 1–Vol. 8; November 1933–June 1937. Nanking: Sun Yat-sen Institute for the Advancement of Culture and Education 南京中山文化教育館. Monthly.

This index to periodical literature was divided into two parts: (1) an index to the titles of articles, and (2) an index to the names of the authors of articles. In the first two numbers, the index to titles was divided into eleven sections and many subsections, the titles being arranged under each heading according to the number of strokes. After the second number appeared, the system of classification and the arrangement of titles and names was changed several times. One half of the third, fourth, fifth, and sixth numbers (January to April, 1934) was given over to an index to newspaper articles, although the newspaper index was published separately as the *Jih-pao so-yin* after April 1934. From Vol. 2, No. 1 (May 1934) to Vol. 3, No. 2 (December 1934), the magazine index was divided into three parts: authors' names, titles of articles, and subjects, the arrangement of all three being according to the number of strokes. Vol. 3, No. 3 (January 1935), was a special index to articles on jurisprudence which appeared in Chinese magazines from 1904 to 1934. Nos. 4–6 of Vol. 3 (February to April, 1935), indexed the titles of magazine articles according to the Dewey Decimal system, the titles being arranged under each subject heading by the form-of-character system outlined in the *Han-tzu hsing-wei p'ai-chien-fa* 漢字形位排檢法 of Tu Ting-yu 杜定友; in these numbers there is no author index. Beginning with Vol. 4, No. 1 (May 1935), an author index was re-introduced, this time arranged according to Tu's form-of-character system; the title index inaugurated in February of the same year was continued.

In the index to articles, each title was followed by the author's name, the abbreviated name of the periodical, the volume, number, and page, and the date of publication. The same material was given in the author index, except that it was placed under the author's name. Translations were placed under the names of translators, which were in each case followed by the name of the author and the original title. There were 568 periodicals indexed in the first number; in May 1936 (Vol. 5, No. 6), the number was 433. There was a list of the periodicals indexed at the beginning of each number, with the abbreviation used in the index, the publisher's name, the volume and number, and the date of publication. Beginning Vol. 3, No. 4, the index to titles was divided as follows: (1) general, philosophy, religions, education; (2) social sciences;

(3) economics; (4) arts, natural sciences, medicine, public health; (5) agriculture, labor, commerce, industry, communications; and (6) languages, literature, history, and geography. The *Ch'i-k'an so-yin* indexed more magazines than any other index published in China, but its rather complicated arrangement tends to make it inconvenient to use.

Ch'üan-kuo chu-yao pao-k'an tzu-liao so-yin 全國主要報刊資料索引. No. 1+; 1955+. Shanghai: Municipal Newspaper and Periodical Library 上海市報刊圖書館. Bi-monthly, March 1955–June 1956; monthly, since July 1956. Called **Ch'üan-kuo chu-yao ch'i-**(期) **k'an tzu-liao so-yin,** March–November, 1955. Nos. 1–57 (1955–1960), Washington: Library of Congress, 1966. 30 vols. (photocopy).

This voluminous periodical index is the most important reference tool of its kind produced in mainland China. Numbers 1–6 index some 200 periodicals. Since No. 7 (April, 1956), both newspapers (*pao-k'an*) and periodicals (*ch'i-k'an*) have been indexed, including 216 of the latter. From No. 39 (January, 1959), two volumes were issued each month, one on natural sciences and the other on humanities and social sciences, but beginning with volume 51 (January, 1960), humanities, social sciences, and natural sciences have been combined in a single volume.

The arrangement of entries in this index series follows the "Chinese library classification scheme 圖書分類法" designed by the Chinese People's University Library 中國人民大學圖書館. A modified decimal system is used, with articles arranged under seventeen topics: Marxism-Leninism and Mao Tse-tung's works, philosophy, dialectical and historical materialism, social and political sciences, economics, national defense and military affairs, jurisprudence, culture and education, fine arts, linguistics, history, geography, natural sciences, medicine and health, engineering and technology, agriculture, and reference works. Under each heading the entries are listed by title, name of author or translator, name of periodical, volume and page.

Ch'i-k'an lun-wen so-yin 期刊論文索引. Compiled and published by the National War College Library (Kuo-fang yen-chiu yüan t'u-shu-kuan 國防研究院圖書館). Taiwan: Yang-ming-shan 陽明山. Vol. 1, No. 1+, February 1950+.

This monthly index to about 160 Chinese periodicals published in Taiwan, Hong Kong, and Macao is classified as follows: 0 general works, 1 philosophy, 2 religion, 3 natural sciences, 4 applied sciences, 5 social sciences, 6 history, 7 geography, 8 linguistics and literature, and 9 fine arts. At the end of each issue there are a few pages listing articles dealing with current Chinese Communist affairs. Each entry is preceded by a library classification number which seems unnecessary for the general consultant of this index. After the number are given the title of the article, the name of the author or translator, the name of the magazine, the volume and the first page number, but the last page is omitted making it impossible to tell the length of the article. Editorials, short comments, special articles and translated essays are included.

Chung-wen ch'i-k'an lun-wen fen-lei so-yin 中文期刊論文分類索引. Compiled and published by the National Taiwan University Library 國立臺灣大學圖書館. Series I+ ; 1960+.

This is a cumulative index to Chinese academic journals published mostly in Taiwan, of which thirty are covered in Series I and forty-seven in Series VI (1967). Unlike the *Ch'i-k'an lun-wen so-yin* (q.v.), which it complements in some respects, this compilation excludes editorials, correspondence, short comments, book reviews, and "literary pieces." Although the entries are also arranged according to the Chinese Library Classification Scheme, more information is given on each article, including the time of publication and the number of pages. This index is published at irregular intervals.

Index to Chinese Periodicals 中華民國期刊論文. Taipei: National Central Library. January 1970+ . Monthly.

This is intended to be a monthly listing of periodical articles published in Taiwan. Each entry gives title and author's or translator's name, abbreviated periodical name, volume and number, first and last page numbers, and year and month. Titles are arranged by number of strokes under ten broad subject headings. There is a list of the periodicals indexed each month and a number-of-strokes author index. Annual cumulative author and title indexes are expected to appear in the final number each year.

Yu-lien yen-chiu so: fen-lei tzu-liao mu-lu 友聯研究所: 分類資料目錄. Hong Kong: Union Research Institute, 1962, [6] 146 pp.

This is a classified catalogue of the files of mainland Chinese newspapers, periodicals and books collected by the Union Research Institute since 1951. Such important periodicals as *Hsüeh-hsi* 學習 and *Shih-shih shou-ts'e* 時事手冊 are clipped, while others are retained intact. The index is divided into the following sections: general, political, social, military, financial, economic, cultural and educational, and further into subsections. Each entry is given a serial number, which is particularly helpful in ordering microfilms. There is also an English version of this catalogue.

Kuo-hsüeh lun-wen so-yin 國學論文索引. First issue compiled by Wang Chung-min 王重民; second issue (**Hsü-pien** 續編) compiled by Hsü Hsü-ch'ang 徐緒昌; third issue (**San-pien** 三編) and fourth issue (**Ssu-pien** 四編), compiled by Liu Hsiu-yeh 劉修業 and the index department of the National Library of Peiping. Peiping: Library Association of China 中華圖書館協會, 1929, 1931, 1934, 1936. [19] 230 pp.; [16] 196 pp.; [36] 386, 13 pp.; [35] 481, 4 pp. The fifth issue (**Wu-pien** 五編), compiled by Hou Chih-chung 侯植忠. Peking: T'u-shu-kuan ts'an-k'ao yen-chiu tsu 圖書館參考研究組, 1955. 2 vols. [11] 29, 533 pp. (mimeographed edition).

This is a cumulative index to Sinological articles which appeared in Chinese periodicals prior to June 1937. There were 81 magazines and newspapers indexed in the first issue, 77 in the second, 185 in the third, and 200 in the fourth. The periodicals indexed in the first issue date from 1905 to July, 1928, and each of the subsequent issues indexes later numbers of the same periodicals and also earlier articles in periodicals neglected by the earlier indexes. Each index is divided into seventeen sections and numerous subsections, the section headings being: general, classics, languages, archaeology, history, geography, philosophy, literature, natural sciences, political science and law, economics, sociology, education, music, the arts, religions, and bibliography and library science. Under each title the author's name and the name of the magazine or newspaper, with the volume or year and the number, are given. There are also frequent brief notes explaining titles, discussing the contents of articles, or giving dates or conclusions. Although the work is not very carefully done and many articles are incorrectly classified, the selection of magazines is very broad, especially in the last three issues. There is a table of contents and a list of the periodicals indexed at the beginning of each volume. The fifth issue also supplies dates of publication and page numbers.

Chung-kuo shih-hsüeh lun-wen yin-te 中國史學論文引得, 1902–1962. Compiled by Ping-kuen Yu (Yü Ping-ch'üan) 余秉權. Hong Kong: East Asia Institute, 1963. 572 pp.

This is an index to scholarly articles in Chinese magazines not only on history but also on other aspects of Chinese culture including literature, philosophy, the society, and the economy. It is perhaps the best reference work of its kind, not because its coverage is complete but because of the care taken in its compilation and the fact that the compiler has actually examined the journals. It indexes 10,325 articles by 3392 authors in 355 periodicals published between 1902 and 1962 that are available in the Hong Kong area.

Each listing is under the author's name or that of the translator and consists of the title of the article, the name of the periodical, volume and number, date, page numbers, and indication of the location of the magazine. When there is more than one article by an author they are listed in order of the date of publication. In contrast to most Chinese periodical indexes both the first and last pages are given for each article. At the beginning there are indexes to the surnames of authors arranged by the number of strokes and the Wade-Giles romanization. A simple subject index is to be found pp. 477–569.

Chung-kuo shih-hsüeh lun-wen so-yin 中國史學論文索引. Compiled by Chung-kuo k'o-hsüeh-yüan, Li-shih yen-chiu-so 中國科學院, 歷史研究所 and the Department of History, Peking University. Peking: K'o-hsüeh ch'u-pan she, 1957. 2 vols. 421; 8, 676, 115 pp.

This index to more than 30,000 articles in some 1300 periodicals published approximately from 1900 to 1937 is divided into seventeen sections. The first volume indexes articles on all facets of Chinese history, biography, archaeology, and bibliography; the second, articles on academic thought, sociology, government, economics, education, religion, language, literature, fine arts, natural sciences, medicine, agriculture and other matters. There are subject, personal name and place name indexes. One defect of this work is the lack of page indication, only the volume number and the date of the magazine being given. Another is that a large part of its contents was copied from the *Kuo-hsüeh lun-wen so-yin* without checking the original journals.

Chung-kuo ku-tai chi chung-shih-chi-shih pao-k'an lun-wen tzu-liao so-yin 中國古代及中世紀史報刊論文資料索引. Compiled and published by the Department of History, Hua-tung Teachers University (華東師範大學 歷史系). [Shanghai] 1959. 2, 197 pp.

This is an index to articles dealing with Chinese ancient and medieval history (to the end of Ming) published in mainland magazines and newspapers between 1949 and September 1959. The material is divided into two parts: general, such as academic thought, scientific techniques, peasant uprisings, book reviews; and according to the time, essays concerning the Hsia, Shang, Chou and other periods. Pagination is not given for magazine articles; only the month and year of publication are noted.

Wen-hsüeh lun-wen so-yin 文學論文索引. First issue (**Cheng-pien** 正編) compiled by Ch'en Pi-ju 陳璧如, Chang Ch'en-ch'ing 張陳卿 and others; second issue (**Hsü-pien** 續編) and third issue (**San-pien** 三編) compiled by Liu Hsiu-yeh 劉修業. (1) Peiping: Library Association of China 中華圖書館 協會, 1932, 1933, 1936. [33], 314 pp.; [46], 333, [24] pp.; [28] 484 pp. (2) Taipei: Ku-t'ing shu-wu, 1970 (photocopy).

This is a cumulative index to literary productions and articles on literature published in Chinese periodicals. The first issue indexes 160 periodical publications dating from 1905 to the end of 1929, the second, 204 dating from 1928 to May, 1933, and the third, 226 dating from 1933 to October, 1935. Some of the periodicals indexed in the second and third issues were published earlier but were not included in the preceding index. The three issues are arranged roughly in the same way, each being divided into three parts and subdivided into sections and subsections. The first part lists articles on literature; the second, literary productions· (grouped according to their nature, as poetry, drama, short stories, essays, etc.); and the third, articles on men of letters, classified according to nationality. Under each title the author's name, the name of the magazine or newspaper in which it appears, the volume or year, and the number are given. In the second and third issues there are often short notes which explain the title, supply information about the author, or give a brief resumé of the contents. At the beginning of each volume a table of contents and a list of the periodicals indexed in it are to be found.

Chung-kuo hsien-tai wen-hsüeh tso-chia tso-p'in p'ing-lun tzu-liao so-yin 中國現代文學作家作品評論資料索引. Compiled by the Office of Source Material of the Modern Chinese Literature Seminar, the Department of Chinese, Fukien Teachers College (福建師範學院中文系, 中國現代文學教研組, 資料室). (1) Fukien: Jen-min chiao-yü ch'u-pan she 人民教育出版社, 1961. 5, 234 pp.; Supplement (續編), 1, 6, 275 pp. (2) Tokyo: Daian Bookstore, 1967 (photocopy).

This is an index to comments, book reviews, and discussions of current literature and famous writers in mainland periodicals from 1949 to December 1959. Comments on Chairman Mao's poems and prose are presented first (pp. 1–8), followed by comments on works of Lu Hsün and others. The scope was enlarged in the supplement to include the many new writers of labor and farm background whose writings were evaluated during 1960–61.

Chung-kuo ti-hsüeh lun-wen so-yin 中國地學論文索引 and **Hsü-pien** 續編. Compiled by Wang Yung 王庸 and Mao Nai-wen 茅乃文. (1) Peiping: National Normal University 國立北平師範大學 and the National Library of Peiping, 1934–1936. 2 vols. [46], 454, [98] pp. Supplement, 2 vols. [22], 453, 47 pp. (2) Taipei: Ku-t'ing shu-wu, 1970 (photocopy).

This is an index to the articles on Chinese geography which appeared in 123 Chinese periodicals between 1902 and June 1933. The work is divided into eight sections and many subsections, the section headings being: (1) travel notes and other geographical descriptions, (2) physical geography, (3) human geography, (4) political geography, (5) communications, (6) economic geography, (7) historical geography, and (8) bibliography, maps, gazetteers, the study of geography, etc. After each title, the author's name, the name of the periodical, the *chüan* or year, and the number are given. There is a table of contents and a list of the periodicals indexed at the beginning and at the end there are indexes to place names and authors, arranged according to the number of strokes. Articles are often not very satisfactorily classified. In the supplement about 4000 articles published in 1934 and 1935 are indexed.

Fa-lü lun-wen fen-lei so-yin 法律論文分類索引. Compiled by Yüan K'un-hsiang 袁坤祥. Taipei: Soochow University 東吳大學, 1963. 8, 8, 24, 504 pp.

This classified index to legal literature published in Chinese periodicals from 1947 to 1962 was compiled by the acting librarian of the Soochow University Library. Some 6,300 articles are classified under jurisprudence, legal philosophy, legal history, the constitution, civil and criminal codes, and many other headings. Bibliographical data are given for each article and an author index by the number-of-strokes system is placed at the back of the volume.

Chung-wen i-hsüeh wen-hsien fen-lei so-yin 中文醫學文獻分類索引. Compiled by Wu Kuan-kuo 吳觀國 and Chi Hung 吉鴻 of the Nanking Medical College Library 南京醫學院圖書館. Peking: Jen-min wei-sheng ch'u-pan she, 1958. [16] 674 pp.

This is an index to more than 24,000 articles in 82 Chinese medical journals, most of which began publication between 1949 and 1955. The articles are arranged under the detailed subdivisions of the medical sciences. The bibliographical data, though limited, are carefully presented.

Nan-yang yen-chiu Chung-wen ch'i-k'an tzu-liao so-yin 南洋研究中文期刊資料索引. Singapore: Institute of Southeast Asia, Nanyang University 南洋大學; 南洋研究所, 1968. [10] 363 pp.

This is an index to some 10,000 articles that relate to Southeast Asia in more than 500 Chinese magazines. Under each country the articles are classified under (1) general; (2) culture and religion; (3) education; (4) language, literature and the arts; (5) social problems and folklore; (6) politics, public administration and international relations; (7) economics, industry and trade; (8) law; (9) natural and applied sciences; and (10) geography, history, and biography. Under each entry the title, the author's name, the journal, volume number, date of publication and pages (such as 29–56) are indicated in detail.

Nung-yeh lun-wen so-yin 農業論文索引. Compiled by Ch'en Tsu-kuei 陳祖槼, Wan Kuo-ting 萬國鼎, and others. University of Nanking Library 金陵大學圖書館 and the National Library of Peiping, 1933. xxiv, 731, vii,

153 pp. Supplement: **Nung-yeh lun-wen so-yin hsü-pien** 農業論文索引續編. Compiled by Chu Yao-ping 朱耀炳. University of Nanking Library, 1935. xxii, 348, iv, 28 pp.

This is an index to articles on agriculture and related subjects appearing both in Chinese and in English-language periodicals in China. The main work indexes 312 Chinese magazines and eight bulletins dating from 1897 to the end of 1931, and thirty-six English-language periodicals, dating from 1858 to the end of 1931. The supplement indexes articles published during the years 1932–1934 in 553 Chinese magazines and six bulletins, and in thirty English-language periodicals. Section and subsection headings are arranged according to the form-of-strokes system used in Wan Kuo-ting's *Hsin-ch'iao tzu-tien* 新橋字典, and under the title of each article the author's name, the name of the periodical, the volume and page number, and the date of publication are given. When articles contain diagrams or tables, this fact is also indicated. Among the section headings in the supplement are: agricultural economics, production, village and other local studies, the land problem, irrigation, and agricultural co-operatives—all of which have been developed as special studies in China comparatively recently. There are lists of the periodicals indexed and number-of-strokes indexes to the first characters of classification headings at the beginning of the parts written in Chinese in both the main work and the supplement.

Chung-kuo k'uang-yeh ch'i-k'an lun-wen tzu-liao so-yin 中國礦業期刊論文資料索引. Compiled by the library of the Peking Academy of Mining (K'uang-yeh hsüeh-yüan 礦業學院). Peking: K'o-hsüeh ch'u-pan-she, 1960. x, 366 pp.

This is an index to more than 8,000 periodical articles dealing with the Chinese mining industry published from 1917 to 1959. The articles are arranged under such categories as the history of Chinese mineralogy, geological surveys, petroleum drilling, mine equipment, and safety techniques. Only the first page number of an article is indicated. There is neither author nor title index.

Jih-pao so-yin 日報索引. May 31, 1934–July 15, 1937. Nanking: Sun Yat-sen Institute for the Advancement of Culture and Education 中山文化教育館. Monthly. Ceased publication.

This is an index to the articles published in eleven leading Chinese newspapers. The newspapers indexed in the first six numbers were *Shen-pao* 申報, *Hsin-wen-pao* 新聞報, *Shih-shih hsin-pao* 時事新報, *Chung-yang jih-pao* 中央日報, *Wu-han jih-pao* 武漢日報, *Ta-kung pao* 大公報, *Pei-p'ing ch'en-pao* 北平晨報,

Hsiang-chiang kung-shang jih-pao 香港工商日報, *Kuang-chou min-kuo jih-pao* 廣州民國日報 and *Hsing-chou jih-pao* 星州日報. Beginning with Vol. 2 (November 1934) the *Ch'en-pao* 晨報 (of Shanghai) and the *Hsi-ching jih-pao* 西京日報 were added, although the former was dropped after Vol. 4, No. 5 (March 1936). Beginning with Vol. 4, No. 1 (November 1935), the *Kuang-chou min-kuo jih-pao* was replaced by the *Hsiang-chiang hsün-huan jih-pao* 香港循環日報. The *Shen-pao* is indexed in its entirety, and when the same material appears in the other newspapers it is not indexed unless it is presented in more detail. The *Jih-pao so-yin* is, with the exception of a few numbers, divided into two parts: in the first, the headlines of articles are indexed; in the second, the names of writers are indexed. The first part, except in the first two numbers, is divided into ten sections and many subsections, the articles under each subsection heading being arranged in chronological order. After each headline the name of the writer, the abbreviated name of the newspaper, the date of publication, and the page and column are given. Continued articles are marked with a cross. The same information is given in the index to writers, in which the writers' names are arranged according to the number of strokes. There is a table of contents at the beginning of each number.

"Kaihō nippō" kiji mokuroku or **"Chieh-fang jih-pao" chi-shih mu-lu** 解放日報記事目錄. Compiled and published by the Kindai Chūgoku kenkyū iinkai, Tokyo, 1967–1968. 3 vols. 243; 296; 439 pp.

This is a table of contents of the official Chinese Communist newspaper, the *Liberation Daily*, from May 16, 1941 to February 5, 1947.

Kuang-ming jih-pao so-yin 光明日報索引. 1952+. Monthly. Peking: Kuang-ming jih-pao. (Only the volumes for the years 1954–1959 are generally available).

This is an index to the Peking *Kuang-ming Daily*, which pays more attention to cultural and educational affairs than other mainland newspapers and is especially important for its weekly supplements on history, philosophy, literature, and other subjects. Many of the indexed articles were written by famous scholars.

Chung-wen pao-chih lun-wen fen-lei so-yin 中文報紙論文分類索引. 1962 +. Taipei: Social Science Materials Center, National Chengchi University 國立政治大學社會科學資料中心. Annual.

This classified index to Chinese newspapers has been issued annually since 1962. The 1968 issue (published in 1969) indexed twenty Taiwan and Hong

Kong newspapers. The articles are arranged according to the Chinese Library Classification system under such headings as general, philosophy, religion, social sciences, history and geography, languages and literature. Each entry gives the title of the article, the name of the newspaper with date and page number, and occasionally a comment.

II ENCYCLOPEDIAS

Chinese encyclopedias (*lei-shu* 類書) differ from Western encyclopedias in that they consist almost entirely of selected quotations from earlier writings, the name encyclopedia having been applied to them because they embrace the whole realm of knowledge. In the great majority of cases the quoted material is classified according to subject and although quotations were seldom made exactly word for word, changes beyond a slight polishing of the literary style were ordinarily avoided. The earliest Chinese encyclopedias were compiled for the purpose of providing the emperor and ministers of state with conveniently arranged summaries of all that was known at the time. Later they were also compiled as manuals to be used in the writing of essays and poems and as text-books to be used in preparing for the civil service examinations; they were even used as handy resumés of knowledge by those who enjoyed displaying their erudition.

The earliest encyclopedia, the *Huang-lan* 皇覽, was compiled under imperial auspices about 220 A.D., and the *Hua-lin pien-lüeh* 華林遍略, the *Hsiu-wen-tien yü-lan* 修文殿御覽, and a number of similar works were compiled during the period of the Six Dynasties, although none of them has survived to the present time. The earliest encyclopedia extant (only a part of it is supposed to be the original compilation, and there is even some doubt as to the authenticity of that part) is the *Pien-chu* 編珠, which was compiled in the Sui dynasty for the purpose of providing material which would be useful in the writing of poems and essays. The encyclopedias of the T'ang and Sung dynasties were compiled mainly for the practical purposes mentioned in the preceding paragraph, while the greatest encyclopedias of the Ming and Ch'ing periods, the *Yung-lo ta-tien* 永樂大典 (which was compiled between 1403 and 1407, but most of which has since been lost)[1] and the *Ku-chin t'u-shu chi-ch'eng*, were compiled primarily for the purpose of preserving as many as possible of the old writings still in existence.

The earliest classification of works of this kind as *lei-shu* occurred in the bibliographical section of the *Hsin T'ang-shu* 新唐書, and while this category is to be found in most of the bibliographies compiled since, there has never been complete agreement among bibliographers as to which works should be so classified. In choosing the works to be classed as encyclopedias in this biblio-

---

1. The **Yung-lo ta-tien** contained 22,877 *chüan*, with a table of contents of 60 *chüan*, in 11,095 *ts'e*. Two manuscript copies were made, during the Yung-lo (1403–1424) and Chia-ching (1522–1566) periods, but they largely disappeared subsequently, the greatest losses occurring during the Boxer uprising in 1900. A multi-colored collotype reproduction of the surviving volumes preserved in the Peking Library was published by the Chung-hua shu-chü in Peking in 1960, in 202 *ts'e*. Another reproduction of surviving parts was issued in Taipei in 1962 by the Shih-chieh shu-chü, in 100 volumes.

graphy, the compilers have followed the *lei-shu* section of the printed catalogue of the Yenching University Library. The absence of essential differences among most of the works ordinarily called *lei-shu* makes the problem of classifying them a very difficult one. However, there are certain differences in emphasis, and an effort has been made roughly to classify them upon that basis, with the hope that such a classification may prove to be useful to Western students. Approximately one-third of the available encyclopedias are discussed, most of those included being works which are important in themselves, but a few are described which, while not so important in their own right, have so often been quoted from or cited in Chinese writings that the inclusion of a certain amount of information concerning them is imperative.

Although encyclopedias have never been in very high repute among Chinese scholars, both because of their nature as secondary sources and because most scholars have considered it degrading to resort to short cuts to knowledge, the quotations in them have often proved to be more correct than the corresponding passages in the modern editions of the original sources, and furthermore many of the works quoted from in the earlier encyclopedias have been entirely lost. Western students who lack the background in Chinese history and traditions which until recently was the heritage of all well educated Chinese should welcome the short cut provided by encyclopedias and should find them extremely helpful, so long as they keep in mind the limitations of such works. The **Yen-ching ta-hsüeh t'u-shu-kuan mu-lu ch'u-kao: Lei-shu chih pu** 燕京大學圖書館目錄初稿: 類書之部[2] is an annotated catalogue of virtually all of the encyclopedias extant, with the further advantage of having a combined *kuei-hsieh* index to section headings.

A.   GENERAL ENCYCLOPEDIAS

While a certain number of encyclopedias lay stress upon particular fields of knowledge, almost all of the early ones and many of the greatest ones compiled during later dynasties maintain a balance among the different fields of knowledge, the amount of material included on each closely corresponding to the place of that field in the intellectual life of the time. All of the encyclopedias described in this subsection are of this general type, but while there is a marked similarity between the section headings of all of them, each work makes its own peculiar contribution and none of the works included can be ignored. The *Ku-chin t'u-shu chi-ch'eng* is the greatest of all the *lei-shu* now available, being in relation to other encyclopedias what the *Ssu-k'u ch'üan-shu tsung-mu* is to other bibliographies.

---

2. Compiled by Ssu-yü Teng 鄧嗣禹, and published in Peiping in 1935 by the Yenching University Library 燕京大學圖書館. vi, 125, 99 pp. Reprint: Taipei: Ku-t'ing shu-wu, 1970.

Pei-t'ang shu-ch'ao 北堂書鈔, 160 *chüan*. Compiled by Yü Shih-nan 虞世南 (A.D. 558–638). Collated and annotated by K'ung Kuang-t'ao 孔廣陶 and published by him in a block-print edition re-cut from a traced Sung edition in 1888. 20 *ts'e*. (2) Taipei: Wen-hai ch'u-pan-she, 1962, 2 vols. 382 pp. Facsimile of 1888 edition.

This encyclopedia was compiled by a high official of the Sui dynasty for the purpose of providing material which would be useful in the writing of essays. It is divided into nineteen sections and subdivided into many items, and the quotations which form the bulk of its contents deal principally with matters of government, although attention is also paid to such miscellaneous subjects as clothing, food and drink, vehicles, festivals, and seasons. The quotations are drawn from a wide variety of writings, and the compiler usually indicates the source by giving either the title or the author's name. In the present edition the collator has added the full citation wherever possible and also his own notes based upon a comparative study of several manuscript and printed editions and the original sources. The quotations were practically all taken from pre-Sui works, many of which are no longer extant, so that this encyclopedia has been widely used in the re-collection of lost pre-T'ang writings. It is also an important source for material on early political and social systems, little of which can be found elsewhere. There is a table of sections and items at the beginning.

*I-wen lei-chü 藝文類聚, 100 *chüan*. Compiled under Imperial auspices by Ou-yang Hsün 歐陽詢 (A.D. 557–641) and others. (1) Ming Chia-ching block-print edition. 24 *ts'e*. (2) Ming Wan-li block-print edition. 24 *ts'e*. (3) Hua-yang hung-ta-t'ang 華陽宏達堂 re-cut block-print edition of 1879. 32 *ts'e*. (4) Facsimile of a Sung edition, Taipei: Hsin-hsing shu-chü, 1960. 4 vols. 2558 pp. (5) Peking: Chung-hua shu-chü, 1959. 16 *ts'e*. Facsimile of a Sung edition. (6) Peking: Chung-hua shu-chü, 1965. 2 vols. 27, 15, 1733 pp. Facsimile of a Sung edition, with parts from a Ming edition.

The *I-wen lei-chü*, which may be looked upon as typical of nearly all later general encyclopedias, was compiled as a source book to be used in the composition of essays. Its predecessors provided either essential factual information or examples of fine literary style, but Ou-yang sought in this compilation to supply both. The work is divided into forty-seven sections, which are again subdivided into many classified items. The subject matter is extremely miscellaneous and while political affairs occupy more space than other things, almost every subject of possible interest is included. The following is a rough summary of the table of contents, not only of the *I-wen lei-chü* but also of most later encyclopedias: celestial phenomena, geography, emperors and empresses, human nature and conduct, government, rites, music, law, officialdom, ranks of nobility, military affairs, domestic economy, property, clothing, vehicles, tools, food, utensils, crafts, chess, Taoism, Buddhism, spirits, medicine, and natural history.

Under each item in the *I-wen lei-chü* there are a number of brief factual extracts, chiefly from the classics and histories, after which relevant passages are quoted from poems and essays to supply material for literary purposes. By Sung times most of the sources quoted had been lost, and efforts made during the Ming dynasty to recover early poems and essays depended to a large extent upon this collection. The system of classification is only moderately satisfactory, and it is sometimes necessary to look for material on a particular subject under several related items. The work is reasonably complete, however, and sources are clearly stated, so that the *Ssu-k'u* editors considered it one of the two best encyclopedias of the T'ang period. Since the work, as it is now known, includes quotations from the writings of Su Wei-tao 蘇味道, Li Chiao 李嶠, Shen Ch'üan-ch'i 沈佺期, and Sung Chih-wen 宋之問, all of whom wrote after the original compilation was completed, it is possible that other additions have also been made, and therefore the whole work should be used with a certain amount of caution.

★Ch'u-hsüeh chi 初學記, 30 *chüan*. Compiled under imperial auspices by Hsü Chien 徐堅 (A.D. 659–729) and others. (1) Chin-fu 晉府 block-print edition of the Ming Chia-ching period. 12 *ts'e*. (2) Hsi-shan an-kuo fang-sung 錫山 安國仿宋 block-print edition of 1513. 14 *ts'e*. (3) *Ku-hsiang-chai hsiu-chen shih-chung* 古香齋袖珍十種, *ts'e* 270–281. +(4) Punctuated edition collating the Hsi-shan an-kuo, Ku-hsiang-chai and other editions. Peking: Chung-hua shu-chü, 1962. 3 vols. (5) Taipei: Hsin-hsing shu-chü, 1966. 424 pp.

This encyclopedia, written with the intention of providing beginning students with a general foundation of knowledge, is divided into twenty-three sections and subdivided into a total of 313 items. While the primary interest is in political affairs, attention is also paid to geography and celestial phenomena, religions, household arts, animal and plant life, and other subjects. At the beginning of each section there is a survey of general facts and a history of the subject discussed. Under each item there is first a brief statement of facts, then a number of relevant *tui-tzu* 對子 (two parallel phrases) of four or six characters in smaller-sized type, and finally selected illustrative extracts from poems and essays. The first part under each item—the statement of facts —is composed, like the rest, of extracts from other sources, but these are carefully fitted together as if written by the compiler, in order to present a unified picture. Although some quotations from early T'ang poems and essays are included, most of the sources used were pre-T'ang. The *Ssu-k'u* editors considered this work and the *I-wen lei-chü* the two best encyclopedias compiled during the T'ang dynasty. While less comprehensive than the other, the *Ch'u-hsüeh chi* is better organized and its quotations are more carefully selected. And like the two preceding works, it is one of the principal sources from which lost pre-T'ang writings have been re-collected in modern times. There is a table of items at the beginning. At the end of each *chüan* in the 1962 edition there is a table comparing differences in wording between this and two other editions.

Pai-shih liu-t'ieh shih-lei-chi 白氏六帖事類集, 30 *chüan*. Compiled by Pai Chü-i 白居易 (A.D. 772–846). (1) [Peiping] Ch'in-pu 近圃 [Chang Ch'in-po 張芹伯] edition of 1933, being a photolithographic reproduction of a Sung edition from Fu Tseng-hsiang's 傅增湘 collection. 12 *ts'e*. (2) Taipei: Hsin-hsing shu-chü, 1969. 2 vols. [35] 1110 [35] pp.

The material in this encyclopedia was collected from pre-T'ang writings and filed under general headings over a long period of years by Pai Chü-i, the great T'ang poet. Finally, with the help of some of his students, he put the collected material into book form, with a view to its being useful in the writing of poetry and essays. But the work was not very systematically done, with the result that the arrangement of material is not orderly, the source references are not infrequently missing, and occasionally there are mistakes in the quotations. Each of the thirty *chüan* is divided into a number of related items, the arrangement under each item being not unlike that in the *Pei-t'ang shu-ch'ao*. The work contains much material on customs, and is especially useful for tracing the early history of certain folk-ways. Rich in literary allusions which are clearly explained in brief commentaries, it is also a useful guide to the language of pre-T'ang writers. Important phrases which might be useful in the composition of essays or poems appear in large-sized characters; material in smaller-sized characters consists either of additional quotations or brief commentaries. There is a table of items at the beginning of the work, and there is also one for each *chüan*.

Pai-K'ung liu-t'ieh 白孔六帖 (also called **T'ang-Sung Pai-K'ung liu-t'ieh** 唐宋白孔六帖), 100 *chüan*. Compiled by Pai Chü-i 白居易 (A.D. 772–846) and K'ung Ch'uan 孔傳. (1) Ming Chia-ching block-print edition. 50 *ts'e*. (2) Taipei: Hsin-hsing shu-chü, 1969. 2 vols. 72, 1417 pp. Photocopy of the same edition.

During the reign of Emperor Kao-tsung 宋高宗 of the Sung dynasty (1127–1162), a thirty-*chüan* supplement to the *Pai-shih liu-t'ieh shih-lei chi* was compiled by a scholar named K'ung Ch'uan, bringing Pai Chü-i's work down to the middle of the twelfth century. The present work is a combination of the compilations of Pai and K'ung, arranged by an unknown person before the end of the Sung dynasty. The same classification is employed as that used by Pai, and under each item the material from the earlier work appears first, followed by that from K'ung's supplement. There is a general table of items, and at the beginning of each *chüan* there is a table of items. While this work contains all of the material from Pai's collection, one wishing to use only that part should consult the *Pai-shih liu-t'ieh shih-lei-chi* itself, since it is available in a photolithographic copy of a Sung edition which is probably much more reliable than the only existing edition of the *Pai-K'ung liu-t'ieh*.

★**Tai-p'ing yü-lan** 太平御覽, 1000 *chüan*; table of contents, 15 *chüan*. Compiled under Imperial auspices by Li Fang 李昉 (A.D. 925–996) and others, and completed in 983. +(1) Hsi-hsien Pao-shih 歙縣鮑氏 block-print edition of 1807. 80 *ts'e*. (2) Japanese movable-type edition of 1855. 156 *ts'e*. (3) Shanghai: Commercial Press, 1935. 136 *ts'e*. Facsimile of a collated Sung edition. +(4) Shanghai: Chung-hua shu-chü, 1960. 4 vols. Facsimile of a Sung edition. (5) Taipei: Commercial Press, 1968. 7 vols. 4560 pp.

This encyclopedia, which was compiled to provide the Sung Emperor T'ai-tsung 宋太宗 with a broad foundation of general knowledge, is divided into fifty-five sections and subdivided into about five thousand items and sub-items. The subjects dealt with do not differ greatly from those to be found in encyclopedias of the T'ang period, but the amount of material quoted is very much greater than that in any earlier work. The *T'ai-p'ing kuang-chi* was compiled at the same time and by the same scholars as this work; the quoted material is divided between the two collections by including in the *Yü-lan* all material of the type generally recognized as suitable for standard historical writing, and by putting the remainder in the *Kuang-chi*. In modern times these two great encyclopedias have been among the principal sources from which lost pre-Sung writings have been re-collected.[3]

Under each item or sub-item of the *T'ai-p'ing yü-lan* quotations from the classics, histories, and belles-lettres appear in chronological order from earliest historical times down to the end of the T'ang dynasty, historical material being arranged according to the period dealt with and non-historical material according to the time when it was written. Each quotation is preceded by the citation of its source, and although quotations are not necessarily taken directly from the original sources, they are nevertheless always based on pre-Sung manuscripts or editions There is an important bibliography at the beginning which lists 1690 titles, although actually more than two thousand works are cited in the text itself—approximately seven out of ten of which have since been lost. There is a table of items near the beginning of the work, and an index has been published by the Harvard-Yenching Institute.[4]

3. For a detailed discussion of the compilation, organization and editions of the *T'ai-p'ing yü-lan*, see the *Sung ssu ta-shu k'ao* 宋四大書考, compiled by Kuo Pai-kung 郭伯恭 (Commercial Press, 1940).

4. **T'ai-p'ing yü-lan yin-te** 太平御覽引得. (1) Peiping: Harvard-Yenching Institute, 1935. (Index No. 23) xcviii, 261 pp. (2) Taipei: Ch'eng Wen Publishing Co., 1966 (photocopy). This *kuei-hsieh* index is to both the item headings and the titles of the works from which all quotations were derived.

★Ts'e-fu yüan-kuei 冊府元龜, 1000 *chüan;* table of contents, 10 *chüan.* Compiled under Imperial auspices by Wang Ch'in-jo 王欽若, Yang I 楊億, and others. The work was ordered in 1005 and completed eight years later. (1) Ming block-print edition of 1642. 320 *ts'e.* (2) Hong Kong: Chung-hua shu-chü, 1960. 12 vols., with a subject index. (3) Peking: Chung-hua shu-chü, 1960. 12 vols. (4) Taipei: Chung-hua shu-chü, 1967. 20 vols. 11741 pp. The last three are based on the 1642 edition.

This collection of material on the lives and activities of early emperors and ministers was compiled to serve as a guide for those in positions of official responsibility, and it is still useful as a treatise on pre-Sung government and political history. The compilers, fifteen in number, were all important scholars, and most of them had had previous experience compiling the *T'ai-p'ing yü-lan* and the *T'ai-p'ing kuang-chi.* This work is famous for the great pains taken to include only authoritative material, only the classics, the dynastic histories, and a few selected philosophers being quoted in it. There are thirty-one sections, each with a general introduction, and 1104 items, each preceded by a brief introduction describing its contents. Except for the introductions and occasional interlinear notes indicating cross references and the compilers' interpretations and opinions, the work consists entirely of quotations arranged chronologically under each item. The sources are seldom given, since practically all quotations were taken from well known works and so were easy to identify.

Early critics complained that the *Ts'e-fu yüan-kuei* was not sufficiently exhaustive, but the *Ssu-k'u* editors felt that the care taken in selecting only authentic and relevant material more than made up for any possible shortcomings. The work is extremely important for any study of the history of the Five Dynasties period, for it contains much material not to be found in the dynastic histories or in any other works now available. The official documents quoted from that period are even more accurately reproduced than those appearing in the *Wen-hsien t'ung-k'ao.* T'ang dynasty material is quoted from the *Chiu T'ang-shu* 舊唐書, but from an earlier edition than those now available. There is a table of items at the beginning, and two indexes have been published.[5]

5. **Ts'e-fu yüan-kuei yin-te** 冊府元龜引得, compiled by Ch'en Hung-fei 陳鴻飛. *Wen-hua t'u-shu-kuan-hsüeh chi-k'an* 文華圖書館學季刊, Vol. 5, No. 1 (March 1933), 97–126. **Sappu genki hōshibu gaishinbu sakuin** or **Ts'e-fu yüan-kuei feng-shih-pu wai-ch'en-pu so-yin** 冊府元龜奉使部外臣部索引. Compiled by Utsunomiya Kiyoyoshi 宇都宮清吉 and Naitō Shigenobu 內藤戊申. (Kyoto: Tōhō bunka kenkyūjo 東方文化研究所, 1938). 2, 16, 994, 21 pp. This is an index of the names, titles, technical terms, terms from foreign languages, etc., in the *Feng-shih-pu* section (*chüan* 652–664) and the *Wai-ch'en-pu* section (*chüan* 956–1000) of the *Ts'e-fu yüan-kuei.* These are the sections which deal with foreign countries and diplomatic affairs. The index is arranged by the number-of-strokes system, and has a table of contents at the beginning and a romanized index at the end.

*Ch'ün-shu k'ao-so 羣書考索 (also called **Shan-t'ang k'ao-so** 山堂考索), first collection 前集, 66 *chüan;* second collection 後集, 65 *chüan;* third collection 續集, 56 *chüan;* and fourth collection 別集, 25 *chüan*—making a total of 212 *chüan*. Compiled by Chang Ju-yü 章如愚 (*chin-shih*, between 1195 and 1200). (1) Shen-tu shu-chai 愼獨書齋 block-print edition of 1518. 64 *ts'e*. (2) Taipei: Hsin-hsing shu-chü, 1969. 8 vols. 20, 5548 pp. Photoprint of the same edition.

This encyclopedia was compiled to supply material for the use of those competing in the civil service examinations. It is remarkable for its critical approach to the material, representing an attitude which was rather unusual in the Southern Sung period during which it was compiled. The four collections—each divided into sections and again into items and sub-items—were not written at the same time, material left out of an earlier one being included in a later one under an item dealing with the same or with a related subject. The titles of corresponding items are not always the same in the different collections, and although the work is carefully classified and there is a table of items at the beginning of each collection, material sought is not always easily found.

The material is collected from a great number of sources, many of which no longer exist, and at the end of each item there is a critical summary written by the compiler. The scope is not as broad as that of most encyclopedias, although the subjects dealt with include classics, history, bibliography and literature, geography, economics, official and military systems, rites and music, law, public revenue, and border affairs. The *Ssu-k'u* editors complained of the frequent inconsistencies between material and ideas in the different collections, and occasionally even within one collection, but they considered the work fairly complete in view of its avowed purpose. They considered the *Ch'ün-shu k'ao-so* less well organized than the *Wen-hsien t'ung-k'ao*, but superior in its interpretation of the classics; not as complete or as condensed as the *Yü-hai*, but containing more material on Sung political activities; and fuller in its treatment of the historical evolution of the subjects discussed than the *Li-tai chih-tu hsiang-shuo*. Sources are always cited, and charts and diagrams are frequently introduced to simplify the explanations.

Ku-chin shih-wen lei-chü 古今事文類聚 (also called **Shih-wen lei-chü** 事文類聚 and **Hsin-pien ku-chin shih-wen lei-chü** 新編古今事文類聚), first collection 前集, 60 *chüan;* second collection 後集, 50 *chüan;* third collection 續集, 28 *chüan;* fourth collection 別集, 32 *chüan;* fifth collection 新集, 36 *chüan;* sixth collection 外集, 15 *chüan;* and seventh collection 遺集, 15 *chüan* —making a total of 236 *chüan*. First four collections compiled by Chu Mu 祝穆, Chu Mu's preface dated 1246. Fifth and sixth collections compiled by Fu Ta-yung 富大用, and seventh collection by Chu Yüan 祝淵, both of the

Yüan period. (1) Ching-ch'ang 經厰 large-sized character block-print edition of the Ming period. 160 *ts'e*. (2) Chi-hsiu-t'ang 積秀堂 block-print edition of 1763. 46 *ts'e*.

The *Ku-chin shih-wen lei-chü* is made up of extracts of a factual nature taken from various sources and of quotations from poems and essays, and was intended to be used in the writing of other poems and essays. It consists of seven collections, each of which is divided into items and preceded by a table of items. According to Chu Mu's preface, he copied the material in the first four collections from works he happened to be reading, merely to supplement his poor memory; the last three collections were compiled later in the same style. Each of the ninety-one items into which the work is divided consists of: (1) miscellaneous cardinal phrases selected from the whole body of literature, (2) factual material quoted from ancient and more recently written sources, and (3) quotations of a literary nature. The last is usually divided into examples of ancient poetry, critical studies of poetry, and miscellaneous quotations. Poems are usually quoted in their entirety, making this compilation important as a source from which have been re-collected many lost and partially lost poems. Unfortunately in reproducing poems and essays only the title and the name of the author are given, without mention of the source from which it was copied, and in biographies only the name of the man and the time in which he lived are indicated. For other types of quoted material the source is sometimes given and sometimes not. The first collection is devoted to such miscellaneous subjects as are common to all of the early general encyclopedias, the second to plants and animals, the third to household matters, the fourth to scholarship and writing, and the last three to the organization and administration of government.

Ku-chin ho-pi shih-lei pei-yao 古今合璧事類備要, first collection 前集, 69 *chüan*; second collection 後集, 81 *chüan*; third collection 續集, 56 *chüan*; fourth collection 別集, 94 *chüan*; fifth collection 外集, 66 *chüan*—making a total of 366 *chüan*. Compiled by Hsieh Wei-hsin 謝維新, compiler's preface dated 1257. (1) San-ch'ü hsia-hsiang 三衢夏相 block-print edition of 1556, re-cut from a Sung edition. 48 *ts'e*. (2) Taipei: Hsin-hsing shu-chü, 1969. 4 vols. 2104 pp. Photocopy of the same edition.

The five collections which make up this encyclopedia are divided into forty, fifty-three, fifteen, twenty, and nineteen sections respectively. Each section is subdivided into a number of items, each of which includes quoted material of a factual nature followed by extracts from poems and essays. Quotations are taken from works dating from ancient times down to the period in which the compiler lived; occasionally sources are not mentioned. Of special value are the many anecdotes recorded concerning people and events of the Sung period, and quotations from important works since lost, such as the *Sung shih-lu* 宋實錄. A poem by Su Shih 蘇軾 entitled 詠雪詩, which does not appear in his collected works, is an example of the sort of thing preserved in this compilation. The second collection, which is concerned entirely with the official system of the Sung dynasty and its historical background, is more thorough and easier to understand than the corresponding section in the *Sung-shih* 宋史. There is no section on geography because Chu Mu's 祝穆 *Fang-yü sheng-lan* 方輿勝覽, devoted entirely to that subject, was being written at about the same time. At the beginning of the fourth and fifth collections the name of Yü Tsai 虞載 is given as that of the compiler but since that name is mentioned in neither the supplementary bibliography of the *Sung-shih*, nor in the *Ssu-k'u ch'üan-shu tsung-mu*, there is probably an error in this edition. There is a table of sections at the beginning of each collection.

Ku-chin yüan-liu chih-lun 古今源流至論 (also called the **Yüan-liu chih-lun** 源流至論 and the **Hsin-chien chüeh-k'o ku-chin yüan-liu chih-lun** 新箋決科古今源流至論), first 前集, second 後集, third 續集, and fourth 別集 collections, each 10 *chüan*. First three collections compiled by Lin Kung 林駉 of the Sung period; fourth collection by Huang Li-weng 黃履翁. Prefaces written by Huang dated 1233 and 1237. (1) Yüan dynasty block-print edition. 26 *ts'e*. (2) Ming dynasty re-cut block-print edition. 12 *ts'e*. (3) Taipei: Hsin-hsing shu-chü, 1970. 2 vols. 1212 pp. (Photocopy of Ming re-cut block-print edition).

During the reign of the Sung Emperor Shen-tsung 宋神宗 (1068–1085), the poetry requirement in the civil service examinations was replaced by the *ts'e-lun* 策論, a kind of essay on current events in which the candidate had to trace the background of the subject assigned and also express his own point of view. This encyclopedia was compiled to meet the new need by supplying a resumé of the historical background of social and political institutions, as well as of current events. Each of the forty *chüan* contains several essays, each essay being a comprehensive study of one subject. Special attention is paid to political developments, and the Sung period is particularly well handled, this work now being the only available source for not a little of the information recorded. Of added interest are the frequent comparisons made between related works among classics, histories, and belles-lettres, in the course of which their similarities and differences are carefully pointed out and explained. There is a table of contents at the beginning of each collection, and in the first two collections additional related topics are indicated here and there in the top margin. The *so-yin* at the beginning of the 1970 edition is actually a seven-page table of contents.

★Yü-hai 玉海, 200 *chüan*. Compiled by Wang Ying-lin 王應麟 (1223–1296). (1) K'ang Chi-t'ien 康基田 re-cut block-print edition of 1806. 92 *ts'e*. (2)

Chekiang shu-chü 浙江書局 re-cut block-print edition of 1883. 122 *ts'e*. (3) Taipei: Hua-wen shu-chü, 1964. 8 vols. 4876 pp. Facsimile of a 1337 edition.

This excellent encyclopedia was compiled by the most learned scholar of the Sung dynasty, a man of extensive knowledge and remarkable memory. His purpose in compiling it was to supply material which would assist candidates for the degree of *po-hsüeh hung-tz'u* 博學宏詞, which demanded very broad knowledge and understanding. The work is divided into twenty-one sections and subdivided into numerous items. Quotations are taken from the classics, histories, philosophers, belles-lettres, personal biographies, and from many other types of sources. All works of importance extant at the time, even secret archives, were consulted and essential parts were quoted from them. The Sung material quoted was derived from the *Shih-lu* 實錄, *Kuo-shih* 國史, *Jih-li* 日曆, and *Hui-yao*, and much of it does not appear in the *Sung-shih* 宋史. The material under each item is arranged chronologically from ancient times down to the end of the Sung dynasty. Sources are clearly indicated and less reliable supplementary material is frequently included in smaller-sized characters. Unfortunately the arrangement of the items under each section heading is unsystematic, and even though there is a table of items at the beginning of the work it is often difficult to locate material. Furthermore, because the work circulated in manuscript for a long time before it was finally published under imperial auspices in the Yüan period, many errors crept into the text. However, in spite of these faults, the *Ssu-k'u ch'üan-shu chien-ming mu-lu* says that of all the important encyclopedias compiled during the T'ang and Sung dynasties, only the *T'ung-tien* is the equal of this one.

T'ien-chung chi 天中記, 60 *chüan*. Compiled by Ch'en Yao-wen 陳耀文 (*chin-shih*, 1550). +(1) Block-print edition, latest dated preface 1569. 60 *ts'e*. (2) Block-print edition of 1589. 30 *ts'e*. (3) T'ing-yü shan-fang 聽雨山房 edition of 1878. 60 *ts'e*. (4) Taipei: Wen-hai ch'u-pan she, 1964. 4 vols. 10, 1999 pp.

This encyclopedia, compiled by a learned scholar of the Ming dynasty, is divided into 808 items, each one of which is a separate essay. The subjects treated are very miscellaneous in character, among the general fields being astronomy, geography, family relations, official systems, Buddhism, Taoism, festivals, musical instruments, architecture, and gardening. Extracts are derived from a great variety of works, sources being clearly indicated either before or after the quotation. Editorial notes are freely used, indicating mistakes of earlier commentators, misinterpretations in dictionaries, and errors perpetuated in earlier encyclopedias. These notes are the most useful feature of the work. The *Ssu-k'u* editors considered the *T'ien-chung chi* too miscellaneous, both as to subject matter and as to sources, to be very useful, but for modern scholars this would seem to be an advantage rather than a weakness. There is a table of items at the beginning.

T'u-shu pien 圖書編, 127 *chüan*. Compiled by Chang Huang 章潢 (1527–1608). (1) 1613 edition. 120 *ts'e*. (2) Block-print edition, latest preface dated 1623. 110 *ts'e*.

This work is classified as an encyclopedia both by the editors of the *Ming-shih* 明史 and by the compilers of the *Ssu-k'u ch'üan-shu*, although in style it corresponds more closely to those works ordinarily classed under miscellaneous philosophers 子部雜家. According to the preface of Yo Yüan-sheng 岳元聲, the work was written over a period of fifteen years, from 1562 to 1577, Chang's purpose being to make available information which would be useful both to research scholars and to men of letters. His material is first outlined by means of charts and diagrams, after which there are full explanations and criticisms. At the beginning there is a bibliography of 213 sources. The material is well arranged and the explanations are clear and are written in a good literary style. *Chüan* 1 to 15 are in general concerned with the classics, 16 to 28 with celestial phenomena and the calendar, 29 to 67 with geography, and 68 to 125 with human conduct and political and social institutions. The last two *chüan* are independent works unrelated to the rest. In the geographical discussions, material is presented on the history, customs, strategic points, population, and products of specific geographical areas, much as it would be in a modern text book on the subject. Unfortunately sources are not clearly indicated, materials are very unevenly distributed among the various subjects, and the opinions expressed sometimes represent a very narrow point of view. The work was proscribed during the Ch'ien-lung period, possibly because the Ming dynasty is praised in it at every possible opportunity.

★Yüan-chien lei-han 淵鑑類函, 450 *chüan;* table of contents, 4 *chüan*. Compiled under Imperial auspices by Chang Ying 張英 and others, and presented for the emperor's approval in 1701. +(1) Palace block-print edition of 1710. 140 *ts'e*. +(2) T'ung-wen shu-chü 同文書局 edition of 1926. 64 *ts'e*. (3) Shanghai Tien-shih-chai 上海點石齋 lithographic edition of 1883. 10 *ts'e*. (4) *Ku-hsiang-chai hsiu-chen shih-chung, ts'e* 5–164. (5) Taipei: Hsin-hsing shu-chü, 1967. 7 vols. Photocopy of the Palace edition.

This work is based upon the Ming encyclopedia, *T'ang lei-han* 唐類函, and probably includes all of that compilation. Additional material is drawn from seventeen other encyclopedias, twenty-one dynastic histories, and from innumerable works of other kinds. Material copied from the *T'ang lei-han* appears under the incised character *yüan* 原, and that from all other sources under the incised character *tseng* 增. In both cases the material is arranged in the following order: (1) an explanation of the title and a study of the origin and evolution of the subject; (2) detailed factual material quoted from all varieties of sources and arranged in chronological order; (3) relevant *tui-ou* 對偶 (parallel phrases), chosen for the excellence of their literary style; (4) selected sentences from all branches of literature, also chosen because of their literary style; and (5) quoted poems and essays and parts of poems and essays. Although the *T'ang lei-han* cites the encyclopedias from which the material in it was copied, as well as the original sources, this work cites only the original sources. It is exceedingly comprehensive in its scope, practically every subject of possible interest being discussed and traced from the time of its origin down to 1566. There is a table of items at the beginning. The *Yüan-chien lei-han* and the *Ku-chin t'u-shu chi-ch'eng* are the two most comprehensive Chinese encyclopedias still in existence.

★Ku-chin t'u-shu chi-ch'eng 古今圖書集成, 10,000 *chüan*; table of contents, 40 *chüan*; list of errata, 44 *chüan*. Compiled under Imperial auspices by [Ch'en Meng-lei 陳夢雷], Chiang T'ing-hsi 蔣廷錫 and others, and presented to the emperor in 1725. (1) Palace bronze movable-type edition of the Yung-cheng period. 5020 *ts'e*. (2) Shanghai T'u-shu chi-ch'eng chü 上海圖書集成局 movable-type edition of 1884 (table of contents only 32 *chüan*). 1628 *ts'e.* +(3) Chung-hua shu-chü 中華書局 photolithographic reproduction of the Palace edition, 1934. 800 *ts'e*; **K'ao-cheng** 考證, 8 *ts'e*. (4) Taipei: Wenhsing shu-tien 文星書店, 1964. 100 vols. plus an index vol.

This is the largest and most useful encyclopedia that has ever been compiled in China, with the exception of the *Yung-lo ta-tien* 永樂大典, which, save for a few hundred odd volumes, is no longer extant. As its title indicates, it is intended to be all-inclusive. Its 6109 items are classified under thirty-two section headings, which are in turn grouped under six major categories: Heavenly Phenomena, Geography, Human Relationships, Arts and Sciences, Literature, and Political Economy. In each item the quoted material is arranged in eight classes: (1) *Hui-k'ao* 彙考, important quotations of a factual nature derived from standard sources. If dateable they are arranged chronologically; if not, they are arranged in the traditional order of classics, histories, philosophers, and belles-lettres. Each quotation is headed by a topic sentence which expresses the central idea. Frequently there are also included in this class pictures, maps, diagrams, and charts, particularly in those items dealing with geography, plants, animals, clothing, tools, calculation of the calendar, and navigation. (2) *Tsung-lun* 總論, general ideas and discussions of an orthodox nature, gathered from the four great branches of standard Chinese writings. (3) *Lieh-chuan* 列傳, biographies. This part does not appear in all items. (4) *I-wen* 藝文, literary compositions, emphasis being laid upon style rather than content. (5) *Hsüan-chü* 選句, selected sentences, chosen for their literary quality. (6) *Chi-shih* 紀事, factual material of a less important nature than that under *hui-k'ao* but still worth preserving. (7) *Tsa-lu* 雜錄, miscellaneous quotations, such as factual material only indirectly related to the subject, discussions and opinions too vague or too complicated to be placed under *tsung-lun*, and literary selections whose poor style precludes their being included in *i-wen*. (8) *Wai-pien* 外編, fabulous and unorthodox material which would have been omitted had the compilers not been particularly interested in making the collection complete, for example: fiction and quotations from Buddhist and Taoist writings. The most important material is usually to be found in the first two classes, but for the modern scholar there is also much of value in the others. There is a detailed table of contents at the beginning of the work and a bibliography and summary of the contents at the beginning of each *chüan*; sources are clearly indicated throughout. Two indexes have been published.[6]

B. ENCYCLOPEDIAS ELUCIDATING PHRASES AND LITERARY ALLUSIONS

While most of the works discussed in this subsection were compiled to provide material which could be used in writing, they are useful to modern scholars principally for the information they give about phrases and literary allusions. In most of them passages in which the various phrases and names are used are quoted from early writings, and in all of them the sources of the quotations or of the original phrases or allusions are indicated. The system of classification in some of these works differs from that used in most encyclopedias: for example, the items in the *Ch'i-ming chi-shu* are arranged by number, and the phrases in the *P'ei-wen yün-fu*, which is the most important work of its kind, are grouped according to the rhyme of their final characters.

Shih-lei-fu t'ung-pien 事類賦統編, (also called **Tseng-pu shih-lei-fu t'ung-pien** 增補事類賦統編), 93 *chüan*. Edited by Huang Pao-chen 黃葆眞, editor's preface dated 1846. (1) Chü-sheng-t'ang 聚盛堂 block-print edition of 1849. 48 *ts'e*. (2) Hung-chien shu-lin 鴻漸書林 block-print edition of 1867. 48 *ts'e*. (3) Tan-yang Huang-shih 丹陽黃氏 block-print edition of 1860. 48 *ts'e*. (4) (**Tseng-pu ta-tzu**) **shih-lei t'ung-pien** (增補大字) 事類統編. Taipei: Shih-wen shu-she 詩文書舍, 1960. 2 vols. 2004 pp.

This is a combination of the **Shih-lei-fu** 事類賦, a collection of factual information and literary allusions written in a beautiful poetic style by Wu Shu 吳淑 (A.D. 947–1002), the **Kuang shih-lei-fu** 廣事類賦, written in 1699 by Hua Hsi-min 華希閔 and adding material down to the beginning of the Ch'ing

---

6. **An Alphabetical Index to the Chinese Encyclopaedia, Ch'in Ting Ku Chin T'u Shu Chi Ch'eng.** Compiled by Lionel Giles. (British Museum, 1911) xx, 102 pp. Reprinted, Taipei: Ch'eng Wen Publishing Co., 1969. This is an alphabetical index to the translated item headings, giving the section heading and *chüan* number of each. **T'u-shu chi-ch'eng fen-lei so-yin** 圖書集成分類索引. Compiled by Takizawa Toshisuke 瀧澤俊亮. (Dairen: Yu-wen-ko 右文閣, 1933). 62 pp. This is a classified index to the encyclopedia, giving the section headings and the *chüan* and *ts'e* numbers.

dynasty, the **Hsü-kuang shih-lei-fu** 續廣事類賦 by Wang Feng-chieh 王鳳喈, that appeared in 1798, and the **Kuang-kuang shih-lei-fu** 廣廣事類賦 written by Wu Shih-chan 吳世旃 in 1808. Huang Pao-chen added material in the form of *tui-chü* 對句 (parallel sentences), based upon beautiful examples of *shih* 詩 and *fu* 賦 from the *Yüan-chien lei-han*, the *Fen-lei tzu-chin* 分類字錦, and various collections of poetry. The classification follows that of the *Shih-lei-fu*, which was divided into fourteen sections and subdivided into one hundred items, though a number of subjects have been added. Under each item the material from the original work and the three supplements are arranged in the order of their writing, Huang's additions being placed last. For ordinary reference purposes consultation with the *Shih-lei-fu t'ung-pien* is sufficient, the earlier works being necessary only for purposes of checking.

Hai-lu sui-shih 海錄碎事, 22 *chüan*. Compiled by Yeh T'ing-kuei 葉廷珪, compiler's preface dated 1149. (1) Block-print edition, latest dated preface 1598. 14 *ts'e*. (2) Taipei: Hsin-hsing shu-chü, 1969. 4 vols.

This work is based upon reading notes made by the compiler from a wide range of literature and over a long period of years. The subjects dealt with are of a general nature, although the compiler's principal interest was in unusual forms of literary expression, and allusions not commonly used in essays and poems. The present edition is divided into sixteen sections and 584 items, although the work has evidently been reorganized since it was first compiled, as the earliest preface mentions 175 sections. Under each item there are numerous topic phrases of two or three characters, each followed by two or three very brief quotations which concisely illustrate the use of that phrase. Originally the work was intended as a guide to rarely used literary allusions, but now it is more useful as a reservoir of material not commonly found in other works. Sources are clearly indicated and there is a table of items at the beginning. The *Ssu-k'u* editors criticised this work because they felt that some of the allusions were not properly classified, but regardless of this, the *Hai-lu sui-shih* is a useful encyclopedia, particularly when compared with other works compiled during the Southern Sung period.

*P'ei-wen yün-fu 佩文韻府, 106 *chüan;* with supplement: **Yün-fu shih-i** 韻府拾遺, 106 *chüan*. Compiled under Imperial auspices by Chang Yü-shu 張玉書 and others, and published in 1711. +(1) Palace block-print edition of 1711 and 1720. 115 *ts'e*. (2) Undated Kwangtung re-cut block-print edition. 115 *ts'e*. +(3) T'ung-wen shu-chü 同文書局 lithographic edition of 1891. 60 *ts'e*. (4) *Wan-yu wen-k'u ti-erh-chi*. 6 vols. 4785 pp., plus an index vol. Photocopy of the Palace edition. (5) Taipei: Hsin-hsing shu-chü, 1960. 4 vols. 4785 pp. Photocopy of the Palace edition. (6) Taipei: Commercial Press, 1966. 6 vols. 4785 pp., plus an index vol.

Because he believed that the *Yün-fu ch'ün-yü* 韻府羣玉, a collection of rhyming phrases compiled in the Yüan dynasty, and the *Wu-ch'e yün-jui* 五車韻瑞, a similar work compiled during the Ming dynasty, were incomplete and frequently in error, the Emperor K'ang-hsi, in 1704, ordered that the two be revised and new material added to make up a new work, to be called the *P'ei-wen yün-fu*. Phrases and allusions are classified under their last characters, which are arranged according to their rhyme. Under each phrase quotations illustrating its use are arranged in four categories: (1) *yün-tsao* 韻藻, the extracts derived from the *Yün-fu ch'ün-yü* and the *Wu-ch'e yün-jui;* (2) *tseng-tzu* 增字, quotations from other sources; (3) *tui-yü* 對語, pairs of parallel phrases with from two to eight, and sometimes more, characters in each phrase; and (4) *tse-chü* 摘句, selected sentences useful in writing poems. In the first two categories, the numerous quotations are arranged in the traditional order of classics, histories, philosophers, and belles-lettres, and original sources are always indicated, although occasionally incorrectly.

The supplement, the *Yün-fu shih-i*, was ordered by the emperor in 1716 and completed in 1720. It contains about one-twentieth as much material as the original work, although the phrases are classified under the same *chüan*, with the consequence that the *chüan* are very much smaller. Illustrative material left out of the *yün-tsao* and *tseng-tzu* categories of the *P'ei-wen yün-fu* is placed in the supplement under *pu-tsao* 補藻. Additional commentaries are arranged under *pu-chu* 補註.

Whenever names or phrases are met with which are not understood, this is the first work which should be consulted. In using it, the last character of the phrase or name sought should be looked up for its rhyme in the *Trindex (q.v.)*, Giles' *Dictionary*, or some such work. The character will be found under the corresponding rhyme in the *P'ei-wen yün-fu*, and it is probably safe to say that in most cases the phrase or allusion will be found under that character. It should be pointed out that a few characters are under the wrong rhyme, but on the whole the work is very reliable. According to the *Yün-fu chi-tzu* 韻府紀字 of Wang Chi 汪汲, there are 10,257 characters in the *P'ei-wen yün-fu*, arranged under 106 rhymes.

Pien-tzu lei-pien 駢字類編, 240 *chüan*. Compiled under Imperial auspices by Ho Ch'o 何焯 and others, and completed in 1726. (1) Palace block-print edition of 1728. 120 *ts'e*. (2) Shanghai: T'ung-wen shu-chü lithographic edition of 1887. 48 *ts'e*. (3) Taipei: Hsüeh-sheng shu-chü, 1963. 8 vols. Photocopy of the Palace edition.

This collection of phrases and literary allusions (*pien-tzu* 駢字 are two-character phrases) was ordered in 1719 by Emperor K'ang-hsi, and is divided into twelve sections, besides one supplementary section. Three of the sections are rather unusual, phrases being classified in them which are related to numbers, directions, and colors. The two-character phrases classified under each section are arranged according to their rhyme, although in this work the rhyme of the first, rather than that of the last character of the phrase is used, thus differing from the *P'ei-wen yün-fu*. Under each phrase passages in which it is used are quoted in smaller-sized characters from classics, histories, philosophers, and belles-lettres. The names of the works quoted from are always indicated, and often the specific chapters or stanzas as well. The *Pien-tzu lei-pien* contains considerably less material than the *P'ei-wen yün-fu*, but it is easier to use, both because of its division into thirteen classified sections, and because each new phrase is put at the top of a new line. The *Ssu-k'u* editors considered the two works complementary and they say that between them it is possible to locate any literary or historical allusion. An index has been published.[7]

Tzu-shih ching-hua 子史精華, 160 *chüan*. Compiled under Imperial auspices by Yün-lu 允祿 and others and published in the Palace in 1727. +(1) Wu-ying-tien 武英殿 block-print edition of 1727. 64 *ts'e*. (2) Re-cut block-print edition of 1729. 48 *ts'e*. (3) Ch'ao-chi shu-chuang 朝記書莊 undated lithographic edition. 8 *ts'e*. (4) Taipei: Hsin-hsing shu-chü, 1967. 3 vols. 1856 pp.

The Emperor K'ang-hsi felt that there were far too many books on history and that the books on philosophy were too miscellaneous in character, so he ordered the compilation of this work, which was to include only the essentials of history and philosophy. There are thirty sections and 279 items; related quotations are grouped under each item with those on history first, arranged chronologically, and those on philosophy second, arranged in the traditional order. Each quotation is preceded by a key-phrase in large characters. Sources are always indicated, philosophic works by title, and historical works by title and subdivision. The *Tzu-shih ching-hua* is commonly used by old-fashioned scholars to trace the source and meaning of literary allusions, and to obtain material which can be used in the writing of essays and poems. Because only important extracts have been included, the work is not bulky, and material can usually be located without great difficulty. There is a table of sections at the beginning.

Tu-shu chi-shu lüeh 讀書記數略, 54 *chüan*. Compiled by Kung Meng-jen 宮夢仁, compiler's preface dated 1707. (1) Privately printed block-print edition of 1707. 12 *ts'e*. +(2) Palace block-print edition of 1708. 16 *ts'e*. (3) Block-print edition of 1880. 10 *ts'e*.

7. **Pien-tzu lei-pien yin-te** 駢字類編引得. Compiled by Chuang Wei-ssu 莊爲思. Taipei: Ssu-k'u shu-chü 四庫書局, 1966. 24, 261 pp.

This encyclopedia was compiled with the intention of making factual information easier to remember by associating it with numbers. It is based upon the *Hsiao-hsüeh kan-chu* 小學紺珠, compiled during the Sung dynasty by Wang Ying-lin, who, incidentally, was also the compiler of the *Yü-hai*. Wang's work was very much enlarged by Kung and presented to Emperor K'ang-hsi in 1707. There are fifty-four classified sections, under each of which the material is arranged according to a numerical system. For instance, in the section on geography, the ten *tao* 道 (political divisions) of the T'ang dynasty are listed by name under the number ten, and the twenty-two *chou* 州 (political divisions) of the Sung dynasty under the number twenty-two. The five punishments are discussed under number five in the section on law, and the history of the four-branch system of Chinese bibliography is given under number four in the section on bibliography. Under each item there are brief but adequate explanations written by Kung and frequent relevant quotations; the sources of the latter, unfortunately, are not always indicated. There is a detailed table of contents at the beginning of each section.

T'ung-su pien 通俗編, 38 *chüan*. Compiled by Chai Hao 翟灝 (*chin-shih*, 1754). (1) Wu-pu-i-chai 無不宜齋 block-print edition, latest dated preface 1751. 10 *ts'e*. (2) Peking: Commercial Press, 1958. 11, 920, 67 pp., with a four-corner index. (3) Taipei: Shih-chieh shu-chü, 1963. (4) Taipei: Kuang-wen shu-chü, 1968. 3 vols.

This is a compilation of material on games, customs, proverbs, common idioms, and literary allusions frequently used in ordinary speech and writing. It is made up entirely of quotations from other works, and is divided into thirty-eight sections and subdivided into many items. The compiler was a learned and diligent scholar who traveled all over China during a period of more than ten years. Whenever he met with a proverb, custom or idiom with which he was not acquainted he made every effort to trace its origin, consulting books of every kind. The results of his researches he recorded in the *T'ung-su pien*, carefully indicating the source of each quotation. The work is extremely useful for tracing the evolution of language and customs, particularly those phrases to which ordinarily little or no attention is paid. It has been read extensively by people in all walks of life, for the material is simply presented and is very interesting.

Shih-wu i-ming-lu 事物異名錄, 38 *chüan*. Compiled by Li Ch'üan 厲荃, and enlarged and edited by Kuan Huai 關槐, compiler's preface dated 1776. (1) Yüeh-tung 粤東 block-print edition of 1788. 16 *ts'e*. (2) Taipei: Hsin-hsing shu-chü, 1969. 2 vols. 1748 pp.

While reading the *Erh-ya* 爾雅 as a boy, the compiler of this work was impressed with the fact that things may have more than one name, and thereafter he kept a record of the various names for things which he met with in the course of his reading. Finally his notes were brought together and classified under thirty-eight section headings. Each item is headed by the most commonly used name for an object or function, and under it are listed all other names known to the compiler, each name being followed by a brief quotation illustrating its use. The subjects included are as miscellaneous as are those in a general encyclopedia, and the number of different names assembled under each item is quite large. Sources are always indicated, and there is a table of sections at the beginning.

Ch'i-ming chi-shu 齊名紀數, 12 *chüan*. Compiled by Wang Ch'eng-lieh 王承烈, compiler's preface dated 1806. Huan-shan-lou 環山樓 block-print edition of 1813. 4 *ts'e*.

This encyclopedia lists the names of men who have come to be associated in Chinese literature in groups of a certain number, as, for instance, the three commentators on the *Chou-li* 周禮三家, the eight scholars of Chou 周八士, and the 72 disciples of Confucius 七十二賢. It also lists the names of men who are connected with a numerically identified thing or place, as the compilers of the *San-t'ung* and the rulers of the Sixteen Kingdoms 十六國. There are no sections, because the names are classified by numbers—from two to 309—and arranged chronologically under each number. The work is based upon dynastic histories, biographies, and collections of essays and poems. Sources are usually indicated unless they are very well-known writings.

Hsiao-chih lu 小知錄, 12 *chüan*. Compiled by Lu Feng-tsao 陸鳳藻 and completed in 1804. (1) Ch'in-ya-t'ang 琴雅堂 block-print edition of the same year. 6 *ts'e*. (2) Taipei: Hsin-hsing shu-chü, 1969.

This encyclopedia pays particular attention to unusual matters. The material collected is, as a rule, in explanation of unusual terms, and is of a type not ordinarily found in more general collections. In the section on astronomy, for example, there are listed the thirty-six names of heaven as given in the *Yün-chi ch'i-ch'ien* 雲笈七籤 and the thirty-three names of heaven as given in the *Yin-pen-ching* 因本經. In the section on officials comparatively little attention is paid to the traditional divisions of government, terms related to the customs and ideas of special periods evidently being of much greater interest to the compiler. Sources of quotations are sometimes indicated and sometimes not. There is a list of the forty section headings at the beginning.

Ching-chuan i-i 經傳繹義, 50 *chüan*. Compiled by Ch'en Wei 陳煒 during the Ch'ien-lung period. Chiao-tzu-chai 校字齋 block-print edition of 1804. 24 *ts'e*.

This encyclopedia is based entirely upon the classics and commentaries on the classics, with occasional explanations quoted from modern scholars or written by the compiler himself. According to the publisher's preface, besides the classics themselves, there are quotations from all Han and Wei dynasty commentators, from the notes on the classics in the *Shang-shu ta-ch'uan* 尚書 大傳, the *Pai-hu t'ung-i* 白虎通義, the *Shih-chi* 史記, and the *Han-shu* 漢書, from ancient commentaries quoted in the *T'ung-tien* and the *T'ai-p'ing yü-lan*, and also selections from the writings of T'ang, Sung, and later classical scholars. A good general survey is presented under each of the nineteen topics. The material on official systems, for example, is very full from the beginning down to about 300 B.C. Charts and tables are frequently introduced to make the classics more comprehensible. There is a table of contents at the beginning.

C. ENCYCLOPEDIAS GIVING MATERIAL ON ORIGINS

The works described in this subsection are devoted primarily to tracing the origin of all manner of things, from tools, garments, and customs, to political and social institutions. The *Yüeh-jih chi-ku* traces the origins of customs and festivals related to the calendar. Some of the encyclopedias described in subsection D also contain a certain amount of material on origins.

Shih-wu chi-yüan 事物紀原, 10 *chüan*. Compiled by Kao Ch'eng 高承, who is known to have been alive in the Sung Yüan-feng 宋元豐 period (1078–1085). (1) *Hsi-yin-hsüan ts'ung-shu* 惜陰軒叢書, *ts'e* 73–82. (2) Ming block-print edition. 10 *ts'e*. (3) *Ts'ung-shu chi-ch'eng*. 4 *ts'e*. (4) Taipei: Hsin-hsing shu-chü, 1969.

The prefaces to this encyclopedia, written by Ming scholars, claim that it is a short cut to knowledge which tells the beginner the origin of almost everything. While this may be somewhat of an exaggeration, the origins of a great many things are traced in it, and on the whole the work is quite reliable. There are fifty-five sections and 1764 items, among the general categories being: emperors, ministers, politics, punishments, ceremonies, music, clothing, customs, games, animals, fish, insects, and tools. Under each item quotations are fitted together in such a way as to give a well-rounded explanation. Being one of the earliest encyclopedias of its kind, it was necessary for the compiler to go directly to original sources, and since many of the works quoted from have since been lost, modern Chinese scholars frequently quote directly from this work. Sources are always indicated. Earlier bibliographical references would seem to show that the organization and perhaps the size of this work have been different at different times. In 1806 (清嘉慶十一年) a revised edition, called the **Shih-wu chi-yüan pu** 事物紀原補, was prepared and published by Na-lan-yung-shou 納蘭永壽, in 12 *ts'e*. It is not known which edition of the original work it is based upon, but there are only fifty-two sections, three of the earlier sections having been combined with others. 119 of the original items have had new material added to them, and there are eighty new items. There is a detailed table of contents at the beginning of all four editions.

Shih-wu yüan-hui 事物原會, 40 *chüan*. Written by Wang Chi 汪汲, earliest dated preface 1796. *Ku-yü lao-jen hsiao-hsia lu* 古愚老人消夏錄, *ts'e* 1–9.

The *Shih-wu yüan-hui* is a study of the origins of a great variety of things. The author felt that previous works of the same nature were either not sufficiently broad in their scope or did not show sufficient care in the selection of source material, so he sought in this work to avoid both of those weaknesses. It is divided into 2052 items which, while not grouped under section headings, are so arranged that related subject-matter comes together. The work is based upon material derived from histories, the *Chiu-t'ung*, various *hui-yao*, and a few general encyclopedias, and virtually all branches of knowledge are represented. The entire work was written by Wang Chi himself, and the style is simple and clear. The material upon which he based his conclusions is reasonably well selected, and the sources are always indicated. The *Shih-wu yüan-hui* may be said to be broader in scope than earlier writings of the same kind, but it is probably less accurate in its use of source materials. There is a table of items at the beginning.

I-shih chi-shih 壹是紀始, 22 *chüan*, with one supplementary *chüan*. Compiled by Wei Sung 魏崧 (*chin-shih*, 1823). +(1) Yung-pei chi-lu 甬北寄廬 re-cut block-print edition of 1888. 8 *ts'e*. (2) Peking: Wen-k'uei-t'ang 文奎堂 block-print edition of 1891. 6 *ts'e*.

This encyclopedia traces the origins of things. It is divided into twenty-two sections and there are more than fifteen hundred items, besides a supplement of ten sections and fifty items. Each item is headed by a topic sentence, as, for example: "The *shu-yüan* 書院 system (medieval public school system) began in the T'ang dynasty," after which there are explanatory quotations and usually notes by the author. Even though the sources of the quotations are frequently omitted, the work repays consultation because of the general excellence of Wei's explanatory notes. His research was careful and frequently produced significant results, although he repeated many of the traditional errors, such as the attributing of a number of inventions to Huang-ti 黃帝. There is a table of items at the beginning of the work itself and also one at the beginning of the supplement.

Ku-chin hsing-shih-shu pien-cheng 古今姓氏書辨證, 40 *chüan*. Compiled by Teng Ming-shih 鄧名世 and presented to the emperor in 1134. (1) *Shou-*

shan-ko ts'ung-shu, ts'e 128–137. (2) Ch'en-shih tai-nan-ko 陳氏岱南閣 block-print edition of 1802. 10 *ts'e*. (3) *Ts'ung-shu chi-ch'eng, ts'e* 3297–3304.

This study of the origin of surnames is based upon the *Kuo-yü* 國語, the *Tso-chuan* 左傳, the *Five Classics*, the dynastic histories, the *Feng-su t'ung* 風俗通, the *Yüan-ho hsing-tsuan* 元和姓纂, the *Hsi-ning hsing-tsuan* 熙寧姓纂, the *Huang-ch'ao* [*Sung*] *po-kuan kung-ch'ing chia-p'u* 皇朝[宋]百官公卿家譜, and many other works. The names are arranged according to their rhyme, and besides the historical and explanatory material quoted under each surname, there are valuable critical notes written by the compiler. The work was highly praised both by Chu Hsi and other Sung scholars and by the editors of the *Ssu-k'u ch'üan-shu*.

The *Ku-chin hsing-shih-shu pien-cheng* was lost sight of for a few centuries during the Ming and Ch'ing dynasties, but was finally re-collected from the *Yung-lo ta-tien* 永樂大典 by the compilers of the *Ssu-k'u ch'üan-shu*. Later, in 1823, a scholar named Ch'ien Hsi-tso 錢熙祚 discovered an incomplete edition (*chüan* 1–4, 19–21, 31–40) dating from the beginning of the Southern Sung period which is much better than the corresponding parts of the *Ssu-k'u* edition. It is the *Ssu-k'u* edition which is reprinted in the *Shou-shan-ko ts'ung-shu*, but to it there is added a three-*chüan* appendix, called the *Ku-chin hsing-shih-shu chiao-k'an chi* 古今姓氏書校勘記, which includes all of the incomplete edition found by Ch'ien Hsi-tso and also Ch'ien's notes. This work is of particular use to students interested in Chinese customs, the feudal system, and the introduction of different foreign names into China during periods of alien domination. The passages quoted from the *Feng-su t'ung* and the *Pei-wei kuan-shih-chih* 北魏官氏志 differ somewhat from modern editions of those works. In the *Shou-shan-ko ts'ung-shu* there is a table of surnames at the beginning of both the main work and the appendix, the latter following the Sung edition and differing very much from the other.

Yüeh-jih chi-ku, Hsin-tseng 月日紀古, 新增, 12 *chüan*. Compiled by Hsiao Chih-han 蕭智漢, original compilation made in 1794; compiler's preface to the enlarged edition dated 1834. (1) Original block-print edition of 1794 or 1795. 12 *ts'e*. (2) T'ing-t'ao shan-fang 聽濤山房 block-print edition of about 1834. 36 *ts'e*. (3) Taipei: Hsin-hsing shu chü, 1969. 2 vols.

This is a collection of material on seasons, festivals, and customs and events related to particular days, compiled with the intention of supplying the lack of such material in general encyclopedias. It is divided into twelve *chüan*, to each of which is assigned one month of the year. At the beginning of each month the festivals which fall within it are listed, detailed material concerning them is presented, and their significance is explained. Then each individual day is taken up and important events which have occurred on that day in the past are listed, and poems and essays written about it are quoted. Material is derived from histories, classics, belles-lettres, and other works, the source being indicated at the beginning of each quotation. This work is particularly well supplied with material on natural calamities, seasonal phenomena, varieties of climate and weather, the history of customs and festivals, and the birthdays of emperors and famous ministers of history.

D. ENCYCLOPEDIAS OF ARTS AND SCIENCES

The first work described in this subsection contains much material on natural history, the next two are filled with practical information on a wide variety of subjects, and the fourth is devoted entirely to the subject of jade.

Kuang po-wu-chih 廣博物志, 50 *chüan*. Compiled by Tung Ssu-chang 董斯張, earliest dated preface 1607. (1) Block-print edition of about the same time. 32 *ts'e*. (2) Kao-hui-t'ang 高暉堂 block-print edition of 1761. 36 *ts'e*.

This encyclopedia covers a wide range of subjects extending from very early times down to the end of the Sui period, although it pays more attention to natural history than to any other one subject. The compiler used as its basis the Chin 晉 dynasty work *Po-wu-chih* 博物志 by Chang Hua 張華 (A.D. 232–300), adding to the original material and dividing it into twenty-two sections and 167 items. A disproportionately greater amount of material is quoted in some items than in others, and in no case is there a really thorough examination of a subject, although it is only fair to say that in comparison with most Ming encyclopedias, this is a good one. Sources are always indicated, but many of the quotations were taken second-hand from earlier encyclopedias, in which cases only the names of the secondary sources are given. The *Ssu-k'u* editors pointed out that there are occasional errors in the *Kuang po-wu-chih*, but they nevertheless praised it as a useful work.

San-ts'ai t'u-hui 三才圖會, 106 *chüan*. Compiled by Wang Ch'i 王圻 and his son Wang Ssu-i 王思義, Wang Ch'i's preface dated 1607. (1) Huai-yin ts'ao-t'ang 槐蔭草堂 block-print edition, latest dated preface 1609. 60 *ts'e*. (2) Taipei: Ch'eng Wen Publishing Co., 1970. 6 vols.

This encyclopedia, of a type which is rare in China, is made up of pictures, maps, charts and tables, each one of which is followed by a brief explanation. It is divided into fourteen sections and many items, and the subject matter is extremely miscellaneous. The work contains a very large collection of maps, pictures of all the Chinese emperors, and illustrations of such varied things as games, clothing, tools, buildings, precious stones, ceremonies, flowers and plants, animals, and the human body. It is sometimes difficult to determine whether illustrations were derived from other sources or were drawn by the compilers. Sometimes both illustration and explanation were taken directly from one work, and sometimes they were derived from different sources. Many of the explanations and even more of the illustrations are the compilers' own. The organization of the work leaves much to be desired, and many of the drawings are extremely crude, but Wang Ch'i was a learned scholar and the material included is interesting and suggestive. The *Ssu-k'u* editors declared it to be too broad in scope, but still they considered it useful for purposes of research in many fields. Most of the illustrations in the *Ku-chin t'u-shu chi-ch'eng* were taken from it.

*Ko-chih ching-yüan 格致鏡原, 100 *chüan*. Compiled by Ch'en Yüan-lung 陳元龍, compiler's latest preface dated 1735. Block-print edition of the same year. 24 *ts'e*.

This work differs very much from most Chinese encyclopedias in that it was compiled primarily for the purpose of providing practical information. It covers, in general, the arts and natural sciences, among the subjects treated being geography, human anatomy, plants and animals, tools and utensils, vehicles and weapons, musical, ceremonial and writing instruments, clothing, and architecture. Under geography, for instance, territories and boundaries are not discussed, but such things as wells, bridges, city walls, sand, dust, mud, kinds of stones, fossils, and waterfalls. Useful material on the origin and spread of printing and stone rubbing appears in this, but probably in no other encyclopedia. Special attention is paid to origins and evolution, and material is quoted from a wide variety of books, original sources always being carefully indicated. There is a table of the thirty sections at the beginning of the work and a table of items at the beginning of each section.

Yü-p'u lei-pien 玉譜類編, 4 *chüan*. Compiled by Hsü Shou-chi 徐壽基, who is known to have been alive in 1875. Yüan-yang kuan-shu 源陽官署 block-print edition of 1889. 4 *ts'e*.

The purpose of the compiler of this encyclopedia was to bring together material on jade from all branches of Chinese literature. The work is divided into twenty-eight sections, each of which, with the exception of the last one, is subdivided into many items. Practically all of the items are headed by a two-character phrase, one of which is that for jade (*yü* 玉) or a character one element of which is *yü*; occasionally an item is headed by only one character, one element of which is *yü*. Material is included on the names, appearance, and quality of different kinds of jade, on the mining of jade, on the tools used in working jade, and on objects made of jade. Literary abstractions and metaphors such as those which compare a good man or a beautiful woman to jade are also included. Almost everything written which relates to jade, whether in the concrete or abstract meaning of the word, and nearly all phrases containing the word *yü* or a word in which *yü* is one element, are to be found in this work. In the last section the compiler lays down a few general principles for judging the value, workmanship, age, etc., of jade objects. There is a table of sections at the beginning, and the sources of quotations are always indicated.

E. ENCYCLOPEDIAS DEALING WITH GOVERNMENT

While most Chinese encyclopedias contain a large amount of material on government, the works included in this subsection are almost exclusively devoted to that subject. Material is presented not only on governmental organization and administration, but also on related social and economic matters. In general the *t'ung* deal primarily with the political system in its various aspects over a long period of time, while the *hui-yao* are somewhat broader in scope but are limited to single dynasties. The other works described present political, social, and economic material from various points of view. The *Ta-ming hui-tien* 大明會典 and the *Ta-ch'ing hui-tien* 大清會典, which are not included in this bibliography because of their special nature, are useful supplements to those works herein described which are primarily concerned with the Ming and Ch'ing periods.

I. THE *T'UNG*

Chiu-t'ung 九通. (1) Palace block-print edition of the Ch'ien-lung period. 898 *ts'e*.+(2) *Chiu-t'ung ch'üan-shu* 九通全書, block-print edition published by the Chekiang shu-chü 浙江書局, between 1882 and 1896. 999 *ts'e*. (3) Shanghai: T'u-shu chi-ch'eng chü 上海圖書集成局 movable-type edition of 1901. 272 *ts'e*. (4) Hung-pao shu-chü 鴻寶書局 lithographic edition of 1902. 200 *ts'e*. **Shih-t'ung**[8] 十通: (5) Shanghai: Commercial Press photocopy of the Palace edition, 1936. 20 vols. 21,735 pp., with a four-corner index. (6) Taipei: Hsin-hsing shu-chü photocopy of the Palace edition, 1958-9. 24 vols. plus an index vol.

This is not a single work, but a collection of nine works which are classed together, usually appear together, and are described one by one below. The nine works are *T'ung-tien, T'ung-chih, Wen-hsien t'ung-k'ao, Hsü t'ung-tien, Hsü t'ung-chih, Hsü wen-hsien t'ung-k'ao (Ch'in-ting), Huang-ch'ao t'ung-tien,*

8. Besides the *Chiu-t'ung*, the *Shih-t'ung* includes the *Huang-ch'ao hsü wen-hsien t'ung-k'ao.*

Huang-ch'ao t'ung-chih, and *Huang-ch'ao wen-hsien t'ung-k'ao.* The first three are usually referred to together as the **San-t'ung** 三通, the last three as the **Huang-ch'ao san-t'ung** 皇朝三通, the last six as the **Liu-t'ung** 六通, and the whole nine as the *Chiu-t'ung.* A useful work called the *San-t'ung k'ao-cheng* 三通考證, which was compiled under imperial auspices during the Ch'ien-lung period and published in 1902 in one *ts'e* by the Kuan-wu-chai 貫吾齋, makes a comparison of the modern texts of the *San-t'ung* with both earlier editions and the original sources. This work is broken up into three parts in the *Chiu-t'ung ch'üan-shu* and the Commercial Press edition, and each part is appended to the work for which it was intended to serve as a list of errata. A work performing the same function for the *Liu-t'ung,* called the *Liu-t'ung ting-wu* 六通訂誤, was compiled toward the end of the nineteenth century by Hsi Yü-fu 席裕福 and others and published in 1901 in a two-*ts'e* movable-type edition by the T'u-shu chi-ch'eng chü.

★T'ung-tien 通典, 200 *chüan.* Compiled by Tu Yu 杜佑 (A.D. 735-812). (1) Palace block-print edition of 1747. 36 *ts'e.* (2) *Chiu-t'ung ch'üan-shu,* *ts'e* 1-50. (3) T'u-shu chi-ch'eng chü edition. 16 *ts'e.* (4) Hung-pao shu-chü edition. 12 *ts'e.* (5) *Shih-t'ung.* 1 vol. or 4 *ts'e.*

The *T'ung-tien* is a great reservoir of source material on the political and social history of China prior to the middle of the T'ang dynasty. The compiler, who was both a diligent scholar and an experienced official, was not so much interested in the mere recording of phrases which could be used in literary composition as in the collection of practical material which would be useful to those governing the country. Believing that the *Cheng-tien* 政典, an earlier work which had been compiled for the same purpose, was far from complete, Tu Yu compiled the *T'ung-tien,* taking thirty-six years to complete it. The work is now divided into nine sections, each of which is preceded by an introduction and is subdivided into many items. The material is carefully selected from a wide variety of sources, among them classics, histories, memorials to the throne, and belles-lettres. The items are arranged in chronological order, and within each item general material precedes that of a more specific character. The quotations are joined together in the fluent style of the compiler, and are followed by the quoted discussions and criticisms of other writers, assembled in such a way as to indicate Tu Yu's own opinions.

The nine sections into which the *T'ung-tien* is divided deal, respectively, with the economic system, the examination system, the official system, rites, music, the military system, the legal system, political geography, and border affairs. In each the period covered extends from the time of the legendary emperor Huang-ti 黃帝 down to the end of the T'ang t'ien-pao 唐天寶 period (755). A certain amount of material from 755 to 801 is added in interlinear notes. The section on rites is much fuller than any other, and the commentaries on the *Shang-shu* 尚書 and *Chou-li* 周禮 quoted are earlier than and superior to any others now available. Although the *Ssu-k'u* editors found it necessary to point out a few minor defects in the *T'ung-tien*, they praised it very highly, saying that it is made up entirely of solid material, that it contains all information essential to a knowledge of the period it covers, and that it clearly and systematically traces the evolution of each of the subjects it deals with. There is a table of sections at the beginning of the work and a detailed table of contents at the beginning of each section.

T'ung-chih 通志, 200 *chüan*. Compiled by Cheng Ch'iao 鄭樵 (1104-1162). (1) Palace block-print edition of 1747. 118 *ts'e*. (2) *Chiu-t'ung ch'üan-shu, ts'e* 51-250. (3) T'u-shu chi-ch'eng-chü edition, 60 *ts'e*. (4) Hung-pao shu-chü edition. 40 *ts'e*. (5) *Shih-t'ung*. 3 vols. or 12 *ts'e*.

The compiler of the *T'ung-chih* was a great critical historian of the Sung period who looked upon history as a continuous stream and felt that it was a mistake arbitrarily to divide it into periods corresponding to the dynasties. He modeled the *T'ung-chih* after the *Shih-chi* 史記 and classified his material according to four categories: *chi* 紀 (annals), *p'u* 譜 (chronological tables, of which there is only one section), *lüeh* 略 (monographic studies), and *chuan* 傳 (biographies). The period covered extends from earliest historical times down to the end of the Sui dynasty in the *chi* and *chuan* sections, and down to the end of the T'ang dynasty in the *lüeh* and *p'u* sections. Most of the material was derived from dynastic histories, although not infrequently other sources which are no longer available were made use of.

The *lüeh* were written, for the most part, by Cheng Ch'iao himself, and they are the most important part of the work, representing as they do, an attempt to summarize all that was known at that time about the subjects treated.[9] The other three categories are of comparatively little value. The topics of five of the *lüeh*, those on family and clan, philology, phonetics, political subdivisions, and flora and insects, were original with Cheng, none of them having been dealt with as independent subjects before. The subjects covered in the other fifteen *lüeh* had been discussed in earlier works, but in no case as clearly or as fully as in the *T'ung-chih*. The sections on the collation of books, on charts and tables, and on archaeology, are particularly good and are frequently referred to in modern studies. The section on bibliography is well classified and is a very convenient list of the pre-Five Dynasties works available in Cheng Ch'iao's time. At the beginning of the work there is an excellent introduction in which Cheng discusses his theory of history; there is also a short introduction at the beginning of each section. There is a table of contents at the beginning.

9. There is an edition of only the twenty *lüeh*, called the **T'ung-chih lüeh** 通志略, 52 *chüan*, published as part of the *Ssu-pu pei-yao*. 12 *ts'e*.

*Wen-hsien t'ung-k'ao 文獻通考, 348 *chüan*. Compiled by Ma Tuan-lin 馬端臨, who lived at the end of the Sung and the beginning of the Yüan dynasty. (1) Punctuated block-print edition of 1524. 120 *ts'e*. +(2) Palace block-print edition of 1747. 88 *ts'e*. (3) *Chiu-t'ung ch'üan-shu*, *ts'e* 251–400. (4) *Shih-t'ung*. 1 vol. or 3 vols.

This work is divided into twenty-four sections, nineteen of which were expanded from the nine of the *T'ung-tien* (as it was divided in Ma's time), the remaining five, on annotated bibliography, imperial genealogies, the feudal system, astronomy, and unusual phenomena, being added by Ma Tuan-lin. The material on the period before A.D. 756 was almost all taken from the *T'ung-tien*, although a certain amount of material neglected by that work was supplied from other sources. The material for the period between 756 and 1224 was collected by Ma, his sources being standard histories, *hui-yao*, such individual records as he considered reliable, and writings of the kind generally classified as belles-lettres. The Sung dynasty is more fully treated than any other, valuable material frequently being included which does not appear in the *Sung-shih* 宋史.

Ma Tuan-lin wrote an introduction to each section, explaining his approach, discussing the material made use of, and presenting a brief survey of the whole subject. These introductions are grouped together at the beginning of the work, and they are of such value that they have sometimes been memorized in their entirety by students preparing to take the civil service examinations. Quoted material is generally presented in the following order: first, quotations of a strictly factual nature, followed by the compiler's interpretations when necessary; then, relevant memorials to the throne, and the opinions and criticisms of other writers, some earlier but mostly contemporary; and finally, summaries of less reliable and even of unsound opinions, together with Ma's conclusions regarding them. There is a table of contents at the beginning.

The *Wen-hsien t'ung-k'ao*, which is usually referred to by Chinese scholars simply as the *T'ung-k'ao*, is grouped with the *T'ung-tien* and the *T'ung-chih* to form the *San-t'ung*. The *T'ung-tien* is known particularly for the comprehensiveness and thoroughness with which its contents are presented, the *T'ung-chih* for the critical treatment of the material presented in its twenty *lüeh* sections, and the *T'ung-k'ao* for Ma Tuan-lin's criticisms and interpretations. The second and third are based to a large extent upon the first, and in order of comparative importance the *T'ung-tien* probably should be placed first, the *Wen-hsien t'ung-k'ao* second, and the *T'ung-chih* last.

Hsü t'ung-tien 續通典, 150 *chüan*. Compiled under Imperial auspices, having been ordered in 1767. (1) Palace block-print edition of the Ch'ien-lung period. 64 *ts'e*. (2) *Chiu-t'ung ch'üan-shu*, *ts'e* 401–440. (3) T'u-shu chi-ch'eng-chü edition. 12 *ts'e*. (4) Hung-pao shu-chü edition. 8 *ts'e*. +(5) *Shih-t'ung*. I vol. or 3 *ts'e*.

This supplement to the *T'ung-tien*, classified according to the same nine sections, merely continues the earlier work from 756 to the end of the Ming dynasty. There are occasional differences in the items and in the method of presenting the material, but on the whole it is a faithful imitation. Material is drawn from dynastic histories, various *hui-yao*, the *T'ai-p'ing yü-lan*, *Ts'e-fu yüan-kuei*, *Shan-t'ang k'ao-so*, *Ch'i-tan kuo-chih* 契丹國志, *Ta-Chin kuo-chih* 大金國志, *Yüan tien-chang* 元典章, *Ming chi-li* 明集禮, *Ta-Ming hui-tien* 大明會典 and the collected writings of a few individuals.

Hsü t'ung-chih 續通志, 640 *chüan*. Compiled under Imperial auspices, having been ordered in 1767. (1) Palace block-print edition of the Ch'ien-lung period. 192 *ts'e*. (2) *Chiu-t'ung ch'üan-shu*, *ts'e* 441–640. +(3) *Shih-t'ung*. 3 vols. or 13 *ts'e*.

This supplement to the *T'ung-chih* follows it very closely both in style and in organization. Certain of Cheng Ch'iao's sections have been combined and new ones have been added, so that this work has a total of forty-eight, although the number of *lüeh* 略 remains the same: twenty. There are a number of changes in the items, and the *p'u* 譜 section is omitted. All material is carried down to the end of the Ming dynasty, the *chi* 紀 and *chuan* 傳 beginning with the T'ang dynasty, and the *lüeh* with the Five Dynasties. The material in the *chi* and *chuan* was taken from dynastic histories, the *Chi-shih pen-mo* 紀事本末 of the Sung and later dynasties, the *T'ung-chien kang-mu* 通鑑綱目, biographies, and belles-lettres. All of the *lüeh*, except the one on bibliography which is based upon the *Ssu-k'u ch'üan-shu tsung-mu*, depend for their source material upon the *chih* 志 of the various dynastic histories. One of the most marked differences between this work and the *T'ung-chih* is to be found in the biographical sections. The biographies in the earlier work were always quoted in their entirety, whereas those in the *Hsü t'ung-chih* are abridged from the original sources. There is a detailed table of contents at the beginning.

Hsü wen-hsien t'ung-k'ao 續文獻通考, 254 *chüan*. Compiled by Wang Ch'i 王圻, compiler's preface dated 1586. Block-print edition, latest dated preface 1603. 80 *ts'e*.

This supplement to the *Wen-hsien t'ung-k'ao* applies Ma Tuan-lin's technique to the history of the Liao, Chin, Yüan and Ming dynasties, and also adds a certain amount of new material for the period from 1224 to the end of the Sung dynasty. The *Wen-hsien t'ung-k'ao* classification and section headings are followed, although six new sections and a number of new items are added. Items which merely supplement those of Ma Tuan-lin are indicated in the table of contents at the beginning by the character *hsü* 續 whereas entirely new items are indicated by the character *tseng* 增. The Ming period is more fully treated than any other, the most valuable material coming from reports of law cases which are, for the most part, no longer accessible. The two sections on foreign relations contain considerable material not to be found in other works. Extracts from other sources are accurately quoted but because of the poor arrangement it is often difficult to distinguish readily between the quotations and the compiler's comments. The *Ssu-k'u* editors severely criticised this work but praised the *Hsü wen-hsien t'ung-k'ao, Ch'in-ting*, which is largely based upon it. The two differ somewhat, and as each is better on certain subjects than the other, it is wise to use them together.

Hsü wen-hsien t'ung-k'ao, Ch'in-ting 續文獻通考, 欽定, 250 *chüan*. Compiled under Imperial auspices having been ordered in 1747. +(1) Palace block-print edition of the Ch'ien-lung period. 128 *ts'e*. (2) *Chiu-t'ung ch'üan-shu, ts'e* 641–760. (3) *Shih-t'ung*. 2 vols.

There are two reasons why a second *Hsü wen-hsien t'ung-k'ao* was compiled: first, the compilers considered Wang Ch'i's work to have been badly done, and second, Emperor Ch'ien Lung wished to achieve eternal fame for having sponsored the compilation of supplements to all of the *San-t'ung*. The work is similar to the *Wen-hsien t'ung-k'ao* in style and arrangement, although there are two new sections, making a total of twenty-six. There is a general introduction to each section, and the period covered extends from 1224 down to the end of the Ming dynasty. This *Hsü wen-hsien t'ung-k'ao* is more carefully arranged than Wang's, although it is made up to a large extent of abridgments of Wang's quotations, with the addition of a certain amount of new material from other sources. This is the better work from the point of view of comprehensibility, but in Wang's the original sources are more accurately quoted. Each is better on certain subjects than the other, and they should be used together.

Huang-ch'ao t'ung-tien 皇朝通典 (also called **Ch'ing-ch'ao t'ung-tien** 清朝通典), 100 *chüan*. Compiled under Imperial auspices, having been ordered in 1767. +(1) Palace block-print edition of the Ch'ien-lung period, 48 *ts'e*. (2) *Chiu-t'ung ch'üan-shu, ts'e* 761–800. +(3) *Shih-t'ung*. 1 vol.

This work, which is a continuation of the *Hsü t'ung-tien* and which follows the same arrangement, covers the period from the beginning of the Ch'ing dynasty to the year 1785. Its section headings are the same as those of its predecessor, although there is an occasional change in the items. Materials are based chiefly upon the *Ta-Ch'ing t'ung-li* 大清通禮, the *Ta-Ch'ing lü-li* 大清律例, the *Ta-Ch'ing i-t'ung-chih* 大清一統志, the *Ta-Ch'ing hui-tien* 大清會典, the various *tse-li* 則例 of different branches of the government, the *Jih-hsia chiu-wen k'ao* 日下舊聞考, and the writings of a few individuals. There is a table of sections at the beginning.

Huang-ch'ao t'ung-chih 皇朝通志 (also called **Ch'ing-ch'ao t'ung-chih** 清朝通志), 126 *chüan*. Compiled under Imperial auspices, having been ordered in 1767. +(1) Palace block-print edition of the Ch'ien-lung period. 48 *ts'e*. (2) *Chiu-t'ung ch'üan-shu, ts'e* 801–840. +(3) *Shih-t'ung*. 1 vol. or 2 *ts'e*.

This work is a continuation of the twenty *lüeh* 略 sections of the *Hsü t'ung-chih*, and it contains neither *chi* 紀 nor *chuan* 傳. Among the sections, some are broader in scope than the corresponding ones in the *Hsü t'ung-chih*, and some are narrower; and whereas some of the items in the earlier work are omitted, some entirely new ones are added, such as those in *chüan* 11–17 on the Manchu, Mongol, Tibetan, and other Central Asian languages. The period covered extends from the beginning of the Ch'ing dynasty to 1785. There is a table of sections at the beginning.

Huang-ch'ao wen-hsien t'ung-k'ao 皇朝文獻通考 (also called **Ch'ing-ch'ao wen-hsien t'ung-k'ao** 清朝文獻通考), 300 *chüan*. Compiled under Imperial auspices, having been ordered in 1747. +(1) Palace block-print edition of the Ch'ien-lung period. 176 *ts'e*. (2) *Chiu-t'ung ch'üan-shu, ts'e* 841–999. +(3) *Shih-t'ung*. 2 vols. or 10 *ts'e*.

This work is classified in the same way as the *Hsü wen-hsien t'ung-k'ao, Ch'in-ting,* the period covered extending from the beginning of the Ch'ing dynasty to 1785. Some items in the earlier work which dealt with matters no longer significant in the Ch'ing period were not included in this work, and a number of new items were added in which subjects such as the Eight Banner system are discussed. The material is, to a certain extent, the same in all of the *Huang-ch'ao san-t'ung,* for they were compiled to perpetuate the tradition and style of the *San-t'ung* rather than to make available new material. In comparing the three, the material in the *Huang-ch'ao t'ung-tien* is the most compact and that in the *Huang-ch'ao t'ung-chih* the most scattered; the *Huang-ch'ao wen-hsien t'ung-k'ao* is the best, for it is the most intelligible and the most convenient to use. Unfortunately its so-called critical notes are of little significance, as it was not possible to be critical in dealing with the dynasty during which it was compiled.

Huang-ch'ao hsü wen-hsien t'ung-k'ao 皇朝續文獻通考 (also called **Ch'ing-ch'ao hsü wen-hsien t'ung-k'ao** 清朝續文獻通考), 400 *chüan*.[10] Compiled by Liu Chin-tsao 劉錦藻, compiler's preface dated 1921. +(1) Movable-type edition of about the same time. 100 *ts'e* (2) *Shih-t'ung*. 4 vols. or 14 *ts'e*.

This work was compiled as a supplement to the *Huang-ch'ao wen-hsien t'ung-k'ao* and follows it closely in arrangement, dealing with the period between 1786 and 1911. There are thirty sections, including four new ones: on foreign affairs, on the postal system, on industry, and on the constitution. New items include those on import duties, opium, and likin in the section on taxation, that on modern education in the section on the school system, and that on the navy in the military section. Sources are not indicated, although probably most of the material was taken from the *Tung-hua hsü-lu* 東華續錄, the *Ta-Ch'ing hui-tien shih-li* 大清會典事例, and other works of the same general nature. The style is simple and readable, and a fairly reliable picture of the second half of the Ch'ing dynasty is presented, although it is probably fair to say that this work fails to come up to the standard set by the *Chiu-t'ung*. There is a table of sections at the beginning of the work.

Erh-shih-ssu shih chiu-t'ung cheng-tien lei-yao ho-pien 二十四史九通政典類要合編, 320 *chüan*. Compiled by Huang Shu-lin 黃書霖 (1862–19 ?). (1) Yüeh-ya-t'ang 約雅堂 movable-type edition of 1902. 60 *ts'e*. (2) Taipei: Hung-ch'iao shu-tien 虹橋書店, 1968. 14 vols. 16, 8596 pp.

Altogether there are more than 5400 *chüan* in the *Chiu-t'ung* and the twenty-four dynastic histories, and useful material on particular subjects is so scattered through them that it can be located only with the expenditure of much time and labor. The compiler of this work picked out what he considered to be the most important material in all of them, and classified and arranged it first by dynasties and then by sections and items. For purposes of classification he divides Chinese history into fourteen dynasties, with pre-Han as the first and Ch'ing as the last, the Ch'ing material extending through most of the Ch'ien-lung period. The section headings under each dynasty are usually as follows: emperors, the system of nobility, the official system, the land and taxation systems, population, public service, coinage, rites, music, the military system, the legal system, geography, and foreign affairs. Maps, charts, stories and anecdotes, and material on natural history, archaeology and bibliography, are not included. Under each item the material is briefly and intelligibly presented,

---

10. A 320-*chüan* edition of this work was published in 1905, covering the period 1786–1904. The enlarged edition described above, however, is much the better of the two, for it not only brings the material down to the end of the dynasty but also adds new material for the period covered in the earlier edition.

with sources indicated in detail. This work is particularly valuable because of the inclusion of material which is scattered through the biographical sections of the dynastic histories, a type of material which is ordinarily difficult to locate. There is a table of the dynasties into which the work is divided at the beginning, and a table of items at the beginning of each dynasty.

2.   THE *HUI-YAO*

Ch'in hui-yao 秦會要. Compiled by Sun K'ai 孫楷 (1871–1907), revised by Shih Chih-mien 施之勉 and Hsü Fu 徐復. Taipei: Chung-hua ts'ung-shu wei-yüan-hui, 1956. [4] 16, 294 pp.

The *Ch'in hui-yao*, like a small encyclopedia, contains all essential information about the Ch'in kingdom and dynasty (246–207 B.C.), in one volume. It is divided into fourteen sections including genealogy, geography, administration, finance and population, economics, military system, legal system, education, ceremonies, music, official costumes, and frontier affairs. The book consists mostly of quotations from Ssu-ma Ch'ien's *Shih-chi* and from many other ancient writings and encyclopedias, with indication of sources. It was first published in Hunan in 1905, but enjoyed very limited circulation. Shih Chih-mien, a specialist on the Han period, obtained a copy and in cooperation with Hsü Fu made corrections and revisions and republished the work in Taipei.

Hsi-Han hui-yao 西漢會要, 70 *chüan*. Compiled by Hsü T'ien-lin 徐天麟, and completed in 1211. (1) *Wu-ying-tien chü-chen-pan ts'ung-shu*, Fukien edition of 1895, *ts'e* 357–368. +(2) Kiangsu shu-chü 江蘇書局 block-print edition of 1884. 10 *ts'e*. (3) *Wan-yu wen-k'u ti-erh-chi*. 6 *ts'e*. (4) Peking: Chung-hua shu-chü, 1955. 723 pp. (5) Taipei: Shih-chieh shu-chü, 1960. 15, 723 pp.

Because of the bulkiness and the somewhat involved literary style of the *Ch'ien Han-shu* 前漢書, it is often difficult to locate material in it. For this reason Hsü T'ien-lin compiled the *Hsi-Han hui-yao*, using the *T'ang hui-yao* as a model. All of the contents are quoted from the *Ch'ien Han-shu*, the material being arranged in fifteen sections and 367 items. The section headings are: imperial genealogies, rites, music, vehicles and clothing, the school system, astronomy and the calendar, unusual natural phenomena, the official system, the examination system, governmental affairs, economic matters, the military system, the legal system, political geography, and foreign affairs. Since it is much easier to find material in this work than in the *Ch'ien Han-shu*, and since in it the original location of all quotations is given, the *Hsi-Han hui-yao* is a very convenient key to that work. There is a table of items at the beginning.

Tung-Han hui-yao 東漢會要, 40 *chüan*. Compiled by Hsü T'ien-lin 徐天麟, compiler's preface dated 1226. (1) 1868 Fukien edition of the *Wu-ying-tien chü-chen-pan ts'ung-shu, ts'e* 272–279. (2) 1895 Fukien edition of the same *ts'ung-shu, ts'e* 369–376. +(3) Kiangsu shu-chü 江蘇書局 block-print edition of 1884. 8 *ts'e*. (4) *Wan-yu wen-k'u ti-erh-chi.* (5) Taipei: Shih-chieh shu-chü, 1960. 21, 438 pp.

This work was compiled by the same scholar who compiled the *Hsi-Han hui-yao*, and the material is arranged under the same section headings. Although the most important source is the *Hou Han-shu* 後漢書, material is also drawn from other works, and the compiler frequently adds his own interpretation and criticism at the end of an item. Quotations are carefully selected and classified, and the compiler's notes are of considerable value. There is a table of the 384 items at the beginning.

San-kuo hui-yao 三國會要, 22 *chüan*. Compiled by Yang Ch'en 楊晨, who lived during the latter half of the nineteenth century. +(1) Kiangsu shu-chü 江蘇書局 block-print edition of 1900. 6 *ts'e*. (2) Huang-yen Yang-shih 黃巖楊氏 block-print edition of 1900. 6 *ts'e*. (3) *T'ai-chou ts'ung-shu hou-chi* 台州叢書後集, *ts'e* 3–7. (4) Peking: Chung-hua shu-chü, 1956. 2, 8, 396 pp. (5) Taipei: Shih-chieh shu-chü, 1960. 8, 396 pp.

This work, similar in style to the *Tung-Han hui-yao*, is divided into sixteen sections and subdivided into many items. Material is largely derived from the *San-kuo chih* 三國志 and its commentaries, although many other works are quoted. Sources are always carefully indicated. As the *San-kuo chih* has no *chih* 志, this work fills that need. The section on political geography is based on the *San-kuo chiang-yü chih* 三國疆域志, and that on the official system on the *San-kuo chih-kuan piao* 三國職官表. There are a list of 245 sources and a table of sections at the beginning.

T'ang hui-yao 唐會要, 100 *chüan*. Final compilation by Wang P'u 王溥 completed in A.D. 961. (1) *Wu-ying-tien chü-chen-pan ts'ung-shu*, Fukien edition of 1895, *ts'e* 299–330. (2) Kiangsu shu-chü block-print edition of 1884. 24 *ts'e*. +(3) Kuang-ya shu-chü 廣雅書局 block-print edition of the Kuang-hsü period. 28 *ts'e*. (4) *Wan-yu wen-k'u ti-erh-chi.* 16 *ts'e*. (5) Taipei: Shih-chieh shu-chü, 1960. 3 vols. 23, 1804 pp.

Su Mien 蘇冕, a T'ang scholar, wrote a forty-*chüan* work entitled *Hui-yao* 會要, in which he assembled under classified items material dating from the beginning of the T'ang dynasty (A.D. 618) down to 804. In 853 Yang Shao-fu 楊紹復 and others, under imperial auspices, compiled a forty-*chüan* supplement to this work, bringing the material down to 852. Near the end of the Five

Dynasties period, Wang P'u collected material for the period between 853 and the end of the T'ang dynasty (907), and combined it with that in the two earlier works to compose the *T'ang hui-yao*.

The *T'ang hui-yao* contains important factual material of all kinds, although it is chiefly devoted to the political and social institutions of the T'ang dynasty. It is divided into 514 items, to a number of which less important miscellaneous material is added in the form of a supplement. Much of the material is quoted from an early edition of the *Chiu T'ang-shu* 舊唐書 which differed in many respects from the editions now extant. Sources are never indicated except in four *chüan* (7 to 10 inclusive) which were completed by later scholars from material from the *T'ung-tien, Wen-hsien t'ung-k'ao, Ts'e-fu yüan-kuei,* and other works. Because four-fifths of the *T'ang hui-yao* was compiled during the T'ang period, it is as important a work as the two T'ang dynastic histories, in spite of the fact that modern editions are not exactly the same as the original compilation. Not a little material is preserved in it which is not to be found elsewhere, and it is often quoted from directly as a first-hand source. There is a table of items at the beginning.

Wu-tai hui-yao 五代會要, 30 *chüan*. Compiled by Wang P'u 王溥, and completed in A.D. 961. (1) 1868 Fukien edition of the *Wu-ying-tien chü-chen-pan ts'ung-shu, ts'e* 281–286. (2) 1895 Fukien edition of the same *ts'ung-shu, ts'e* 331–336. (3) *Wan-yu wen-k'u ti-erh-chi.* 4 *ts'e.* (4) *Ts'ung-shu chi-ch'eng.* 4 *ts'e.* (5) Taipei: Shih-chieh shu-chü, 1960. 14, 369 pp.

The *Wu-tai hui-yao* was compiled by the same scholar and in the same style as the *T'ang hui-yao*. It is divided into 270 items and the scope of the material included is somewhat broader than that of the two official Five Dynasties histories. The fifty-two year period of the Five Dynasties (907–959) was one of great disorder, and most of the primary sources dating from that time were destroyed. Fortunately this work and the *Ts'e-fu yüan-kuei* were compiled very soon after the end of the period, and a great deal of valuable material has been preserved in them. The *Wen-hsien t'ung-k'ao* also preserves some, but in that work the literary style of original documents has been so polished that their value as original source materials is somewhat lessened. There is a table of items at the beginning of this work.

Sung hui-yao kao 宋會要稿, 460 *chüan*. Re-collected from the *Yung-lo ta-tien* 永樂大典 in 1809–1810 by Hsü Sung 徐松. (1) Photolithographic edition published in 1936 by the Ta-tung shu-chü for the National Library of Peiping. 200 *ts'e.* (2) Peking: Chung-hua shu-chü, 1957. 8 vols. 7898 pp. (3) **Sung hui-yao chi-pen** 宋會要輯本, Taipei: Shih-chieh shu-chü, 1964. 16 vols.

This is a large collection of miscellaneous source material on the history of the Sung dynasty. According to the *Sung hui-yao yen-chiu* 宋會要研究 of T'ang Chung 湯中, ten different *Sung hui-yao* 宋會要 were compiled during the Sung period, all organized in the same way but each covering the history of a certain number of reigns, and having altogether a total of 2400 *chüan*. Seven of these *hui-yao*, each with a different title, were broken up and copied into various sections of the *Yung-lo ta-tien*, and except for the material scattered through that compilation the work had entirely disappeared by the middle of the Ming dynasty.

In 1809 Hsü Sung was appointed a chief compiler of the *Ch'üan T'ang-wen* 全唐文, and while assembling material for that work he also undertook to re-collect the *Sung hui-yao*. He copied five or six hundred *chüan*, but died before he had had time to rearrange and edit them. His manuscript fell into the hands of the Kuang-ya shu-chü 廣雅書局 shortly after its establishment (in 1887) by Chang Chih-tung 張之洞, the governor-general in Canton, and Miao Ch'üan-sun 繆荃孫 and T'u Chi 屠寄 were asked by Chang to prepare it for publication. Although they went through and annotated the whole manuscript, they had only had time to finish editing the section on the official system when Chang was transferred to another post and the work was discontinued. In 1915 the manuscript was purchased by Liu Ch'eng-kan 劉承幹, who employed Liu Fu-chin 劉富晉 and others to rearrange it. The work was so poorly done, however, that when the two copies were examined by the National Library of Peiping with the idea of reproducing them, only the original manuscript, partly revised by Miao and T'u, was considered worth perpetuating.

The material included in the *Sung hui-yao* is not very evenly distributed among the different sections, those on economic matters and on the official system being much fuller than any others. Furthermore, the arrangement in this edition is still far from satisfactory, for much material remains wrongly located (for example, a certain amount of material on imperial genealogies appears at the end of the section on the school system), and some material is included which was copied from the *Yung-lo ta-tien* but which has no place in the *Sung hui-yao*. The *Sung-shih* 宋史 was originally based in part upon the *Sung hui-yao*, but the material on the subjects discussed in the latter is naturally much fuller than that in the *Sung-shih*.

Ming hui-yao 明會要, 80 *chüan*. Compiled by Lung Wen-pin 龍文彬 (*chin-shih*, 1865). (1) Yung-huai-t'ang 永懷堂 block-print edition of 1887. 20 *ts'e*. (2) Undated Kuang-ya shu-chü 廣雅書局 block-print edition. 20 *ts'e*. (3) Peking: Chung-hua shu-chü, 1956. 2 vols. 24, 1563 pp. (4) Taipei: Shih-chieh shu-chü, 1960. 2 vols.

The style and organization of this work, which is divided into fifteen sections and 498 items and which is devoted to an exposition of the political and social institutions of the Ming dynasty, are the same as those of its immediate predecessors. According to the introduction, the most important sources from which the material in this work was taken are the *Ming-shih* 明史 and the *T'ung-chien kang-mu san-pien* 通鑑綱目三編, although altogether more than two hundred works were used, many dating from the Ming dynasty. Quotations were carefully chosen and their sources are always indicated. In most of the items there is a criticism and a final conclusion written by the compiler, and whenever there is a conflict between the sources he gives his own opinion. This is probably the best of the *hui-yao*, for the compiler was able to avoid many of the weaknesses of the earlier ones. There is a table of items at the beginning.

3.   THE *CHING-SHIH-WEN* COLLECTIONS

The movement among scholar-officials to emphasize knowledge for practical use, generally referred to as the "statecraft 經世 school," was inspired by such early Ch'ing scholars as Ku Yen-wu 顧炎武 (1613–1682) and Yen Yüan 顏元 (1635–1704) and was most active during the last century of the Ch'ing dynasty. Scholars of this persuasion compiled a number of collections of material on practical governmental problems, commencing with the *Huang-ch'ao ching-shih wen-pien*, which was itself modeled to a certain extent on the *Huang-Ming ching-shih wen-pien*. The *Huang-ch'ao ching-shih wen-pien* was compiled by Ho Ch'ang-ling, an innovative and energetic provincial governor and governor-general of the first half of the nineteenth century, assisted by Wei Yüan 魏源, a vigorous advocate of practical scholarship and a leading scholar of the period. This very important collection of research data was followed by many compilations of the same type. Seventeen different *ching-shih-wen* collections presently available in Japanese libraries have been indexed by the Center for Modern Chinese Studies at the Tōyō bunko.[11] Included in this subsection are the four most useful, or in any event most accessible, of this type of late Ch'ing collections of material relating to problems of government, and one from the early Republican period.

Huang-Ming ching-shih wen-pien 皇明經世文編, 504 *chüan*, supplement 4 *chüan*. Compiled by Hsü Fu-yüan 徐孚遠 (1599–1665), Ch'en Tzu-lung 陳子龍 (1608–1674), *et al*. Taipei: Kuo-feng ch'u-pan she, 1964. 30 vols. Photocopy of a Ming Ch'ung-chen 崇禎 (1628–1643) edition.

11.   **Keisei bumpen sō mokuroku** or **Ching-shih wen-pien tsung-mu-lu** 經世文編總目錄. Tokyo: Kindai Chūgoku kenkyū iinkai, 1956. 3 vols. 197, 371, 6, 149, 13 pp. The first two volumes reprint the titles of essays and other writings included and the names of their authors, in the order in which they appear in the seventeen collections covered. The third volume is an index to the names of all authors whose writings are reproduced in the seventeen collections, arranged by the Japanese system, but with a Wade-Giles romanization key.

This is a collection of 3145 memorials, essays, and other compositions written by 442 authors who sought to improve political, economic, and intellectual conditions under the declining Ming dynasty. The bringing together of such writings was perhaps a reaction against both the prevalent Wang Yang-ming philosophy which stressed intuitive knowledge and the academic tendency to enjoy empty discussion and factional criticism, neither of which contributed to the solution of political and social problems. The collection was assembled by a member of the Fu-she 復社 and a few associates during 1638. The essays are not arranged by subject matter but according to the chronological order of the authors. Thumbing through these volumes, one finds that the 3000-odd pieces deal with such matters as ceremonies and music, military affairs, punishments, and religious and moral instructions, as well as statecraft (*chih-tao* 治道), generalship, financial and taxation measures, civil service examinations, water conservancy, and frontier and barbarian affairs. In the last two categories there are passages critical of the Manchus, for which reason the whole work was banned by the rulers of the Ch'ing dynasty and so had very limited circulation.

Huang-ch'ao ching-shih wen-pien 皇朝經世文編. 120 *chüan*. Compiled by Ho Ch'ang-ling 賀長齡 (1785–1848), compiler's preface dated 1826. (1) Shanghai: Chung-hsi shu-chü 中西書局, 1899. 12 *ts'e*. (2) Taipei: Shih-chieh shu-chü, 1964. 8 vols.

This is a collection of 2120 essays and excerpts from memorials, reports, and other writings, by some 600 writers of the Ch'ing dynasty. It is a kind of guide to government, intended to assist officials with the day-to-day problems of public administration. The selections are arranged under eight section headings: (1) theories of government, (2) substance of government, and the names of the six boards into which the central administration was divided: (3) civil appointments, (4) finance, (5) ceremonies, (6) military affairs, (7) punishments and (8) public works. Each section is subdivided, for example civil appointments includes subsections on different aspects of the bureaucratic system, the selection and evaluation of officials, the duties and emoluments of officials, local government, the staffs of provincial and local officials, etc. The punishments section, among a variety of materials, includes summaries of their experience in the handling of criminal cases by such eminent jurists as Wang Hui-tsu 汪輝祖.

At the beginning of each *chüan* there is a table of contents listing the selections included therein, with authors' names. The first volume has several tables of the writers quoted in the collection, one listing those who were still alive in 1826, giving brief biographical data and their major publications together with the selections included in the *Huang-ch'ao ching-shih wen-pien*, and others listing the writers of different kinds of excerpts as from collections of essays or memorials to the throne, generally also including brief biographical information.

Huang-ch'ao ching-shih wen hsü-pien 皇朝經世文續編. 120 *chüan*. Compiled by Ko Shih-chün 葛士濬, preface dated 1888. (1) Shanghai: Sao-yeh shan-fang, 1897. 24 *ts'e*. (2) Shanghai: Wen-sheng shu-chü 文盛書局, 1898. 10 *ts'e*. (3) Taipei: Kuo-feng ch'u-pan-she, 1964. 2 vols. 1070; 1172 pp.

This supplement to the *Huang-ch'ao ching-shih wen-pien*, consisting largely of materials written later than 1826, is arranged with the same section headings as the Ho Ch'ang-ling compilation except that a ninth has been added, foreign affairs 洋務, which fills the final 20 *chüan*. There is a table of contents for the whole collection at the beginning, but none of the kinds of biographical and bibliographical data supplied in the earlier work.

Huang-ch'ao ching-shih wen san-pien 皇朝經世文三編. 80 *chüan*. Compiled by Ch'en Chung-i 陳忠椅, prefaces dated 1898. (1) Shanghai: Sao-yeh shan-fang, 1897. 6 *ts'e*. (2) Taipei: Kuo-feng ch'u-pan she, 1965. 2 vols. 835; 738 pp.

This collection, which follows the model of the *Huang-ch'ao ching-shih wen hsü-pien*, having been compiled after the first Sino-Japanese War includes considerable useful material on foreign relations and on reform. It appears to have been hastily compiled.

Huang-ch'ao ching-shih wen hsin-pien 皇朝經世文新編. 21 *chüan* (some of them subdivided). Compiled by Mai Chung-hua 麥仲華, preface dated 1898. (1) Shanghai: Shang-hai shu-chü 上海書局, 1902. 12 *ts'e*. (2) Taipei: Kuo-feng ch'u-pan she, 1965. 2 vols. 665; 587 pp.

This collection of material, presumably compiled at the same time as the previous work, is organized under an entirely different set of section headings though it contains the same kinds of data.

Min-kuo ching-shih wen-pien 民國經世文編. Compiled by T'ang Shou-ch'ien 湯壽潛. (1) Shanghai: Ching-shih wen-she 經世文社, 1914. 40 *ts'e*. (2) Taipei: Wen-hsing shu-tien 文星書店, 1962. 4 vols. 1284 pp. (photocopy).

This compilation of useful essays relating to problems of statecraft at the beginning of the Republican period is patterned after Ho Ch'ang-ling's *Huang-ch'ao ching-shih wen-pien* (q.v.). It consists of essays and editorials written by leading contemporary writers, and official documents that deal with politics, law, internal and external affairs, public finance, the military, education, industry, communications, religion, and ethics. Emphasis is on legal and political matters such as the constitution, and on the political struggle between Yüan Shih-k'ai and members of the Kuomintang. Considerable attention is also paid to the autonomy claims of Mongolia and Tibet. Although these essays deal only with the 1912–13 period, the compilation is a handy reference to public opinion on many fundamental problems of the early Republican era. There is neither author-title index nor indication of sources, but there is a detailed table of contents.

4. OTHER ENCYCLOPEDIAS DEALING WITH POLITICAL, LEGAL, AND ECONOMIC MATTERS

Li-tai chih-tu hsiang-shuo 歷代制度詳說, 15 *chüan*. Written by Lü Tsu-ch'ien 呂祖謙 (1137–1181). *Hsü chin-hua ts'ung-shu* 續金華叢書, *ts'e* 9–11.

This work, presumably by a famous Sung scholar, was written to provide material in a simple and brief form which could be easily memorized by students planning to take the civil service examinations. Each *chüan* is a separate item, and each item is an essay in itself. Among the subjects are: the examination system, the school system, taxation, the salt monopoly, coinage, famine relief, and the land system. The whole of Chinese history up to the middle of the Southern Sung period is covered, and the author presents both material of a factual nature and his own interpretations and explanations. Each item gives a clear and accurate survey of the subject under discussion, written in a simple colloquial style not unlike that employed in modern lecture notes. The *Ssu-k'u* editors suggested the possibility that the work might be a forgery, since it is mentioned neither in the bibliographical section of the *Sung-shih* 宋史 nor in Lü Tsu-ch'ien's *nien-p'u* 年譜, but even if it is by another hand, it is none the less useful.

Ching-chi lei-pien 經濟類編, 100 *chüan*. Compiled by Feng Ch'i 馮琦 (1558–1603). (1) Block-print edition of 1604. 56 *ts'e*. (2) Taipei: Ch'eng Wen Publishing Co., 1969. 20 vols. 11,492 pp. (photocopy).

This work is not unlike the *Ts'e-fu yüan-kuei*, in that it was compiled with the intention of providing material which would be of practical value to those engaged in governing the country, but it contains a wider variety of material. The Sung work is a collection of factual information derived mainly from dynastic histories, but this, although presenting some factual material, is more a collection of the ideas expressed in essays and in works of a philosophic nature. There are about four hundred items, arranged under twenty-three section headings, and although the principal concern is with governmental affairs, there are also a few *chüan* on religions and other subjects. The *Ssu-k'u* editors praised the work—which was rather unusual for anything written during the Ming dynasty—although they also pointed out a few inconsistencies and minor mistakes which probably were the result of the compilation having been completed after Feng's death by his son and two of his pupils. There is a table of items at the beginning.

Pa-pien lei-tsuan 八編類纂 (also called **Ching-shih pa-pien lei-tsuan** 經世八編類纂, and **Pa-pien ching-shih lei-tsuan** 八編經世類纂), 285 *chüan*. Compiled by Ch'en Jen-hsi 陳仁錫, compiler's preface dated 1626. (1) Block-print edition of about the same time. 100 *ts'e*. (2) Taipei: Hua-wen shu-chü, 1968. 8 vols. 4687 pp.

This is a combination of eight earlier compilations of practical material on political affairs: *Ta-hsüeh yen-i pu* 大學衍義補, *Shih-tsuan tso-pien* 史纂左編, [*Shih-tsuan*] *yu-pien* [史纂] 右編, *Pai-pien*, *T'u-shu pien*, *Han-shih pien* 函史編, *Shih-yung pien* 實用編, and *Ching-chi lei-pien*. All of the original items are preserved, although obviously some of the material must have been omitted. The items are classified and arranged under thirty-six section headings. The *Pa-pien lei-tsuan* is much easier to use than any of the works included in it because of the more careful arrangement of the material; and in it the location in the earlier work from which material has been copied is always carefully specified. The prefaces of all eight are reprinted in the first *ts'e*, and the text is punctuated throughout. At the end of each paragraph there is a summarizing sentence, and brief criticisms by Ch'en Jen-hsi are occasionally placed in the top margin. The work was intended as a practical guide for those dealing with the problems of government and society, and since it was compiled by Ming scholars it contains more useful material from that period than from any other, although it contains some material dating from earliest historical times. The work was proscribed in its entirety during the literary inquisition of the Ch'ien-lung period.

Ku-chin hao-i-lun 古今好議論, 10 *chüan*. Compiled by Lü I-ching 呂一經 (*chin-shih*, 1631). Block-print edition of about 1641. 10 *ts'e*.

This is a collection of quotations chosen from among the most important expressions of ideas and opinions written between the beginning of the Han dynasty and the end of the Ming. It is divided into two sections: the first, of twenty-two items, deals with the classics and philosophers, and with miscellaneous subjects; the second, of twenty-four items each dealing with a different branch of government, is devoted to political theory. Each item is made up entirely of long quotations, of which there are 556 in the whole work, and each quotation is followed by a detailed reference to its source. The critical marginal notes of the compiler are concerned only with the literary style. There is a table of items at the beginning.

Huang-ch'ao chang-ku hui-pien 皇朝掌故彙編, 100 *chüan*. Compiled by Chang Shou-yung 張壽鏞 (1879–19 ?) and others. (1) Ch'iu-shih shu-she 求實書社 movable-type edition of 1902. 60 *ts'e*. (2) Taipei: Wen-hai ch'u-pan she, 1964. 3 vols. 12, 1881 pp.

This work is divided into a *nei-pien* 內編 of forty sections and a *wai-pien* 外編 of forty-five sections. The *nei-pien* deals with internal political affairs, from the beginning of the Ch'ing dynasty down to about 1900, and the *wai-pien* with foreign affairs for the same period. The material included was derived from the *Sheng-hsün* 聖訓, the *Huang-ch'ao san-t'ung*, the *Tung-hua lu* 東華錄, and other works of similar nature, although sources are seldom indicated. There is a table of sections at the beginning of each *pien*.

Huang-ch'ao cheng-tien lei-tsuan 皇朝政典類纂, 500 *chüan*. Compiled by Hsi Yü-fu 席裕福 and others, compiler's preface dated 1903. (1) T'u-shu chi-ch'eng chü movable-type edition of 1903. 119 *ts'e*. (2) Taipei: Ch'eng Wen Publishing Co., 1969. 30 vols. 14,796 pp.

This work, concerned with political, social, and diplomatic affairs from the beginning of the Ch'ing dynasty down to about 1900, is divided into twenty-two sections and 132 items. Material was derived from the *Ta-Ch'ing hui-tien* 大清會典, the *Huang-ch'ao san-t'ung*, the *Sheng-hsün* 聖訓, the *Tung-hua lu* 東華錄, the *Peking Gazette* 邸鈔, and also from memorials to the throne, biographies, gazetteers, and the collected writings of individuals. The source of every quotation is indicated, and there are a table of sections and a list of the works quoted from at the beginning. This work is of more importance to Ch'ing scholars than the *Huang-ch'ao chang-ku hui-pien* because it contains more material and because the sources are more carefully indicated. However, the other work is better classified, and the material on certain subjects is more lucidly presented.

Hsiu-chen hsin liu-fa ch'üan-shu 袖珍新六法全書. Compiled by Kuo Wei 郭衛. Shanghai: Hui-wen-t'ang hsin-chi shu-chü 會文堂新記書局, 1946. [14] 752 pp.

This handbook purports to contain a complete collection of the latest official versions of the six classes of modern Chinese laws: the constitution, civil law, criminal law, commercial law, law of civil procedure, and law of criminal procedure. Actually it also includes laws concerning the income tax, the census, sales stamps, and criminal affairs in connection with American military personnel in China. There is a thumb-index and a detailed table of contents, as well as various useful appendixes.

F. COLLECTIONS OF ANECDOTES AND STORIES

The two encyclopedias described in this subsection are collections of anecdotes, short stories, fables, etc. While they are of considerable interest to students of folk-lore and fiction, they are of even greater interest to historians, for they contain much valuable supplementary historical material.

★**T'ai-p'ing kuang-chi** 太平廣記, 500 *chüan*. Compiled under Imperial auspices by Li Fang 李昉 and others; ordered in 977 and finished the next year. (1) Hsü Tzu-ch'ang 許自昌 block-print edition of the Ming Chia-ching period. 32 *ts'e*. (2) Huang Hsiao-feng 黃曉峯 small-sized block-print edition of 1753. 40 *ts'e*. +(3) Peiping: Wen-yu-t'ang 文友堂 photoprint of a Ming edition, 1934. 60 *ts'e*. (4) Peking: Jen-min wen-hsüeh ch'u-pan she, 1959. 5 vols. (5) Taipei: Hsin-hsing shu-chü, 1958. 3 vols. 972 pp.

This encyclopedia was compiled to make available a large amount of useful information not generally included in orthodox writings. It contains many quotations from weird tales and stories of the supernatural, although there is also much material on political institutions, customs, names of things, etc. The work is divided into ninety-two sections, most of which are subdivided into numerous items. Quotations are taken mainly from historical fiction, short stories, and other writings of a miscellaneous nature, although there are also some extracts from the dynastic histories. Sources are indicated in all but about 150 of the items. Many famous novels and short stories have been re-collected from this encyclopedia, although the re-collecting unfortunately has been carelessly done, with the result that not all the parts actually scattered through the *T'ai-p'ing kuang-chi* have been brought together again. Besides its value as a repertory of important works which otherwise would have been lost, this encyclopedia is a great source of material on the social history of early China, and also a valuable supplement to the official dynastic histories from the Chin 晉 to the Sung. At the beginning there is a bibliography listing 343 titles, although in reality there are quotations from 475 books in the body of the work. Of these, 240 have since been lost. There is a table of items at the beginning and a table of the items included therein at the beginning of each *chüan*. The Harvard-Yenching Institute has published an index.[12]

12. **T'ai-p'ing kuang-chi p'ien-mu chi yin-shu yin-te** 太平廣記篇目及引書引得. Compiled by Ssu-yü Teng 鄧嗣禹. (1) Peiping: Harvard-Yenching Institute, 1934. (Index No. 15) xi, 60, 43 pp. (2) Taipei: Ch'eng Wen Publishing Co., 1966 (photocopy). A *kuei-hsieh* index to item headings and to the titles of works quoted from.

Ch'ing-pai lei-ch'ao 清稗類鈔. Compiled by Hsü K'o 徐珂, compiler's preface dated 1917. (1) Shanghai: Commercial Press, 1917. 48 *ts'e*. (2) Taipei: Commercial Press, 1966. 12 vols. 12, 8544, 13 pp.

This is a collection of material derived from stories, anecdotes, fables, and similar sources, it being Hsü K'o's purpose to do for the Ch'ing dynasty what the compilers of the *T'ai-p'ing kuang-chi* did for the pre-Sung period. The material included is, for the most part, *yeh-shih* 野史, and as such must be used with great caution, but still it may be regarded as a valuable supplement to the contents of more orthodox works. There are ninety-two sections, and the items are arranged chronologically under each, the material presented dating from 1644 down to 1908. Practically every subject of interest is included, although possibly the work is of more use to the sociologist than to anyone else. Although sources are never indicated, the compiler says that some of the material is quoted from works in his own library, some is the result of his own observations, and some is mere hearsay. There is a table of sections at the beginning of the work and a table of items at the beginning of each section. On the front cover of each *ts'e* are listed the titles of the sections it contains.

G. ENCYCLOPEDIAS USEFUL FOR RAPID REFERENCE

Most of the works described in this subsection were compiled as manuals to be used by those preparing for the civil service examinations. The subject matter is miscellaneous, with more stress laid on political subjects than on any others, and the history of each subject is presented as concisely and clearly as possible, usually with interpretations and criticisms.

Han T'ang shih-chien 漢唐事箋, first collection 前集 12 *chüan*, second collection 後集 8 *chüan*. Written by Chu Li 朱禮 who lived in the Yüan period. (1) Nan-ch'eng Hu Sen 南城胡森 block-print edition of 1822. 4 *ts'e*. (2) *Yüeh-ya-t'ang ts'ung-shu, ts'e* 308–311.

This work was written to provide information for those preparing for the civil service examinations. The first collection, consisting of ninety-nine items, is concerned with the Han dynasty, and the second, of twenty-six items, is concerned with the T'ang dynasty. Material is presented on the official, economic, and military systems, on rites and music, and on other such subjects. Each item is a brief, accurate and very well written essay. Commentaries, consisting largely of quotations, are cleverly arranged in interlinear notes in such a way that whether they are read as part of the text or not there is no violation of the literary style. The essential points in the evolution of the subjects under discussion are clearly pointed out, and the writer contributes a number of original and suggestive ideas. There is a table of items at the beginning of each collection.

Kuang chih-p'ing-lüeh, Hsin-k'o 廣治平略, 新刻, 44 *chüan*. Compiled by
Chu Chien 朱健 (d. 1646) and edited by Ts'ai Fang-ping 蔡方炳, preface
dated 1664. (1) Block-print edition of about 1664. 16 *ts'e*. (2) Block-print
edition between 1723 and 1734. 16 *ts'e*. (3) Hsiao-lang-hsüan-kuan 小琅嬛館
block-print edition (36 *chüan*). 10 *ts'e*. (4) Ssu-ming Ju-ku-chai 四明茹古齋
edition of 1882. 10 *ts'e*.

This work, in forty-four sections each of which is subdivided by dynasties,
is actually an enlargement and rearrangement of Chu Hsi's 朱熹 *Chih-p'ing-
lüeh* 治平略. The purpose of the work is to present general historical surveys
of the various political, social, and economic institutions of China, and there
are also included some sections on literature. Each item is a long essay in which
factual material is briefly presented in the author's own words, followed by
discussions and criticisms, sometimes quoted and sometimes written by Ts'ai.
The principal sources are the *chih* 志 of the dynastic histories, although in
using them, the author was more interested in opinions and ideas than in plain
historical facts. The work, which is punctuated throughout and provided with
a table of items at the beginning, is a useful introduction to material on the
development of Chinese political, social, and economic systems.

Jih-yung pai-k'o ch'üan-shu, Ch'ung-pien 日用百科全書, 重編. Compiled
by Huang Shao-hsü 黃紹緒 and others. Shanghai: Commercial Press, 1934.
3 vols. [11] 6221 [170] pp.

This encyclopedia for every day use closely follows the style of Western
encyclopedias and presents material on almost every conceivable subject of
current interest. It was first compiled by Wang Yen-lun 王言綸 and others in
1919, but the present edition represents a complete revision of the earlier one.
The articles which make up this edition are classified under thirty section
headings, and among the general subjects treated of are the natural and physical sciences, the arts, the social sciences, industry and commerce, agriculture,
and communications. The work is based upon a wide selection of books,
magazines, and newspapers, both Chinese and foreign, but sources are very
seldom indicated in the text. As a rule each article gives the historical background of the particular subject under discussion and traces its evolution to
the end of 1933. Modern conditions and implications are stressed, and explanations are frequently supplemented by charts and statistical tables. There is a
table of sections at the beginning of the first volume, and a four-corner index
at the end of the third volume.

Chung-kuo li-shih ts'an-k'ao t'u-p'u 中國歷史參考圖譜. Compiled by
Cheng Chen-to 鄭振鐸 (1897–1958). Shanghai: Ch'u-pan kung-ssu 出版
公司, 1947–1951. 24 *ts'e*.

This is a pictorial history of China, prepared for use in visual education classes in high schools and colleges. The first *ts'e* illustrates earliest China; the second the Yin or Shang dynasty; the third and fourth, Chou; the fifth, Ch'in; the sixth and seventh, Former and Later Han and the Three Kingdoms; the eighth and ninth, Western and Eastern Chin and the Southern and Northern Dynasties; the tenth to twelfth Sui, T'ang, and the Five Dynasties; the thirteenth to fifteenth, Sung; the sixteenth and seventeenth, Yüan; the eighteenth to twentieth, Ming; and the last four, Ch'ing. Each *ts'e* consists of 24 pages, with 80 illustrations. The pictures show historical relics, portraits of famous persons, tomb tablets, vessels and utensils, coins, costumes, paintings, calligraphy, oracle bones, wood carvings, scrolls, rare books, sculpture, stone inscriptions, pottery and porcelain, embroideries and silks, and other objects which illustrate the cultural life of China. In general, the selections appear to have been well made, and the source of each picture is carefully indicated. The material has been collected from five or six hundred Chinese, Japanese, and Western sources, and reproduced by the photolithographic process. Each set of pictures is accompanied by a booklet which summarizes the history of the period and the significance of each picture. The style of the summaries is simple and clear, though not always fluent, and they are not entirely free from misinterpretation.

III DICTIONARIES

The works described in this section are of three types: dictionaries which give the pronunciation and meaning of individual characters and phrases, etymological dictionaries and other philological works helpful to students who are seeking facility in the use of the Chinese language, and dictionaries concerned with special fields. The works included represent only a small proportion of the number available, it being the intention of the compilers to present only the more important ones of each type.

A. DICTIONARIES OF WORDS AND PHRASES

The dictionaries described in this subsection give the meaning and usage and often the pronunciation of characters and phrases. The *K'ang-hsi tzu-tien* is the model upon which almost all later dictionaries have been based, the *Chung-hua ta-tzu-tien* is the largest modern dictionary of single characters, and the *Chung-wen ta-tz'u-tien* and the *Dai Kan-Wa jiten* are the largest modern dictionaries of words and phrases. The *Tz'u-hai* is probably the most widely used phrase dictionary today.

★**K'ang-hsi tzu-tien** 康熙字典. Compiled under Imperial auspices by Chang Yü-shu 張玉書 (1642–1711), Ch'en T'ing-ching 陳廷敬 and others, and completed in 1716. +(1) Palace block-print edition of 1716. 40 *ts'e*. +(2) T'ung-wen shu-chü lithographic edition of 1887. 6 *ts'e*. (3) Commercial Press movable-type edition. 6 *ts'e* or 1 vol. (4) Peking: Chung-hua shu-chü, 1958. [71] 1562, 2, 47 pp. Photocopy of T'ung-wen edition. (5) Revised edition by Watanabe Atsushi 渡部溫 (1837–1898), Taipei: I-wen yin-shu kuan, 1965. 2 vols. 6, 3598 pp.

The *K'ang-hsi tzu-tien* has been the standard Chinese dictionary for more than two hundred and fifty years, the Emperor K'ang-hsi having ordered its compilation in 1710. It was partly based upon two earlier dictionaries, the *Tzu-hui* 字彙 of Mei Ying-tso 梅膺祚 (preface dated 1615), and the *Cheng-tzu t'ung* 正字通 of Chang Tzu-lieh 張自烈 (originally published in 1627). The characters in the *K'ang-hsi tzu-tien* are grouped under 214 radicals, and under each radical the characters are arranged in the order of the number of strokes in the part not included in the radical. The dictionary proper is divided into twelve sections, each of which is identified by a character which indicates the number of strokes in the radicals of the characters included in it. *Tzu* 子 has one- and two-stroke radicals, *ch'ou* 丑 and *yin* 寅 three-stroke radicals, *mao* 卯, *ch'en* 辰 and *ssu* 巳 four-stroke radicals, *wu* 午 five-stroke radicals, *wei* 未 and *shen* 申 six-stroke radicals, *yu* 酉 seven-stroke radicals, *hsü* 戌 eight-and nine-stroke radicals, and *hai* 亥 radicals of ten or more strokes. Each section is subdivided into three parts: *shang* 上, *chung* 中, and *hsia* 下.

Under each character variant forms, if any, are given first, followed by different early *ch'ieh* spellings and the modern pronunciation (*yin*), the latter being indicated by a common character which has the same sound and tone. Finally, the different variations in meaning are explained and each variation is illustrated by a quotation from a well known work. The abbreviated titles of the sources of early *ch'ieh* spellings and of all explanations and illustrations are given immediately after the quotations. Borrowed meanings, shortened forms, and different pronunciations of the same character are always indicated. There are two supplements included in the work, one, 備考, containing characters the meaning, or both the meaning and pronunciation, of which has been lost, and the other, 補遺, containing characters which were inadvertently omitted from the dictionary proper.

According to the *Tzu-tien chi-tzu* 字典紀字 of Wang Chi 汪汲, the *K'ang-hsi tzu-tien*, including its two supplements, lists 49,030 characters. Of these, 1995 are variant forms, leaving a total of 47,035 different characters. Because of K'ang-hsi's demand that the compilation be completed within five years, the work was necessarily somewhat hastily done and many errors were allowed to creep into it. A board set up for the purpose of revision by Emperor Tao-kuang published a supplement in which 2588 mistakes were corrected, for the most part mistakes made in quoting or citing other works.[1] Besides errors, there are many other serious weaknesses, such as the inconvenient arrangement, the complicated and occasionally inaccurate indication of pronunciation, and the frequently illogical classfication of characters under certain radicals. In spite of its age and defects, the *K'ang-hsi tzu-tien* is still an important and useful dictionary. Moreover its choice of radicals and its arrangement of characters have been followed by most dictionaries compiled since. There is a *kuei-hsieh* index to nearly fourteen thousand of its most commonly used characters.[2]

---

1. *Tzu-tien k'ao-cheng* 字典考證, compiled under Imperial auspices by I-hui 奕繪, Wang Yin-chih 王引之 and others. Ai-jih-t'ang 愛日堂 block-print edition of 1831. 6 *ts'e*. Corrections follow the order of the original work and in each case quote both the mistake from the *K'ang-hsi tzu-tien* and the correct version from the original source.

2. **Trindex** 三字典引得. Compiled by Vernon Nash, with material supplied by the Harvard-Yenching Institute Sinological Index Series. (1) Peiping: Index Press, Yenching University, 1936. lxx, 576 pp. (2) Taipei: Ch'eng Wen Publishing Co., 1967. lxx, 584, 6, 10 pp. This is a combined index to the 13,848 characters in Giles' *Chinese-English Dictionary* and to the same characters in the *K'ang-hsi tzu-tien* and in the *P'ei-wen yün-fu*, arranged in numerical sequence according to the *kuei-hsieh* system. Each page is divided into six columns: in the first is the number of the character according to the *kuei-hsieh* system; in the second appears the character itself; in the third there is given the romanization according to the Wade system as used in Giles' *Dictionary*; in the fourth are the number of the radical, the section and sub-

*Chung-hua ta-tzu-tien 中華大字典. Compiled by Hsü Yüan-kao 徐元誥 and others, and published in 1916 by the Chung-hua shu-chü. (1) Large size, fourth printing, 1927. 4 vols. Small size, fourth printing, 1932. 2 vols. Both sizes: [325] [2997] 42 pp. (2) Taipei: Chung-hua shu-chü, 1960. 2 vols. 224, 3044 pp. Facsimile copy of the 1916 edition. (3) Peking: Chung-hua shu-chü, 1958. 3262 pp.

This dictionary of individual characters is the best and the most nearly complete dictionary of its kind that has yet been published. It contains more than 48,000 characters, including a great many which have been invented since the *K'ang-hsi tzu-tien* was compiled. It is based upon that dictionary and is arranged according to its radical system, with some modification. After each character there are generally given the *ch'ieh* spelling which appears in the *Chi-yün* and the modern pronunciation (*yin*), the latter indicated by a well-known character having the same sound and tone. The different meanings of each character are explained in separate numbered columns, each explanation being followed by a quotation which illustrates that particular usage taken from one or another branch of Chinese literature. As many different meanings are given as possible, there sometimes being more than forty for a single character. The sources of all quotations are indicated in detail, those taken second-hand from the *K'ang-hsi tzu-tien* having been carefully checked with the original sources. Different pronunciations of the same character are dealt with separately as though they were different words. After the explanations of all the possible meanings of a single character have been recorded, two-character phrases made up of that character and other closely related characters are frequently added and explained in the same manner as are the individual characters. At the beginning of the work there is an index to all characters, arranged according to the number of strokes.

Although the *Chung-hua ta-tzu-tien* is very comprehensive and is very carefully compiled, three defects should be pointed out. The index is not convenient to use because of the great number of characters listed in each subdivision, for instance, there are 2189 characters which are made up of nine strokes. There are no characters printed in the margin, with the result that it

---

section in the *K'ang-hsi tzu-tien* in which the character appears, the number of strokes in the radical, the radical itself, and the number of strokes in the remainder of the character; the fifth gives the rhyme under which the character is classified in the *P'ei-wen yün-fu;* the sixth gives the number of the character in Giles' *Dictionary*. By looking in the table which appears in Section VI under the rhyme given in the fifth column, the tone and the *chüan* in which the character appears in the *P'ei-wen yün-fu* are to be found. The letter "s" appearing after the number in the sixth column indicates that that character is included in Giles' supplementary list of surnames. Section IV provides a transcription table from the Wade-Giles system of romanization to the French system used in the *Bulletin de l'École Française d'Extême-Orient*. Those who use the *kuei-hsieh* system will find this an extremely convenient handbook.

is very difficult to locate characters by radical in the body of the work. Finally, a two-character phrase may be placed under either of the characters, frequently making it necessary to look for it under both. These defects are of comparatively little consequence, however, and they can scarcely be considered as seriously detracting from the general excellence of the dictionary. The 1958 Peking edition is legible though the type is small and the binding is weak.

Tz'u-yüan 辭源. Compiled by Lu Erh-k'uei 陸爾奎 and others, and published by the Commercial Press in 1915. Large size, 12 *ts'e* or 2 vols.; medium and small size, 2 vols. [15] [2974] [98] pp. **Tz'u-yüan hsü-pien** 辭源續編. Compiled by Fang I 方毅 and others. Commercial Press, 1931. [14] [1568] [120] pp.

The *Tz'u-yüan* is the earliest modern Chinese phrase dictionary, and it is based chiefly upon material derived from the *K'ang-hsi tzu-tien* and the *Ching-chi tsuan-ku*. Individual characters are arranged in the same order as in the *K'ang-hsi tzu-tien*, and following each character the *ch'ieh* spelling, a common character with the same sound and tone which indicates the modern pronunciation (*yin*), and the modern rhyme are given in heavy parentheses. Then a few of the more common meanings of the word are given, often with brief quotations from well known writings as illustrations. The phrases are grouped under their first character, and are arranged first according to the number of characters in the phrase, and second according to the radical system. Varied meanings of phrases are explained separately, and these are often illustrated by quotations. Besides ordinary phrases, the titles of books, modern technical terms, and Chinese and foreign personal and place names are included. The supplementary volume is made up of new terms invented after the first two volumes were compiled, and of terms accidentally omitted from them. The *Tz'u-yüan* is far from exhaustive, and most of its illustrative quotations were taken from secondary sources without being checked. The sources of quotations are cited very briefly in the main work and in detail in the supplement. At the beginning of the first volume there is an index to radicals and a table of characters difficult to find. Only 9952 different characters are used in the *Tz'u-yüan* and 5662 in the *Hsü-pien*; most of the latter also appear in the main work.

Tz'u-yüan cheng-hsü-pien ho-ting-pen 辭源正續編合訂本. Compiled by Fang I 方毅 and others. (1) Shanghai: Commercial Press, 1939. [12] 1739 [205] pp. (2) Changsha: Commercial Press, 1950. 982, [16] 143 pp. (3) Taipei: Commercial Press, 1968. 6, 1739, 216 pp.

This is a combination of the *Tz'u-yüan* and the *Tz'u-yüan hsü-pien* in which duplications are eliminated, errors corrected, and some new characters added. At the end there is an index to all characters and phrases, arranged by the four-corner system, and a list of changes in place names during the Republican period. While this combination is easier to use than its predecessors, the characters are very small, and the work of combining was done so hastily that some errors still remain. Moreover, the translations of many new terms derived from Western languages are not given. For these reasons the work is inferior to the *Tz'u-hai*. The publisher of the 1950 edition claims to have omitted hundreds of obsolete translations and seldom-used phrases and to have added new terms.

★Chung-wen ta-tz'u-tien 中文大辭典. Compiled by a commission with Chang Ch'i-yün 張其昀 as chief editor and Lin Yin 林尹 and Kao Ming 高明 as editors. Taipei: Institute of Advanced Chinese Studies 中國文化研究所, 1962–1968. 38 vols., plus 2 index vols.

The Encyclopedic Dictionary of the Chinese Language is probably the most complete and the best Chinese dictionary in existence. The evolution of each character is given from its earliest known to its latest pre-modern form, the sound is indicated, and sources are given in chronological order. The entries under each character and phrase are unusually rich, even more so in many cases than are those in Morohashi Tetsuji's *Dai Kan-Wa jiten*,[3] upon which it appears to be partly based. The characters are arranged according to the radical system, and numbered consecutively from 1 to 49,905 (including a page of addenda at the end of volume 38). Under each character the phrases which it begins are arranged according to the number of strokes in the second and (if more than two) third and subsequent characters. There are many phrases under some characters, for example 3,417 under 一, the first in the dictionary, and 1,398 under 黃, in volume 38. At the beginning of each volume there is a radical index to the characters therein, and these are brought together for all 38 volumes in the 39th. The 40th volume is a number-of-strokes index to all characters.

★Tz'u-hai 辭海. Compiled by Shu Hsin-ch'eng 舒新城 and others. (1) Shanghai: Chung-hua shu-chü, 1938. 2 vols. [12] [1903]; [1495] [379] pp. (2) Taipei: Chung-hua shu-chü, 1956. 2 vols. [13] [1903]; [1495] [376] pp.

3. **Dai Kan-Wa jiten** 大漢和辭典. Compiled by Morohashi Tetsuji 諸橋轍次. (Tokyo: Taishūkan shoten 大修館書店, 1957–1960). 13 vols. Text: 13,757 pp.; index vol. 1101 pp. This outstanding Sino-Japanese dictionary of Chinese characters and phrases is particularly strong for poetry and classical literature and for its biographical notices of historical figures; it is weakest on Buddhist terms. A total of 49,964 characters are described, including variant forms, and sources are indicated more accurately than in more popular dictionaries. There are four indexes: by the number of strokes, by Japanese *on* readings, by Japanese *kun* readings, and by the four-corner system. Besides these four indexes, the thirteenth volume supplies lists of 1062 additional characters, the official list of 1850 "characters for daily use" used in Japan, and the 517 abbreviated characters used in the People's Republic of China.

In this outstanding dictionary the phrases are assembled under their initial characters, which are themselves arranged according to the system of the *K'ang-hsi tzu-tien*. Their second and later characters are arranged in order according to the number of strokes. In addition to a definition, if the phrase is an old one its use will be illustrated by one or more quotations from named sources. The initial characters are also defined and their pronunciation indicated. There is a table of characters at the beginning of the first volume, arranged by the number of strokes, and on the end papers of each volume there are indexes to the K'ang-hsi radicals. Among the appendixes are a *kuo-yin* pronunciation table of common characters and an index to the translations of foreign nouns and names.

*Kuo-yü tz'u-tien 國語辭典. Compiled by the Chung-kuo ta-tz'u-tien pien-tsuan-ch'u 中國大辭典編纂處 under the auspices of the Ministry of Education of the Chinese Government. Compilers' prefaces dated 1936. (1) Shanghai: Commercial Press, 1937. 8 vols. [31] 4485 [220] pp. (2) Taipei: Commercial Press, 1953. 4 vols. [66] 4485 [361] pp. (3) Hong Kong: Commercial Press, 1961. 8, 1254, 27 pp. (4) **Han-yü tz'u-tien** 漢語辭典. Shanghai: Commercial Press, 1957. 18, 1254, 27 pp.

This is a dictionary of words and phrases arranged according to the Chinese phonetic alphabet. Special attention is said to have been paid to correct pronunciation and to explanations in a simple and clear-cut *pai-hua* style. The most common form of each character is used, but abbreviated and alternative forms are also given. Under each character or phrase the pronunciation is indicated, first in Chinese phonetic symbols, then in a romanization similar to the Y. R. Chao system; there is also a brief explanation of the meaning. At the top of each page appear the romanized and phonetic symbols for the words below. The last volume contains an index arranged according to the phonetic alphabet and another by the system of the *K'ang-hsi tzu-tien*. In addition, there are a brief list of terms and proper names from Western languages and Sanskrit arranged alphabetically with Chinese transliterations, lists of chemical elements, measurements, and Chinese emperors with their reign titles, and a Western calendar. Editions (3) and (4) are abridgements of the original edition.

Wang Yün-wu ta-tz'u-tien 王雲五大辭典. Compiled by Wang Yün-wu 王雲五. (1) Shanghai: Commercial Press, 1928. 1384, 154, 45, 53 pp. (2) Hong Kong: Wan-t'ung shu-tien 萬通書店, 1963. 5, 1384, 40, 44, 53 pp.

This combined dictionary of single characters and phrases is arranged according to the four-corner system. The National Language pronunciation of each character is indicated in the National phonetic script, in the National

Romanization, and by a common character, placed in parentheses, which has the same sound and tone. The very brief explanations of the different meanings of the single characters are grouped under each character by parts of speech, and following each explanation there is an equally brief example of that particular usage. Different pronunciations of the same character are given separate treatment. The phrases are always arranged under the first character, in the numerical order of the second character according to the four-corner system. The number of phrases included in this dictionary is astonishingly large considering its size, and the explanations of phrases are as succinct and simple as are those of the individual characters, though it is not free from mistakes. In the appendix there are thirty-one lists and tables, among them a list of English terms with their Chinese equivalents. At the end there is an index to characters, arranged first according to the number of strokes and then by radicals, in which both page numbers and four-corner numbers are given.

Chung-hua ch'eng-yü tz'u-tien 中華成語辭典. Compiled by Wu Lien-ming 吳廉銘. (1) Shanghai: Chung-hua shu-chü, 1936. [23], 723 pp. (2) Taipei: Chung-hua shu-chü, 1956. 21, 721 pp.

This is a dictionary of Chinese idiomatic phrases, technical terms, and peculiar expressions. The brief definitions are in simple *pai-hua*, and their sources are given. The entries are arranged by number of strokes, and characters having the same number of strokes are arranged within their groups by the *K'ang-hsi tzu-tien* system. At the beginning there is an index to the first characters of the phrases. There are six short appendixes, including one on the use of punctuation marks in modern Chinese.

Ching-chi tsuan-ku 經籍纂詁, 106 *chüan*, with a supplement. Compiled by Juan Yüan 阮元 and others, and completed in 1798. (1) Lang-hsüan hsien-kuan 琅環僊館 block-print edition of the Chia-ch'ing period. 8 *ts'e*. (2) Undated lithographic edition of the Hung-chang shu-chü 鴻章書局. 12 *ts'e*. (3) Shanghai: Kuo-hsüeh cheng-li she 國學整理社, 1936. [82] 1072 pp. (4) Taipei: Shih-chieh shu-chü, 1956. [82] 1072 pp.

This is a dictionary of characters used in the classics. A board of about forty scholars, set up for the purpose at the end of the eighteenth century, gathered all relevant explanations and illustrative examples from almost a hundred works, including the classics themselves and commentaries on them, histories, important philosophic writings, and other works written before the middle of the T'ang dynasty. The collected material is arranged under the proper individual characters. The meaning of each character is indicated by a more common character, after which full extracts are quoted to demonstrate

its use, with sources cited in detail. The characters themselves are arranged
·according to their rhyme, and different meanings of a character are treated
separately. This is a very convenient dictionary for students of the classics or
of any type of pre-T'ang writing, for while the work is by no means exhaustive, there is gathered into it a great deal of useful material on the ancient
meanings of characters. There is an index to characters at the beginning of
the Hung-chang shu-chü edition, arranged by radicals, and an index to characters, including variant forms, in the 1936 and 1956 editions.

Chung-kuo wen-hsüeh ta-tz'u-tien 中國文學大辭典. Compiled by Chiang
Heng-yüan 江恒源 and Yüan Shao-ku 袁少谷. Taipei: Wen-hai ch'u-pan-
she, 1967. 3, 8 [1002] pp.

The initial characters of the phrases in this dictionary of Chinese literature
are arranged according to the system of the *K'ang-hsi tzu-tien*. Each phrase
is succinctly explained, and the sources of examples are given. Though the
work is not bulky, its contents are unusually rich, particularly in historical
terms. It was published originally in Shanghai, as the **Kuo-wen ch'eng-yü
tz'u-tien** 國文成語辭典. The real author's name is Chuang Shih 莊適.

Shih-tz'u ch'ü-yü tz'u hui-shih 詩詞曲語辭匯釋. Compiled by Chang
Hsiang 張相. (1) Hong Kong: Chung-hua shu-chü, 1962. 788 pp. (2) Taipei:
Chung-hua shu-chü, 1962. 4, 782 pp. (3) **Shih-tz'u ch'ü-yü tz'u-tien**
詩詞曲語辭典. Taipei: I-wen yin-shu-kuan, 1957. 10, 16, 730 pp.

There are many dictionaries of classical Chinese but few of colloquial
literature. Chang Hsiang's scholarly compilation is devoted to the explanation
of local expressions in the poetry, fiction, and drama of the T'ang, Sung,
Chin, Yüan, and Ming periods. In his avid reading he confronted a large
number of phrases which were hard to understand and to comment upon.
Spending years on this work, he accumulated numerous similar examples
and undertook to establish definitions which would explain the peculiar
usages. The third edition listed seems less close to Chang Hsiang's original
manuscript than the other two, evidently having undergone some changes
in the original order. There is a full list of terms at the beginning of each edition.

Hsiao-shuo tz'u-yü hui-shih 小說辭語彙釋. Compiled by Lu Tan-an 陸澹
安. Shanghai: Chung-hua shu-chü, 1964. 2, 2, 172, 916 pp.

This is a phrase dictionary of colloquial expressions used in Chinese novels
written from the Yüan to the end of the Ch'ing dynasty. All entries (estimated
8400) are listed at the beginning of the volume, arranged by the number of
strokes. Each entry is given a simple definition followed by a quotation, with
indication of source.

Yüan-ch'ü su-yü fang-yen shih-li 元曲俗語方言釋例. Compiled by Chu Chü-i 朱居易. Shanghai: Commercial Press, 1956. 350 pp.

This is a dictionary of about one thousand colloquial and slang expressions used in the dramas of the Yüan dynasty. Some two hundred of the items also appear in Chang Hsiang's *Shih-tz'u chü-yü tz'u hui-shih* (q.v.), but with different illustrations. Under each phrase is given a simple definition with its equivalent in literary Chinese, or an explanation followed by a few examples with indication of sources. There is a four-corner index.

Tz'u-t'ung 辭通. Compiled by Chu Ch'i-feng 朱起鳳. (1) Shanghai: K'ai-ming shu-tien, 1934. 2 vols. [44] 2847, 362 pp. (2) Taipei: K'ai-ming shu-tien, 1960. 2 vols. 65, 2814, 340 pp.

This is a dictionary of variant forms of names, historical and classical terms, and literary phrases. These are collected from all branches of Chinese literature, and all variations of any one term or phrase are grouped under its most commonly used form. The most commonly used key forms are arranged in the dictionary according to the rhyme of the final character. Under each variant, sentences are quoted to illustrate its proper, and often improper, use. Thus the compiler, by comparing the different forms, is able to determine and point out different shades of meaning. The compiler's notes, which are clear and concise, show the result of long years of careful research, and although there are some mistakes, and no Buddhist terms are included, this is a very useful guide to literary allusions as well as to other names and phrases. The sources of all quotations are indicated in full, and there are two indexes: one to all terms, arranged according to the four-corner system, and the other to first characters, arranged according to the number of strokes.

Li-tai hui-tzu p'u 歷代諱字譜, 2 *chüan*; **Chia-hui k'ao** 家諱考, 1 *chüan*. Compiled by Chang Wei-hsiang 張惟驤, compiler's preface dated 1928. Hsiao shuang-ch'i-an 小雙寂庵 block-print edition of 1931. 2 *ts'e*.

The main part of this work lists characters which were forbidden during a particular dynasty because they occurred in the personal names of emperors of that dynasty or, in some dynasties, in the reign titles, the names of members of the imperial family, or the names of imperial tombs. When a character was declared taboo, either another having the same sound or meaning was chosen to be used in its place, or the original character was used with one stroke omitted. In this work the characters are arranged in two tables, the taboo characters being placed first in one and the substitute characters first in the other. In both tables the characters are arranged according to their rhyme, and under each the reason for the prohibition and brief illustrations of the proper use of the substitute are given. The *Chia-hui k'ao* lists characters which were avoided by certain writers because of their occurrence in the names of their parents or grandparents. While this work is not exhaustive, it is the most satisfactory work of its kind available.[4]

Tzu-pien 字辨. Compiled by Ku Hsiung-tsao 顧雄藻. Shanghai: Sheng-huo shu-tien, 1933. [14] [236] pp. **Tzu-pien pu-i** 字辨補遺. Compiled by Yang Hsieh-ling 楊燮酈. Shanghai: Sheng-huo shu-tien, 1935. 21, 176 pp.

This is a guide to the correct use of characters which are frequently misused. It was compiled with the intention of helping students to distinguish between characters which have a very slight difference in meaning, characters which are pronounced in more than one way (each pronunciation having a different meaning), and characters which may be written in different ways; it also explains many literary allusions which are often misread and misused. The work is divided into twenty-three sections, within which the characters are roughly arranged according to the radical system. Pairs of characters which are commonly confused are grouped together, the definition and proper pronunciation of each are given, their misuse is explained, and many examples are given of their correct usage. Even though the *Tzu-pien* is rather inconveniently arranged and also contains a number of errors, it is a very useful guide to correct usage. The supplement, compiled by one of Ku's students, is arranged in much the same way and adds characters omitted from the original work. There is an index to characters at the beginning of each, arranged according to the radical system.

Tzu-pieh tz'u-tien 字別辭典. Compiled by T'ao Yu-pai 陶友白. Shanghai: San-chiang shu-tien 三江書店, 1936. [6] 226 [56] pp.

This dictionary of characters which present special difficulties consists of three parts: distinctions of meaning, distinctions of forms, distinctions of pronunciation. It also contains three appendixes: a list of characters which are commonly used in abbreviated form, a list of commonly used characters which are sometimes written in archaic form in modern literature, and a list of miscellaneous words which are used in daily speech but which many people do not know how to write correctly. Finally there is an index to the approximately two thousand characters, arranged by number of strokes. This dictionary was compiled for the use of high school students and grade school teachers. The entries have been selected with a view to correcting common errors and eliminating difficulties frequently met with, and the *pai-hua* explanations are simple and clear.

4. See *Shih-hui chü-li* 史諱舉例, by Ch'en Yüan 陳垣. Peking: Chung-hua shu-chü, 1962. 175 pp

B. DICTIONARIES OF NEW TERMS

Many new terms have been introduced into recent Chinese literature. Some of them are easily understandable, but many others need definition. Two dictionaries useful for this purpose are listed below.

Hsien-tai yü tz'u-tien 現代語辭典. Compiled by Li Ting-sheng 李鼎聲. Shanghai: Kuang-ming shu-chü 光明書局, first edition 1933, eighth edition 1941. [77] 722 pp.

This is a dictionary of about 5000 modern Chinese terms relating to the social and natural sciences, philosophy, literature, and international relations. Under each term the corresponding English term and a brief explanation is furnished. This dictionary is useful for students of modern Chinese, especially for those concerned with the literature of the social sciences, where the adaptation of Western terms has been very common.

Hsien-tai yung-yü ta tz'u-tien 現代用語大辭典. Compiled by Chang I-ch'ü 張一渠. Hong Kong: Chung-kuo ch'u-pan kung-ssu 中國出版公司, 1956. [4] 6, 714 pp.

This dictionary of new terms used elsewhere than on the mainland, is divided into twelve sections: international, political, military, economic, legal, educational, social, scientific, historical, geographic, literary, and fine arts. Explanations are brief—from two to twelve characters in length—but to the point. The use of large print for the terms defined and inclusion of a number-of-strokes index facilitate consultation, even though sources are not indicated. Another edition, which omits the compiler's name, was published the same year by the Tung-ya hua-pao she 東亞畫報社.

C. ETYMOLOGICAL AND CALLIGRAPHISTS' DICTIONARIES

The *Shuo-wen*, which is the basic Chinese etymological dictionary, has been the object of much study and annotation since the beginning of the Sung dynasty, especially during the Ch'ing period. The first work described below is a comprehensive and widely used annotated edition of the *Shuo-wen* in a convenient size. The second is a collation of practically all the available material on the *Shuo-wen* and is the largest and best dictionary of its kind that has been published in China. These are followed by works described as guides to the correct writing of various styles of Chinese script, and finally there are guides to the abbreviated forms of characters, including the official abbreviations authorized by the People's Government.

Shuo-wen chieh-tzu chu 說文解字注, 15 *chüan*, each divided into two parts; supplement: **Liu-shu yin-yün piao** 六書音韻表, 2 *chüan*. Compiled by Hsü Shen 許慎, and annotated by Tuan Yü-ts'ai 段玉裁 (1735–1815). (1) Hupeh: Ch'ung-wen shu-chü 湖北崇文書局 block-print edition of 1872. 20 *ts'e*. (2) Shanghai: Sheng-wen shu-chü 上海盛文書局 lithographic edition of 1914, with a supplement: **Shuo-wen t'ung-chien** 說文通檢 by Li Yung-ch'un 黎永椿. 8 *ts'e*. (3) *Ssu-pu pei-yao*, 12 *ts'e*. (4) Taipei: I-wen yin-shu-kuan, 1955. 3, 877 pp. (5) Peking: Chung-hua shu-chü, 1963. 5, 328, 62 pp., with a number-of-strokes index. (6) *Kuo-hsüeh chi-pen ts'ung-shu*. 18 *ts'e*. (7) Taipei: Ssu-k'u shan-pen ts'ung-shu kuan 四庫善本叢書館, 1959, containing a photocopy of a Sung edition of the *Shuo-wen chieh-tzu* from the Seikadō 靜嘉堂 collection. 4 vols.

The **Shuo-wen chieh-tzu** 說文解字 (better known as the **Shuo-wen** 說文), which was compiled by Hsü Shen about A.D. 100, is the earliest Chinese etymological dictionary. It originally was divided into fifteen *p'ien* 篇, but each of these was later subdivided into two parts. According to Hsü's postface, there were originally 9353 different characters (besides 1163 variant forms) arranged under 540 radicals, although in modern editions there are 9431 different characters and 1279 variants. In the *Shuo-wen* the characters appear in the "seal" 篆文 form, and under each character the "greater seal" 籀文 form is also given if there is one, and the sound is frequently indicated by another character which at the time of compilation had the same pronunciation. The *ch'ieh* spelling, which is based upon the *T'ang-yün*, was added by later scholars. For each character a very brief explanation of its structure and meaning is given, the latter usually consisting of material quoted from other sources. One of the great specialists on the *Shuo-wen* was Tuan Yü-ts'ai, of the Ch'ing period. He collected the comments made by earlier scholars and after adding the results of his own research in the form of commentaries, he published them under the title: *Shuo-wen chieh-tzu chu*. Many revolutionary ideas were introduced by Tuan, although at many points his interpretations are too dogmatic.

*Shuo-wen chieh-tzu ku-lin 說文解字詁林. Compiled by Ting Fu-pao 丁福保, compiler's preface dated 1928. (1) Shanghai: I-hsüeh shu-chü 醫學書局, 1928. 66 *ts'e*. **Shuo-wen chieh-tzu ku-lin pu-i** 說文解字詁林補遺. (1) Shanghai: I-hsüeh shu-chü, 1932. 16 *ts'e*. (2) Taipei: Commercial Press, 1959. 12 vols. (photocopy of both works).

The *Shuo-wen chieh-tzu ku-lin* is a collection of all the available material on the *Shuo-wen*, arranged in the order of the original dictionary. The compiler clipped the material which he intended to include, arranged it, and reproduced it by the photolithographic process. Under each of the original *Shuo-*

wen characters relevant material taken from the following works is arranged in the following order: (1) a photolithographic copy of a Sung edition of Hsü Hsüan's 徐鉉 collation of the *Shuo-wen*, (2) a modern edition of Hsü Ch'ien's 徐鍇 collation of the *Shuo-wen*, (3) the *Shuo-wen chieh-tzu chu* by Tuan Yü-ts'ai, (4) the *Shuo-wen chieh-tzu i-cheng* 說文解字義證 by Kuei Fu 桂馥, (5) the *Shuo-wen chieh-tzu chü-tou* 說文解字句讀 and *Shuo-wen shih-li* 說文釋例 by Wang Yün 王筠, (6) the *Shuo-wen t'ung-hsün ting-sheng* 說文通訓定聲 by Chu Chün-sheng 朱駿聲, (7) all other writings on the *Shuo-wen* (107 works), (8) studies of quotations in the *Shuo-wen* taken from the classics and other early writings (21 works), (9) studies of a single character or of a single phrase in the *Shuo-wen*, taken principally from the collected writings of individuals and from modern periodical publications, and (10) characters on stone, bronze, tortoise shell, and bone, with explanations, taken from seven selected works. All prefaces, introductions, and general discussions of either the *Shuo-wen* or of the six ways of word-formation, 六書, are grouped together in the *ch'ien-pien* 前編 at the beginning of the work. Studies of more than two thousand characters which were in use at the time of the compilation of the *Shuo-wen* but which were not included in it are grouped together in the *hou-pien* 後編, and material accidentally left out of the work is placed in the *pu-pien* 補編. After each quotation the source is indicated very briefly, the full titles of the 182 sources being listed together near the beginning of the work. The material on tortoise shell and bone inscriptions is far from adequate, but the work is on the whole an excellent one, representing the fruit of many years of labor on the part of an outstanding specialist. In spite of its bulk, it is conveniently arranged and easy to use. At the end there is an index to all characters, arranged by radicals. The separately published supplement, arranged in the same way, adds material omitted from the main work or published after 1928, and also provides a full bibliography for each of the thirty parts into which the work is divided.

Chung-kuo shu-fa ta-tzu-tien 中國書法大字典. Compiled by Hsieh Tsung-an 謝宗安. Taipei: Chung-hang 中行 shu-chü, 1963. 2, 27, 1459 pp.

This is a dictionary of the various styles of Chinese characters as they were written at different times in Chinese history. The individual characters are arranged in the order of the *K'ang-hsi tzu-tien*, with the *k'ai-shu* (standard) form at the top of a page and other versions in series below, with sources indicated.

Cheng ts'ao li chuan ssu-t'i tzu-hui 正草隸篆四體字彙. Compiled by Shen Ya-kung 沈亞公. Shanghai: Chung-yang shu-tien 中央書店, 1936. [6] 66, 615 pp.

This collection of 4478 different characters gives four forms of each character: standard model, cursive or "grass," square, and seal. According to the compiler, the examples were reproduced on copper plates from photographs of the writing of famous calligraphers, the sources being indicated by the initials of the calligraphers. There is an index to characters at the beginning, arranged by radicals.

Ts'ao-shu ta-tzu-tien 草書大字典 (subtitle: *Li-tai ming-jen fa-t'ieh hui-hsüan* 歷代名人法帖彙選), 24 *chüan*, with a one-*chüan* supplement. Compiled and published in Shanghai by the Sao-yeh shan-fang, 1924. 24 *ts'e*. (2) Taipei: I-wen yin-shu-kuan, 1964. 2 vols. 1790 pp.

In this work, which is more a calligraphist's handbook than a dictionary, are collected examples of the cursive script (*ts'ao-shu* 草書) chosen from the handwriting of more than seven hundred calligraphers who have lived since the beginning of the Han dynasty. Modeled after the *Ts'ao-tzu hui* 草字彙 (compiled by Shih Liang 石梁 in 1787), in which the examples are fewer in number but more accurately reproduced, the *Ts'ao-shu ta-tzu-tien* lists approximately 6070 different characters, which are arranged according to the radical system. Each character appears first written in the standard script (*k'ai-shu* 楷書) and enclosed in a circle; this is followed by selected examples of the cursive script, each example followed by the name, or at least the dynasty, of the writer. These examples, of which there are altogether about 49,500, were reproduced from stone inscriptions and other original or traced records. Because of the wide freedom of self-expression which has always been allowed in the writing of the cursive script, the examples reproduced in this work vary from the so-called running script (*hsing-shu* 行書) which is near enough to the formal style to be quite easily recognized, to forms which are so "grassy" that they are readily recognizable only by a specialist. The formal form and also abbreviated forms (*chien-t'i* 簡體) of each character are printed in the margin opposite the part of the text devoted to it, adding to its convenience as a reference work. At the beginning there is a list of the calligraphers whose handwriting is included, arranged in chronological order, and at the beginning of each *chüan* there is a list of the characters included in it.

Chien-t'i tzu-piao 簡體字表. Compiled by the Tzu-t'i yen-chiu-hui 字體研究會. National Research Institute of Peiping 國立北平研究院, 1935. 94 pp.

This is a list of about 5000 characters, giving the abbreviated, obsolete, alternative, borrowed, or vulgar forms which appear often in modern Chinese literature. Arrangement is according to the outstanding stroke or the stroke that appears first in writing the character.

Chien-t'i tzu-tien 簡體字典. Compiled by Jung Keng 容庚. Peiping: Harvard-Yenching Institute, 1936. 4, 50, 4 pp.

This is a dictionary of frequently abbreviated characters. The correct form is given first, followed by the abbreviated form. The characters are arranged by the number of strokes.

Han-tzu chien-hua piao 漢字簡化表. Hong Kong: Sun kiu Publishing Co. 新僑出版社, 1965. 52 pp.

This is a pocket table of the 515 abbreviated forms of 544 Chinese characters authorized by the People's Government and used on the mainland and by some publishers in Hong Kong and Japan. The abbreviated characters with the corresponding standard forms are arranged by number of strokes, then according to the first stroke from pp. 27–39, and the standard characters with their abbreviated forms are similarly arranged from pp. 40–52. There is also a list of 54 simplified radicals. A more useful dictionary of the new abbreviated characters has been published in English.[5]

D. WORKS ON GRAMMAR

While the works described in this subsection are not dictionaries in the strict sense of the word, the grammatical information they contain makes them indispensable aids to students of the Chinese language.

Ching-chuan shih-tz'u 經傳釋詞, 10 *chüan*. Compiled by Wang Yin-chih 王引之 (1766–1834), compiler's preface dated 1798. (1) *Huang-Ch'ing ching-chieh, ts'e* 305–306. (2) *Shou-shan-ko ts'ung-shu, ts'e* 26–28. (3) Ch'eng-tu shu-chü 成都書局 block-print edition of 1928, with two supplements. 4 *ts'e.* (4) Shanghai: Ch'ün-hsüeh shu-she 羣學書社, 1929. 2 *ts'e.* +(5) Peking: Chung-hua shu-chü, 1956. With supplements. 350 pp. (6) Taipei: Shih-chieh shu-chü, 1956. 4, 132 pp. (7) Taipei: Commercial Press, 1968. 11, 81, 85 pp.

---

5. **Dictionary of Simplified Chinese** 簡體字彙. Compiled by Ronald Hsia [夏冷漪] and Peter Penn [彭錫恩]. Hong Kong: Oriental Book Co., 1959. 122 pp. Tables A and B give the 425 simplified characters authorized by the People's Government at the time of publication. Table A is arranged by the number of strokes, and table B is arranged in the alphabetical order of the new official Latin transcription. In each table, besides the standard form of each character, the official romanization, the Wade-Giles transcription, the radical, and English meanings are given. Appendix 1 lists 116 additional simplified characters that were still in trial circulation at the time of publication, and Appendix 2 lists the 54 simplified radicals. There are indexes by the radical system and by the Wade-Giles transcription.

This study of 160 grammatical particles was made by one of the greatest classical scholars of the Ch'ing dynasty. Under each character he briefly defines varying usages and illustrates each usage with quotations from classics and commentaries written before the end of the Han dynasty, each quotation being followed by his own interpretation. Common and easily understood usages are not given, but early misinterpretations are corrected and many new interpretations based upon the results of a life time of careful study are added. The work was compiled as a guide to the understanding of early texts, but it is also a great aid to the understanding of the same particles as they appear in later writings. At the beginning there is a table of particles in the order in which they appear in the text. Two supplements, published toward the end of the nineteenth century, add further material on fourteen particles and apply Wang's technique to one additional particle.[6]

Chu-tzu pien-lüeh 助字辨略, 5 *chüan*. Compiled by Liu Ch'i 劉淇, earliest dated preface 1711. (1) Hai-yüan-ko 海源閣 re-cut block-print edition of 1855. 5 *ts'e*. (2) Changsha Yang Shu-ta 長沙楊樹達 block-print edition of 1925. 5 *ts'e*. (3) *Kuo-hsüeh chi-pen ts'ung-shu*. (4) Peking: Chung-hua shu-chü, 1954. 8, 10, 315, 12 pp. (5) Taipei: K'ai-ming shu-tien, 1958. 345 pp.

This work on grammatical particles includes adverbs, prepositions, conjunctions, and interjections. The author examined all available classical works and compared all possible cases. The result is that many obscure meanings and commonly mispronounced words are made known and corrected. The book ranks high in Chinese philology. The arrangement is according to rhyme. Besides the main text, supplementary materials are presented in postscripts to the second and third editions.

Ku-shu tu-fa lüeh-li 古書讀法略例, 6 *chüan*. Compiled by Sun Te-ch'ien 孫德謙, compiler's preface dated 1925. Shanghai: Commercial Press, 1936. [9] 372 pp.

This guide to the reading of early Chinese writings deals not only with grammatical difficulties but also with such things as differences in editions, the problem of interpreting tables, the background of authorship, and various methods of study. A general principle is first laid down, followed in each case by selected examples and the compiler's explanations. Although the compiler's point of view tends to be somewhat conservative, the work is well compiled and presents much useful material. There is a table of contents at the beginning.

6. **Ching-chuan shih-tz'u pu** 經傳釋詞補, 1 *chüan;* and **Ching-chuan shih-tz'u tsai-pu** 經傳釋詞再補, 1 *chüan*. Compiled by Sun Ching-shih 孫經世. Ch'ang-chou Chiang Feng-tsao hsin-chü-chai 長洲蔣鳳藻心矩齋 block-print editions of 1888 and 1885 respectively, each 1 *ts'e*.

Ma-shih wen-t'ung 馬氏文通, 10 *chüan*. Compiled by Ma Chien-chung 馬建忠, compiler's preface dated 1898. (1) Shanghai: Commercial Press, 1927. [404] pp. (2) *Kuo-hsüeh chi-pen ts'ung-shu*. 3 *ts'e*. (3) Peking: Chung-hua shu-chü, 1954. 2 vols. 263 pp. (4) Peking: Chung-hua shu-chü, 1961. 2 vols. 22, 558 pp.

This was the first important work to be written in Chinese in which Western rules of grammar were applied to the Chinese language. It is divided into three parts: in the first, the different parts of speech are discussed; in the second, individual characters which have grammatical usages are analyzed; in the third, sentence structure and punctuation are studied. The explanations are simple and clear, and abundant illustrations are drawn from various types of writing from the earliest still extant in China down to that of Han Yü 韓愈, who lived in the T'ang dynasty. Although it contains numerous errors and is rather difficult to use as a rapid reference work, this book is of great assistance in understanding and writing Chinese. The Peking editions include notes by Chang Hsi-shen 章錫琛. There are shorter editions that are more convenient to use.[7]

Tz'u-ch'üan 詞詮, 10 *chüan*, with an appendix. Compiled by Yang Shu-ta 楊樹達. (1) Shanghai: Commercial Press, 1928. [42] [618] pp. (2) Peking: Chung-hua shu-chü, 1954. 626 pp. (3) Taipei: Commercial Press, 1959. [42] [618] pp.

This is a study of those Chinese characters which act in certain connections as prepositions, conjunctions, auxiliary verbs, interjections, or as one or another of the various kinds of pronouns. Many characters have several of these grammatical uses, depending upon their place in the sentence. Under each character the different usages are explained separately, and each is illustrated with quotations from early literature. While the work is probably based to a large extent upon the *Ching-chuan shih-tz'u* and the *Ma-shih wen-t'ung,* much new material has been added. There are two indexes to characters at the beginning, one arranged according to the National phonetic system and the other according to the radical system.

Ku-shu hsü-tzu chi-shih 古書虛字集釋, 10 *chüan*. Compiled by P'ei Hsüeh-hai 裴學海. (1) Shanghai: Commercial Press, 1934. [19] 918 [16] pp. (2) Peking: Chung-hua shu-chü, 1954 (photocopy). (3) Taipei: Kuang-wen shu-chü, 1962 (photocopy).

7. **Ma-shih wen-t'ung i-lan** 馬氏文通易覽. Edited by Shao Ch'eng-hsüan 邵成萱. Fang-ku yin-shu fen-chü 仿古印書分局, 1934. [12] 148 pp. **Ma-shih wen-t'ung k'an-wu** 馬氏文通刊誤 by Yang Shu-ta 楊樹達. (1) Peking: K'o-hsüeh ch'u-pan-she, 1958. 126 pp. (2) Peking: Chung-hua shu-chü, 1962. 126 pp. The first contains numerous typographical errors; the second corrects Ma's mistakes.

This is a study of some 500 *hsü-tzu* 虛字 (empty words), including grammatical particles, prepositions, and interjections. The work is based mainly on the *Ching-chuan shih-tz'u, Chu-tzu pien-lüeh,* and *Tz'u ch'üan* (q.q.v.). The material is arranged according to articulatory groups, such as gutturals, dentals, palatals, retroflexes, and labials. Under each character examples from pre-Han works are given, as well as definitions or explanations which are helpful to the study of Chinese classics and early literature. Since this work was compiled later than other works of the same nature, it is more compact and convenient for general reference, but as the compiler has not tried to incorporate all other materials into one volume, it cannot replace the earlier compilations. The characters are arranged according to rhyme, without an index other than the table of contents. An index is available in a hectographed edition.[8]

E. WORKS ON PRONUNCIATION

Many rhyming dictionaries and studies of early pronunciations have appeared in China, but only a few are included in this bibliography as they are of comparatively little value to Western scholars other than specialists. For the modern pronunciation of Chinese words, the dictionaries described in subsection A should be consulted.

Kuang-yün 廣韻 (also called **Ta-Sung ch'ung-hsiu kuang-yün** 大宋重修 廣韻), 5 *chüan*. Originally compiled in A.D. 601 by Lu Fa-yen 陸法言 under the title **Ch'ieh-yün** 切韻. Annotated in 677 by Chang-sun No-yen 長孫訥 言, collated by Sun Mien 孫愐, and republished in 751 under the title **T'ang-yün** 唐韻. Revised and enlarged under Imperial auspices in 1011 by Ch'en P'eng-nien 陳彭年, Ch'iu Yung 邱雍 and others, and published under the present title. (1) *Ku-i ts'ung-shu* 古逸叢書, *ts'e* 24–25. (2) *Tse-ts'un-t'ang wu-chung* 澤存堂五種, *ts'e* 4–6 (the fullest edition). +(3) *Ssu-pu ts'ung-k'an.* 5 *ts'e.* +(4) Taipei: Kuang-wen shu-chü, 1961. 106, 243 pp. Photocopy with marginal corrections. (5) **Sung-pen kuang-yün** 宋本廣韻. Taipei: I-wen yin-shu-kuan, 1956.

This is the oldest rhyming dictionary still extant in its entirety. In it there is a total of 26,194 characters, which are arranged under 206 final sounds, with different forms of the same character, characters having the same meaning, and characters having the same radical grouped together. Under each character brief notes give its various meanings, and passages are quoted from a wide

---

8. **Ku-shu hsü-tzu chi-shih so-yin** 索引. Compiled by K. L. Thern and others, with a preface by Chow Tse-tsung (Madison: Department of Chinese, University of Wisconsin, 1965). 2, 5, 81 pp.

variety of early writings by way of illustration. If a character has more than one pronunciation, those differing from that of the final sound under which the character is classified are indicated by the *ch'ieh* or by another common character with the same sound and tone. Because this dictionary is made up of many earlier ones, it is the most important one available for tracing early changes in the pronunciation of Chinese characters. Most later works of the same nature are based upon it. There is a table of final sounds at the beginning of each *chüan*. Chang Shih-lu 張世祿 has made a study of the *Kuang-yün*.[9]

Chi-yün 集韻, 10 *chüan*. Compiled under Imperial auspices by Ting Tu 丁度 and others in 1037 and possibly completed by Ssu-ma Kuang 司馬光 in 1067. +(1) *Lien-t'ing wu-chung* 揀亭五種, *ts'e* 25–42. +(2) T'ung-ch'eng Fang-shih Yang-chou 桐城方氏揚州 block-print edition of 1814. 10 *ts'e*. (3) *Ssu-pu pei-yao*. 5 *ts'e*. (4) *Wan-yu wen-k'u ti-erh chi*. 20 *ts'e*. (5) *Wan-yu wen-k'u ti-i-erh-chi chien-pien* 萬有文庫第一二集簡編, vols. 66–69.

This rhyming dictionary is less important than the *Kuang-yün*, although the number of characters included in it is approximately double the number in the earlier work, amounting to 53,525, arranged under 206 final sounds. The sound of each character is indicated by the *ch'ieh* of the Sung period, and the explanations are based, as far as possible, upon those given in the *Shuo-wen*. There is a table of final sounds at the beginning of each *chüan*.

Ch'ieh-yün chih-chang t'u 切韻指掌圖, 1 *chüan*. Attributed to Ssu-ma Kuang 司馬光 (1019–1089). **Chien-li** 檢例, 1 *chüan*. Compiled by Shao Kuang-tsu 邵光祖, who lived at the beginning of the Ming dynasty. (1) *Mo-hai chin-hu* 墨海金壺, *ts'e* 38. (2) Feng-ch'eng Hsiung-shih chiu-pu shih-t'ang 豐城熊氏舊補史堂 block-print edition of 1910. 1 *ts'e*. +(3) *Ssu-pu ts'ung-k'an hsü-pien*. 1 *ts'e*. (4) Taipei: Hsin-hsing shu-chü, 1963. 114 pp.

In this set of twenty tables of Chinese phonetic sounds, the *ch'ieh* of 3130 different sounds of characters are indicated. The thirty-six initial sounds are placed at the top of each table, grouped according to their nature, for example, as dentals, supradentals, light labials, and heavy labials. The final sounds are placed in the first vertical column of each table, grouped according to their tones. The combination of each of the initials with each of the finals gives a sound, and when there are Chinese characters pronounced in the same way as the sound resulting from the combination, one of them is printed in the square opposite the corresponding initial and final; when there is no character having that pronunciation, a circle is inserted. Rhymes are indicated in the

9. **Kuang-yün yen-chiu** 廣韻研究. (1) Shanghai: Commercial Press, 1933. 5, 274 pp. (2) Hong Kong: T'ai-p'ing shu-chü, 1964. 5, 274 pp.

last vertical column of each table. In the *Chien-li* the use of Ssu-ma Kuang's tables is explained, and 760 additional sounds are indicated, making a total of 3890.

Yin-hsüeh wu-shu 音學五書 (also called **Ku-shih yin-hsüeh wu-shu** 顧氏音學五書). Written by Ku Yen-wu 顧炎武 (1613–1682). +(1) Ssu-hsien chiang-she 思賢講舍 block-print edition of 1890. 12 *ts'e*. (2) Ch'ing-fu shan-t'ang 清符山堂 undated block-print edition. 10 *ts'e*. (3) Ku-min Lin-shih fu-t'ien shu-she 古閩林氏福田書舍 bronze movable-type edition, also un-dated. 4 *ts'e*. (4) Taipei: Kuang-wen shu-chü, 1966. 8 vols. (Photocopy of 1933 Ch'eng-tu: Wei-nan Yen-shih 渭南嚴氏 edition.)

Five important studies of ancient sounds, all written by an eminent scholar of the early Ch'ing period, are included under this title: the **Yin-lun** 音論, 3 *chüan*; the **Shih-pen-yin** 詩本音, 10 *chüan*; the **I-yin** 易音, 3 *chüan*; the **T'ang-yün cheng** 唐韻正, 20 *chüan*; and the **Ku-yin piao** 古音表, 2 *chüan*. The *Yin-lun* is a general discussion of the history of Chinese pronunciation, with an analysis of three old rhyming dictionaries, and special studies of the four tones, of the *ch'ieh* system, and of the differences between the final sounds used in the T'ang and Sung dynasties. The *Shih pen-yin* and the *I-yin* are studies of the original pronunciation of the characters in the *Mao-shih* 毛詩 and the *Chou-i* 周易, and the *T'ang-yün cheng*, which is the most important of the five, is a systematic correction of the T'ang final sounds, based upon a study of the classics, classical commentaries, and pre-Han poetry. The *Ku-yin piao* is a table of all ancient sounds, arranged under ten divisions, in each of which the characters are grouped according to the four tones. Ku Yen-wu's was the first important systematic study of ancient Chinese sounds, and it has been the foundation upon which all later work of the same kind has been built.

F. DICTIONARIES FOR SPECIAL FIELDS

The encyclopedic dictionaries included in this subsection represent a com-paratively recent development in China, since they are modeled after works of the same nature in the West. Names and terms relating to the following subjects are defined in the books described below: library science, history, education, Buddhism, botany, pharmacology, medicine, science and tech-nology, music, law, and diplomacy. Besides these works and the geographical and biographical dictionaries included in chapters IV and V, there are a number of other dictionaries of special fields which are not included in this bibliography because they are largely concerned with non-Chinese material.

T'u-shu-hsüeh ta-tz'u-tien 圖書學大辭典. Compiled by Lu Chen-ching 盧震京. (1) Hong Kong: Commercial Press, 1940. 2 vols. [86] 595; 763, 51 pp. (2) Revised edition, entitled **T'u-shu-kuan-hsüeh tz'u-tien** 圖書館學辭典. Peking: Commercial Press, 1958. 26, 898 pp.

The material in the first volume of the 1940 edition of this encyclopedia of library science appears under some two thousand technical terms relating to the history of public and private book collections, library buildings, book binding, Chinese classification systems, cataloguing and other aspects of library science. The terms are arranged according to the number-of-strokes system. Under each term a clear explanation is given, followed by indication of the sources on which the explanation is based. If a term is translated from a foreign language the original is supplied. In the second volume are 24 appendixes, of which the more significant are: a list of Chinese periodicals, a bibliography of important Chinese reference works, a list of foreign newspapers in China, a catalogue of the alternative names of Chinese and foreign writers, a list of the studio names of famous book collectors of different dynasties, and a list of the libraries and academic institutions of China at the time of publication.

The revised edition is based largely on the 1940 edition, almost the only new material being that derived from Russian sources. It consists largely of definitions and elaborations of library science terms, with Russian, English, German, and French equivalents when known. Most of the earlier appendixes have been dropped.

Chung-hua li-shih ti-li ta-tz'u-tien 中華歷史地理大辭典. Compiled by Chang Ch'in 張嶔. Chung-hua t'u-shu-kuan 中華圖書館 movable-type edition of 1913. 12 *ts'e*.

This is a very miscellaneous collection of rather sketchy material on history and geography, which is designed as a reference work for teachers and students. Among its diversified contents are to be found the genealogies of all emperors, tables of important events arranged under the name of each emperor, lists of famous persons grouped according to their surnames, brief descriptions of important books, descriptions of all types of political and economic institutions, evolution of place names and official and reign titles. The work is illustrated with charts, pictures, and diagrams, and the explanations are so simple and clear that besides being useful as a general reference work it is also a handy glossary of the terms used in connection with history, geography, and related subjects. The first characters of item headings are arranged according to the radical system, but often so many different items are classified under the same character that it is difficult to find the information one is looking for. Sources are only occasionally mentioned.

Chung-kuo li-shih hsiao-tzʻu-tien 中國歷史小辭典. Compiled by Chou Mu-chai 周木齋. (1) Shanghai: Hsin-sheng-ming shu-chü 新生命書局, 1934. 11, 144 pp. (2) Hong Kong: Kuang-hua shu-tien 光華書店, 1963. 11, 144 pp. (3) Taipei: Hua-lien chʻu-pan-she 華聯出版社, 1968. 11, 144 pp.

This dictionary of historical terms is more convenient to use than the *Chung-hua li-shih ti-li ta-tzʻu-tien* because of its smaller size. More than six hundred historical terms are defined in it, arranged according to the number of strokes.

Chiao-yü ta-tzʻu-shu 教育大辭書. Compiled by King Chu 朱經農, Yueh Tang 唐鉞, and Kao Chiue Fu 高覺敷. (1) Shanghai: Commercial Press, 1930. 2 vols. [35], 1692, 25 pp. (2) Taipei: Commercial Press, 1964. 35, 1693, 26, 31 pp.

This is a dictionary of educational terms, theories, and writings, both ancient and modern, with about the same amount of space devoted to Chinese material as to foreign. One of the aims of the work is to try to standardize the Chinese translations of foreign educational terms, but it also gives brief statements of various educational theories, reproduces the essential parts of contemporary laws and mandates having to do with education, briefly describes important Western writings on education, presents short biographies of important Chinese and foreign educators giving their most significant contributions, and describes Chinese and foreign educational systems and the most important schools in China. Such historical subjects as the development and nature of the Chinese examination system and the Chinese medieval school system are included, and there are biographies of such educators as Confucius, Tung Chung-shu, Wang An-shih, and Tseng Kuo-fan. There are nearly 3400 items included, arranged in order according to the number of strokes; those which are signed were written by specialists in the particular fields dealt with. There is a table of items at the beginning of each volume, and the Taipei edition has a four-corner index at the end.

Fo-hsüeh ta-tzʻu-tien 佛學大辭典. Compiled by Ting Fu-pao 丁福保. (1) Shanghai: I-hsüeh shu-chü 醫學書局, 1921, 1925. 16 *tsʻe*. (2) Taipei: Hua-yen she 華嚴社, 1956. 4 vols.

This is a dictionary of Buddhist terms which is based largely upon a Japanese work with the same title compiled by Oda Tokuno 織田得能, which in turn is probably based upon the *I-chʻieh ching yin-i* 一切經音義 and the *Fan-i ming-i-chi* 翻譯名義集, Buddhist dictionaries dating from the Tʻang and Sung dynasties respectively. The terms are arranged according to the number of strokes, and under each the meaning is first given as briefly as possible, followed by a much more detailed explanation made up largely of quotations from the

Buddhist canon, from poems and songs, and from the miscellaneous writings of individuals. The Sanscrit pronunciation of names and terms taken over from that language is given in romanization, and the abbreviated title and *chüan* number of the source are given after each quotation. The different items vary greatly in length, and many names and terms are included which have only a slight connection with Buddhism. There is an index to terms at the beginning, arranged according to the number of strokes, and at the end there are descriptive notes on thirty-eight Buddhist sutras.

Fo-hsüeh tz'u-tien 佛學辭典 (also called **Shih-yung Fo-hsüeh tz'u-tien** 實用佛學辭典). Compiled by Kao Kuan-lu 高觀廬 and others. (1) Shanghai: Fo-hsüeh shu-chü 佛學書局, 1934, 1935. 4 vols. [21] 1936 pp. (2) Shanghai: Fo-hsüeh shu-chü, 1947. 16, 252, 1936 pp. (3) Taipei: Jui-ch'eng shu-chü 瑞成書局, 1956. 4 vols. 1939 pp.

This is a more popular and practical Buddhist dictionary than the one described above because the explanations of the various terms are much simpler and the material presented concerning each term is much less extensive. The arrangement and indexing are very similar.

Chih-wu ming-shih t'u-k'ao ch'ang-pien 植物名實圖攷長編, 22 *chüan;* **Chih-wu ming-shih t'u-k'ao** 植物名實圖攷, 38 *chüan*. Compiled by Wu Ch'i-chün 吳其濬 (1789–1847). The *T'u-k'ao* was edited by Lu Ying-ku 陸應穀. Both were first published by Lu, his preface being dated 1848. (1) Shanghai: Commercial Press, 1919. 2 vols. 4, 1129 pp.; 892, 38 pp. (2) Peking: Commercial Press. *Ch'ang-pien*, 1959. 14, 1251 pp. *T'u-k'ao*, 1957. [12] 892, 68 pp. (3) Peking: Chung-hua shu-chü, 1963 (same as Peking Commercial Press editions). (4) *Ch'ang-pien*. Taipei: Shih-chieh shu-chü, 1962. 2 vols. 14, 1251 pp. (5) *T'u-k'ao. Kuo-hsüeh chi-pen ts'ung-shu*. 18 vols.

This botanical dictionary is divided into two parts: the *Ch'ang-pien* gathers together, under 838 names of different kinds of plant life, material from all branches of Chinese literature; the *T'u-k'ao* describes and pictures 1714 different kinds of plants studied by Wu Ch'i-chün in the course of his extensive travels in China. In the *Ch'ang-pien*, which is divided into eleven sections dealing, for example, with grains, vegetables, various kinds of grasses, and fruits, material is quoted from the *Pen-ts'ao kang-mu* 本草綱目, *Ch'i-min yao-shu* 齊民要術, *Erh-ya* 爾雅, *Shuo-wen*, and many other works, particular attention being paid to places of origin, characteristics, places where grown, and uses. After each quotation the source is clearly stated. The *T'u-k'ao*, which is divided into twelve sections, gives the different names of each plant, describes it in detail, and illustrates it with an accurate picture. A table of contents precedes each *chüan*, and at the end of the work there is an index arranged by the number of strokes. The post-war editions correct a number of earlier errors and have four-corner indexes. For foreign equivalents of Chinese botanical terms, see the **Chih-wu-hsüeh ta-tz'u-tien.**[10]

Chung-kuo yao-hsüeh ta-tz'u-tien 中國藥學大辭典. **Chung-kuo yao-wu piao-pen t'u-ying** 中國藥物標本圖影. Compiled by Ch'en Ts'un-jen 陳存仁. (1) Shanghai: Shih-chieh shu-chü, 1935. 3 vols. [40] 944 pp.; 1981, [72] pp.; 13 pp., 247 plates. (2) Peking: Jen-min wei-sheng ch'u-pan-she, 1957. 2 vols. [9] 26, 914; 1120 pp. (3) Kaohsiung: Ta-chung shu-chü 大衆書局, 1958. 6 vols. (4) Hong Kong: Commercial Press, 1962. 2 vols.

This pharmaceutical dictionary presents material on the nature, origin, and uses of virtually all Chinese medicines. In the first and second volumes, under the modern name of each medicine, there are given: the meaning of the name; the prescription form of the name; earlier names, with Latin, English, German, and Japanese equivalents if they exist; a description of the plant, animal or mineral from which it is derived; the place of production; the appearance and characteristics; the chemical formula, as determined by means of modern research; uses, dosage, and methods of determining the genuine article; and relevant quotations from old writings and modern research reports, with sources indicated. Often an essay on an important kind of medicine will consist of as many as three thousand characters, although discussions of less common medicines are much shorter. The third volume consists of more than five hundred colored plates illustrating an equal number of commonly used medicines. The items in the first and second volumes are arranged according to the number of strokes, and there is an index to first characters at the beginning of the first volume and an index to the plates in the third volume at the end of the second volume, both arranged according to the same system. At the beginning of the third volume there is a classified table of plates. A bibliography of the nearly 400 books and articles upon which the work is based appears after the index at the end of the second volume.

Chung-yao ta-tz'u-tien 中藥大辭典. Compiled by Lu Hung-min 盧宏民. Taipei: Wu-chou ch'u-pan she 五洲出版社, 1967. 4, 8, 539, 53 pp.

This is a dictionary of medicinal herbs frequently mentioned in Chinese literature and still widely used in China and Japan. The names of some 700 different herbs are arranged by the number of strokes. Each is illustrated and described simply and clearly, its characteristics and uses being explained and its Latin name given. There is a list of diseases in the appendix with indication

---

10. 植物學大辭典. (Shanghai: Commercial Press, 1918). [24] 1590, 110 pp. Small-size edition, with a four-corner index (Shanghai: Commercial Press, 1933). [16] 1590, 104, 62, 48 pp.

of the herbs that are appropriate for the treatment of each. At the beginning there is a brief general discussion of Chinese medicine.

Chung-kuo i-hsüeh ta-tz'u-tien 中國醫學大辭典. Compiled by Hsieh Kuan 謝觀. (1) Shanghai: Commercial Press, 1921, 1933. 2 vols. [34] 4690, 127, [248] pp. (2) Taipei: Commercial Press, 1958. 4 vols. 33, 4817, 245 pp. (3) Peking: Commercial Press, 1967. 4 vols.

This dictionary of Chinese medical terms includes names of diseases and medicines, names of parts of the body, biographies of famous Chinese medical practitioners, and descriptive notes on medical books. More than seventy thousand items are included, arranged according to the number of strokes. Explanations are brief and lucid, and the sources from which the information was derived are frequently indicated. Of particular interest to the bibliographer are the notes on more than two thousand old Chinese medical works. At the beginning there is an index to first characters, arranged according to the number of strokes; there is a four-corner index to items at the end.

Chien-ming k'o-chi tz'u-tien 簡明科技辭典. Compiled by a committee consisting of Ch'iu Ch'i-ch'in 仇啟琴 *et al.* Shanghai: K'o-hsüeh chi-shu ch'u-pan she 科學技術出版社, 1958. 49, 2050, 57 pp.

This is a dictionary of scientific and technical terms that was prepared to help cadres understand the terminology used in current periodical literature and official documents relating to economic, industrial, scientific, and sociocultural developments. It can be helpful for foreigners too who may read publications from the People's Republic. While the work appears to have been done somewhat hurriedly, and there is no indication of sources, the coverage is wide. There is a number-of-strokes index at the end.

K'o-hsüeh ming-tz'u hui-pien 科學名詞彙編. Compiled by the National Institute of Compilation and Translation 國立編譯館, Wang Feng-chieh 王鳳喈, director, under the auspices of the Ministry of Education. Taipei: Cheng-chung shu-chü, 1959. 7 vols.

This is a dictionary of scientific and technical terms compiled for the purpose of standardizing modern terminology, which has been quite chaotic because of the number of different translations that have been used for the same foreign word in thousands of cases. The work is divided by subject: mathematics, chemistry, and physics in vol. 1; astronomy, meteorology, and forestry in vol. 2; anatomy, bacteriology, embryology, and immunology in vol. 3; pathology, psychopathology, and pharmacology in vol. 4; mineralogy and agricultural sciences in vol. 5; engineering terminology in vol. 6;

and sociology, economics, statistics, pedagogy, and athletics in vol. 7. There is a general index at the end of the last volume.

Yin-yüeh tz'u-tien 音樂辭典. Compiled by Liu Ch'eng-fu 劉誠甫. (1) Shanghai: Commercial Press, 1935. [73] 447, 59 pp. (2) Taipei: Ch'i-ming shu-chü 啟明書局, 1957. 420 pp.

This is a dictionary of musical terms, ancient and modern, although more attention is paid to traditional Chinese terms than to those introduced from the West. Nearly five thousand items are included, among them the names of musical instruments and of famous musicians and composers, the titles of plays, musical dramas, ballads, songs, dances, and books on music, technical terms for tone, pitch, etc., theories of music, and many other related matters. In each case the origin is given, and the meaning or nature is simply and clearly explained. Pictures are frequently inserted into the text, and at the end of the work there are many charts and diagrams of particular interest to the specialist. While the sources of information are frequently not mentioned, the work is a very useful one, not only to those who specialize in the field of music but also to students of Chinese history and literature. Music held a cardinal place in the educational system of ancient China, and without a guide such as this much of the writing on music which has survived until the present day is unintelligible to the layman. The terms are arranged according to the number of strokes, both in the body of the work and in an index at the beginning, and there is another index at the end which is arranged according to the four-corner system.

Fa-lü ta-tz'u-shu 法律大辭書. **Fa-lü ta-tz'u-shu pu-p'ien** 法律大辭書補篇. Compiled by Cheng Ching-i 鄭競毅. Shanghai: Commercial Press, 1936. 3 vols. [24] 2339, 81 [245] pp.; 449, 148, [25] pp.

The dictionary of Chinese legal terms which fills the first and second volumes of this work is based upon a broad selection of old Chinese works on law and modern investigations and writings of a legal nature. In it the meaning and evolution of both early and modern legal terms are explained in considerable detail, and foreign equivalents are given wherever possible. The arrangement of items is according to the number of strokes; under each term there is an indication as to whether it is a historical or modern one, and if the latter, whether it is related to the civil, criminal, commercial, or another of the codes. Explanations are simple and clear, and the full titles and *chüan* numbers of the sources of quotations are usually given. Of particular value are the analyses and definitions of historical terms, the discussions of the legal system and of law offices under different dynasties, and the copious notes on books on law. The last are of unequal length, depending upon the importance of the work described, but in many cases material is presented on the history of compilation, on different editions, and on the nature and value of the work; there is always an indication as to whether or not the book is still extant. There is an index to first characters, arranged according to the number of strokes, at the beginning of the first volume, and at the end of the second volume there is a four-corner index to the approximately sixteen thousand terms and an alphabetical index to foreign equivalents (chiefly English and German, and occasionally Latin). The third volume, the *Fa-lü ta-tz'u-shu pu-p'ien*, is given over to examples of legal forms and to biographies of famous legalists of all nationalities. The biographies were written by P'eng Shih 彭時 and are arranged by countries. There is a four-corner index to all names and also an alphabetical index to foreign names.

Fa-lü tz'u-tien 法律辭典. Compiled by Sa Meng-wu 薩孟武, Lin Chi-tung 林紀東, and others. Taipei: Chung-hua ts'ung-shu pien-shen wei-yuan-hui 中華叢書編審委員會, 1963. 83, 1357 pp.

This dictionary of 3101 legal terms was compiled by twenty-one experts, some of whom were professors of law and several judges and lawyers. It is divided into thirteen sections: (1) the constitution, (2) administrative law, (3) civil law, (4) commercial law, (5) civil suits, (6) criminal law, (7) criminal suits, (8) international law, (9) international private law, (10) jurisprudence, (11) history of legal systems, (12) Anglo-Saxon law, and (13) social legislation. The entries are from 200 to 600 characters in length, and each is followed by the contributor's name. Some of the terms are supplied with English translations and others with German or French equivalents. The terms are arranged in each section according to the number of strokes.

Wai-chiao ta-tz'u-tien 外交大辭典. Compiled by Wang Cho-jan 王卓然 and others. (1) Shanghai: Chung-hua shu-chü, 1937. 34, 1160, 162, 29 pp. (2) Taipei: Wen-hai ch'u-pan-she, 1965. [7] 25, 1160, 162, 29 pp.

This dictionary of diplomacy includes approximately 2100 technical terms and phrases used in laws, regulations, treaties, and names of personalities. China's foreign relations are taken as the basis of the compilation, but international diplomacy is also given attention. The entries are arranged by the number of strokes, and there is an alphabetical index to the European-language equivalents of Chinese terms. The five appendixes contain useful source material.

IV GEOGRAPHICAL WORKS

With the assistance of the various works described in this section, it is possible to identify almost any place name or name of a political subdivision, whether modern or dating from earlier times. For a much fuller list of atlases and maps the *Kuo-li Pei-p'ing t'u-shu-kuan Chung-wen yü-t'u mu-lu* (q.v.) should be consulted.

A. GEOGRAPHICAL DICTIONARIES

Li-tai ti-li-chih yün-pien chin-shih 歷代地理志韻編今釋, 20 *chüan*. Compiled by Li Chao-lo 李兆洛 and others, compiler's preface dated 1837. (1) Block-print edition of 1871. 7 *ts'e*. (2) *Li-shih wu-chung ho-k'an* 李氏五種合刊, *ts'e* 1–8. (3) *Ssu-pu pei-yao*. 6 *ts'e*. (4) *Wan-yu wen-k'u ti-i-chi*, *ts'e* 1800–1805. (5) *Kuo-hsüeh chi-pen ts'ung-shu*. 6 vols.

This work brings together under the names of provinces, prefectures, and districts, important material derived from the geographical sections of fourteen dynastic histories and from the *Huang-ch'ao yü-ti-t'u* 皇朝輿地圖 and the *Ta-Ch'ing i-t'ung-chih* 大清一統志. The names are arranged according to their rhyme, and under each name the material is arranged by dynasties, each notation being preceded by the name of its source in incised characters. For each dynasty it is indicated whether the name represented a prefecture, district, or some other political subdivision, and in each case the name of the next larger political subdivision of which it formed a part is given. While the Ch'ing material is fuller than that for any other dynasty, the definite location of the places named is not always indicated exactly. The names of rivers and mountains are entirely omitted, but border and specially administered areas and tributary states are included. Material concerning different places having the same name appears under the one name, but separated by circles. While this work is somewhat limited by being entirely dependent upon the dynastic histories for pre-Ch'ing material, it was the most important geographical handbook available before the modern geographical dictionaries were compiled. In spite of its inconvenient arrangement, it is still a useful work, not only because of the simple and clear presentation of material, but also because of its function as a key to the geographical material in the dynastic histories and because it gives the proper pronunciation of all names contained in it, a particularly helpful service for those names which are pronounced differently from the usual pronunciation of the characters forming them. All but the first edition listed above include a two-*chüan* supplement, the **Huang-ch'ao yü-ti yün-pien** 皇朝輿地韻編, also compiled by Li Chao-lo, in which the

Ch'ing dynasty names of districts and prefectures are listed, arranged according to their rhyme, indicating in each case the province in which the prefecture is located and the province and prefecture in which the district is located.

*Chung-kuo ku-chin ti-ming ta-tz'u-tien 中國古今地名大辭典. Compiled by Tsang Li-ho 臧勵龢 and others. (1) Shanghai: Commercial Press, 1931. [27] 1410, 11 [348] pp. (2) Taipei: Commercial Press, 1960. 27, 1410, 11, 287 pp.

This geographical dictionary lists approximately forty thousand place names, including the names of mountains and rivers, all names being arranged according to the number of strokes. Under each name previous changes in name are given, and boundaries and geographical features are indicated; as a rule the modern name is also given, and in nearly half of the items there are quotations from other works, with sources cited. There is an index to first characters at the beginning of the work, arranged according to the number of strokes, and a four-corner index to all names at the end. The explanations not only are fuller than those in the *Chung-kuo ti-ming ta-tz'u-tien*, but about twice as many names are included. The appendix of the 1931 edition has tables of modern district (*hsien*) names, arranged under the provinces in which they are located, of railroads, of commercial cities, and of the variant names of *hsien*. These are provided in the 1960 edition as of 1947, except the railroad table is as of 1960. The chief defects of the work are its inadequate treatment of border areas and its imprecision which often makes it difficult to know the exact location of a place mentioned in pre-Ch'ing writings. A Japanese work, the **Shina rekidai chimei yoran,**[1] is a particularly useful supplement because it gives the modern equivalents of early place names with reasonable accuracy.

1. 支那歷代地名要覽 (also called **Tu-shih fang-yü chi-yao so-yin chih-na li-tai ti-ming yao-lan** 讀史方輿紀要索引支那歷代地名要覽). Compiled by Aoyama Sadao 青山定雄. (1) Tokyo: Tōhō bunka gakuin (Tokyo) kenkyūjo 東方文化學院 (東京) 研究所, 1932. [23] 721 [70] pp. (2) Tokyo: Daian Bookstore, 1967 (photocopy). This index to the second and third parts of Ku Tsu-yü's 顧祖禹 *Tu-shih fang-yü chi-yao* 讀史方輿紀要 (Szechwan T'ung-hua shu-wu 四川桐華書屋 block-print edition of 1879; Peking: Chung-hua shu-chü, 1955. 6 vols.), is a very handy guide to the modern equivalents of more than thirty thousand pre-Ch'ing place names. Each half-page is divided into three horizontal columns in which are given: (1) the historical name and frequently the dynasty during which that name was used, (2) the location of the place during the Ch'ing dynasty, and (3) the location of the material on that particular place in the *Tu-shih fang-yü chi-yao*. Names are arranged according to the *kana* of the Chinese pronunciation, and there are two indexes to first characters, one by the *kana* system, at the beginning of the work, and one according to the number of strokes at the end. While the compiler not infrequently confuses different places which have the same name and occasionally assigns a name to two places which belongs only to one, generally he has succeeded in listing each name separately.

Chung-kuo ti-ming ta-tzʻu-tien 中國地名大辭典. Compiled by Liu Chün-jen 劉鈞仁. (1) Peiping: Kuo-li Pei-pʻing yen-chiu-yüan 國立北平研究院, 1930. [22], 1118, 232 pp. (2) Taipei: Wen-hai chʻu-pan-she, 1967. 8, 1118, 232 pp. (Compiler's name is given as 劉君任)

In this geographical dictionary the place names are arranged according to the radical system, and after each character in each name the *chʻieh* spelling and rhyme are given and also the romanization used by the Chinese Post Office. About twenty thousand place names are included, and under each the following information is given: the present name, previous changes in the name, the present location, the area, and political boundaries. Although sources are usually not indicated, the work as a whole is based upon the geographical sections of the fourteen dynastic histories having them, the *Ta-Chʻing i-tʻung-chih* 大清一統志, and some twenty other geographical works. The work is very clearly printed and there is an alphabetical index at the end. The chief defects are its omission of the names of provinces, rivers, and mountains, and in the weakness of the material on the Six Dynasties and on modern changes. It is exceedingly convenient to use, however, because of the alphabetical index. It lists some names which do not appear in the *Chung-kuo ku-chin ti-ming ta-tzʻu-tien*, but the latter includes thousands of names which were omitted from this work.

Wai-kuo ti-ming tzʻu-tien 外國地名辭典. Compiled by Lu Ching-yü 陸景宇. Taipei: Wei-hsin shu-chü 維新書局, 1966. 3, 9, 878, 30, 166 pp.

A dictionary of foreign place names is sometimes needed when reading Chinese documents in which only Chinese transliterations and not the original names are given. In this dictionary the Chinese transliteration is given first, then the original name and an explanation. There is an index to Chinese characters at the beginning and an index to the original foreign names at the end of the volume.

B. HISTORICAL ATLASES

Although the technique of map making was known in China as early as the third century A.D. and reached a comparatively high degree of excellence during the Tʻang dynasty, little progress was made in the following centuries owing to the absence of surveys and of an adequate engraving technique. In modern times scientific methods have been introduced, and while the works described in this and the following subsection do not quite measure up to the highest Western standards, they are reasonably well prepared and most of them are indispensable to geographers and historians.

Li-tai yü-ti-t'u 歷代輿地圖. Compiled by Yang Shou-ching 楊守敬 (1839–1915), maps drawn by Hsiung Hui-chen 熊會貞. Yang-shih kuan-hai-t'ang 楊氏觀海堂 block-print edition of 1906–1911. 42 *ts'e*.

This is the best historical atlas published to date in China. The first *ts'e* contains seventy-one general maps, showing the whole of China at different times from the geographical configuration described in the *Yü-kung* 禹貢 to the end of the Ming dynasty. The general maps are followed by forty-five sets of sectional maps, showing the different subdivisions of the country at different times from the *Ch'un-ch'iu* 春秋 period to the end of the Ming, most of the sets being preceded by a preface. The last eight *ts'e* contain maps drawn to illustrate the *Shui-ching chu* 水經注. Each map is divided into squares, those on the subdivisional maps of China proper representing fifty square *li*, and those on the subdivisional maps of outlying territories such as Mongolia and Tibet representing 800 square *li*. Names, boundaries, rivers, and mountains printed in red are as of the Ch'ing period, and throughout the work the Ch'ing material is probably based upon the *Nei-fu yü-t'u* 內府輿圖, which was in turn based upon the surveys made by Jesuit missionaries during the K'ang-hsi period. Names and geographical features indicated in black are as of the historical period dealt with in that particular map or set of maps. The historical material is based upon a careful examination of the geographical sections of such dynastic histories as contain them, and of maps and descriptions selected from a large number of other works to supply for those periods whose geography is neglected in the dynastic histories. This atlas is rather cumbersome to use because the sectional maps are not adequately labeled. There are occasional omissions of important names, and places are frequently located with insufficient exactness, but the work is indispensable to anyone making a study of Chinese historical geography.

Chung-kuo li-shih ti-t'u chi 中國歷史地圖集. Compiled by Ch'eng Kuang-yü 程光裕, and Hsü Sheng-mo 徐聖謨. Taipei: Chung-hua wen-hua shih-yeh ch'u-pan wei-yüan hui 中華文化事業出版委員會, 1955. 2 vols. [6] 110; 3, 223 pp.

The first volume of this historical atlas is made up of maps arranged under five different headings: (1) territorial maps, (2) maps of capital cities, (3) rivers, (4) lines of communication, and (5) battle-fields. The second volume is devoted to descriptive material, arranged in the same order as the maps. While many of the maps are well prepared, some are too crowded and all are too small for easy consultation. Shorter descriptions directly following the maps they explain would be more useful.

Chung-kuo li-tai chiang-yüeh chan-cheng ho-t'u 中國歷代疆域戰爭合圖.
Compiled by Ou-yang Ying 歐陽纓. Wuchang: Ya-hsin ti-hsüeh she 亞新
地學社, 1920, 1933. 12 pp., 46 plates.

This historical atlas has forty-six double-page plates, each of which is related
to a single historical period. The first is a map of China as it is supposed to
have been in the mythological time of the Five Emperors 五帝, and the last
is a map of the country during the early 1930's. As a rule each plate bears a
large general map of China and also several smaller maps, including those of
battle-fields, capitals, and political subdivisions. Names and geographical
features printed in red are those of modern times, and those in black are as of
the particular period being dealt with. Each plate is followed by an explanatory
note discussing political subdivisions, changes in boundaries, specific rivers,
canals, and historical sites. While this atlas would be more helpful if the maps
had been more accurately drawn and more clearly printed, it does give more
place names than any other work of its kind and has been widely used as a
reference work by Chinese scholars.

C. MODERN ATLASES

Ta-Ch'ing i-t'ung yü-t'u 大清一統輿圖 (also called **Huang-ch'ao chung-
wai i-t'ung yü-t'u** 皇朝中外一統輿圖). Compiled by Hu Lin-i 胡林翼, Yen
Shu-sen 嚴樹森 and others, Yen's postface dated 1863. (1) Hupeh Fu-shu
湖北撫署 block-print edition of 1863. 12 or 32 *ts'e*. (2) Soochow: Ching-
hsiang-ko 蘇州經香閣 block-print edition of 1863. 26 *ts'e*.

This contemporary atlas of the Ch'ing period, if taken apart and the pages
pieced together on a flat surface, would form a large map of that part of Asia
extending from the Pacific Ocean on the east to the Caspian Sea on the west,
and from the Arctic Ocean on the north to Indo-China and India on the south.
The pages are so arranged that they form continuous strips, covering two
degrees of latitude (approximately 400 *li*), and extending from east to west.
The longitude and latitude of Peking are taken as the center, with the maps
numbered east and west and the long strips numbered north and south from
that center. The geographical features indicated on the various maps are based
upon the Jesuit surveys made during the K'ang-hsi period, but as this is the
third or fourth re-cutting of the original map it is by no means as accurate
as the original. In addition to the geographical markings, including dotted
lines of longitude which were taken from the Jesuit map, posthouses, strategic
and famous places are marked, and the various types of political subdivisions
are indicated by different symbols. Finally, each map is divided into squares,
each of which represents 10,000 square *li*. The lack of an index and even a
satisfactory table of maps makes this atlas somewhat inconvenient to use.

Chung-hua yu-cheng yü-t'u 中華郵政輿圖. Chinese Directorate-General of Posts 交通部郵政總局, Nanking, 1936. 30 plates [15] pp.

This postal atlas of China, which was first published in 1903 and revised in 1908, 1919, and 1933, shows the postal routes and postal establishments in each province. The one general map of China is drawn to the scale of 1: 7,500,000, and the twenty-nine provincial maps to the scale of 1: 900,000. All cities, towns, and villages which have post offices or postal agencies are marked, the former with both Chinese characters and the romanized name used by the postal authorities, and the latter with only the characters. In addition, telegraph offices and air, motor, and other mail routes are indicated, and also the class of each post office, the frequency of its service, and the method by which mail is dispatched to and from it. Perhaps the most useful feature of this atlas is the care taken to indicate the exact distance in Chinese *li* between postal establishments. At the end there are two indexes, one to the Chinese names of all places having postal establishments, arranged according to the radical system, and the other to the romanized names of all cities and towns having post offices, arranged alphabetically.

*Chung-hua min-kuo hsin ti-t'u 中華民國新地圖. Compiled by V. K. Ting 丁文江, Wong Wen-hao 翁文灝, and Tseng Shih-ying 曾世英. Shanghai: Shen-pao kuan 申報館, 1934. [21] pp., 53 plates, 180 pp.

This probably is still the best modern atlas of China, though now somewhat out-of-date. The maps were drawn by specialists and are based upon between seven and eight thousand Chinese maps and more than fifteen hundred foreign maps of China, supplemented by the results of surveys made by the Geological Survey of China. There are seven plates of general maps: political divisions, physical geography, communications, weather, agricultural population and distribution of dialects, mines, and agricultural products. There are twenty-two physical maps and twenty-two political maps of subdivisions, either kind of which, if pieced together, would form a complete map of China and its outlying dependencies. Before each sectional map there is a small outline map of the whole country showing the location of that particular section in relation to the whole. The last two plates have on them separate small maps of sixty-one cities drawn to the scale of 1: 100,000. The sectional maps are drawn on the polyconical projection; the scale of the four largest general maps is 1: 15,000,000, and that of the sectional maps is 1: 2,000,000 for China proper and 1: 5,000,000 for outlying areas. The units of measure in all the maps are kilometer and *li*. At the back of this atlas there is a radical index to all geographical names, and there are also four-corner and Wade–Giles romanization keys to all first characters.

*Chung-hua min-kuo ti-t'u chi 中華民國地圖集. Compiled by Chang Ch'i-yün 張其昀, Hsü Sheng-mo 徐聖謨, and others. Taipei: National War College 國防研究院, in cooperation with the Chinese Geographical Institute, 1959–62. 5 vols.

The first volume of the *National Atlas of China* is devoted to Taiwan. Besides ten topographical maps dividing up the island and one of the Pescadores, there are four large and twelve small detailed maps of cities and their environs, a number of large maps showing such aspects as climate, soils, land use, communications, population, minerals, and industry, and smaller ones showing such things as crop and domestic animal distribution. Volume II, devoted to Outer Mongolia, Sinkiang and Tibet, has topographical and political maps of these regions, small maps of cities and their environs, and a few special maps showing soils, minerals and climate. Volumes III and IV, North China and South China respectively, consist of topographical and political maps of the various provinces of China proper, Inner Mongolia, and Manchuria, with inserted small maps of the environs of the principal cities. Volume V is made up of specialized maps of all of China devoted to such topics as climate, soils, crops, communications, and population and language distribution. Although the names and the political subdivisions established by the Central Government before 1949 are retained throughout, the latest available data of other kinds appear to have been used, as, for example, the location of railroads. There are indexes to place names, one arranged by number of strokes and one by the Post Office romanization, in all but the fifth volume. There are lists of sources in each volume. The cartography is clear and the colors are distinctive.

Chung-hua jen-min kung-ho-kuo fen-sheng ti-t'u 中華人民共和國分省地圖. Compiled by the Ya-kuang yü-ti hsüeh-she 亞光輿地學社. Shanghai: Ti-t'u ch'u-pan she 地圖出版社, 1953. Revised edition, 1964. 50 plates, approximately 120 pp.

This simple atlas of the People's Republic of China has twenty national maps presenting material on such topics as topography, climate, rivers, crops, industries, minerals, and various means of transportation, and thirty plates of maps of all or parts of all Chinese provinces and border regions, and fifty-two cities. After each map there are two or more pages of explanation. The maps are poorly printed and too small for reference purposes. There are no indexes.

D. GEOGRAPHICAL TABLES

The works described in this section contain tables which give the names of political subdivisions used at different times in Chinese history.

Li-tai ti-li yen-ko piao 歷代地理沿革表, 47 *chüan*. Compiled by Ch'en Fang-chi 陳芳績, compiler's preface dated 1667; edited by Huang T'ing-chien 黃廷鑑, editor's introduction dated 1833. *Kuang-ya ts'ung-shu, ts'e* 176–182.

This table of changes in place names is divided into three sections: provinces, prefectures, and districts. Each page is divided into twelve horizontal columns, in which appear the names used for the same political subdivision during twelve different periods in Chinese history, pre-Han material appearing in the first column and Ming in the last. The arrangement of names follows the geographical section of the *Ch'ien Han-shu* 前漢書, and when there is little or no change, the name is repeated in each successive column. New names and new political subdivisions in the same area are given together. Besides the names, notes are inserted giving the number of smaller subdivisions and the time when changes took place, and pointing out mistakes which appeared in earlier works. Pre-Ming material was taken from dynastic histories, gazetteers, and a few special geographical works, and the Ming material from the *Ta-Ming i-t'ung chih* 大明一統志, much of which was derived from gazetteers. While it is difficult to locate individual names in the body of this work because of its arrangement, the graphic way in which the history of changes in place names is shown and the significant material included in the notes make it a useful reference work. There is a historical introduction at the beginning of each section, and at the beginning of the work there is a table of all names, in which the Ming name, if different, is always given in smaller sized characters, and if the same, is so marked. Names of political subdivisions which have been abolished are marked with the character *fei* 廢.

Li-tai yen-ko piao 歷代沿革表, 3 *chüan*. Compiled by Tuan Ch'ang-chi 段長基, compiler's preface dated 1814. (1) Wei-ku shan-fang 味古山房 block-print edition of about the same time. 6 *ts'e*. (2) Hsiao-yu shan-fang 小酉山房 block-print edition of 1815. 6 *ts'e*. (3) *Ssu-pu pei-yao.* 8 *ts'e* or 2 vols. (4) *Kuo-hsüeh chi-pen ts'ung-shu.*

In this table of the changes in the names of political subdivisions, the names used during the Ch'ing dynasty are placed first, and under each are listed the names for the same area in use at different times from the time of the earliest records down to the end of the Ming dynasty. The names are arranged by provinces, with the districts grouped under their prefecture and the prefectures under their province, and before each of the provinces there is a general introduction discussing the size, boundaries, the number of political subdivisions included in it, and the history of changes. In the top margin, above the Ch'ing name, the literary name for each political subdivision is given, and at the end of each *chüan* there is a table of the names included in it which are common to two or more places.

Chia-ch'ing i-t'ung-chih piao 嘉慶一統志表, 20 *chüan*. Collected by Chang Yüan-chi 張元濟 and others from the *Ta-Ch'ing i-t'ung-chih* 大清一統志 compiled during the Chia-ch'ing period (1796–1820). Shanghai: Commercial Press, 1935. 10 *ts'e*.

This table of changes in the names of political subdivisions is arranged in much the same way as the *Li-tai yen-ko piao*, although the material in the two works differs considerably in detail. More names are recorded in this work and it is probably somewhat more reliable, having been taken from an official compilation, but the print is small and the columns are not marked with the names of the different dynasties except at the beginning of each *chüan*—making it somewhat inconvenient to use. There is a table of contents at the beginning.

Li-tai chiang-yü piao 歷代疆域表, 3 *chüan*. Compiled by Tuan Ch'ang-chi 段長基, compiler's preface dated 1813. (1) Wei-ku shan-fang 味古山房 block-print edition of the same year. 6 *ts'e*. (2) *Ssu-pu pei-yao*, 6 *ts'e* or 2 vols. (3) *Kuo-hsüeh chi-pen ts'ung-shu*.

This is also a table of changes in the names of political subdivisions during different dynasties. At the beginning there are eleven maps of the whole empire, showing the political boundaries at different times. Each dynasty is treated separately in the main part of the work, each page being divided into three parts, as follows: (1) changes in the capital; (2) political subdivisions, giving names and indicating changes; (3) miscellaneous notes, particularly on changes during or after rebellions, and changes effected under independent dynasties. The particular importance of this work lies in the general view it gives of the changes which took place under different dynasties and in the material it contains on the periods of change at the end of different dynasties.

E. INDEXES TO GEOGRAPHICAL WORKS

Shui-ching-chu yin-te 水經注引得. Compiled by Cheng Te-k'un 鄭德坤. (1) Peiping: Harvard-Yenching Institute, 1934. (Index No. 17) 2 vols. lvi, 260; 267 pp. (2) Taipei: Ch'eng Wen Publishing Co., 1966 (photocopy).

This is a *kuei-hsieh* index to the names in the famous commentary on the *Shui-ching* 水經 written by Li Tao-yüan (d. A.D. 527). The *Shui-ching*, which is said to have been written by Sang Chin 桑欽 who lived just before the beginning of the Christian era, but the compiler of which actually is unknown, discusses nearly fourteen hundred rivers and streams, and the commentary adds considerable material not only on rivers but on all types of physical features and historical sites. The work, including the commentary, is a very important source book on historical geography, and the index (to the Wang

Hsien-ch'ien 王先謙 edition published in Changsha in 1892) is a useful key to it. In an introduction the compiler discusses the author and commentator, earlier studies of the work, and the different editions.

Chia-ch'ing ch'ung-hsiu i-t'ung-chih so-yin 嘉慶重修一統志索引. (1) Shanghai: Commercial Press, 1934. 10 *ts'e*. (2) Taipei: Commercial Press, 1966. 11 vols.

This is an index to the Commercial Press photolithographic edition of the original manuscript of the third revision of the *Ta-Ch'ing i-t'ung-chih* 大淸一統志 (*Chia-ch'ing ch'ung-hsiu i-t'ung-chih* 嘉慶重修一統志, 560 *chüan*, 200 *ts'e*), which contains material down to 1820 and was presented to the emperor in 1842. The *Ta-Ch'ing i-t'ung-chih* is a geographical work dealing first with China as a whole, and then with each of the different political subdivisions into which the country was divided during the Ch'ing dynasty. It is rather inconvenient to use, and this index provides a useful key. Among the various things indexed are: official titles, customs, products, population, maps, tables, boundaries, political subdivisions, names of persons, and names of places, mountains, rivers, imperial tombs, and temples and monasteries. The arrangement is according to the four-corner system, and after each entry are given the number of the *ts'e*, the political subdivision, and the *chüan* and page numbers.

V BIOGRAPHICAL WORKS

Although many works of various kinds have been published in China to which one may turn for biographical information, it is still impossible to locate information about a great many persons of historical importance, and it is often impossible even to determine during which dynasty some of them lived. An effort is made to include in this section most of the biographical works which are likely to be useful to the average student, and to arrange the different kinds of works in a more or less natural order. Collections of brief biographies are described first; these are followed by indexes to collections of biographies. Works in which persons having the same names are listed and works identifying alternative and posthumous names follow, and at the end there are several studies of Chinese surnames.

A. BIOGRAPHICAL DICTIONARIES

1. GENERAL

While some of the works included in this section are not biographical dictionaries in the strict sense of the term, all are collections of brief biographical notes and all are primarily useful as rapid reference works. The first is very broad in scope, while the others contain biographies of writers, book collectors, painters or Buddhist monks.

★Chung-kuo jen-ming ta-tz'u-tien 中國人名大辭典. Compiled by Fang I 方毅 and others. (1) Shanghai: Commercial Press, 1921; 1934. [19] 1833 [423] pp. (2) Taipei: Commercial Press, 1958. 191, 1808, 385 pp.

This biographical dictionary contains 1833 pages of biographies, including a 25-page supplement; the appendix contains an 83-page study of surnames, a 34-page list of alternative names, and a 15-page table of reign titles. According to the compilers' figures, the work includes the biographies of more than forty thousand persons and is based upon material in the biographical sections of dynastic histories and gazetteers, the *Wan-hsing t'ung-p'u* 萬姓統譜, the *Shang-yu lu* 尚友錄, and many other works. The biographies are comparatively short, dates of birth and death are seldom given exactly, and sources are never indicated. It should be pointed out that the material presented is not always reliable, and that the biographies of men who lived in ancient times and those who lived during the latter part of the Ch'ing dynasty are particularly inadequately handled. Names are arranged according to the number of strokes, although later editions have a four-corner index which adds greatly to the ease with which biographies can be located. The first edition was more clearly printed than later ones have been. There is a romanized index to surnames.[1]

*Chung-kuo wen-hsüeh-chia ta-tz'u-tien 中國文學家大辭典. Compiled by T'an Cheng-pi 譚正璧. (1) Shanghai: Kuang-ming shu-chü 光明書局, 1934. 1746 [55] pp. (2) Taipei: Shih-chieh shu-chü, 1962. 2, 1746, 3, 50 pp. (3) Hong Kong: Wen-shih ch'u-pan she 文史出版社, 1961. 2, 1746, 1, 2, 50 pp.

This work, according to the compiler, contains 6851 biographies of men famous in Chinese history for their literary accomplishments. The compiler states that writers who specialized in classics and philosophy have been excluded, but since biographies for Lao-tzu 老子 and for a number of famous classicists are included, the work would seem to be broader in scope than is claimed by T'an. The biographies are short, but each contains the following facts, in so far as they are available: alternative names, exact, or when that is not ascertainable, approximate dates of birth and death according to the Western calendar, place of birth, chief activities, and most important writings. The principal sources are the sections on biographies of men of letters and arts 文苑 and on bibliography 藝文 in the dynastic histories, and the brief biographical notes in the *Ssu-k'u ch'üan-shu tsung-mu*. The arrangement is chronological, the first biography being that of Lao-tzu and the last that of a scholar who died in 1931. While this biographical dictionary is much more limited in scope than the *Chung-kuo jen-ming ta-tz'u-tien*, it is more conveniently arranged and the individual biographies contain more material. There is an index at the end of the work in which the names are arranged according to the number of strokes.

Chung-kuo ts'ang-shu-chia k'ao-lüeh 中國藏書家攷略. Compiled by Yang Li-ch'eng 楊立誠 and Chin Pu-ying 金步瀛. Chekiang Sheng-li t'u-shu-kuan 浙江省立圖書館, 1929. [10] 150 fol.

This is a collection of biographical notes about some 740 Chinese book collectors, dating from the Ch'in dynasty to the end of the Ch'ing dynasty. The names are arranged according to the number of strokes, and under each name alternative names, the native place, a brief outline of the collector's official career, notes on his collection, and a list of his important writings and publications are given. These biographical notes are sometimes long, but more

1. M. Jean Gates, *A Romanized Index to the Surnames in the Chinese Biographical Dictionary* (Washington, 1942). 32 pp.

often they are very brief. Sources are frequently indicated, but dates of birth and death are usually not given and there are many collectors for whom biographies are not included. However, the work is of considerable use to librarians and scholars who wish brief notes about Chinese book collectors and their collections and writings. There is an index to names at the beginning, arranged according to the number of strokes. See also the *Ts'ang-shu chi-shih-shih yin-te.*

Chung-kuo hua-chia jen-ming ta-tz'u-tien 中國畫家人名大辭典. Compiled by Sun Ta-kung 孫鮚公. (1) Shanghai: Shen-chou kuo-kuang she 神州國光社, 1934. [14] [760] pp. (2) Taipei: Tung-fang shu-tien 東方書店, 1959. 4, 752 pp.

This is a biographical dictionary of Chinese painters. The names are arranged according to the number of strokes, and under each name the dynasty, the native place, and alternative names are given, as well as the branch of painting in which that person specialized. Anecdotes and other relevant materials are also presented, and an effort is made to correct the errors made or perpetuated in earlier works. This work is chiefly based upon the *Li-tai hua-shih hui-chuan* 歷代畫史彙傳, the *P'ei-wen shu-hua p'u* 佩文書畫譜, the *Ming-hua lu* 明畫錄, the *Li-tai ming-hua chi* 歷代名畫記, a few other works of the same order, and the collected writings of many individuals. Sources are always indicated. The notices are quite brief, and there are numerous typographical and copying errors, but the work is useful for purposes of rapid reference. There is an index to surnames at the beginning, arranged according to the number of strokes.

T'ang-ch'ien hua-chia jen-ming tz'u-tien 唐前畫家人名辭典. Compiled by Chu Chu-yü 朱鑄禹. Peking: Jen-min mei-shu ch'u-pan she, 1961. 2, 2, 4, 76 pp.

The 192 biographies in this dictionary of pre-T'ang painters are arranged by the number of strokes. Under each name, besides a short biography, there is a list of the artist's most famous paintings with sources indicated. Of the several appendixes, lists of pre-T'ang mural paintings and of the alternate names of pre-T'ang painters are the most useful.

T'ang Sung hua-chia jen-ming tz'u-tien 唐宋畫家人名辭典. Compiled by Chu Chu-yü 朱鑄禹, assisted by Li Shih-sun 李石孫. Peking: Chung-kuo ku-tien i-shu ch'u-pan she 中國古典藝術出版社, 1958. [4] 29, 492 pp.

This is a biographical dictionary of some 1500 painters of the T'ang and

Sung dynasties; it also includes painters of the Wu-tai, Liao, and Chin periods. In each biography the artist's social background, his teachers, and the characteristics of his painting are given briefly. Among the appendixes a list of Sung court painters and an index to the alternate names of artists from T'ang to the end of Chin are particularly useful.

Kao-seng chuan 高僧傳. Includes: **Kao-seng chuan (ch'u-chi)** 高僧傳 (初集), 15 *chüan*, written by Hui-chiao 慧皎 (A.D. 497–554); **Hsü kao-seng chuan** 續高僧傳 (also called **T'ang kao-seng chuan** 唐高僧傳 and **Kao-seng chuan erh-chi** 高僧傳二集), 40 *chüan*, written by Tao-hsüan 道宣 (A.D. 596–647); **Sung kao-seng chuan** 宋高僧傳 (also called **Kao-seng chuan san-chi** 高僧傳三集), 30 *chüan*, written by Tsan-ning 贊寧, author's preface dated 988; **Ming kao-seng chuan** 明高僧傳 (also called **Kao-seng chuan ssu-chi** 高僧傳四集), 6 *chüan*, written by Ju-hsing 如惺, author's preface dated 1617. (1) Chin-ling K'o-ching-ch'u 金陵刻經處 punctuated block-print edition of 1884–1892. 24 *ts'e*. (2) *Taisho Shinshu Daizokyo*, Vol. 50, Nos. 2059–2062.[2]

This work is made up of the biographies of Chinese and a few Indian Buddhist monks, the first collection covering the period from A.D. 67 to 519, the second the period from 502 to 645, the third the period from 618 to about 988, and the fourth the Sung, the Yüan, and the early part of the Ming dynasty. Each collection is divided into ten sections, with such headings as Translators of the Canon, Interpreters of the Canon, Upholders of the Doctrine, and Teachers of the Canon. In each section the biographies are arranged chronologically. Besides presenting information relating to the lives of individual monks, the biographies frequently contain more general material on Buddhist history and doctrine. The first two collections are considered particularly important by students of Chinese Buddhism, and they are frequently quoted in modern writings. There is an index based on the Wade-Giles romanization.[3]

Hsin-hsü kao-seng chuan ssu-chi 新續高僧傳四集, 65 *chüan*. Written by Yü-ch'ien 喻謙. Pei-yang yin-shua-chü 北洋印刷局 movable-type edition of 1923. 16 *ts'e*.

2. This edition differs somewhat from the Chin-ling K'o-ching-ch'u edition collated by Yang Wen-hui 楊文會, the number of *chüan* in the four collections being 14, 30, 30, and 8, respectively. Furthermore, there are fewer biographies in the second collection, and there are occasional differences in the text and in the punctuation.

3. H. Hackmann, *Alphabetisches Verzeichnis zum Kao Seng Ch'uan* (Leiden: E. J. Brill, 1923). [32] pp. (*Acta Orientalia*).

Because the *Ming kao-seng chuan* is incomplete and rather poorly written, this work was written to provide supplementary biographies of Buddhist monks who lived in the Sung, Yüan, Ming, and Ch'ing dynasties. The form and style follow very closely those of the first two collections of the *Kao-seng chuan*. There is a table of contents at the beginning, and there is also a table of contents for each *chüan*.

2. REPUBLICAN PERIOD

Tsui-chin kuan-shen li-li hui-lu 最近官紳履歷彙錄. Peking: Fu-wen-she 敷文社, 1920. [90] 258 pp.

This is a directory of officials, which contains brief biographical notes concerning some four thousand persons who were holding positions in the central government or in various local governments in 1920. The names are arranged according to the number of strokes, and under each name are given the *hao*, age in 1920, native place, record of higher education, record of official career, and position at the time of compilation. The notes are, with some exceptions, very brief; nevertheless they frequently contain information which is not readily obtainable elsewhere. There is an index to names (also giving *hao*) at the beginning, arranged according to the number of strokes.

Hsin Chung-kuo fen-sheng jen-wu chih 新中國分省人物志. Compiled by Sonoda Ikki 園田一龜, translated into Chinese by Huang Hui-ch'üan 黃惠泉 and Tiao Ying-hua 刁英華. Shanghai: Liang-yu t'u-shu yin-shua kung-ssu 良友圖書印刷公司, 1930. [24] 578 pp.

This is a collection of biographies arranged province by province, which also traces the development of modern Chinese provincialism and nepotism. The author was an expert on Manchuria and Mongolia, but he was also well acquainted with Chinese political conditions in 1926, so that his analysis of Chinese government personnel is very good. Unfortunately this Chinese translation has no index.

Tang-tai Chung-kuo ming-jen-lu 當代中國名人錄. Compiled by Fan Yin-nan 樊蔭南. Shanghai: Liang-yu t'u-shu yin-shua kung-ssu 良友圖書印刷公司, 1931. [11] 460 pp.

This is a "who's who" containing brief biographical notes on approximately four thousand prominent modern Chinese. In general the following information is given under each name: alternative names, age, native place, higher education, official and professional positions previously held, and present position; sometimes the titles of writings are also listed. The material used in the compilation of this work was derived from newspapers and magazines, from various official directories, and from personal inquiries. In no sketch are there more than one hundred characters, and there are often as few as ten. The names are arranged according to the number of strokes, and there is an index to surnames at the beginning, arranged in the same way.

Tang-tai tang-kuo ming-jen chuan 當代黨國名人傳. Compiled by Yüan Ch'ing-p'ing 袁清平 and others. Canton: Ku-chin t'u-shu she 古今圖書社, 1936. 2 vols. 24, 524 pp.

This is a collection of brief biographies of prominent members of the Kuomintang. The first volume treats 259 military officers; the second contains biographies of 122 civil officials and politicians, 30 diplomats, 30 financiers, 24 educators, 26 persons noted for work in reconstruction, and 10 jurists. The book, while not scholarly, is useful for quick reference. There are 48 photographs at the beginning of each volume.

Chung-hua min-kuo ming-jen chuan 中華民國名人傳. Compiled by Chia I-chün 賈逸君. Peiping: Wen-hua hsüeh-she 文化學社, 1932–1933. 2 vols. [18] [484] pp.; [8] [367] [125] pp.

This is a "who's who" of 318 Chinese who had been prominent since the 1911 Revolution. It is divided according to professions into twelve sections, and within each section the names are arranged according to the number of strokes, except that Sun Yat-sen's name appears first. Short biographies or autobiographies which already existed were incorporated into this work wherever possible; when such did not exist, new biographical sketches were written by the compiler, giving dates of birth and death according to the Western calendar, alternative names, and important facts about the person's career. Occasionally the titles of important writings are also included. There is a list of twenty-nine works which were used as sources. At the beginning of each volume there is a list of the biographies included in it. There are two appendixes: one, a list of persons who died between 1911 and 1932 (including many who were not considered sufficiently important to have biographies in the main part of the work), giving after each name the *hao*, a few words concerning the man's career, and the date of death if known; the other, a list of more than two thousand persons still alive at the time of compilation giving in each case the *hao*, the native province and district, and the highest official position held. The names in the first appendix are arranged in the order of the date of death, while those in the second are arranged according to the number of strokes in the name.

Min-kuo ming-jen t'u-chien 民國名人圖鑑. Compiled by Yang Chia-lo 楊家駱. Nanking: Tz'u-tien kuan 辭典館, 1937. 2 vols. [139] 132 pp. illus. [836] pp.; 104 pp. illus. [676] pp.

This is an illustrated "who's who" of the Republican period, not confined to persons living at the time of publication. According to the compiler, about 20,000 biographies and 1500 pictures are included. Names are arranged by the number of strokes. For those who read Japanese there is a useful collection of the biographies of more than 4500 Chinese intellectuals who lived during the Republican period.[4]

Chung-kuo tang-tai ming-jen chuan 中國當代名人傳. Compiled by Fu Jun-hua 傅潤華 and Ting Ti-sheng 丁滌生. Shanghai: Shih-chieh wen-hua fu-wu she 世界文化服務社, 1948. 12, 310 pp.

This is a "who's who" of prominent persons in Kuomintang China at the time of publication. There are two hundred biographies, which are arranged according to the number of strokes in the names, except for those of the president and vice president of the Central Government, which come first. Sources are not given.

Hsien-tai hua-ch'iao jen-wu chih 現代華僑人物志. Compiled by Hsiang Ch'eng 向誠. Taipei: Ta Chung-hua ch'u-pan she 大中華出版社, 1964. 16, 380 pp.

This is a collection of 185 biographies of overseas Chinese who are presumably *persona grata* to the Taipei government. Sixty live in Thailand, the Philippines or South Vietnam, thirty-seven in Latin America, twenty-four in Hong Kong or Macao, fourteen in the United States, and the rest are scattered elsewhere around the world. Sources are not given.

Tung-nan-ya jen-wu chih 東南亞人物志. Compiled by Koh Kow Chiang 許敎正. Singapore: New Life Co. 新生有限公司, 1965. [17] 274 [64] pp.

This is a biographical dictionary of more than 500 prominent overseas Chinese in Southeast Asia. While most are biographies of persons still alive,

---

4. **Chūgoku bunkakai jimbutsu sōkan** 中國文化界人物總鑑. Compiled by Hashikawa Tokio 橋川時雄. (1) Peiping: Chung-hua fa-ling pien-i kuan 中華法令編譯館, 1940. [8] 82, 815 [48] pp. (2) Taipei: Ku-t'ing shu-wu, 1969 (photocopy). Each brief biography includes ordinary name and *hao*, date of birth, date of death if appropriate at time of compilation, native place, education, special interests, public services performed, publications, and photograph when available. The work is based on earlier publications of the same kind and on personal research. There is a number-of-strokes index to names.

a number are of historical figures, including Cheng Chao 鄭昭, who was king of Siam for thirteen years during the second-half of the eighteenth century. Though sources are not given, this is a useful reference work.

3.   COMMUNIST CHINA

Chung-kung jen-ming tien 中共人名典. Compiled by Chang Ta-chün 張大軍. Hong Kong: Tzu-yu ch'u-pan she 自由出版社, 1957. 2, 224 pp.

This biographical dictionary supplies brief but informative notes on some twenty-one hundred leaders of Communist China during the 1940's and 1950's, many of whom have since disappeared from view. A number of biographies are of persons who were not members of the Communist Party though they lived and worked in the People's Republic.

Chung-kung jen-ming lu 中共人名録. Compiled by an *ad hoc* committee 中共人名録編修委員會 headed by Kuo Hua-lun 郭華倫, Fang Hsüeh-shun 方雪純, *et al.* Taipei: Institute of International Relations 國際關係研究所, 1967. 4, 24, 756, 94 pp.

This is a "who's who" of Communist China compiled from the enormous research resources in Taiwan. It contains 2013 short biographies of party and government figures down to the provincial level and military officers down to the division level, as well as important persons in scientific, educational, artistic, and other circles. Of particular value is the large amount of political background and inside information supplied on the Chinese Communist Party and its leaders, the compilers being mostly professional experts on the subject.

Chung-kung chün-jen chih 中共軍人誌. Compiled by Huang Chen-hsia 黃震遐. Hong Kong: Research Institute of Contemporary History 當代歷史研究所, 1968. 5, 20, 790, 11 pp.

This "who's who" of Chinese Communist military personnel has as an English title *Mao's Generals*. It was compiled by an ex-army officer who is a veteran journalist. Each of the 726 sketches begins with a brief statement of the most recent events in the person's life and of his importance, followed by the place and date of birth and a narration of his career. The length varies from twelve pages in the case of Lin Piao to a few lines for relatively unimportant figures. Sources are occasionally indicated and there is a bibliography at the end. There was some inconsistency in the selection of biographies to be included, for whereas Mao Tse-tung and Chou En-lai are excluded, presumably because they are not professional military men, there are biographies of the scientist Ch'ien Hsüeh-sen and the wife of Lin Piao, Yeh Ch'ün. The biographies are arranged by the number-of-strokes system, and there is a Wade-Giles romanization index.

B. WORKS USEFUL FOR DATING IMPORTANT PERSONS

Very few Chinese biographical dictionaries indicate the year in which a man was born or the year in which he died, and it is the function of the first three works described below to give the years of birth and death for all persons of importance for whom such information is available. The other three works are sometimes helpful in approximately dating persons who lived during the Ming and Ch'ing dynasties but for whom more exact dates are not known.

I-nien-lu hui-pien 疑年錄彙編, 16 *chüan*, with supplement, rhyme index to names, 1 *chüan*. Compiled by Chang Wei-hsiang 張惟驤. (1) Hsiao-shuang ch'i-an 小雙寂庵 block-print edition of 1925. 8 *ts'e*. (2) *Hsiao-shuang ch'i-an ts'ung-shu, ts'e* 1–8.

This is a combination of six tables of dates of birth and death, listing a total of approximately four thousand persons of importance, beginning with Confucius and ending with persons born in 1885. The works combined in the *I-nien-lu hui-pien* are: (1) **I-nien-lu** 疑年錄 by Ch'ien Ta-hsin 錢大昕, (2) **Hsü i-nien-lu** 續疑年錄 by Wu Hsiu 吳修, (3) **Pu i-nien-lu** 補疑年錄 by Ch'ien Chiao 錢椒, (4) **San-hsü i-nien-lu** 三續疑年錄 by Lu Hsin-yüan 陸心源, (5) **I-nien keng-lu** 疑年賡錄 by Chang Ming-k'o 張鳴珂, and (6) **Wu-hsü i-nien-lu** 五續疑年錄 by Min Erh-ch'ang 閔爾昌. Of these, the first, second and sixth are the most reliable; the others are marred by errors, Lu Hsin-yüan's *San-hsü i-nien-lu* being the least reliable. In the *I-nien-lu hui-pien* the names are arranged in chronological order according to the year of birth, and each page is divided into four horizontal columns, which give the following information: (1) surname, *hao*, length of life, *ming*, and years of birth and death; (2) the abbreviated title and *chüan* number of the original table from which the material was derived, or, if supplied by Chang Wei-hsiang, an indication of that fact; (3) notes indicating original sources or discussing doubtful points, copied from the original tables; and (4) notes of the same nature supplied by Chang. In *chüan* 16, sixty-eight famous women and sixty-two Buddhist and Taoist monks are listed separately, Although the names of many persons of importance whose dates of birth and death are ascertainable were omitted from it, and the dates should be used with some caution, this is still a helpful work. There is an index to names, arranged according to rhyme.

Shih-shih i-nien-lu 釋氏疑年錄, 12 *chüan*. Compiled by Ch'en Yüan 陳垣. (1) *Fu-jen ta-hsüeh ts'ung-shu* 輔仁大學叢書, No. 5, 1939. 4 *ts'e*. (2) Peking: Chung-hua shu-chü, 1964. [6] 472, 38 pp.

This is a list of 2800 Buddhist monks in China, giving the dates of their births and deaths, and covering the period from the third century A.D. to 1698. To avoid confusion because of more than one person having the same name, the name of his native place or of his temple is placed before the name of each monk. All entries are arranged chronologically. Sources are carefully indicated in each case. Ch'en Yüan is noted for his accuracy, and this work is no exception. A number-of-strokes index has been published to the final characters of the monks' names.[5]

Li-tai ming-jen nien-li pei-chuan tsung-piao 歷代名人年里碑傳總表. Compiled by Chiang Liang-fu 姜亮夫. (1) Shanghai: Commercial Press, 1937. [11] 555, 42 pp. (2) Peking: Chung-hua shu-chü, 1959. 8, 753, 87 pp. (uses character 綜 instead of 總 in the title). (3) Taipei: Commercial Press, 1965. [13] 589 [56] pp.

This is the largest compilation of the years of birth and/or death of Chinese historical figures that has appeared, supplying such information for more than 9,000 persons (the compiler claims to have included more than 12,000). Names are arranged chronologically according to the year of birth, or if that is not known, the year of death, and there is a four-corner index to all names. The 1959 edition corrects many of the factual and typographical errors that mar the first edition, and the 1965 edition claims to be an enlarged version.

Kuo-ch'ao li-k'o t'i-ming pei-lu (ch'u-pien) 國朝歷科題名碑錄 (初編) (also called **Chin-shih t'i-ming pei-lu** 進士題名碑錄); including a supplement listing the names of persons granted the *chin-shih* degree between 1371 and 1643. Compiled by Li Chou-wang 李周望, and supplemented by Ch'ien Wei-ch'eng 錢維城 and, later, others; Li's preface dated 1720; Ch'ien's preface dated 1746. (1) Block-print edition of the Ch'ien-lung period, containing material down to 1778. 10 *ts'e*. (2) Block-print edition of the T'ung-chih period, containing material down to 1862. 13 *ts'e*.

5. "**Shih-shih i-nien-lu t'ung-chien**" 釋氏疑年錄通檢. Compiled by Chao Wei-pang 趙衛邦 and Yeh Te-lu 葉德錄. *Fu-jen hsüeh-chih* 輔仁學誌, 9, No. 2 (December 1940). 16 pp.

This is a list of the names of persons who received the *chin-shih* degree (as a result of having passed the regular triennial and occasional special metropolitan examinations), from the beginning of the Ming dynasty down to the time of publication. The names of all persons passing a single examination are grouped together in the order of the ranking given their examination papers by the examiners. Under each name the successful candidate's province, prefecture, and district are given. There are occasional copying mistakes and the order of names sometimes differs from the original order, but on the whole this work is very useful because a large majority of the scholars and Chinese officials of the Ming and Ch'ing dynasties received the *chin-shih* degree, and definite knowledge of the years in which they received it makes it possible approximately to date many whom it might not otherwise be possible to date at all.

Tseng-chiao Ch'ing-ch'ao chin-shih t'i-ming pei-lu fu yin-te 增校清朝進士題名碑錄附引得. Enlarged, edited, and furnished with an index by Fang Chao-ying 房兆楹 and Tu Lien-che 杜聯喆. (1) Peiping: Harvard-Yenching Institute, 1941. (Supplement No. 19) xxvi, 434 pp. (2) Taipei: Ch'eng Wen Publishing Co., 1966 (photocopy).

This is a collection of 112 lists of *chin-shih*, the persons who passed the regular or special civil sevice examinations held in Peking from 1646 to 1904. There are also lists of graduates of foreign universities and of two Chinese universities who were awarded the *chin-shih* between 1905 and 1911. Altogether 26,747 *chin-shih* are listed, arranged under the examinations in which they acquired this degree. 259 received the award after the traditional examinations were abolished. Besides the name, the native place is given. There is a *kuei-hsieh* index to names and number-of-strokes and Wade-Giles romanization keys to surnames.

Tz'u-lin chi-lüeh 詞林輯略, 11 *chüan*. Compiled by Chu Ju-chen 朱汝珍. Chung-yang k'o-ching-yüan 中央刻經院 movable-type edition, undated, but probably published about 1927. 5 *ts'e*.

This is a list of the scholars who passed the triennial palace examination between 1646 and 1905 and who were then admitted to membership in the Hanlin Yüan 翰林院. The names of 114 persons who graduated from foreign or Chinese universities and were admitted to membership in the Hanlin Yüan between 1905 and 1911 are also recorded. The names are arranged under the different examinations in the order of the ranking given the papers by the examiners, with those admitted between 1905 and 1911 grouped at the end. Under each name alternative names, native province and district, official position while in the Hanlin Yüan, later official career, and important writings are indicated. An index to names at the end, arranged according to the rhyme, gives the year of the examination under which each name is to be found.

C. INDEXES TO *NIEN-P'U*

These works serve as indexes to persons for whom there are *nien-p'u* 年譜, chronological biographies. In other words, they are bibliographies of *nien-p'u*, arranged under the names of their subjects.

Chung-kuo li-tai ming-jen nien-p'u mu-lu 中國歷代名人年譜目錄. Compiled by Li Shih-t'ao 李士濤. Shanghai: Commercial Press, 1941. [9] 60 [20] pp.

This bibliography of *nien-p'u* lists chronological biographies of persons living from the Chou period to the twentieth century. Altogether 1108 biographies of 964 people are included, arranged according to the years of birth of the persons. The names and dates of compilers and information on editions are supplied. This catalogue is more nearly complete, particularly with respect to bibliographical data, than other similar works, though there are some mistakes and typographical errors. At the end there is a four-corner index.

Li-tai ming-jen nien-p'u tsung-mu 歷代名人年譜總目. Compiled by Wang Pao-hsien 王寶先. Taichung: Tunghai 東海 University Library, 1965. 46, 353 pp.

This index to the chronological biographies of some 1200 eminent Chinese is arranged according to time sequence from the Duke of Chou to Feng Chien 馮簡, who died in 1962. Under each name the title of the biography and its source are given, followed by the person's alternative names, native place and years of birth and death. At the beginning of the volume there is a list of names arranged by the number of strokes, each name furnished with dates of birth and death according to the Western calendar. Near the end there are lists of biographies of Buddhists, Koreans, and a few Italian and French Jesuits in China. There is also an index to alternative names.

Rekidai meijin nempu mokuroku or **Li-tai ming-jen nien-p'u mu-lu** 歷代名人年譜目錄. Compiled and published in Kyoto by the Jimbun kagaku kenkyūjo, 1951. [6] 163 pp.

This is a catalogue of 1013 Chinese chronological biographies, beginning with that of the Duke of Chou and ending with Wen I-to 聞一多 (1899–1946). With its various indexes, this is a useful checklist.

D. INDEXES TO GENERAL COLLECTIONS OF BIOGRAPHIES OR TO BIOGRAPHICAL MATERIAL IN OTHER COLLECTIONS

The first two works listed in this subsection are indexes to the biographies in all the dynastic histories except the *Ch'ing-shih*, which has its own index. The others are indexes to collections of biographies or to biographical data in other kinds of collections, all limited to particular dynasties.

★Erh-shih-wu shih jen-ming so-yin 二十五史人名索引. (1) Shanghai: K'ai-ming shu-tien, 1935. 518 pp. (2) Peking: Chung-hua shu-chü, 1956. 518 pp. (3) Taipei: K'ai-ming shu-tien, 1961. 518 pp.

This is a four-corner index to the names of all persons having biographies or biographical notes in the *pen-chi* 本紀, *shih-chia* 世家, or *lieh-chuan* 列傳 sections of the twenty-five dynastic histories, which include the *Hsin Yüan-shih* 新元史 that was given official recognition during the Republican period. Under each name are given the abbreviated title of the history or histories in which the biographical data are to be found, the *chüan* number, and the page and column in the K'ai-ming edition of the *Erh-shih-wu shih*. There is a key to surnames at the end, which is arranged by the number of strokes.

Nien-ssu-shih chuan-mu yin-te 廿四史傳目引得. Compiled by Liang Ch'i-hsiung 梁啓雄. (1) Shanghai: Chung-hua shu-chü, 1936. [34] 440 pp. (2) Taipei: Chung-hua shu-chü, 1960.

This is an index to the biographies in the twenty-four dynastic histories. In the main body of the work names are arranged according to the number of strokes, with the *chüan* number of the dynastic history following. There are also a number of lists of special categories of persons in which the names are arranged chronologically. These include heroines or chaste women, empresses and imperial concubines, imperial princes, imperial princesses, foreigners, adventurers, eunuchs, assassins, hermits, Buddhists, Taoists, and so forth. This index is not as complete as the *Erh-shih-wu shih jen-ming so-yin* (q.v.), but its lists of special categories of persons are useful. There are number-of-strokes and Wade-Giles romanization keys to surnames at the beginning.

Liang Han pu-lieh-chuan jen-ming yün-pien 兩漢不列傳人名韻編, 10 *chüan*. Compiled by Chuang Ting-i 莊鼎彝, compiler's preface dated 1885. Shanghai: Commercial Press, 1935. [10] [298] pp.

This is an index to the names of persons mentioned in the *Ch'ien Han-shu* 前漢書 and the *Hou Han-shu* 後漢書, but who do not have separate biographies in those works. The index is divided into four sections: members of the royal family mentioned in the *Ch'ien Han-shu*, ordinary persons mentioned in the *Ch'ien Han-shu*, members of the royal family mentioned in the *Hou Han-shu*, and ordinary persons mentioned in the *Hou Han-shu*. In each section the names are arranged according to their rhyme. After each name the following information is usually given: relationship to some more prominent person, official titles, and the section of the dynastic history in which the person is referred to—more often than not another person's biography. Alternative names are occasionally given and sometimes brief biographical facts. There is a four-corner index at the end, but Chuang's failure to indicate *chüan* numbers makes the work inconvenient to use.

San-kuo-chih jen-ming lu 三國志人名錄. Compiled by Wang Tsu-i 王祖彝. Shanghai: Commercial Press, 1957. 5, 6, 229, 18, 38, 4 pp.

This is an index to 4065 personal names of the third century referred to in the terse text of the *San-kuo-chih*, written by Ch'en Shou 陳壽, and more importantly in the much longer, scholarly and informative commentaries on that work by P'ei Sung-chih 裴松之. Neither the *Erh-shih-wu shih jen-ming so-yin* nor the *Nien-ssu-shih chuan-mu yin-te* (qq.v.) indexes the biographical material in P'ei's commentaries. The names are arranged by the number of strokes and there is a four-corner index. The sources cited in P'ei's commentaries are listed in an appendix.

Ssu-shih-ch'i-chung Sung-tai chuan-chi tsung-ho yin-te 四十七種宋代傳記綜合引得. (1) Peiping: Harvard-Yenching Institute, 1939. (Index No. 34). xxiv, 199 pp. (2) Tokyo: Japan Council for East Asian Studies, 1959 (photocopy).

This is a combined index to forty-seven collections of Sung dynasty biographies. It consists of two parts: an index to alternative and fancy names, supplying the ordinary name in each case, and an index to ordinary names, giving the location of the biographies. Altogether the biographies of 9204 persons are indexed. The compiler, Nieh Ch'ung-ch'i 聶崇岐, was a specialist on this period.

Liao Chin Yüan chuan-chi san-shih-chung tsung-ho yin-te 遼金元傳記三十種綜合引得. (1) Peiping: Harvard-Yenching Institute, 1940. (Index No. 35) xxiv, 207 pp. (2) Tokyo: Japan Council for East Asian Studies, 1960 (photocopy).

This is a combined *kuei-hsieh* index to thirty collections of biographies of persons who lived during the Liao, Chin and Yüan periods. After alternative or fancy names the ordinary name of the person is given, and after ordinary names the location of the biographies is mentioned.

Sōjin denki sakuin or **Sung-jen chuan-chi so-yin** 宋人傳記索引. Compiled by the Japanese Committee for Cooperation with the Sung Project 宋史提要編纂協力委員會. Tokyo: Tōyō bunko 東洋文庫, 1968. [16] 274, 15 pp.

This index to some 8,000 biographies of the Sung, Liao, and Chin dynasties is an important supplement to the Harvard-Yenching Institute indexes: *Ssu-shih-ch'i-chung Sung-tai chuan-chi tsung-ho yin-te* and *Liao Chin Yüan chuan-chi san-shih-chung tsung-ho yin-te* (qq.v.). It covers many more sources, indexing the biographical information in 312 collections of essays, 28 collections of epigraphs, and 28 local gazetteers. The persons indexed are not necessarily eminent historical figures, and include many women, Buddhists, and Taoists. The arrangement is compact, informative, and clear, and it is easy to locate a person's name, the entries being listed according to the number of strokes. Each page is divided into seven vertical columns: the first gives each person's name; the second, alternative name (*tzu*); the third, native place; the fourth, dates of birth and death; the fifth, the person's parentage (three generations if known); the sixth, degrees and official posts; and the last the sources of relevant biographical material. There is a preface by Aoyama Sadao 青山定雄. At the end of the volume there are two indexes to surnames, one arranged by the Japanese pronunciation and the other by the Wade-Giles system.

Yüan-yen-chi shan-ts'un fu yin-te 琬琰集刪存附引得. (1) Peiping: Harvard-Yenching Institute, 1938. (Supplement No. 12) 3 *ts'e*. (2) Taipei: Ch'eng Wen Publishing Co., 1966 (photocopy).

This is a selection from Tu Ta-kuei's 杜大珪 *Ming-ch'en pei-chuan yüan-yen chih-chi* 名臣碑傳琬琰之集, which consists of biographies and epitaphs of 221 ministers of the Sung dynasty. Much of the material is no longer available in Sung editions. The Harvard-Yenching Institute secured a Sung copy of Tu Ta-kuei's work, from which valuable materials were selected, edited, and indexed to facilitate their use by scholars studying this period.

Sung Yüan ti-fang-chih chuan-chi so-yin 宋元地方志傳記索引. Compiled by Chu Shih-chia 朱士嘉. Peking: Chung-hua shu-chü, 1963. 9, 182 pp.

The many biographies located in Chinese gazetteers all too frequently remain unnoticed and unused. This is an index to several hundred biographies in more than thirty gazetteers compiled during the Sung and Yüan dynasties. The names of the subjects of these biographies are arranged by the number of strokes system, and there is a four-corner index at the end.

Pa-shih-chiu-chung Ming-tai chuan-chi tsung-ho yin-te 八十九種明代
傳記綜合引得. Compiled by T'ien Chi-tsung 田繼綜. (1) Peiping: Harvard-
Yenching Institute, 1935. (Index No. 24) 3 vols. xxxii, 138; 326; 281 pp.
(2) Taipei: Ch'eng Wen Publishing Co., 1966 (photocopy).

This is a combined index to eighty-nine important collections of biographies
of persons who lived under the Ming dynasty or who were loyal to it after
it was superseded by the Ch'ing. The names of approximately thirty thousand
persons are indexed by the *kuei-hsieh* system: ordinary names are indexed in
the second and third volumes, and alternative names in the first.

Ming-jen chuan-chi tzu-liao so-yin 明人傳記資料索引. Compiled by
Ch'ang Pi-te 昌彼得, Ch'iao Yen-kuan 喬衍琯, Sung Ch'ang-lien 宋常廉, *et
al*. Taipei: National Central Library, 1965–66. 2 vols. [20] 963, 6, 73, 116
pp.

This is an index to the biographical material on personalities of the Ming
period that is to be found in nearly a thousand collections of Ming and early
Ch'ing belles-lettres preserved in the National Central Library in Taipei. The
names are arranged according to the number of strokes, with the regular name
supplied for alternative names and the regular name itself followed by a brief
biographical resumé and the location of biographical data in the collections
indexed.

Ku-chin t'u-shu chi-ch'eng chung Ming-jen chuan-chi so-yin 古今圖
書集成中明人傳記索引. Compiled by Chang Ch'ün 章羣 under the supervision of Mou Jun-sun 牟潤孫. Hong Kong, n.p., 1963. [16] 222 pp.

This index to the biographies of Ming personalities included in the *Ku-
chin t'u-shu chi-ch'eng* (q.v.) was compiled under the auspices of the Project
Committee for the Ming Biographical Dictionary. The more than 20,000
biographical references are arranged alphabetically in accordance with the
Wade-Giles romanization. At the beginning of the volume there is an alphabetical list of romanized Chinese surnames.

San-shih-san-chung Ch'ing-tai chuan-chi tsung-ho yin-te 三十三種清代
傳記綜合引得. Compiled by Tu Lien-che 杜聯喆 and Fang Chao-ying 房兆楹.
(1) Peiping: Harvard-Yenching Institute, 1932. (Index No. 9) xxi, 392 pp.
(2) Tokyo: Japan Council for East Asian Studies, 1960 (photocopy).

This is a combined *kuei-hsieh* index to thirty-three collections of biographies
of persons who lived during the Ch'ing dynasty. At the beginning are Wade-
Giles romanization and number-of-strokes indexes to surnames.

Ch'ing-tai pei-chuan-wen t'ung-chien 清代碑傳文通檢. Compiled by Ch'en Nai-ch'ien 陳乃乾. Peking: Chung-hua shu-chü, 1959. [5] 410 pp. **Ch'ing-jen pieh-chi ch'ien-chung pei-chuan-wen yin-te chi pei-chuan-chu nien-li p'u** 清人別集千種碑傳文引得及碑傳主年里譜. Compiler's name given as Yang Chia-lo 楊家駱. Yangmingshan, Taiwan: Institute for Advanced Chinese Studies 中國文化學院, 1965. [4] 3, 410 pp.

This is an index to some 13,000 biographical notes on persons who lived and died during the Ch'ing dynasty (after 1644). It also includes some who were born before 1911 but have been active since. These biographic essays, funeral speeches, birthday eulogies, and other accounts are selected from 1,025 *wen-chi* (collections of essays and poems, usually by an individual writer). The entries are arranged by the number of strokes. For each entry the following information is supplied: the person's name, his alternative names (*tzu* and *hao*), native province and district, dates of birth and death (according to both Chinese and Western calendars), and the sources, including enough bibliographic data for identification and location. There are three supplements: (1) a list of alternative names including cases of more than one personal name (*ming*) and of other adopted names, (2) conflicting dates of birth and death when such appear in different sources, and (3) a bibliography of works cited, with a total of 1153 titles, 128 of which contain no biographies. Compiled during the 1940's by Ch'en Nai-ch'ien, this is an excellent biographical reference work, complementing the *San-chih-san-chung Ch'ing-tai chuan-chi tsung-ho yin-te* and the *Ch'ing-tai wen-chi p'ien-mu fen-lei so-yin* (qq.v.). Except for a few sentences in the preface and the title and publication data, the Taiwan edition is an exact reproduction of the Peking edition.

Hakki tsūshi retsuden sakuin or **Pa-ch'i t'ung-chih lieh-chuan so-yin** 八旗通志列傳索引. Compiled and published by the Seminar on Manchu History, Tōyō bunko 東洋文庫: 滿文老檔研究會, Tokyo, 1965. iii, 206 pp.

This is an index to biographical material on some 4,000 Manchu bannermen in the biographical sections of the *Pa-ch'i t'ung-chih*. There are number-of-strokes and romanization keys.

E. INDEXES TO BIOGRAPHIES OF WRITERS AND PAINTERS

The indexes in this section, except the last two, are to scattered biographical material on pre-Ming writers, and also incidentally to selected compositions of the same writers that are to be found in the various anthologies indexed. The last two works index collections of biographies of Ch'ing dynasty painters and calligraphers.

Ch'üan shang-ku San-tai Ch'in Han San-kuo Liu-ch'ao wen tso-che yin-te 全上古三代秦漢三国六朝文作者引得. Compiled by William Hung 洪業, Nieh Ch'ung-ch'i 聶崇岐 and others. (1) Peiping: Harvard-Yenching Institute, 1932. (Index No. 8) vi [40] pp. (2) Taipei: Ch'eng Wen Publishing Co., 1966 (photocopy).

This is a *kuei-hsieh* index to brief biographical notes about 3497 pre-T'ang authors whose writings are collected in the *Ch'üan shang-ku San-tai Ch'in Han San-kuo Liu-ch'ao wen* 全上古三代秦漢六朝文, a 746-*chüan* anthology of pre-T'ang prose collected by Yen K'o-chün 嚴可均 (1762–1843). The index is to the 1893 Kuang-ya shu-chü 廣雅書局 edition, of which a photocopy was published in 1963 in Taipei by the Shih-chieh shu-chü. Besides the usual number-of-strokes and Wade-Giles romanization keys, there is one arranged according to the rhyme.

Ch'üan Han San-kuo Chin Nan-pei-ch'ao shih tso-che yin-te 全漢三國晉南北朝詩作者引得. Compiled by Ts'ai Chin-chung 蔡金重. (1) Peiping: Harvard-Yenching Institute, 1941. (Index No. 39) x, 14 pp. (2) Taipei: Ch'eng Wen Publishing Co., 1966 (photocopy).

This is a *kuei-hsieh* index to the authors included in the *Ch'üan Han San-kuo Chin Nan-pei-ch'ao shih*, a collection of poems written between the beginning of Han and the beginning of Sui compiled in 54 *chüan* by Ting Fu-pao 丁福保.

Ch'üan T'ang-shih-wen tso-chia yin-te ho-pien 全唐詩文作家引得合編. Compiled by Lin Ssu-te 林斯德, and published in 1932 by the Library of the National Tsingtao University 國立青島大學圖書館. 215 pp.

This is a combined number-of-strokes index to the names of the writers of the poems collected in the *Ch'üan T'ang-shih* 全唐詩 (900 *chüan*) and of the essays collected in the *Ch'üan T'ang-wen* 全唐文 (1000 *chüan*). The first of these great collections was compiled under imperial auspices by Ts'ao Yin 曹寅 (imperial preface dated 1707), and the second was compiled under imperial auspices by Tung Kao 董誥 and others (in 1814). In both collections the poems or essays of each writer are grouped together, preceded by a short biographical sketch. Each page of the index is divided into three horizontal columns: the first gives the writer's full name, or, if that is not known, his pen name; the second gives the *han, ts'e, chüan,* and page of his biography in the 1887 T'ung-wen shu-chü 同文書局 lithographic edition of the *Ch'üan T'ang-shih;* and the third similarly gives the location of his biography in the 1901 Kuang-ya shu-chü 廣雅書局 block-print edition of the *Ch'üan T'ang-wen*. Although there are frequent errors and omissions, this index is a very useful one, serving as a key both to the biographical information and to the poems and essays contained in those two collections.

Tōdai no sambun sakka 唐代の散文作家. Compiled by Hiraoka Takeo 平岡武夫 and Imai Kiyoshi 今井清. Kyoto: Jimbun kagaku kenkyūjo, 1954. 28, 120 pp.

This is an author index to the T'ang prose writers in the *Ch'üan T'ang-wen* 全唐文, *T'ang-wen shih-i* 唐文拾遺 and *T'ang-wen hsü-shih* 唐文續拾. A total of 3,812 writers' names are arranged according to the four-corner system. Under each name the author's alternative names, place and time of birth and death, and degrees or official posts held (if known) are given. Every essay in the three collections is given a serial number under which its exact location is indicated. The *Ch'üan T'ang-wen*, in 1000 *chüan*, is a great reservoir of literary and historical material for the T'ang period, and this index is an indispensable key to it and to the two supplements. A separate index to alternative names, general tables of the royal families of T'ang and the Five Dynasties, and a comparative chronology of the Five Dynasties are furnished. A number-of-strokes index to characters is appended.

Tōdai no shijin 唐代の詩人. Compiled by Hiraoka Takeo 平岡武夫 and Ichihara Ryōkichi 市原亨吉. Kyoto: Jimbun kagaku kenkyūjo, 1960. 16, 178 pp.

This index to 2955 T'ang poets is arranged in the same way as the *Tōdai no sambun sakka* (q.v.).

T'ang-shih chi-shih chu-che yin-te 唐詩紀事著者引得. Compiled by William Hung 洪業, Nieh Ch'ung-ch'i 聶崇岐 and others. (1) Peiping: Harvard-Yenching Institute, 1934. (Index No. 18) xii, 15 pp. (2) Taipei: Ch'eng Wen Publishing Co., 1966 (photocopy).

This is a *kuei-hsieh* index to the names of 1150 writers whose best poems are collected in the *T'ang-shih chi-shih* 唐詩紀事. In that anthology of T'ang poetry, which was compiled during the Southern Sung period by Chi Yu-kung 計有功, the poems of each writer are grouped together, and a certain amount of material relating to the poems and to the writer is added. This index is to the *Ssu-pu ts'ung-k'an* edition.

Sung-shih chi-shih chu-che yin-te 宋詩紀事著者引得. Compiled by William Hung 洪業, Nieh Ch'ung-ch'i 聶崇岐 and others. (1) Peiping: Harvard-Yenching Institute, 1934. (Index No. 19) xviii, 127 pp. (2) Taipei: Ch'eng Wen Publishing Co., 1966 (photocopy).

This is a *kuei-hsieh* index to the names of more than 6800 writers whose best poems are collected in the *Sung-shih chi-shih* 宋詩紀事 and in the *Sung-shih chi-shih pu-i* 宋詩紀事補遺. In those anthologies of Sung poetry, which were compiled by Li Ao 厲鶚 (1692–1752) and Lu Hsin-yüan 陸心源 (1834–1894) respectively, the poems of each writer are grouped together and preceded by a short biographical notice. This index is to the 1746 block-print edition of the *Sung-shih chi-shih*, and to the 1893 block-print edition of the *Sung-shih chi-shih pu-i*.

Yüan-shih chi-shih chu-che yin-te 元詩紀事著者引得. Compiled by William Hung 洪業, Nieh Ch'ung-ch'i 聶崇岐 and others. (1) Peiping: Harvard-Yenching Institute, 1934. (Index No. 20) xii, 16 pp. (2) Taipei: Ch'eng Wen Publishing Co., 1966 (photocopy).

This is a *kuei-hsieh* index to the names of 1000 writers whose best poems are collected in the *Yüan-shih chi-shih* 元詩紀事. In that anthology of Yüan dynasty poetry, which was compiled in recent years and published by the Commercial Press 商務印書館 in 1921, the poems of each writer are grouped together and preceded by a brief biographical sketch. This index is to the Commercial Press edition.

Ch'ing-tai shu-hua-chia tzu-hao yin-te 清代書畫家字號引得. Compiled by Ts'ai Chin-chung 蔡金重. (1) Peiping: Harvard-Yenching Institute, 1934. (Index No. 21) xxxii, 179 pp. (2) Taipei: Ch'eng Wen Publishing Co., 1966 (photocopy).

This work consists of two combined *kuei-hsieh* indexes: the first, to the ordinary names of persons whose biographies are to be found in one or more of eight important collections of Ch'ing dynasty painters and calligraphers, and the second, to the alternative names of the same persons. The names of 5787 persons are indexed.

Ch'ing-hua-chuan chi-i san-chung fu yin-te 清畫傳輯佚三種附引得. (1) Peiping: Harvard-Yenching Institute, 1941. (Supplement No. 8) 42, 18 pp., 4 l. (2) Taipei: Ch'eng Wen Publishing Co., 1966 (photocopy).

This work reproduces three rare collections containing 373 short biographies of Ch'ing painters. Their names and alternative names are indexed.

F. WORKS ON IDENTICAL NAMES

Because of the limited number of Chinese surnames, it is quite common for several persons to have the same full name, and in reading Chinese books one frequently encounters a name which might belong to any one of several persons. The works described in this section were compiled to aid the reader in distinguishing between such persons.

Chiu-shih t'ung-hsing-ming lu 九史同姓名錄, 72 *chüan*, supplement 遺補, 4 *chüan*. Compiled by Wang Hui-tsu 汪輝祖, compiler's preface dated 1792. (1) *Kuang-ya ts'ung-shu, ts'e* 213–217. (2) *Ts'ung-shu chi-ch'eng*, vols. 3284–3291.

This is an index to the biographies of Chinese with identical names published in nine dynastic histories: the *Chiu T'ang-shu* 舊唐書, *Hsin T'ang-shu* 新唐書, *Chiu Wu-tai-shih* 舊五代史, *Hsin Wu-tai-shih* 新五代史, *Sung-shih* 宋史, *Liao-shih* 遼史, *Chin-shih* 金史, *Yüan-shih* 元史, and *Ming-shih* 明史. Names are arranged first by the rhyme of the surname, and under each surname the given names 名字 are arranged according to their radicals. Men are listed under each name in the order of the appearance of their biographies in the nine histories. There are also some included who have no biographies, and these are listed in their proper place in chronological order. When there is only one man with a particular name in any one dynasty, and he has a biography in one or more of the nine histories, only the reference to the biography or biographies is given with his name. When there are two or more men with the same name in one period who have biographies or who have no biographies in the nine histories, sufficient information is given about each one to identify him. The supplement introduces men omitted from the main body of the work.

Liao Chin Yüan san-shih t'ung-hsing-ming lu 遼金元三史同姓名錄 (also called **San-shih t'ung-hsing-ming lu** 三史同姓名錄), 40 *chüan*. Compilation begun by Wang Hui-tsu 汪輝祖 and completed by his son Wang Chi-p'ei 汪繼培. Wang Hui-tsu's postface dated 1801. (1) *Kuang-ya ts'ung-shu, ts'e* 218–219. (2) *Ts'ung-shu chi-ch'eng*, vols. 3292–3295.

This work is an index to all biographies in the *Liao-shih* 遼史, the *Chin-shih* 金史, and the *Yüan-shih* 元史 of non-Chinese whose full names were the same for two or more persons. The tribes which established the Liao and Chin dynasties had each only one surname for the whole tribe, and these are seldom mentioned in Chinese dynastic histories; the surnames of Mongols and certain other tribesmen are never mentioned in Chinese histories. Consequently all the names in this work are arranged by the rhyme of the first character of the name commonly recorded.

This work is divided into five parts: (1) names common to two or more persons appearing in the *Liao-shih*, 5 *chüan*; (2) names common to two or more persons appearing in the *Chin-shih*, 10 *chüan*; (3) names common to two or more persons appearing in the *Yüan-shih*, 20 *chüan*; (4) a combined list of the names appearing only once in each of two or three of the histories, and those appearing more than once in one history and also in one or both of the other histories; (5) names appearing in one or more of these three histories and also in one or more of the following: *Chiu Wu-tai-shih* 舊五代史, *Hsin Wu-tai-shih*

新五代史, *Sung-shih* 宋史, and *Ming-shih* 明史. The arrangement of the names in each of the five parts is first, according to the rhyme of the first character, and second, according to the radical of the second character. Under each name the name and *chüan* number of the work or works in which biographies appear are indicated. When there is a possibility of confusing persons of the same name, certain distinguishing facts are also included, and occasionally when a man has a surname which appears in his biography, it is also indicated here. The system of transliteration of non-Chinese names followed in this work is that which was current in China before the revision made during the Ch'ien-lung period. The last *chüan* consists of a table of all the names, arranged in the order of their appearance.

Li-tai t'ung-hsing-ming lu 歷代同姓名錄, 22 *chüan*; supplement 補遺, 1 *chüan*. Compiled by Liu Ch'ang-hua 劉長華, compiler's preface dated 1871, and his preface to the supplement dated 1880. (1) *Ch'ung-ch'uan Liu-shih ts'ung-shu* 崇川劉氏叢書, *ts'e* 6–12. (2) Hai-ning Ch'en-shih shen-ch'u-t'ang 海寧陳氏慎初堂 edition reprinted in 1926 from the original block-print edition, preface dated 1880. 6 *ts'e*.

This work lists together all important persons with identical names from earliest historical times down to end of the Ming dynasty. It is divided according to dynasties, although under each dynasty the names are arranged in no definite order beyond that of placing together those having the same surname. Under each full name are arranged the men bearing it, beginning with the earliest in that dynasty and including all of those in that and later dynasties, arranged in chronological order. Only enough information is given about each man definitely to identify him. The work is based principally upon the dynastic histories and the classics, although sources are not indicated in much detail. Names are difficult to find in the *Li-tai t'ung-hsing-ming lu* itself because they are always placed under the dynasties during which the first men to bear them lived. However, the Harvard-Yenching Institute has published an index which makes the location of all names very easy.[6]

★Ku-chin t'ung-hsing-ming ta-tz'u-tien 古今同姓名大辭典, 6 *chüan*. Compiled by P'eng Tso-chen 彭作楨. Peiping: Hao-wang shu-tien 好望書店, 1936. [39] 1239 pp.

This list of full names borne by more than one person is more nearly complete than any other work of its kind. According to the compiler's preface 16,000 full names are included, representing 56,700 different persons. The

---

6. **Li-tai t'ung-hsing-ming lu yin-te** 歷代同姓名錄引得. (1) Peiping: Harvard-Yenching Institute, 1931. (Index No. 4) iv, 28 pp. (2) Taipei: Ch'eng Wen Publishing Co., 1966 (photocopy).

work is based upon the *Ku-chin t'ung-hsing-ming lu* 古今同姓名錄 of the Liang Emperor Yüan 梁元帝, the *T'ung-hsing-ming lu* 同姓名錄 of Yü Yin 余寅, the *T'ung-hsing-ming p'u* 同姓名譜 of Ch'en Shih-chuang 陳士莊, the *Li-tai t'ung-hsing-ming lu*, the *Chiu-shih t'ung-hsing-ming lu*, and a few other works of the same nature, supplemented by material from more than twenty provincial gazetteers and a number of modern publications of various kinds. Surnames are arranged according to the number of strokes, and given names according to the radical. Each name is preceded by a numeral which indicates the number of persons listed under it; enough information is given concerning each person definitely to identify him, and the sources of the information are frequently given in some detail. There is an index to surnames at the beginning, arranged according to the number of strokes, and at the end there are a table of the persons listed in the *Ku-chin t'ung-hsing-ming lu* and an index to the names in Yü Yin's *T'ung-hsing-ming lu*, the latter arranged according to the number of strokes.

G. WORKS GIVING ALTERNATIVE AND POSTHUMOUS NAMES

In Chinese writings persons are often referred to by their alternative or by their posthumous names, and although these are sometimes given in some of the works described earlier, the works in this section are entirely devoted to the presentation of this type of material.

Ku-chin jen-wu pieh-ming so-yin 古今人物別名索引. Compiled by Ch'en Te-yün (Chan Tak Wan) 陳德芸. (1) Canton: Lingnan University Library 嶺南大學圖書館, 1937. 2, 630 pp. (2) Taipei: I-wen yin-shu-kuan, 1965. 630 pp.

This *Synonymy of Names of Distinguished Chinese, Ancient and Modern* lists the fancy, study, pen and other alternative names that are often used in Chinese literature instead of the ordinary name of the person referred to. The names are arranged by Ch'en's own system, in which characters are classified under thirteen outstanding strokes, but there is a number-of-strokes index at the end. Under each alternative name the person's ordinary name and the dynasty under which he lived are given. There is no indication of sources and the collection is far from complete.

Chung-kuo ti-hao piao-t'i i-lan 中國帝號標題一覽. Compiled by Hu Cheng-chih 胡正支. Peiping: Index Press, Yenching University, 1939. [vii] 86, 26 pp.

This is an index to the personal and other names and the reign titles of 373 Chinese emperors, from Huang-ti to Yüan Shih-k'ai. The names are arranged according to the number of strokes, with cross references. An appendix gives a chronological list of the emperors, with their dynasties and the length of each reign.

Shih-ming pieh-hao so-yin 室名別號索引. Compiled by Ch'en Nai-ch'ien 陳乃乾. (1) Peking: Chung-hua shu-chü, 1957. 20, 351 pp. (2) **Pieh-shu chü-ch'u ming t'ung-chien** 別署居處名通檢. Compiler's name given as Yang Chia-lo 楊家駱. Taipei: Shih-chieh shu-chü, 1962. 20, 351 pp. (3) **Li-tai jen-wu shih-ming pieh-hao t'ung-chien** 歷代人物室名別號通檢. Hong Kong: T'ai-p'ing shu-chü, 1964. 20, 351 pp.

This is a combined index to some 6000 *shih-ming* 室名, the names of private studies, libraries, gardens, and residences which have been used as parts of the titles of books or as alternative names of persons, and *pieh-hao* 別號, fancy names written in three or more characters which were generally adopted by persons themselves. Indexes to *shih-ming* and *pieh-hao* had been published as separate books in 1933 and 1936 respectively, but in 1957 the compiler, Ch'en Nai-ch'ien, combined the two into one. All entries are arranged by the number of strokes. The Taipei and Hong Kong editions, though bearing different titles, are photocopies of the Peking edition.

Chung-kuo li-tai shu-hua chuan-ko chia tzu-hao so-yin 中國歷代書畫篆刻家字號索引. Compiled by Shang Ch'eng-tso 商承祚 and Huang Hua 黃華. Peking: Jen-min mei-shu ch'u-pan-she, 1960. 2 vols. 1, 4, 1, 28, 1826; 8, 1128 pp.

This is an index to the alternative names of some 16,000 calligraphers, painters, seal artists, and engravers from the Ch'in dynasty to the Republican period. Volume One lists alternative names (*tzu* 字 and *hao* 號) which were used by many artists in their seals and signatures without indicating their family names. Some artists, such as Fu Shan 傅山, might use as many as forty different names, causing art collectors tremendous trouble in identifying their works. By locating in the first column the name used, one finds in the other columns the ordinary name of the artist, his native place, his specialty in art, his academic background, and the biographical source. Volume Two supplies the alternative names of artists whose ordinary names are known. Under each alternative name an arabic number refers to the page in Volume One where more information about the artist is available. The compiler is a specialist on oracle bones whose training in paleography enables him to read later seal characters without difficulty. At the beginning of each volume there is a list of characters arranged by the number of strokes, and at the end of Volume One there is a list of errata.

Hsien-tai Chung-kuo tso-chia pi-ming lu 現代中國作家筆名錄. Compiled by Yüan Yung-chin 袁湧進. (1) Peiping: Library Association of China, 1936. 144 pp. (2) Tokyo: Daian Bookstore, 1968. 144 pp.

This is a list of the names and pseudonyms of some 550 modern Chinese authors. The names are arranged by the number-of-strokes system, real names appearing in the first column on each page, followed by the corresponding pseudonyms in the second column. There is a number-of-strokes index to all the names, including pseudonyms, and an alphabetic index of those written in romanization.

Ch'ing shih-fa k'ao 清諡法考, 2 *chüan*. Compiled by Lei Yen-shou 雷延壽 and others, preface dated 1924. Movable-type edition. *2 ts'e.*

This collection of posthumous names of princes and ministers of the Ch'ing dynasty is based upon several earlier works of the same nature. Approximately eighteen hundred names are listed, divided into three sections: princes, civil officials, and military officials. There is no order of arrangement beyond the grouping together of names which have the same first character. Under each posthumous name the official title, the surname and *ming*, and the reign during which the person was granted the posthumous name are given. The rules for the granting of posthumous names are reproduced, those to princes before the first *chüan* and those to officials before the second *chüan*. An appendix lists persons whose posthumous names were later withdrawn, and also a few who for various reasons were not included in the body of the work.

H. IDENTIFICATION OF JAPANESE NAMES

In using Chinese source materials one frequently encounters difficulty in transliterating Japanese personal or place names from Chinese characters into romanization, or vice versa. To assist with this process, *Japanese Personal Names* and *Japanese Surnames*, compiled by I. V. Gillis and Pai Ping-ch'i and published in Peking in 1939 and 1940, are indispensable tools. These two volumes, however, do not solve all problems and may be supplemented by the following works.

Jih-pen hsien-tai ming-jen Chung-hsi-wen hsing-ming tui-chao-piao 日本現代名人中西文姓名對照表. Nanking: Intelligence and Publicity Department of the Ministry of Foreign Affairs, 1936. [4] 124 pp.

The student of modern Chinese history frequently confronts the difficulty of transcribing Japanese personal names from romanization into Chinese characters, or vice versa. This difficulty has been partially removed by the appearance of this *Vocabulary of Japanese Proper Names in Romanization and Chinese*. About two thousand names are included. The Japanese pronunciation in romanization is given first, followed by the Chinese characters, and then, in parentheses, indication of the profession of the person named. The names are arranged alphabetically. There is an index to the Chinese characters, arranged according to the number of strokes. This book is convenient to use and is very helpful in identifying the names of modern Japanese. It is, of course, far from complete.

Chung-hsi tui-i Jih-pen hsien-tai jen-ming ti-ming piao 中西對譯日本現代人名地名表. Compiled by Li Chi 李籍. Nanking: Cheng-chung shu-chü 正中書局, 1945. 2, 185 pp.

This collection of Japanese names is divided into two sections: (1) personal names and (2) place names. In each section the names are given first in romanization, arranged alphabetically, and followed by the proper characters; and then in a second part they are given first in characters, arranged by number of strokes, with the romanization following. Although this list also is incomplete and seems to have been hastily compiled, it is better than the one previously described.

I-pai ch'i-shih-wu chung Jih-pen ch'i-k'an-chung tung-fang-hsüeh lun-wen p'ien-mu, fu yin-te 一百七十五種日本期刊中東方學論文篇目，附引得. Compiled by Yü Shih-yü 于式玉 and Liu Hsüan-min 劉選民. (1) Peiping: Harvard-Yenching Institute. 1940. (Supplement No. 13) xliv, 198, 124, 36 pp. (2) Taipei: Ch'eng Wen Publishing Co., 1966 (photocopy).

This work includes an alphabetized author index in which the difficult readings of many Japanese personal names were checked by the renowned scholar Torii Ryūzō 鳥居龍藏.

VI TABLES

A. CONCORDANCES WITH THE WESTERN CALENDAR

Many tables have been published in China which may be used in transferring Chinese dates into the Western calendar and Western dates into the Chinese calendar; a few of the more important ones are included in this section.

Ou-Ya chi-yüan ho-piao 歐亞紀元合表. Compiled by Chang Huang 張璜.
(1) Shanghai: T'u-shan-wan tz'u-mu-t'ang 土山灣慈母堂, 1904. xlii, 488, 99 pp. (2) Tokyo: Daian Bookstore, 1968 (photocopy).

This is a combined chronological table for the years from B.C. 2357 to A.D. 1905, giving the corresponding years for China, Japan, Korea, Annam, Siam, and various Central Asian countries. The table is based upon the Western calendar, and the corresponding cyclical characters are given for each year. The reign titles and years are given not only for the recognized dynasties in China, but also for those of usurping and rebellious dynasties which existed at the same time. The work is very simply arranged, with the years according to the Western calendar indicated at the left-hand side of each page. At the beginning there are indexes to the names of all emperors: first those of recognized Chinese dynasties, then those of other Chinese dynasties which existed at the same time, followed by those of the other countries included—the names in each index being arranged chronologically. At the end of the work there is an index to all reign titles, arranged according to rhyme, giving the first and last years of each according to the Western calendar; and there is a key to the rhymes, arranged according to the number of strokes.

*Chung-hsi-hui-shih jih-li 中西回史日曆, (also called **Ch'en-shih Chung-hsi-hui-shih jih-li** 陳氏中西回史日曆), 20 *chüan*. Compiled by Ch'en Yüan 陳垣. (1) Peking: Sinological Research Institute of the National University of Peking, 1926. 5 *ts'e* (movable type). (2) Peking: Chung-hua shu-chü, 1962. 1034 pp. (revised and enlarged).

This is a comparative daily calendar of Chinese, Western and Mohammedan dates, from the year A.D. 1 to 1940. The Julian calendar is followed before 1582, after which the Gregorian calendar is used; years according to the Roman calendar are indicated down to A.D. 476, and the Mohammedan calendar begins in A.D. 622. On each leaf there are black arabic numerals representing 1441 days (roughly four years in the Western calendar). In the top margin the years according to the Western calendar, and the corresponding cyclical characters and Chinese emperors' names, and reign titles and years are all given in red Chinese characters; the years according to the Roman calendar or the Mohammedan calendar are given in red arabic numerals. In the tables of black arabic figures, those figures printed in bold-face indicate the month, and they are placed in the table in the place of the number "1" which would otherwise represent the first day of the month. The interlinear red Chinese numerals indicate the first day of each Chinese month, which corresponds to the day in the Western calendar beside which the Chinese numeral is placed. The red arabic numerals in the same way indicate the first day of the month according to the Mohammedan calendar. The red character *tung* 冬 marks the winter solstice and the red character *jun* 閏 the Chinese intercalary month. At the lower left-hand corner of each recto sets of red and black arabic numerals relate the preceding 1441 days to two transfer tables in the back of the work: one to foreign days of the week (the red dot marks Sunday), and the other to the Chinese cyclical characters which represent individual days. This work, which was very carefully compiled and which has served as the basis for most later works of the same nature, is in general simply and conveniently arranged, the only complicated features being the transfer tables to days of the week and to the cyclical characters of individual days. At the very end there are two keys to reign titles, one to the Japanese and the other to the Chinese, arranged according to the number of strokes and giving the first year of each according to the Western calendar. The revised edition extends to A.D. 2000.

Liang-ch'ien-nien-lai Chung-hsi li tui-chao piao 兩千年來中西曆對照表. Compiled by Hsüeh Chung-san 薛仲三 and Ou-yang I 歐陽頤. (1) Shanghai: Commercial Press, 1940. xx, 438 pp. (2) Peking: San-lien shu-tien 三聯書店, 1956. 438 pp.

This comparative calendar, extending from A.D. 1 to 2000, is based chiefly on the *Chung-hsi-hui shih jih-li* (q.v.). Each page of the main body of the work is divided horizontally into five sections, one for each year, and vertically into several columns. The first column on the left gives the year according to the Chinese calendar, with the reign-period and number of the year and the appropriate cyclical characters, as well as the year according to the Western calendar. The second column records the lunar months, with their cyclical characters in bold-faced type. Most of the remainder of the page is given over to figures for the days of the month, with the thirty figures across the top representing the days of the Chinese month and the corresponding numerals below the days of the Western month. On the right-hand side of the page are columns by which the days of the week according to the Western calendar and the cyclical characters for the days according to the Chinese calendar may be determined. By using this work it is easy to change a Chinese date into a Western date and vice versa, but close attention must be paid to the compilers' formulas (see English explanation on pages xviii–xx) to determine the day of the week or the cyclical characters for the day. The appendix contains eighteen tables, twelve of them dealing with dates within various kingdoms and reigns that paralleled legitimate dynasties of China. Table 16 is an index to Chinese reign-periods (*nien-hao*), arranged alphabetically.

Chung-kuo nien-li tsung-p'u 中國年曆總譜. Compiled by Tung Tso-pin 董作賓, and published by the Hong Kong University Press, 1960. 2 vols. xvi, 72, 357; 412 pp.

These volumes contain transfer tables for the Chinese, Western, and Moslem calendars. The first volume extends from 2674 (the traditional year of the mythological emperor Huang-ti) to 1 B.C.; the second volume from A.D. 1 to 2000. Beginning with 1384 B.C. (the Chinese calendar is unreliable before that time, and probably for hundreds of years after, too), the pages are divided into yearly horizontal columns, each of which is further divided into three vertical columns. The first vertical column gives the cyclical year, the year B.C. or A.D., the dynasty, emperor, reign period and year, the number of years before the Chinese republic, and the year according to the Julian calendar. After A.D. 622 the year according to the Moslem calendar is also given (in parentheses). The second column lists the months (with cyclical characters) of the Chinese lunar calendar and the cyclical characters of the first day of each month. The third column supplies the corresponding months of the Western solar calendar and the days of the month of the Western and Julian calendars that correspond with the first day of the lunar month. The transfer of exact dates from one calendar to another can be calculated, though the shift to or from the Moslem calendar is somewhat complicated. There are instructions in English as well as in Chinese, and some useful appendixes.

Erh-shih-shih shuo-jun piao 二十史朔閏表. Compiled by Ch'en Yüan 陳垣. (1) Peking: Sinological Research Institute of the National University of Peking, 1925. 1 *ts'e* (lithographed). (2) Peking: Ku-chi ch'u-pan-she 古籍出版社, 1956. 242 pp. (revised). (3) Taipei: I-wen yin-shu-kuan, 1958. 246 pp.

In this work, which is an abridgment of the *Chung-hsi-hui shih jih-li*, the cyclical characters and the corresponding month and day in the Western calendar are given for the first day of each Chinese month. The Chinese reign title and year, as well as the cyclical characters, are given each year; the year, according to both the Western calendar and the Roman or Mohammedan calendar, is indicated only for the first year in each decade. At the beginning of the work there is an index to Chinese reign titles, arranged according to the number of strokes, both to those of the recognized dynasties and to those of coexistent dynasties, giving the first year of each in the Western calendar;

at the end there is a table for determining the days of the week. The first edition extends from 206 B.C. to A.D. 1940, the others to A.D. 2000.

Chin-shih Chung-hsi shih-jih tui-chao piao 近世中西史日對照表. Compiled by Cheng Ho-sheng 鄭鶴聲. (1) Nanking: National Institute of Compilation and Translation 國立編譯館, 1936. [16] 880 pp. (2) Taipei: Commercial Press, 1962. [16] 880 pp.

This handy table for transferring dates between the Chinese and Western calendars covers the years from 1516 to 1941. Every page is divided into six sections, each devoted to one month of the Western calendar. In each section four horizontal columns give: the days of the month according to the Western calendar, the corresponding days of the month according to the Chinese calendar, the days of the week according to the Western calendar, and the cyclical characters for each day. In the margin are printed the cyclical characters for the year, the Western calendar year, and the Chinese dynasty, emperor, reign-period and year. At the beginning there is a chart with six vertical columns giving for each year the designation according to the Chinese, Japanese, Korean and Western calendars, the appropriate cyclical characters, and the number of years before the first year of the Chinese Republic. At the end is the daily calendar of the Taiping kingdom (1851–1864) with, in addition to the cyclical characters, the corresponding days of the month according to the imperial Chinese and Western calendars.

B. MISCELLANEOUS TABLES

Described in this section are chronological tables of important historical events, and tables of dynasties and emperors, official titles and positions, authors and their writings, and artists and art objects.

Li-tai ti-wang nien-piao 歷代帝王年表. Compiled by Ch'i Chao-nan 齊召南, compiler's preface dated 1777. Supplement: **Ming nien-piao** 明年表. Compiled by Juan Fu 阮福, preface dated 1824. (1) *Wen-hsüan-lou ts'ung-shu* 文選樓叢書, *ts'e* 21–22. (2) *Ssu-pu pei-yao*. 2 *ts'e*. (3) Wu-lin yeh-tun-i-t'ang 武林葉敨怡堂 re-cut block-print edition of 1863. 2 *ts'e*. (4) *Yüeh-ya-t'ang ts'ung-shu*, *ts'e* 141–143. (5) *Wan-yu wen-k'u ti-erh-chi*. 3 *ts'e*. (6) *Kuo-shih nien-piao ssu-chung*.[1]

---

1. 國史年表四種. Taipei: Shih-chieh shu-chü, 1963. Besides the Ch'i and Juan compilations, this collection of chronological tables includes the **Ch'ing nien-piao** 清年表, compiled by Hsiao I-shan 蕭一山, covering the period from 1560–1911, in 26 pages, and the **Chung-hua min-kuo nien-piao** 中華民國年表, compiled by the Chung-hua min-kuo nien-chien she 中華民國年鑑社, covering 1911 to 1961, in 16 pages. The last two use rather small type.

This chronological table of important events is arranged by reigns from earliest historical times down to the beginning of the Ch'in dynasty, and by single years from that time down to the end of the Yüan dynasty. It was compiled by one of the great historians of the Ch'ing dynasty, and the material included in it is carefully chosen and simply presented. The cyclical characters and the reign title and year are given for each year, and the factual data are largely concerned with political affairs. The supplement, the *Ming nien-piao*, arranged in the same way, brings the material down to the end of the Ming dynasty. The *Li-tai ti-wang nien-piao* and its supplement are particularly useful to beginning students because of their convenient size and arrangement, and because of the condensed form of the material included in them.

Li-tai t'ung-chi piao 歷代統紀表, 13 *chüan*. Compiled by Tuan Ch'ang-chi 段長基, compiler's preface dated 1813. (1) *Ssu-pu pei-yao.* 15 *ts'e* or 4 vols. (2) *Nien-ssu-shih san-piao* 廿四史三表, *ts'e* 1–13. (3) *Wan-yu wen-k'u ti-erh chi.* (4) *Kuo-hsüeh chi-pen ts'ung-shu.*

This is a chronological table of dynastic changes and other important events, arranged year by year from the supposed time of the legendary Emperor P'an-ku 盤古 down to the end of the Ming dynasty. The pages are divided into four horizontal columns, material on important political events appearing in the first, material on feudal princedoms in the second, material on the careers of high ministers of state in the third, and foreign affairs in the fourth. There are more columns for periods when there were two or more coexistent dynasties, and the data are more condensed. The *Li-tai t'ung-chi piao* is based to some extent upon the *Yü-p'i t'ung-chien chi-lan* 御批通鑑輯覽, which is a much larger work of the same nature.

Chung-kuo ta-shih nien-piao 中國大事年表. Compiled by Ch'en Ch'ing-ch'i 陳慶麒. (1) Shanghai: Commercial Press, 1934. [16] 354 pp. (2) Taipei: Commercial Press, 1963. 16, 354 pp. (3) Hong Kong: Commercial Press, 1964. 16, 348 pp.

This chronological table of important events is arranged by two year periods from earliest (supposedly) historical times down to 842 B.C. and year by year from 841 B.C. down to A.D. 1932. Most of the pages are divided into five or six horizontal columns, giving: (1) the number of years before A.D. 1912, (2) the year according to the Western calendar, (3) the cyclical characters for the year, (4) the emperor's name and the reign title and number of the year, (5) brief notes describing important events which took place within the year (or two years), and (6) the reign titles and years of coexistent dynasties before 221 B.C.

Chung-kuo li-shih nien-piao 中國歷史年表. Compiled by Mo Tzu-fen 莫子奮. Hong Kong: Ta-ch'eng shu-chü 大城書局, 1962. 4, 321 pp.

This chronological list of important events from the time of the mythological Yellow Emperor (assigned the date of 2697 B.C.) to A.D. 1945 furnishes more information than the *Chung-kuo ta-shih nien-piao* (q.v.).

Chung-wai li-shih nien-piao 中外歷史年表. Compiled by Chien Po-tsan 翦伯贊 (chief), Ch'i Ssu-ho 齊思和, Liu Ch'i-ko 劉啟戈 and Nieh Ch'ung-ch'i 聶崇岐. Peking: Chung-hua shu-chü, 1962. iv, 883 pp.

This chronological table of important events from 4500 B.C. to A.D. 1918 in both China and foreign countries was compiled by such first-rank historians as Chien Po-tsan, who is famous as a general historian, Ch'i Ssu-ho, a specialist on the Chou period, and Nieh Ch'ung-ch'i, an authority on Sung. The compilers' preface declares that historical materialism has been influential in the selection of data. They pay particular attention to (1) the tools of production, and improvements in the means of production, (2) the evolution of economic and political systems, including the proclamation of important decrees, (3) class contradictions and struggles, and internal contradictions within the dominating class, (4) interracial and international relations, and (5) dates of important historical figures. The information included in this volume is fuller than in other similar tables. It is surprising to find a modern compilation including millenia for which there is no history, only legends. Sources are not given.

*Chin-tai Chung-kuo shih-shih jih-chih 近代中國史事日誌. Compiled by Kuo Ting-yee 郭廷以. Taipei, 1963. 2 vols. [27] 791; 17, 659, 95 pp.

This carefully compiled chronological history records events in China day by day from 1829 to 1911, after a thirty-five page chronological listing of Chinese-Western relations from the sixteenth century to 1829. In the appendix are lists of the membership of the Grand Council year by year, of governors-general, governors and Tartar generals in chronological order under the names of provinces, of the membership of the Tsungli Yamen year by year from 1861 to 1901, and of Chinese ministers abroad and foreign ministers to China in chronological order under the names of the particular foreign countries.

*T'ai-p'ing t'ien-kuo shih-shih jih-chih 太平天國史事日誌. Compiled by Kuo Ting-yee 郭廷以. (1) Shanghai: Commercial Press, 1946. 2 vols. 1191, 266 pp. (2) Taipei: Commercial Press, 1963. 2, 4, 1191, 266 pp.

This chronological tabulation of historical events is an indispensable tool for students of the Taiping and Nien rebellions, not only because Kuo's notations are accurately dated as a result of repeated checking and revising but also because the work is very informative. Among the various subjects dealt with are the activities of secret societies from 1796 to 1868. Many historical problems relating to the rebellions are discussed in considerable detail. There are eight appendixes, including lists of Taiping dignitaries, imperial military commanders against the Taiping and Nien forces, foreigners who served either side, and major battles with the names of the commanders involved. There are some maps. There is a table for relating the Taiping, imperial Chinese, and Western calendars and an impressive and helpful bibliography of both Chinese and Western sources, with some brief annotations.

Chin-shih Chung-Jih kuo-chi ta-shih nien-piao 近世中日國際大事年表. Compiled by Yang Chia-lo 楊家駱. Chungking: Chung-shan wen-hua chiao-yü kuan 中山文化教育館, 1941. x, 212 pp.

This is a chronology of important events in Sino-Japanese relations from March 28, 1894 to July 7, 1937. In preparing this book the compiler has drawn on private sources hitherto inaccessible to the public. Although it contains some errors, it is an indispensable reference work for students in this field.

Chung-hua min-kuo ta-shih chi 中華民國大事記. Compiled by Kao Yin-tsu 高蔭祖 and Liu Shih-ch'ang 劉世昌. Taipei: Shih-chieh shu-chü, 1957. 6, 4, 704 pp.

Of several books of the same nature, this is the most detailed daily record of important events from 1911 to 1946. Attention is concentrated on Chinese national rather than on international developments, and the selection and interpretation conform to Kuomintang tenets. There is no index, but since the material is arranged strictly chronologically, a patient student can ordinarily locate the items he is looking for. A list of the 127 reference works used in making the compilation is appended.

Tu-shih nien-piao fu yin-te 讀史年表附引得. Compiled by William Hung 洪業, Nieh Ch'ung-ch'i 聶崇岐, and others. (1) Peiping: Harvard-Yenching Institute, 1933. (Supplement No. 1) [111] pp., 24 plates, 8 pp. (2) Taipei: Ch'eng Wen Publishing Co., 1966 (photocopy).

This is a set of chronological tables which show the comparative length of dynasties and reigns from Han to Ch'ing inclusive, and give certain other important historical data. There are nineteen charts of different dynasties, and four supplementary charts showing the relationship between different dynasties during certain periods when several existed simultaneously. At the beginning there is a general chart showing the comparative length of all of the dynasties. On the charts are given names of emperors, reign titles, honorific and posthumous imperial names, names of emperors' tombs, and the words substituted for taboo characters. The book itself is inconveniently large, but the charts can easily be removed and hung on a wall. Not only are the charts accurate and useful, but they are drawn so as to give a graphic picture of the comparative length of reigns. The measurement of years is according to both the Chinese and Western calendars, and there is a *kuei-hsieh* index to all names at the end.

Nien-i-shih ssu-p'u 廿一史四譜, 54 *chüan*. Compiled by Shen Ping-chen 沈炳震 (1679–1737). (1) Undated Hai-ning Ch'a-shih 海寧查氏 block-print edition. 24 *ts'e*. + (2) *Kuang-ya ts'ung-shu, ts'e* 205–212. (3) *Kuo-hsüeh chi-pen ts'ung-shu*. 20 vols.

This work consists of four sets of tables which are based upon material contained in the dynastic histories, from the *Shih-chi* 史記 through the *Yüan-shih* 元史: (1) *Chi-yüan p'u* 紀元譜 (Reign titles, including, besides those of recognized dynasties, those of coexistent, rebel, and a few foreign dynasties). The names of the emperors of each dynasty are arranged chronologically, and their reign titles are grouped under them, giving the date of adoption and the length of each reign title period. (2) *Feng-chüeh p'u* 封爵譜 (Feudatories and princedoms). The names are arranged according to their rhyme, and under each are given the location, the rank, and the names of persons appointed to hold it at different times. (3) *Tsai-chih p'u* 宰執譜 (High officials of the central government). The names are arranged chronologically, giving in each case the office and the years of appointment and retirement. (4) *Shih-fa p'u* 諡法譜 (Posthumous names). This section is subdivided into: (a) names given to emperors immediately after death, (b) names given to emperors by later emperors, (c) names given to empresses immediately after death, (d) names given to empresses by later emperors, (e) names given to princes and princesses, and (f) names given to high ministers. In the last subsection the posthumous names are listed first, and under each are listed the names of the ministers to whom they were given. There are indexes at the end of the first, third, and fourth sections, arranged according to the rhyme system.

Chung-kuo li-tai ti-wang p'u-hsi hui-pien 中國歷代帝王譜系彙編. Compiled by Chia Hu-ch'en 賈虎臣. Taipei: Cheng-chung shu-chü, 1966. 4, 5, 13, 357 pp.

This compilation of imperial rulers in successive dynasties offers quick reference. From the Shang through the Ch'ing dynasty, each emperor's temple name, reign titles, parentage, given name, dates of birth and death, native place, wife and children, length of reign (with Western dates), and capital city are given. There is also a brief, succinct summary of each emperor's merits and demerits. There is an index to reign titles, arranged by the number of strokes.

★**Li-tai chih-kuan piao** 歷代職官表, 72 *chüan*. Compiled under Imperial auspices by Chi Yün 紀昀 and others, the work being ordered in 1780. +(1) Palace block-print edition of the Ch'ien-lung period. 36 *ts'e*. (2) Kuang-ya shu-chü 廣雅書局 block-print edition of 1896. 24 *ts'e*. (3) *Kuang-ya ts'ung-shu, ts'e* 172–182. (4) *Ssu-pu pei-yao.* 16 *ts'e* or 4 vols. (5) *Kuo-hsüeh chi-pen ts'ung-shu.* 8 vols. [2076] pp. +(6) Peking: Chung-hua shu-chü, 1965. 366, 210, 160 pp. (with supplement and index).

This is a set of tables of all Chinese official titles from ancient times down to the time of compilation. The titles are classified under the names of the different boards, bureaus, and other departments of government of the Ch'ing dynasty, the Ch'ing titles appearing at the top of the page in each table with the other eighteen following in order from San-tai 三代 through Ming. There is one table for each department of government and the title of the highest official in the department appears first, followed, in order of rank, by the titles of all of the other officials connected with it. After each table, material is presented on changes in rank and title in that particular branch of government during different periods, and also on changes in the functions performed by it. Except for the Ch'ing period, this supplementary material is quoted from other sources, although there are frequent critical comments and explanations which have been added by the compiler. This is the only comprehensive work available which presents comparative data on official positions during different dynasties, and it is consequently almost indispensable to students of Chinese history—particularly of institutional history. Unfortunately it is by no means free from mistakes and omissions, and it is somewhat difficult for a person who is not already comparatively well acquainted with the official system of the Ch'ing dynasty to use it. An abridged six-*chüan* edition which bears the same title contains only the bare tables.

Ch'ing-tai ko-ti chiang-chün tu-t'ung ta-ch'en teng nien-piao 清代各地 將軍都統大臣等年表. Compiled by Chang Po-feng 章伯鋒. Peking: Chung-hua shu-chü, 1965. 3, 272 pp.

These chronological tables of personnel from 1796 to 1911 are indispensable for study of the military garrison system of the Ch'ing dynasty. There are five tables: (1) chiang-chün 將軍, Manchu generals-in-chief or Tartar generals, and tu-t'ung 都統, lieutenant-generals, (2) fu-tu-t'ung 副都統, deputy lieutenant-generals in Manchuria, (3) deputy lieutenant-generals elsewhere in China, (4) ts'an-tsan pan-shih ta-ch'en 參贊辦事大臣, military governors (ambans) or assistant military governors, and (5) Sheng-ching wu-pu shih-lang 盛京五部侍郎, the five vice-presidents in Sheng-ching (Fengtien), whose positions corresponded with board vice-presidencies in Peking. Much information in these tables is not available in the *Ch'ing-shih* 清史 or in the *Ch'ing-tai hsien-cheng lei-pien* 清代獻徵類編, compiled by Yen Mou-kung 嚴懋功 (Wu-hsi, 1951). The index to names, which supplies some biographical information, is very useful because it includes many minor officials who are not recorded in other sources.

Ch'ing-chi chung-yao chih-kuan nien-piao 清季重要職官年表. Compiled by Ch'ien Shih-fu 錢實甫. Shanghai: Chung-hua shu-chü, 1959. 9, 270 pp.

These tables of high Chinese officials between 1830 and 1911 list all grand secretaries 大學士, grand councillors 軍機大臣, presidents of boards and ministries 部院大臣, governors-general 總督, and provinicial governors 巡撫. Subdivisions are provided for each of the named grand secretaryships and the two assistant grand secretaries; for each of the six boards, the Mongolian superintendency, the censorate and the new ministries after 1900; and for each governor-generalship and province with a governor. The incumbents are listed each year, with indication in each case if the person was an imperial clansman, or a Manchu, Mongol or Chinese bannerman, or a holder of military rather than civil rank, the compiler having done some research on ethnic origins. Also supplied are the dates of appointment to and departure from each post. A number-of-strokes index to names, besides giving alternative names and places of birth, lists the posts held, giving dates of appointment.

Chung-kuo wen-hsüeh nien-piao 中國文學年表, 4 *chüan*. Compiled by Ao Shih-ying 敖士英. Peiping: Li-ta shu-chü 立達書局, 1935. 4 *ts'e*.

This is a table of authors and their writings, with a certain amount of background material, arranged chronologically from 343 B.C. to A.D. 625. Each page is divided into nine horizontal columns, giving the following information: (1) year, according to the Western calendar; (2) dynasty, emperor's name, and reign title and year; (3) important events, particularly those having sociological implications; (4) names of authors born during that year; (5) names of authors who died during that year; (6) biographical notes concerning authors born during that year, with attention paid more to individual characteristics than to official careers; (7) and (8) titles of works written during that year, with very brief descriptive notes, the works listed in (7) being definitely datable and those listed in (8) being only approximately datable; (9) miscellaneous notes. In the top margin there are occasional notes on the economic background of the period. Quoted materials are taken mainly from the dynastic histories and from works of the nature of belles-lettres, with the sources always indicated. In the fourth *chüan* there is a table of authors' birth-places, arranged first by place and then by dynasty. At the end of the work there is an index to authors' names, arranged according to the number of strokes. While this table shows the results of extensive research, it is not very conveniently arranged, and there are many mistakes, particularly in the dating of undatable writings and authors.

Sung Yüan li-hsüeh-chia chu-shu sheng-tsu nien-piao 宋元理學家著述生卒年表. Compiled by Mai Chung-kuei 麥仲貴, and published by the Institute of Advanced Chinese Studies and Research, New Asia College, The Chinese University of Hong Kong, 1968. [8] 4, 443, 20 pp.

This is a chronological table of bibliographical and biographical data on Sung and Yüan neo-Confucian philosophers. Actually it is a chronological survey of the intellectual history of the period from 960 to 1367. Each page is divided into three columns: (1) Chinese and Western dates, (2) socio-political background and academic careers of individual Confucianists, including when they were awarded literary degrees, when appointed to or dismissed from office, when certain of their essays or books were written, and their personal relations with teachers and students, (3) dates of birth and death. A special feature of this book is the careful indication of sources under each entry. A bibliography of the sources cited is provided at the beginning, and at the end there is a number-of-strokes index to the more than 1600 persons included, with dates of birth and death indicated.

Chung-kuo mei-shu nien-piao 中國美術年表. Compiled by Fu Pao-shih 傅抱石. (1) Shanghai: Commercial Press, 1937. [16] 148 pp. (2) Hong Kong: T'ai-p'ing shu-chü, 1963. [12] 148 pp. (3) Taipei: Wu-chou ch'u-pan-she 五洲出版社, 1968 (photocopy; Ch'ien Hsing-hua 錢興華 designated as the compiler).

This is a table summarizing significant facts about Chinese art including architecture, sculpture, painting, craft work, bronze and stone inscriptions, stone tablets, books on art, and biographical information concerning famous artists. The material is arranged chronologically. Seventeen Chinese and 71 Japanese sources are listed at the beginning of the book, but unfortunately individual references to source material are not furnished. Since this chart covers the period from 2697 B.C. to A.D. 1911 there are naturally some omissions and errors; but on the whole the work has been compiled with considerable care and is accordingly a useful checklist for writers and art lovers. A list of Chinese reign titles, arranged chronologically, is furnished at the end.

Li-tai liu-ch'uan shu-hua tso-p'in pien-nien piao 歷代流傳書畫作品編年表.
Compiled by Hsü Pang-ta 徐邦達. Shanghai: Jen-min mei-shu ch'u-pan
she, 1963. 4, 19, 467, 2 pp.

This chronological list of Chinese calligraphy and paintings of all dynasties,
most of which are said still to be in existence, was compiled by a museum
expert and art connoisseur. The work is divided into two parts: (A) by the
names of the artists, under each of which are listed his major pieces chronologically, with indication of sources, (B) by date, in which each painting or piece
of calligraphy is listed and described under the year it was painted (from 1035
to 1900), with those the compiler considers genuine starred. At the beginning
there is a directory of artists arranged by the number of strokes which serves
as an index to all references to each artist in the body of the work. At the end
there is an inventory of pictures painted cooperatively by two or more artists
and a list of the abbreviations of sources cited in the text.

Sung Yüan Ming Ch'ing shu-hua chia nien-piao 宋元明清書畫家年表.
Compiled by Kuo Wei-ch'ü 郭味蕖. Peking: Chung-kuo ku-tien i-shu ch'u-
pan she 中國古典藝術出版社, 1958. [12] 76, 553, 22 [45] pp.

This is a chronological list of events in the lives and careers of more than
4,000 calligraphers and painters who lived from 960 to 1947. Under each
artist's name there are given the years of birth and death, if known, major
artistic events that involved him, and his major dated works that are still
extant, with sources. The book is well indexed and one of the appendixes, a
list of the most important pre-Sung artists, seems particularly useful.

VII YEARBOOKS

Yearbooks were introduced into China rather late, and their caliber generally has not been very high. Some of the most useful supply information from official sources, though the quantity and quality of Chinese statistical data leave much to be desired. Most of the yearbooks in this section were issued only once or a few times, but they still provide useful reference material relating to the periods they cover.

Chung-kuo nien-chien 中國年鑑. Compiled by Yüan Hsiang 阮湘 and others. Shanghai: Commercial Press, 1924. [42] 2123 pp.

This was one of the earliest yearbooks to appear in Chinese, although it was discontinued after the first issue. It is divided into six sections and thirty subsections, the section headings being: (1) land and population, (2) political and military affairs, (3) finance and banking, (4) communications and irrigation, (5) agriculture, industry, and commerce, and (6) education and religions. There is a brief general introduction to each section, and most of the subsections are preceded by a brief statement regarding conditions under the Ch'ing dynasty and a more detailed survey of conditions during the period from 1912 to the time of compilation. The current material appears very largely in the form of statistical tables with explanations, more than half of the space being taken up with such tables. Material was derived from official and private records, foreign yearbooks and investigations, and from direct inquiries made by the compilers. Sources are frequently not indicated and the statistical tables are not very reliable, but the introductions to sections and subsections contain valuable material on the last years of the Ch'ing dynasty and on the early years of the Republic, which is difficult to find elsewhere. There is a table of contents at the beginning, and at the end there is a chronological table of important events, extending from 1903 to 1922.

Shen-pao nien-chien 申報年鑑. Compiled by Chang Tzu-sheng 張梓生, Chang Cho-han 章倬漢, and others, and published by the Shanghai Shen-pao kuan 上海申報館. 1933 issue: [7] 1248 pp. 1934 issue: [27] 1347 pp. 1935 issue: [21] 1225 pp.; supplement, [129] pp. 1936 issue: 1458 pp. 1944 issue: [40] 1527 pp. Taipei: Chung-kuo wen-hsien ch'u-pan she 中國文獻出版社, 1966. [6] 1234 pp. Photocopy of 1935 issue.

This general yearbook is divided into twenty-four sections and more than fifty subsections, the section headings in the 1934 and 1935 issues being: (1) general national and international affairs, (2) geography, astronomy, and population, (3) Kuomintang affairs, (4) government and administration,

(5) diplomatic affairs, (6) national defense, (7) finance, (8) currency, (9) industry, (10) domestic and foreign commerce, (11) agriculture and village affairs, (12) forestry, animal husbandry, and fisheries, (13) mining, (14) labor, (15) affairs of overseas Chinese, (16) communications, (17) floods and other natural calamities, (18) education, (19) intellectual and religious affairs, and affairs related to the publishing field, (20) co-operatives, (21) public health, (22) chronological table of important domestic and international events, (23) world affairs, and (24) tables of weights and measures. The information presented in these yearbooks was secured from government and other publications, and through direct investigations by the compilers. Special attention is paid to political and economic affairs, and much space is devoted to the reproduction of laws and official regulations. Some sections are much better compiled than others, sources are too frequently not indicated, and the statistical tables are often out of date or inaccurate. However, the work showed improvement with each new issue, and its publication by the largest newspaper in China gave its compilers unusual facilities for securing the most important contemporary source materials. There is a table of contents at the beginning. The supplement to the 1935 issue consists of the first and sixth sections, which were not ready for publication as soon as the rest of the yearbook. The 1944 issue is a continuation of the 1936 issue, carrying the material down to the end of 1942. It is an important source of information about conditions during the Second Sino-Japanese War.

Wu-han jih-pao nien-chien 武漢日報年鑑. 1947 issue. Hankow: Editorial Board of the Almanac of the *Wu-han jih-pao*, 1947. 2 vols. [1048]; [1098] pp.

This general yearbook or almanac is divided into six sections: political and military events, domestic affairs, international affairs, important documents, a general review of laws and regulations, and the names of high officials of the Chinese central and local governments, including diplomatic officials serving abroad. Among the more useful subsections are those on important events since the founding of the Republic, political parties, land and population, and educational conditions; it also includes an up-to-date list of Chinese newspapers with their location and the names of their managers. Numerous statistical tables are furnished, with sources indicated in most cases. The strengths of the *Wu-han jih-pao nien-chien* are its richness of information and succinct style; its weaknesses are small-size type and poor printing, occasional inaccuracies, disproportionate presentation of material, and unsatisfactory pagination.

Tung-pei nien-chien 東北年鑑. Compiled by Feng Ch'i-liu 馮啓鏐, Wang Hsiao-yin 王小隱, T'ang Lan 唐蘭 and others. Shenyang: Yearbook Compilation Office of the Northeast Culture Society 東北文化社年鑑編印處, 1931. [10] 1458 pp.

Although only one issue of this Manchurian yearbook appeared before the Japanese occupied Manchuria, it is a very useful compilation of political, economic, and geographical material relating to that area for the period from 1912 to 1931. Considerable attention is paid to the historical background of each subject, and the sources of statistical and other materials are always indicated. There is a table of contents at the beginning.

Tung-pei yao-lan 東北要覽. Compiled and published by the National Northeastern University 國立東北大學, San-t'ai 三台 [Heilungkiang] 1944. [30] 796 [26] pp.

This handbook about Manchuria is a comprehensive survey in twelve sections: historical sketch, geography, population, party affairs and local administration, judicial, military and police affairs, communications, finance, products, commerce, educational and cultural affairs, and social conditions. For the years prior to 1931 the principal source is the *Tung-pei nien-chien* (q.v.); for the period after 1931 the materials were collected by scholars native to the region. There are many tables and charts. Appendix II lists books on the Northeast.

Chung-kuo ching-chi nien-chien 中國經濟年鑑. Compiled by a special committee of the Chinese Ministry of Industry 實業部中國經濟年鑑編纂委員會. Shanghai: Commercial Press. 1932–1933 issue (1934): 2 vols. [12] [4928] pp. 1933–1934 issue (1935): 2 vols. [16] [4259] pp. 1934–1935 issue (1936): 3 vols. [21] [1497]; 8 [1590]; 4 [1207] 44 pp.

The first issue of this economic yearbook is divided into seventeen sections, and the second into twenty sections. The section headings in the first are: (1) governmental economic activities, (2) geography, (3) population, (4) finance, (5) currency, (6) agriculture, (7) land rent, (8) forestry and reclamation, (9) fisheries and animal husbandry, (10) mining, (11) industry, (12) communications, (13) domestic commerce, (14) international trade, (15) labor, (16) floods and other natural calamities, and (17) economic affairs of overseas Chinese. In the second issue the second and last sections were discontinued, but new ones were added dealing with: (1) the land problem, (2) irrigation, (3) co-operatives, (4) prices and the cost of living, and (5) economic activities in Mongolia, Sikang, Tibet and Sinkiang. Each section is divided into subsections and items, many of the latter having been compiled by specialists. More space is devoted to statistical tables than to theoretical discussions, the materials having been derived from government files and from individual studies. Sources are frequently indicated, and the data in the second issue were purportedly more carefully checked than those in the first, although all should be used with caution. Each volume contains a table of contents and a list of newspapers and magazines of economic interest.

Chung-wai ching-chi nien-pao 中外經濟年報, the Third Supplement. Compiled by Chang Hsiao-mei 張肖梅 in the Chung-kuo kuo-min ching-chi yen-chiu-so 中國國民經濟研究所. Shanghai: Shih-chieh shu-chü, 1941. 850 pp.

This is a kind of yearbook on Chinese economic affairs. It consists of thirteen parts, of which the first contains general statements while the others treat economic administration and public organization, financial administration, international exchange, inflation, prices, currency, investments in markets, industry and minerals, agriculture and food stuffs, commerce, reconstruction of communications, and world economics. Most of the fifty-six chapters were written by specialists, so that this volume may be considered a collection of articles or monographic studies on Chinese economic affairs during the war. Although the contributors were not all famous, the work furnishes valuable information on economic conditions during that important period.

Chung-kuo ching-chi nien-chien 中國經濟年鑑. Compiled by Ti Ch'ao-pai 狄超白 and others. (1) Hong Kong: T'ai-p'ing-yang ching-chi yen-chiu-she 太平洋經濟研究社, 1947. [9] 127, 216, 62, 7 pp. (2) Hong Kong: Hua-nan hsin-wen-she 華南新聞社, 1948. (Identical, except for advertising matter.)

This Chinese economic yearbook is different from the earlier one with the same title (q.v.). It deals with the crucial period after the Sino-Japanese war when inflation was beginning to spiral and covers both the part of China under Communist control and that under the Kuomintang. The first of three main divisions (*shang-pien* 上編) deals with industry, mineralogy, agriculture, transportation, banking, currency and foreign exchange, international trade, commodity prices, and famine relief. The second division (*chung-pien* 中編) is concerned with the provincial and regional economies. The third (*hsia-pien* 下編) consists of documents, such as international trade agreements, economic regulations, foreign exchange rates, loan regulations, and land transactions. There is a special section on the economic regulations of Communist China: land policy, rent, agriculture, technology, and industry. The last chapter is a chronology of important events from January to December 1946.

Shang-hai chieh-fang ch'ien-hou wu-chia tzu-liao hui-pien 上海解放前後物價資料彙編 (1921–1957). Shanghai: the Economic Research Institute of Shanghai of the Academy of Sciences of China 中國科學院: 上海經濟研究所, 1958. 4, 8, 600 pp.

This is a compendium of economic data on Shanghai between 1921 and 1957, with particular attention to changes in commodity prices. There are numerous tables of the wholesale prices of articles of daily need, with some analysis and interpretation.

Ch'üan-kuo yin-hang nien-chien 全國銀行年鑑. Compiled and published by the Bureau of Economic Research of the Bank of China 中國銀行管理處 經濟研究室, Shanghai. 1934 issue: 13 [1668] pp. 1935 issue: [11] [1938] pp. 1936 issue: [9] [2103] pp.

This banking yearbook aimed to include every type of information which could possibly be of interest to bankers, and the material was collected for it both by direct inquiry and from published writings of all kinds. Besides many data of general economic significance, it contains lists of all banks and bankers in China, reproduces laws and discusses events and governmental activities which are related to banking, and presents material on pawnshops and old-style banks. In the 1935 issue there is an index to books and articles on banks and banking subjects. At the beginning of each issue there is a general table of contents and a brief explanation of the contents of each chapter, and there is a detailed table of contents at the beginning of each section. This work was more carefully compiled than most Chinese yearbooks, and it is of more general interest than the title would seem to indicate.

Ts'ai-cheng nien-chien 財政年鑑. Compiled by a special committee of the Ministry of Finance 財政部財政年鑑編纂處. 1933–1934 issue. Shanghai: Commercial Press, 1935. 2 vols. [50] 2600 pp. Second issue: [Chungking?] 1944. 3 vols. [14] 2434 pp. Third issue: [Nanking?] 1948. 2 vols. 44 [1625] pp.

The first issue of this financial yearbook is divided into fifteen sections: (1) general financial conditions, (2) the financial administration of the government, (3) the governmental budget, (4) the maritime customs, (5) the salt administration, (6) the consolidated taxes, (7) stamp taxes, (8) wine and tobacco taxes and licenses, (9) miscellanous taxes, (10) government-controlled enterprises and properties, (11) the national debt, (12) the currency, (13) finances of local governments, (14) chronological table of important financial events occurring in China from July, 1933 to the end of 1934, and (15) world financial conditions. The material included was derived largely from the files of the Ministry of Finance, although a certain amount of information was also taken from current books and periodicals. Sources are sometimes indicated, and there is a detailed table of contents at the beginning. The second and third issues have the same arrangement as the first except that they are divided into only fourteen sections. Each brings the material down to the time of publication.

T'ieh-tao nien-chien 鐵道年鑑 1931–1932. Nanking: Committee of the Chinese Ministry of Railways 鐵道部鐵道年鑑編纂委員會, 1933. [23] 1284 [96] pp.

This railway yearbook presents material on the history of Chinese railways, the organization of the Ministry of Railways, the organization, administration, condition and activities of different railways. Regulations, laws, and agreements concerning railways are reproduced, plans for further railway construction are outlined, and numerous maps and tables are included. Material was obtained from the files of the Ministry of Railways and also from the different railway administrations themselves. There is a table of contents at the beginning, and there are indexes to railway laws and agreements at the end.

Chung-kuo lao-tung nien-chien 中國勞動年鑑. First issue compiled by Wang Ch'ing-pin 王清彬, Wang Shu-hsün 王樹勳 and others; second issue compiled by Hsing Pi-hsin 邢必信, Wu To 吳鐸, and others; both edited by L. K. T'ao 陶孟和. Peiping: Institute of Social Research 北平社會調查所, 1928 and 1931. Third and fourth issues: Committee of the Chinese Ministry of Industry 實業部中國勞動年鑑編纂委員會, Nanking, 1933 and 1934. First issue: xvii, 1402, vii pp. Second issue: xviii [718] pp. Third issue [18] [1066] pp. Fourth issue: [19] [1421] pp.

The first issue of this labor yearbook covers the period from 1912 to February, 1927, the second issue from March, 1927 to the end of 1931, the third issue the year 1932, and the fourth issue the year 1933. The first two issues are divided into three sections, dealing with general labor conditions, the labor movement, and laws and practises protecting or otherwise benefitting labor. The third and fourth issues have an additional fourth section which is devoted to the activities of the International Labor Office. Sources are carefully indicated throughout, the material in the first two issues is drawn from the books, periodicals and newspapers listed at the end, and that in the third and fourth issues from the files of the Ministry of Industry and also from a large number of published works. There is a table of contents at the beginning of each issue.

Chung-kuo chiao-yü nien-chien 中國教育年鑑. Compiled by the Education Yearbook Committee of the Ministry of Education. First issue 第一次: Shanghai: K'ai-ming shu-tien, 1934. 2 vols. [24] [848]; [1324] pp. Second issue: Shanghai: Commercial Press, 1948. [29] 1643 pp. Third issue: Taipei: Cheng-chung shu-chü, 1957. 2 vols. [6] 21, 1237 pp.

The first issue of this yearbook deals with the development of education in China from the establishment of the modern school system at the beginning of this century to 1931, with a certain amount of additional material on 1932 and 1933. The second issue carries the story through the Second Sino-Japanese War. The third issue describes Chinese education during the Central Government's last few years on the mainland but is devoted mostly to the educational system developed during the 1950's on Taiwan. The three issues are organized differently, but all provide information on all aspects of public and private education, including elementary, secondary and higher education, vocational education, teacher training, education of overseas Chinese and people in the border areas, scholarship and research, and educational administration and theory. The contents were drawn from the extensive archives of the Ministry of Education, from questionnaires submitted to educational institutions, and from books and periodicals, the last always cited. There are countless tables, a number of useful appendixes, some short biographies, in fact virtually every kind of information one might seek about Chinese education under the Kuomintang. There is a general table of contents at the beginning, and each section is preceded by a more detailed table of contents.

Kuo-min cheng-fu nien-chien 国民政府年鑑. Compiled and published by the Executive Yüan of the National Government of China 國民政府行政院. First issue: Chungking, 1943. 2 vols. 2, 31 [414]; [419] pp. Second issue: Chungking, 1944. 2 vols. 28 [419]; [364] pp. Third issue: Nanking, 1946. 2 vols. 2, 12 [386]; 10 [192] [311] pp.

This yearbook supplies official information concerning many activities of the central and provincial governments. While the statistics should perhaps be taken with caution, the information on government agencies and personnel and on government structure is fuller and more authoritative than that in any other work of a similar nature.

Nei-cheng nien-chien 內政年鑑. Compiled by a special committee of the Chinese Ministry of the Interior 內政部年鑑編纂委員會. Shanghai: Commercial Press, 1936. 4 vols. [9] [5141] [26] pp.

This yearbook of Chinese internal affairs, which appeared only once, deals with central and local government, police administration, land policies, ceremonies and customs, hydraulic engineering, and health and medicine. Excepting the last two sections which terminate in June 1934, the period covered extends from the first year of the Republic to June 1935. Historical background is summarized at the beginning of each section, and statistical tables and charts, laws and regulations are appended at the end. The material was derived from the files of the Ministry of the Interior, the reports of local governments, and publications of learned societies and individuals. Although sources are not carefully indicated, this yearbook is useful owing to its details and analyses. The material on the governmental system of China, and the chapters under police administration on registered societies, organizations, and publications, and the statistical list of proscribed publications, are perhaps the most valuable. At the beginning there is a general table of contents, and each section has its own detailed table of contents. At the end of volume 4 there are two indexes to topics, one arranged according to the four-corner system, the other according to the number of strokes.

Chung-kuo wai-chiao nien-chien 中國外交年鑑. 1933 issue: compiled by Chang Chin 章進 and others. Shanghai: Sheng-huo shu-tien, 1934. [12] pp., 16 plates, 462 pp. 1934 issue: compiled by Hsüeh Tai-ch'iang 薛代强, Chang Chin and others. Shanghai: Shih-chieh shu-chü, 1935. 36 plates [477] pp. 1935 issue: Shanghai: Cheng-chung shu-chü, 1936. 18 plates, 16, 601 pp. 1940–1941 issue: [Shanghai]: San-t'ung shu-chü 三通書局, 1941. 13, 302 pp.

This yearbook of Chinese foreign affairs includes sections on the foreign relations of the National Government, the foreign relations of local governments, the Chinese foreign service, the organization of the Ministry of Foreign Affairs and its subordinate bureaus and establishments, laws, regulations, and treaties bearing on China's foreign relations, and many other related subjects. There are also classified lists of articles and books published in Chinese, Japanese, English, and French dealing with Chinese foreign affairs, and there is a directory of Chinese diplomatic and consular officials. The 1934 issue lists all the publications of the Ministry of Foreign Affairs since its establishment. Most of the material in this yearbook was derived from the files of the Ministry, the sources of material secured elsewhere always being indicated. There is a table of contents at the beginning. The 1940–1941 issue is devoted to the puppet government of Wang Ching-wei.

Chung-hua min-kuo nien-chien 中華民國年鑑. Taipei: Yearbook Editorial Board 中華民國年鑑社編. 1951 (9 plates [51] 1068 pp.) +. Annual.

This general yearbook provides the latest public information on virtually all aspects of life on Taiwan, under such headings as political parties, the various activities of the Central Government, the administration of Taiwan province, cultural and social affairs, education, communications and transportation, finance, business and industry, Chinese-American economic cooperation, overseas Chinese affairs, the off-shore islands, and Communist activities on the mainland. There are statistical tables, charts, maps, biographies, laws and regulations, and a detailed table of contents at the beginning.

Jen-min shou-ts'e 人民手冊. Compiled and published by the *Ta-kung-pao* 大公報. 1950, 1951 and 1952 issues in Shanghai; 1953, 1955 and 1956 issues in Tientsin; subsequent issues annually to 1965 in Peking. 1960 issue, 341 pp.; 1965 issue, 688 pp.

This "People's Handbook," a principal source of general information about mainland China, was published until 1965 by the *Ta-kung-pao*, a semi-official newspaper. It consists mainly of official documents, many of which seem to be unavailable elsewhere. The contents are arranged under such subject headings as: important speeches and sayings of Mao Tse-tung, important meetings, land and population, government and society, external relations, finance and the economy, industry and agriculture, communications and transportation, education and public health, and physical education and athletics. A selected bibliography is appended to many sections. There is a detailed table of contents at the beginning.

Nan-yang nien-chien 南洋年鑑. 1938 issue: compiled by Fu Wu Mun 傅无悶 and others. Singapore: Nan-yang Siang Pau Press 南洋商報出版部, 1939. [1300+] pp. 1951 issue: compiled by Yü Shu-k'un 郁樹錕, Hsü Yün-Ts'iao 許雲樵 and others. Singapore: Nan-yang pao-she 南洋報社, 1951.

Both of these issues bring together information on the different countries of Southeast Asia, and also devote a large section (more than 200 pages) to the overseas Chinese who live in that region. Under each country (or colony, as most of them were in 1938) material is supplied on all subjects one might expect to find in a general yearbook intended primarily for persons engaged in trade and finance. There is a detailed table of contents at the beginning.

Chung-kuo wen-i nien-chien 中國文藝年鑑. 1932 issue: compiled by the Chung-kuo wen-i nien-chien-she 中國文藝年鑑社. Shanghai: Hsien-tai shu-chü 現代書局, 1933. [10] [799] pp. 1936 issue: compiled by Yang Chin-hao 楊晉豪. Shanghai: Pei-hsin shu-chü 北新書局, [1937]. 5, 782 pp. 1967 issue: compiled by Kuo I-tung 郭衣洞, P'eng P'in-kuang 彭品光 and others. Taipei: P'ing-yüan ch'u-pan-she 平原出版社, 1967. 5, 6, 430 pp.

Nearly four-fifths of the pre-war issues of this yearbook of Chinese literature is devoted to an anthology of current literary productions. The first issue is divided into three parts and the second into four: the first part presents general information relating to the Chinese literary world, such as current tendencies in writing, controversial points of view regarding literary style, and news of the deaths of important writers; the second part is an anthology of short stories, poems, essays, sketches, biographies, and dramas; the third part is a classified list of literary productions written during the period covered by the yearbook;

and the fourth part (of the 1934 issue) is a report of literary conditions in different parts of China. In the third part of the 1932 issue there is a list of writers, arranged according to the number of strokes, giving the titles of their writings. The 1967 issue, a completely new compilation, deals primarily with literary activities in Taiwan. There is a section with biographic notes on writers representing the various branches of literature.

VIII   SINOLOGICAL INDEXES

Indexes are among the most important tools for research in Chinese studies. Yet until the twentieth century nearly all Chinese books were published without them. The ideal of the old-fashioned Chinese scholar was to know his books by heart and to carry a sort of index in his head. During the 1930's an extensive project for indexing important Chinese works was carried on by William Hung, Nieh Ch'ung-ch'i, and others at Yenching University in Peiping, and the resulting Harvard-Yenching Institute Sinological Index Series has rendered indispensable service to students of China all over the world. The Harvard-Yenching Institute series used the *kuei-hsieh* system by which characters are converted into numbers with a minimum of duplication, and always added number-of-strokes and Wade-Giles romanization keys.

When the Harvard-Yenching Institute series was interrupted during the Second Sino-Japanese War, Nieh Ch'ung-ch'i was engaged by the Centre franco-chinois d'études sinologiques in Peiping to compile a new index series. Eight indexes were published by this organization prior to 1948, after which seven more appeared in the same series but under a new name: Université de Paris, Centre d'études sinologiques de Pékin. While the method of indexing was similar to that of the Harvard-Yenching Institute series, the number-of-strokes system was used instead of the *kuei-hsieh*, and besides a Wade-Giles key there is one based on the romanization used in the *Bulletin de l'École Française d'Éxtrême-Orient*. All of the Centre d'études sinologiques indexes, all but four of the Harvard-Yenching Institute indexes, and all but three of the Harvard-Yenching Institute supplements have been republished in photocopy by the Ch'eng Wen Publishing Co. of Taipei (Authorized distributor: Chinese Materials and Research Aids Service Center, P.O. Box 22048, Taipei, Taiwan).

Besides these two series, other indexes have appeared since the early 1930's. A number have been introduced earlier in this bibliography, particularly in the geographical and biographical sections, but many useful indexes still remain to be identified in this section. It is taken for granted here that persons who look for an index to a certain book know the value of that book and therefore that it is not necessary to supply a note about it. The indexes in this section are arranged roughly under the well-known four categories of the *Ssu-k'u ch'üan-shu*.

A. CLASSICS

Shih-san-ching so-yin 十三經索引. Compiled by Yeh Shao-chün 葉紹鈞. (1) Shanghai: K'ai-ming shu-tien, 1934. [39] 1718 pp. (2) Taipei: K'ai-ming shu-tien, 1955. [40] 1718 pp. (3) Peking: Chung-hua shu-chü, 1957. [28] 13, 1718 pp.

This is an index to the text of the *Thirteen Classics*, sentence by sentence. The first phrase of each sentence appears in the index, which is arranged according to the number of strokes, and each first phrase is followed by the abbreviated name of the classic, one or two characters indicating the chapter, and the number of the sentence in the original work. Although there are frequent typographical errors, and a certain number of sentences are not properly punctuated with the result that they cannot be found under their proper first character, this is nevertheless a very useful reference work. There is an index to first characters at the beginning, arranged according to the number of strokes. A companion volume, containing the punctuated text of the *Thirteen Classics* with the sentences numbered as they are in the index, has been published by the same company.[1]

Huang-Ch'ing ching-chieh chien-mu 皇清經解檢目, 8 *chüan*. Compiled by Ts'ai Ch'i-sheng 蔡啓盛, compiler's preface dated 1886. Wu-lin 武林 block-print edition of the same year. 2 *ts'e*.

This is a subject index to the approximately 180 Ch'ing works interpreting or otherwise annotating the classics and commentaries which were published together in the *Huang-Ch'ing ching-chieh (Cheng-pien)* 皇清經解 (正編). The various phrases of the *Thirteen Classics* are classified under forty-eight section and many subsection headings, and under each phrase the *chüan* and page numbers in the Hsüeh-hai-t'ang 學海堂 block-print edition of the *Huang-Ch'ing ching-chieh* are indicated. A wide variety of subjects is introduced, the section headings corresponding closely to those found in most Chinese encyclopedias. There is a table of contents at the beginning, and at the end there is a transfer table making it possible to apply the index to the small-sized Hung-pao-chai 鴻寶齋 lithographic edition.

Mao-shih yin-te 毛詩引得. (1) Peiping: Harvard-Yenching Institute, 1934 (Supplement No. 9). xxxii, 243 pp. (2) Tokyo: Japan Council for East Asian Studies, 1962 (photocopy).

This is a concordance to Juan Yüan's *Shih-san-ching chu-su* 阮元十三經註疏 edition of the *Mao-shih* or *Shih-ching*. The index is preceded by the text, with punctuation.

Mao-shih chu-su yin-shu yin-te 毛詩注疏引書引得. (1) Peiping: Harvard-Yenching Institute, 1937. (Index No. 31) vi, 31 pp. (2) Taipei: Ch'eng Wen Publishing Co., 1966 (photocopy).

Commentators on the *Shih-ching* have quoted from several hundred sources, most of which are no longer extant. This index to the titles and authors of

---

1. *Shih-san-ching ching-wen* 十三經經文. 949 pp.

works quoted from is useful to scholars who wish to collect excerpts from old books or to study the availability of particular books at certain times.

Shang-shu t'ung-chien 尚書通檢. Compiled by Ku Chieh-kang 顧頡剛. Peiping: Harvard-Yenching Institute, 1936. iv, 308 pp.

This is a concordance to the *Shang-shu* or *Shu-ching*, prepared by a great modern scholar of ancient China. The text of the *Shang-shu* is given with punctuation, followed by the index in which the number assigned to each character indicates the order of its appearance in the text. The index is arranged by the number-of-strokes system. A chart at the end shows differences in the form of certain characters in different editions. Another chart points out the differences in text and punctuation in the K'ung 孔 and Ts'ai 蔡 versions. For the convenience of scholars, there are indexes according to the four-corner system, by rhyme, and by the Wade-Giles system of romanization. This work is an indispensable tool for students of this important but difficult classic.

Chou-i yin-te 周易引得. (1) Peiping: Harvard-Yenching Institute, 1935. (Supplement No. 10) 185 pp. (2) Taipei: Ch'eng Wen Publishing Co., 1966 (photocopy).

This work provides first a punctuated text of the *Chou-i* or *I-ching*, based on the *Shih-san-ching chu-su* edition, then a concordance to this text.

Chou-li yin-te, fu chu-su yin-shu yin-te 周禮引得附注疏引書引得. (1) Peiping: Harvard-Yenching Institute, 1940. (Index No. 37) xxiv, 174 pp. (2) Taipei: Ch'eng Wen Publishing Co., 1966 (photocopy).

This index to the *Chou-li* and to the titles quoted in its commentaries is based on the *Ssu-pu ts'ung-k'an* edition. References to the text and to the commentaries are distinguished in the index by larger and smaller sized type.

I-li yin-te fu cheng-chu chi chia-su yin-shu yin-te 儀禮引得附鄭注及賈疏引書引得. (1) Peiping: Harvard-Yenching Institute, 1932. (Index No. 6) xxvi, 84 pp. (2) Taipei: Ch'eng Wen Publishing Co., 1966 (photocopy).

This index to the *I-li* and to the titles quoted in its commentaries is based on the text of the *Shih-san-ching chu-su* edition, but a comparative chart of page numbers makes it usable with other editions.

Li-chi yin-te 禮記引得. (1) Peiping: Harvard-Yenching Institute, 1936. (Index No. 27) lxviii, 612 pp. (2) Taipei: Ch'eng Wen Publishing Co., 1966 (photocopy).

This is an index to the nouns and to important verbs and adjectives in the *Li-chi*. It is not a concordance to every word in this text, possibly because the *Li-chi* is not as early as other Confucian classics. There is an important preface by William Hung.

Li-chi chu-su yin-shu yin-te 禮記注疏引書引得. (1) Peiping: Harvard-Yenching Institute, 1937. (Index No. 30) viii, 21 pp. (2) Taipei: Ch'eng Wen Publishing Co., 1966 (photocopy).

This is an index to the titles and authors of works quoted in the commentaries on the *Li-chi* included in Juan Yüan's *Shih-san-ching chu-su*.

Ch'un-ch'iu ching-chuan yin-te 春秋經傳引得. (1) Peiping: Harvard-Yenching Institute, 1937. (Supplement No. 11) 4 vols. cxliv, 502, 2664 pp. (2) Taipei: Ch'eng Wen Publishing Co., 1966 (photocopy).

This combined concordance to the *Ch'un-ch'iu* 春秋, *Kung-yang chuan* 公羊傳, *Ku-liang chuan* 穀梁傳, and *Tso-chuan* 左傳 has an admirable introduction by William Hung and a punctuated text in the first volume, while a word by word index fills the other three volumes. The *Shih-san-ching chu-su* text is followed.

Ch'un-ch'iu ching-chuan chu-su yin-shu yin-te 春秋經傳注疏引書引得. (1) Peiping: Harvard-Yenching Institute, 1937. (Index No. 29) viii, 25 pp. (2) Taipei: Ch'eng Wen Publishing Co., 1966 (photocopy).

This is a combined index to the titles quoted in the commentaries on the *Ch'un-ch'iu*, the *Kung-yang chuan*, the *Ku-liang chuan*, and the *Tso-chuan*, based on Juan Yüan's *Shih-san-ching chu-su* edition.

Ch'un-ch'iu fan-lu t'ung-chien 春秋繁露通檢. (1) Peiping: Centre franco-chinois d'études sinologiques, 1944. (Index No. 4) xix, 114 pp. (2) Taipei: Ch'eng Wen Publishing Co., 1968 (photocopy).

This is an index to the Pao-ching-t'ang 抱經堂 edition of the *Ch'un-ch'iu fan-lu* by Tung Chung-shu 董仲舒, an important interpretive work on the *Spring and Autumn Annals*.

Kokugo sakuin or **Kuo-yü so-yin** 國語索引. Compiled by Suzuki Ryūichi 鈴木隆一. (1) Kyoto: Tōhō bunka gakuin kenkyūjo 東方文化學院研究所, 1933. 16, 276 pp. (2) Tokyo: Daian Bookstore, 1967 (photocopy).

This is an index to proper nouns and to political, economic, military, musical, and other terms used in the *Kuo-yü*. It is arranged by the number of strokes.

Lun-yü yin-te 論語引得. (1) Peiping: Harvard-Yenching Institute, 1940. (Supplement No. 16) xxii, 190 pp. (2) Taipei: Ch'eng Wen Publishing Co., 1966 (photocopy).

This is a concordance to the *Lun-yü*, preceded by a punctuated text.

Meng-tzu yin-te 孟子引得. (1) Peiping: Harvard-Yenching Institute, 1941. (Supplement No. 17) xxvi, 480 pp. (2) Taipei: Ch'eng Wen Publishing Co., 1966 (photocopy).

This is a concordance to the *Meng-tzu*, preceded by a punctuated text based on a photolithographic reproduction of the 1815 Nanchang edition of the *Shih-san-ching chu-su*.

Hsiao-ching yin-te 孝經引得. (1) Peking: Harvard-Yenching Institute, 1950. (Supplement No. 23) x, 27 pp. (2) Taipei: Ch'eng Wen Publishing Co., 1966 (photocopy).

This is a concordance to the *Hsiao-ching*.

Erh-ya yin-te 爾雅引得. (1) Peiping: Harvard-Yenching Institute, 1941. (Supplement No. 18) xxxii, 129 pp. (2) Taipei: Ch'eng Wen Publishing Co., 1966 (photocopy).

This is an index to the *Erh-ya*, preceded by a standard text.

Erh-ya chu-su yin-shu yin-te 爾雅注疏引書引得. (1) Peiping: Harvard-Yenching Institute, 1941. (Index No. 38) viii, 14 pp. (2) Taipei: Ch'eng Wen Publishing Co., 1966 (photocopy).

This is an index to the works quoted in the standard commentaries on the *Erh-ya*.

Fang-yen chiao-chien fu t'ung-chien 方言校箋附通檢. (1) Peking: Centre d'études sinologiques de Pékin, 1951. (Index No. 14) 2 vols. xxx, 95; xlii, 249 pp. (2) Taipei: Ch'eng Wen Publishing Co., 1968 (photocopy).

This is an index to the *Fang-yen*, with a standard text.

B. HISTORY

Chan-kuo ts'e t'ung-chien 戰國策通檢. (1) Peiping : Centre d'études sinologiques de Pékin, 1948. (Index No. 10) xxvi, 90 pp. (2) Taipei : Ch'eng Wen
Publishing Co., 1968 (photocopy).

This is an index to the Shih-li-chü 士禮居 edition of the *Chan-kuo ts'e*,
together with a table applying it to five other editions.

Shih-chi chi chu-shih tsung-ho yin-te 史記及注釋綜合引得. (1) Peiping :
Harvard-Yenching Institute, 1947. (Index No. 40) xxx, 715 pp. (2) Cambridge : Harvard University Press, 1955 (photocopy).

This volume supplies combined indexes for the *Shih-chi* (Shanghai : Wu-
chou t'ung-wen shu-chü 五洲同文書局 edition) and the notes of P'ei Yin 裴駰,
Ssu-ma Chen 司馬貞, Chang Shou-chieh 張守節 and Takigawa Kametaro 瀧川
龜太郎. References to the original text are in large characters, and to the notes
in smaller ones.

Shih-chi so-yin 史記索引. Compiled by Wong Fook-luen [Huang Fu-luan]
黃福鑾. Hong Kong : Research Institute of Far Eastern Studies, Ch'ung-chi
College, The Chinese University of Hong Kong, 1963. [22] 728 pp.

This is the most comprehensive index to the *Shih-chi* that has been published.
It is based on the *Ssu-pu ts'ung-k'an* and *Ssu-pu pei-yao* editions, and it indexes
names, important events, and a great variety of terms, though the material
in the ten charts and tables is excluded. Unfortunately the arrangement, following the classification system of the *T'ai-p'ing yü-lan* (q.v.), makes it awk-
ward to use, the indexed terms being separated among twenty-four sections,
including names of persons, geography, costume, food, public works, technology, functionaries, political and military affairs, communications, economics, minerals, and zoology. Moreover, there are often several hundred page
references under a single name or term, making it very time consuming to
find specific information.

Shih-chi yen-chiu ti tzu-liao ho lun-wen so-yin 史記研究的資料和論文
索引. Compiled by the History Research Institute of the Chinese Academy
of Sciences 中國科學院歷史研究所. Peking : K'o-hsüeh ch'u-pan she, 1957;
second revised edition, 1958. 2, 2, 72 pp. illus.

This so-called index is actually a catalogue of all the available information
on the *Shih-chi*, its editions and its authors. Besides giving thorough coverage

to all kinds of Chinese writings from ancient to modern times, it provides an incomplete list of works in Japanese, Russian, German, and English.

Han-shu chi pu-chu tsung-ho yin-te 漢書及補注綜合引得. (1) Peiping: Harvard-Yenching Institute, 1940. (Index No. 36) xxxii, 846 pp. (2) Taipei: Ch'eng Wen Publishing Co., 1966 (photocopy).

This is a combined index to the 1903 T'ung-wen shu-chü edition of the *Han-shu* and to the 1900 block-print edition of the notes of Yen Shih-ku 顏師古 and Wang Hsien-ch'ien 王先謙. References to the text are in large characters and to the notes in small characters.

Han-shu so-yin 漢書索引. Compiled by Wong Fook-luen [Huang Fu-luan] 黃福鑾. Hong Kong: Research Institute of Far Eastern Studies, Ch'ung Chi College, The Chinese University of Hong Kong, 1966. [6] 10, 963, 26 pp.

This index to the *Han-shu*, based on the *Ssu-pu ts'ung-k'an* and *Ssu-pu pei-yao* editions, uses the same classification system as the compiler's *Shih-chi so-yin* (q.v.) and therefore the index has the same virtues and weaknesses.

Hou Han-shu chi chu-shih tsung-ho yin-te 後漢書及注釋綜合引得. (1) Peiping: Harvard-Yenching Institute, 1949. (Index No. 41) xxxii, 918 pp. (2) Taipei: Ch'eng Wen Publishing Co., 1966 (photocopy).

This is a combined index to the *Hou Han-shu* and to the notes of Liu Chao 劉昭 and Li Hsien 李賢. It is based on the 1903 Shanghai Wu-chou t'ung-wen shu-chü edition, but it may be applied to other editions by means of a conversion chart. Although not a concordance, it is quite a detailed index.

Gokanjo goi shūsei or **Hou Han-shu yü-hui chi-ch'eng** 後漢書語彙集成. Compiled by Fujita Shizen 藤田至善. Kyoto: Jimbun kagaku kenkyūjo, 1962. 3 vols. 6, 3, 3335 pp.

This detailed index to personal and place names, official titles, and many historical events and other terms in the *Hou Han-shu* is based on the *Po-na* collated edition. Whereas the *Hou Han-shu . . . yin-te* (q.v.), which is limited mainly to personal and place names, has some 80,000 entries, this much fuller compilation, which also indexes numerous notes and commentaries on the *Hou Han-shu*, has more than 150,000 entries, which are arranged by the number of strokes. Under each term the sentence in which it was used is quoted, with its exact source indicated. At the beginning of each volume is a list of Chinese characters, arranged by the number of strokes, giving the pages in that volume where names and terms commencing with each character are to be found.

Han-kuan ch'i-chung t'ung-chien 漢官七種通檢. Compiled by Ch'en Tso-lung 陳祚龍. Paris: Centre franco-chinois, University of Paris, 1962. xlii, 49, lxxii pp., maps.

This is an index to the *Han-kuan ch'i-chung*, collated and edited by Sun Hsing-yen 孫星衍, with a preface in French.

San-kuo-chih chi P'ei-chu tsung-ho yin-te 三國志及裴注綜合引得. (1) Peiping: Harvard-Yenching Institute, 1938. (Index No. 33) xxx, 478 pp. (2) Taipei: Ch'eng Wen Publishing Co., 1966 (photocopy).

This is a combined index to the *San-kuo-chih* (Wu-chou t'ung-wen shu-chü 五洲同文書局 edition of the *Twenty-four Histories*, Shanghai, 1903), and to the famous commentary of P'ei Sung-chih 裴松之. The materials indexed include proper nouns, official titles, and key words in the text, as well as additional material and valuable quotations in the commentary. Consequently this is an indispensable tool for the study of one of the best of the dynastic histories.

T'ang-lü su-i yin-te 唐律疏義引得. Compiled by Chuang Wei-ssu 莊爲斯. Taipei: Wen-hai ch'u-pan she. Preface dated December, 1964. 945 pp.

This is a concordance to the important and influential *T'ang Code with Commentary* based on the *Kuo-hsüeh chi-pen ts'ung shu* edition and arranged by the number of strokes. For a simpler index see below.[2]

Hsin T'ang-shu tsai-hsiang shih-hsi-piao yin-te 新唐書宰相世系表引得. Compiled by Chou I-liang 周一良 and others. (1) Peiping: Harvard-Yenching Institute, 1934. (Index No. 16) xl, 207 pp. (2) Taipei: Ch'eng Wen Publishing Co., 1966 (photocopy).

This is a time-saving index to the genealogical tables of the families of chief ministers in the *Hsin T'ang-shu*.

Shiji tsūgan sakuin or **Tzu-chih t'ung-chien so-yin** 資治通鑑索引. Compiled by Saeki Tomi 佐伯富. Kyoto: Tōyōshi kenkyūkai, 1961. xxii, 301 pp.

---

2. **Tōritsu sakuin kō** or **T'ang-lü so-yin kao** 唐律索引稿. (Kyoto: Tōritsu kenkyūkai 唐律研究會, 1958). iv, 116 pp. This index to the text (excluding the commentary) of the *Ku T'ang-lü su-i* 故唐律疏議 in the *Wan-yu wen-k'u* edition is arranged by the four-corner system.

This index to the well-known *Tzu-chih t'ung-chien* has number-of-strokes and four-corner indexes appended.

Shiji tsūgan kochū chimei sakuin or **Tzu-chih t'ung-chien Hu-chu ti-ming so-yin** 資治通鑑胡注地名索引. Compiled by Araki Toshikazu 荒木敏一 and Yoneda Kenjirō 米田賢次郎. Kyoto: Jimbun kagaku kenkyūjo, 1967. vi, 351 pp.

This is an index to geographical names, local officials, and products referred to in the commentary on the *Tzu-chih t'ung-chien* by Hu San-sheng 胡三省, who is famous for his knowledge of historical geography. It is based on the 1956 Chung-hua shu-chü edition punctuated by Ku Chieh-kang 顧頡剛 and others. Included in the volume is a historical map of Sung China.

Sōshi shokukan shi sakuin or **Sung-shih chih-kuan chih so-yin** 宋史職官志索引. Compiled by Saeki Tomi 佐伯富. Kyoto: Tōyōshi kenkyūkai, 1963. 4, 63, 25, 423 pp.

This index to official titles, personal and place names, institutions, and economic terminology of the *Sung-shih chih-kuan chih* 宋史職官志 is arranged according to the Japansese alphabet. However, there is a list of Chinese characters (pp. 413–423) arranged under the number of strokes as a guide to the index.

Ryōshi sakuin or **Liao-shih so-yin** 遼史索引. Compiled by Wakashiro Kyūjirō 若城久次郎. Kyoto: Tōhō bunka gakuin (Kyoto) kenkyūjo 東方文化學院 (京都) 研究所, 1937. 11, 632 pp.

This is an index to the *Liao-shih*, the Liao dynastic history, based on the *Nan-chien* 南鑑 or Nanking palace edition of 1529. Names of persons and places, official titles, reign titles, and key words in important events are indexed by the number-of-strokes system.

Ch'i-tan kuo-chih t'ung-chien 契丹國志通檢. (1) Peiping: Centre d'études sinologiques de Pékin, 1949. (Index No. 12) xxviii, 116 pp. (2) Taipei: Ch'eng Wen Publishing Co., 1968 (photocopy).

This is an index to the *Ch'i-tan kuo-chih* by Yeh Lung-li 葉隆禮 (*chin-shih*, 1274).

Kinshi goi shūsei or **Chin-shih yü-hui chi-ch'eng** 金史語彙集成. Compiled by Onogawa Hidemi 小野川秀美. Kyoto: Jimbun kagaku kenkyūjo, 1960. 3 vols. 2, 2, 2, 1627 pp.

This index to personal and place names and official titles in the Chin dynastic history is based on the 1529 *Nan-chien* text, but it can also be used with other editions by means of a conversion table. The arrangement of entries is the same as that followed in the *Gokanjo goi shūsei* (q.v.)

Ta Chin kuo-chih t'ung-chien 大金國志通檢. (1) Peiping: Centre d'études sinologiques de Pékin, 1949. (Index No. 11) xxviii, 162 pp. (2) Taipei: Ch'eng Wen Publishing Co., 1968 (photocopy).

This is an index to the *Kuo-hsüeh chi-pen ts'ung-shu* edition of the *Ta Chin kuo-chih*, an important source on the Chin dynasty completed in 1234 and attributed to Yü-wen Mou-chao 宇文懋昭.

Genshi goi shūsei or **Yüan-shih yü-hui chi-ch'eng** 元史語彙集成. Kyoto: Bungakubu 文學部, Kyoto University, 1963. 3 vols. [4] 3, 2825 pp.

This index to personal and place names, official titles, and other important data in the Yüan dynasty history is based on the 1529 *Nan-chien* edition and can also be used with the *Po-na* and other editions. The arrangement is the same as that of the *Kinshi goi shūsei* (q.v.).

Ch'ing-tai ch'ou-pan i-wu shih-mo so-yin 清代籌辦夷務始末索引. Compiled by Chang Ch'eng-sun 張誠孫, Ho Ling-hsu 賀凌虛 and others; edited by David Nelson Rowe with the assistance of Yang Shao-tseng 楊紹震 and Sophia S. F. Yen 顏叔暉. Hamden, Conn.: Shoe String Press, 1960. xi, 855 pp.

This index to the important *I-wu shih-mo* documents on mid-nineteenth century foreign relations would be even more useful if the topics into which it is divided were further subdivided. References to England, for example, in chronological order, fill eleven pages, to the Tsungli Yamen four pages, to Kwangtung province nearly eight pages, and to Li Hung-chang a page and a half.

Shih-huo-chih shih-wu-chung tsung-ho yin-te 食貨志十五種綜合引得. (1) Peiping: Harvard-Yenching Institute, 1938. (Index No. 32) xxiv, 441 pp. (2) Taipei: Ch'eng Wen Publishing Co., 1966 (photocopy).

This is a combined index to the economic sections of fifteen standard histories, namely: *Shih-chi* 史記, *Han-shu* 漢書, *Chin-shu* 晉書, *Wei-shu* 魏書, *Sui-shu* 隋書, *Chiu T'ang-shu* 舊唐書, *Hsin T'ang-shu* 新唐書, *Chiu Wu-tai-shih* 舊五代史, *Sung-shih* 宋史, *Liao-shih* 遼史, *Chin-shih* 金史, *Yüan-shih* 元史, *Hsin Yüan-shih* 新元史, *Ming-shih* 明史, and *Ch'ing-shih kao* 清史稿. In these economic sections of the histories, the Chinese land system, taxation, population, transportation, salt tax, currency system, mining, customs duties, and miscellaneous taxes of all dynasties are fairly well treated. But the material is bulky and the items are hard to find. This index is a time-saver. It is based mainly on the T'ung-wen shu-chü edition of the *Twenty-four Dynastic Histories*.

Chu-shih jan-i chiao-ting fu yin-te 諸史然疑校訂附引得. (1) Peiping: Harvard-Yenching Institute, 1932. (Supplement No. 2) iv, 12, iv, 8 pp. (2) Taipei: Ch'eng Wen Publishing Co., 1966 (photocopy).

The *Chu-shih jan-i*, by Hang Shih-chün 杭世駿 (1696–1773), contains notes correcting a number of errors in eight of the dynastic histories. This edited text corrects some of Hang's own errors. It is followed by an index.

C. PHILOSOPHY AND MISCELLANEOUS

Chuang-tzu yin-te 莊子引得. (1) Peiping: Harvard-Yenching Institute, 1947. (Supplement No. 20) xxxvi, 740 pp. (2) Cambridge: Harvard University Press, 1956.

This is a concordance to the *Chuang-tzu*, preceded by a punctuated text of Kuo Ch'ing-fan's 郭慶藩 *Chuang-tzu chi-shih* 莊子集釋 (Ssu-hsien shu-chü 思賢書局 edition, 1895).

Hsün-tzu yin-te 荀子引得. (1) Peking: Harvard-Yenching Institute, 1950. (Supplement No. 22) xxxii, 919 pp. (2) Taipei: Ch'eng Wen Publishing Co., 1966 (photocopy).

This is a concordance to the *Hsün-tzu*.

Lü-shih ch'un-ch'iu t'ung-chien 呂氏春秋通檢. (1) Peiping: Centre franco-chinois d'études sinologiques, 1943. (Index No. 2) xxv, 163 pp. (2) Taipei: Ch'eng Wen Publishing Co., 1968 (photocopy).

This is an index to the *Ssu-pu ts'ung-k'an* edition of the *Lü-shih ch'un-ch'iu*.

Shen-chien t'ung-chien 申鑒通檢. (1) Peiping: Centre franco-chinois d'études sinologiques, 1947. (Index No. 8) xxviii, 24 pp. (2) Taipei: Ch'eng Wen Publishing Co., 1968 (photocopy).

This is an index to the *Ssu-pu pei-yao* edition of the *Shen-chien* by Hsün Yüeh.

Huai-nan-tzu t'ung-chien 准南子通檢. (1) Peiping: Centre franco-chinois d'études sinologiques, 1944. (Index No. 5) xxv, 308 pp. (2) Taipei: Ch'eng Wen Publishing Co., 1968 (photocopy).

This is an index to the *Ssu-pu ts'ung-k'an* edition of the *Huai-nan-tzu*.

Shuo-yüan yin-te 說苑引得. (1) Peiping: Harvard-Yenching Institute [1931]. (Index No. 1) 58 pp. (2) Taipei: Ch'eng Wen Publishing Co., 1966 (photocopy).

This is an index to the *Shuo-yüan* of Liu Hsiang.

Hsin-hsü t'ung-chien 新序通檢. (1) Peiping: Centre franco-chinois d'études sinologiques, 1946. (Index No. 7) xxxix, 39 pp. (2) Taipei: Ch'eng Wen Publishing Co., 1968 (photocopy).

This is an index to the *Ssu-pu ts'ung-k'an* edition of the *Hsin-hsü*.

Lun-heng t'ung-chien 論衡通檢. (1) Peiping: Centre franco-chinois d'études sinologiques, 1943. (Index No. 1) xxix, 163 pp. (2) Taipei: Ch'eng Wen Publishing Co., 1968 (photocopy).

This is an index to the *Ssu-pu ts'ung-k'an* edition of the *Lun-heng* of Wang Ch'ung.

Ch'ien-fu-lun t'ung-chien 潛夫論通檢. (1) Peiping: Centre franco-chinois d'études sinologiques, 1945. (Index No. 6) xxxvii, 95 pp. (2) Taipei: Ch'eng Wen Publishing Co., 1968 (photocopy).

This is an index to the *Ssu-pu pei-yao* edition of the *Ch'ien-fu-lun*.

Feng-su t'ung-i fu t'ung-chien 風俗通義附通檢. (1) Peiping: Centre franco-chinois d'études sinologiques, 1943. (Index No. 3) xx, 97 pp. (2) Taipei: Ch'eng Wen Publishing Co., 1968 (photocopy).

This is the index to the punctuated and supplemented edition of the *Feng-su t'ung-i* that was published by the same publisher at the same time.

Shan-hai-ching t'ung-chien 山海經通檢. (1) Centre d'études sinologiques de Pékin, 1948. (Index No. 9) [87] 99 pp. (2) Taipei: Ch'eng Wen Publishing Co., 1968 (photocopy).

This index is based on Hao I-hsing's 郝懿行 *Shan-hai-ching su-tsuan* 疏纂 edition.

Pai-hu-t'ung yin-te 白虎通引得. (1) Peiping: Harvard-Yenching Institute, 1931. (Index No. 2) xvi, 33 pp.ʹ (2) Taipei: Ch'eng Wen Publishing Co., 1966 (photocopy).

Index to the *Pai-hu-t'ung*.

Shih-shuo hsin-yü yin-te 世說新語引得; supplement: **Liu-chu yin-shu yin-te** 劉注引書引得. (1) Peiping: Harvard-Yenching Institute, 1933. (Index No. 12) xvi, 56 pp. (2) Taipei: Ch'eng Wen Publishing Co., 1966 (photocopy).

This is an index to the *Shih-shuo hsin-yü* of Liu I-ch'ing 劉義慶 (A.D. 403–444), and to the commentary on that work written by Liu Chün 劉峻 (*hao*, Hsiao-piao 孝標, A.D. 462–521). The *Shih-shuo hsin-yü*, which is anecdotal in nature, with Liu's famous commentary on it, provides an excellent source for material on the Three Kingdoms 三國 and the two Chin 晉 periods, derived from other works almost all of which have since disappeared. The supplement is an index to the titles of the works quoted from by Liu Chün, giving both the location of the quotation in the *Shih-shuo hsin-yü*, and the full citation as given by Liu. Both indexes are to the *Ssu-pu ts'ung-k'an* edition, in which the original text and the commentary appear together.

Su-shih yen-i yin-te 蘇氏演義引得. (1) Peiping: Harvard-Yenching Institute, 1933. (Index No. 14) xii, 13 pp. (2) Taipei: Ch'eng Wen Publishing Co., 1966 (photocopy).

This is an index to the *Su-shih yen-i*, by Su E 蘇鶚, who lived during the eighth century.

Feng-shih wen-chien-chi chiao-cheng fu yin-te 封氏聞見記校證附引得. (1) Peiping: Harvard-Yenching Institute, 1933. (Supplement No. 7) 2 *ts'e*. (2) Taipei: Ch'eng Wen Publishing Co., 1966 (photocopy).

This is an index to the miscellaneous notes of Feng Yen 封演 of the T'ang period, reedited by Chao Chen-hsin 趙貞信.

K'an-wu yin-te 刊誤引得. (1) Peiping: Harvard-Yenching Institute, 1934. (Index No. 22) viii, 5 pp. (2) Taipei: Ch'eng Wen Publishing Co., 1966 (photocopy).

An index to the *K'an-wu*, by Li Fou李涪 (fl. 825–835), which preserves much material on T'ang customs.

Jung-chai sui-pi wu-chi tsung-ho yin-te 容齋隨筆五集綜合引得. (1) Peiping: Harvard-Yenching Institute, 1933. (Index No. 13) xxvi, 123 pp. (2) Taipei: Ch'eng Wen Publishing Co., 1966 (photocopy).

A combined index to the five collections of miscellaneous notes of Hung Mai 洪邁 (1123–1202), which are of interest to students of historical and political problems of ancient and medieval China.

K'ao-ku chih-i yin-te 考古質疑引得. (1) Peiping: Harvard-Yenching Institute, 1931, 1941. (Index No. 3) x, 9 pp. (2) Taipei: Ch'eng Wen Publishing Co., 1966 (photocopy).

Index to the *K'ao-ku chih-i* by Yeh Ta-ch'ing 葉大慶 (*chin-shih*, 1205).

Cho-keng-lu t'ung-chien 輟耕錄通檢. (1) Peking: Centre d'études sinologiques de Pékin, 1950. (Index No. 13) lxi, 207 pp. (2) Taipei: Ch'eng Wen Publishing Co., 1968 (photocopy).

This index to the *Cho-keng-lu* by T'ao Tsung-i 陶宗儀 of the Yüan dynasty is to a recut Yüan edition by I-yüan 逸園覆元刊本, which makes the scholarly notes readily available.

Ts'ui Tung-pi i-shu yin-te 崔東壁遺書引得. (1) Peiping: Harvard-Yenching Institute, 1931. (Index No. 5) xiv, 48 pp. (2) Taipei: Ch'eng Wen Publishing Co., 1966 (photocopy).

This is an index to the collected writings of Ts'ui Shu 崔述 (T. Tung-pi, 1740–1816), an advanced scholar with a critical mind and revolutionary ideas.

Chūgoku zuihitsu sakuin or **Chung-kuo sui-pi so-yin** 中國隨筆索引. Compiled by the Tōyōshi kenkyūkai at Kyoto University. Tokyo: Nihongakujutsu shinkōkai 日本學術振興會, 1954. 11, 1018 pp.

This is an index to Chinese essays or headings in some 160 collections of desultory notes (*sui-pi*) written from the T'ang to the end of the Ch'ing dynasty, including Ku Yen-wu's *Jih-chih lu* 顧炎武, 日知錄 and many other well-known titles which are frequently consulted for scholarly comments. A number-of-strokes index makes the work usable by Chinese scholars.

Chūgoku zuihitsu zatcho sakuin or **Chung-kuo sui-pi tsa-chu so-yin** 中國隨筆雜著索引. Compiled by Saeki Tomi 佐伯富. Kyoto: Tōyōshi ken-kyūkai, 1961. 10, 1144 pp.

This is a supplement to the *Chūgoku zuihitsu sakuin* (q.v.), indexing forty-six additional collections of miscellaneous writings. There is a number-of-strokes index.

Ts'ang-shu chi-shih shih yin-te 藏書紀事詩引得. Compiled by Ts'ai Chin-chung 蔡金重. (1) Peiping: Harvard-Yenching Institute, 1937. (Index No. 28) xx, 98 pp. (2) Taipei: Ch'eng Wen Publishing Co., 1966 (photocopy).

This is an index to the *Ts'ang-shu chi-shih shih* (seven *chüan*), which was written and published in 1910 by Yeh Ch'ang-chih 葉昌熾. The book relates, in poetic form, stories and anecdotes about the private libraries, seals, and editions of 1175 book-collectors, from the period of the Five Dynasties (907–960) to the end of the Ch'ing dynasty. A one-*chüan* supplement by Lun Ming 倫明 adds stories of book-collectors in the Republican period. The book is useful to students of bibliography and of old editions, but is not always accurate; this index furnishes a key to its contents and also corrects many errors.

D. BELLES-LETTRES

Wen-hsüan-chu yin-shu yin-te 文選注引書引得. (1) Peiping: Harvard-Yenching Institute, 1935. (Index No. 26) xvi, 145 pp. (2) Taipei: Ch'eng Wen Publishing Co., 1966 (photocopy).

This is a *kuei-hsieh* index to the *Wen-hsüan* 文選, an anthology of poetry and prose written between 246 B.C. and A.D. 502, which was compiled by Hsiao T'ung 蕭統 (Prince Chao-ming 昭明, A.D. 501–531), and to two T'ang commentaries on it which were combined during the Southern Sung period and published with the original text under the title: *Liu-ch'en-chu wen-hsüan* 六臣注文選. The first commentary was written by Li Shan 李善 (d. 689), who included quotations taken from a great many works which have since been lost, and the second commentary, usually called *Wen-hsüan wu-ch'en-chu* 文選五臣注, was compiled by five high officials during the reign of the T'ang Emperor Hsüan-tsung 唐玄宗 (713–755). The index, which is to the *Ssu-pu ts'ung-k'an* photolithographic reproduction of a Sung edition of the *Liu-ch'en-chu wen-hsüan*, is divided into two parts: (1) index to the titles and authors of poems and pieces of prose collected in the *Wen-hsüan*, (2) index to the titles and authors of works quoted in the commentaries.

Monzen sakuin or **Wen-hsüan so-yin** 文選索引. Compiled by Shiba Roku-rō 斯波六郎. Kyoto: Jimbun kagaku kenkyūjo, 1957–1959. 4 vols. 796; 820; 572; 240 pp.

This is a concordance to the *Wen-hsüan*, a *chef-d'oeuvre* of Chinese anthologies, compiled by Prince Chao-ming 昭明 (A.D. 501–531) of the Liang dynasty. In the first three volumes all words and phrases (totaling a quarter million entries) are arranged in the order of the *K'ang-hsi tzu-tien*. The fourth volume has a detailed table of contents, indexes to titles and to authors (with brief biographical information), and a table of genre or style (with terse explanations). There are guides to first characters, arranged by the number of strokes, by the four-corner system and by the Wade-Giles romanization. This superb publication is the product of a life-long study of the *Wen-hsüan* by a former professor of Chinese literature at Hiroshima University.

Wen-hsin tiao-lung hsin-shu t'ung-chien 文心雕龍新書通檢. (1) Peking: Centre d'études sinologiques de Pékin, 1951–1952. (Index No. 15) 2 vols. xxix, 183; xxxvi, 429 pp. (2) Taipei: Ch'eng Wen Publishing Co., 1968 (photocopy).

This concordance to the *Wen-hsin tiao-lung*, based on the Wang Li-ch'i 王利器 edition, consists of a punctuated text, indicating differences from other editions, and a number-of-strokes index, with Wade-Giles and French romanization keys to individual characters. The title is misleading in that the *Hsin-shu* is not indexed and should have been omitted even though Wang Li-ch'i's edition includes both works.

Ch'üan shang-ku San-tai Ch'in Han San-kuo Liu-ch'ao wen tso-che yin-te 全上古三代秦漢六朝文作者引得 (q.v.)

Ch'üan Han San-kuo Chin Nan-pei-ch'ao shih tso-che yin-te 全漢三國晉南北朝詩作者引得 (q.v.)

Ri Haku kashi sakuin or **Li Pai ko-shih so-yin** 李白歌詩索引. Compiled by Hanabusa Hideki 花房英樹. Kyoto: Jimbun kagaku kenkyūjo, 1957. vi, 96, 522 pp.

This concordance to the poems of Li Po is based upon the Miao-yüeh-chi 繆曰芑 edition; a list of differences from the Sung edition is appended. The 52 poems not found in the Miao edition are also appended, making a complete concordance to the 1,049 extant poems composed by Li Po. Every character used in his verse is indexed in accordance with the four-corner system. Phrases and personal and place names are also indexed. At the end are number-of-strokes and Wade-Giles romanization keys.

Tu-shih yin-te 杜詩引得. (1) Peiping: Harvard-Yenching Institute, 1940. (Supplement No. 14) 3 vols. cxci, 915 pp. (2) Taipei: Ch'eng Wen Publishing Co., 1966 (photocopy).

The first volume of this concordance to the poems of Tu Fu (712–760) contains the famous introduction by William Hung. In the second is the text of Tu Fu's poems, with commentaries, based on the Chiu-chia chi-chu tu-shih 九家集注杜詩 edition, which was reproduced from a Sung copy during the Chia-ch'ing period (1796–1820); and a supplement based on the *Tu-shih hsiang-chu* 杜詩詳注, published by the Shanghai Sao-yeh shan-fang 掃葉山房 in 1921. The third volume contains the concordance to the poems. There is a comparative chart of *chüan* and page numbers in volume one by means of which this index may be used with other editions of Tu Fu's poems.

*Ch'ing-tai wen-chi p'ien-mu fen-lei so-yin 清代文集篇目分類索引. Compiled by Wang Chung-min 王重民 and others. (1) Peiping: National Library of Peiping, 1935. [1158] pp. (2) Taipei: Kuo-feng ch'u-pan-she, 1965 (photocopy).

This is a multiple index to the titles of the essays and notes in 428 individual collections and twelve general collections of literary writings, practically all dating from the Ch'ing dynasty. The work is divided into three parts: (1) essays and notes on special subjects, (2) biographical sketches, and (3) miscellaneous writings. The arrangement of the first part very closely follows the *Ssu-k'u* system. The second part is divided into seven sections, each of which lists a different type of biographical study. The third part is divided into four sections: (1) personal letters on special subjects, (2) stone inscriptions, (3) the type of poetry called *fu* 賦, and (4) miscellaneous essays. In the first part the essay titles are arranged in the various subsections according to the nature of the subject. In the second part the names of the persons described in the biographical sketches are arranged under the different section headings according to the number of strokes. In the third part the essay titles are arranged chronologically according to authors in the first, third and fourth sections, and according to the nature of the sites of the stone inscriptions (whether in temples, gardens, schools, or tombs) in the second section. After most titles the name of the writer, the title of the collection, and the *chüan* and page numbers are given. At the beginning of the work there is a list of the collections indexed, arranged chronologically, giving in each case the compiler's name, the number of *chüan* in the collection, and the edition upon which the index is based. This is followed by another list of the same titles of collections, in the same order, in which brief descriptive notes are presented concerning each separate collection. This, in turn, is followed by an author index, arranged according to the number of strokes. Finally, there is a table of contents at the beginning of each of the three parts. The book has some serious defects which it is necessary to point out: (1) it is very inconvenient to use, owing to the complexity of its arrangement (it is necessary in the second part, for instance, to look for a man's name in seven different places); (2) the list of collections is far from exhaustive, the writings of Tai Ming-shih 戴名世, Chang Yü-shu 張玉書, Tso Tsung-t'ang 左宗棠, and Li Hung-chang 李鴻章, for instance, being entirely neglected; and (3) there are frequent mistakes in the classification of titles. However the work is the result of a tremendous amount of labor on the part of the compilers, and it is a very useful guide to a large mass of widely scattered material.

Hu Shih wen-ts'un so-yin 胡適文存索引. Compiled by T'ung Shih-kang 童世綱. Taipei: Hsüeh-sheng shu-chü, 1969. 136 pp.

This is an index to three editions of collected works of Hu Shih. There are subject, title, and key-phrase indexes to his writings in Chinese, and a separate index to his English writings.

INDEX AND GLOSSARY

This combined index and glossary gives the page numbers for the titles and for the names of authors or compilers of all the reference works described in this bibliography. In addition, it supplies the Chinese characters for the names of publishers and the titles of *ts'ung-shu* that have been omitted to save space, it gives minimal bibliographical data on *ts'ung-shu,* and it explains or gives the Chinese characters for a few terms.